Business
in FORTR
and
ANSI FORT
A Structure Approach

BUSINESS PROGRAMMING IN FORTRAN IV AND ANSI FORTRAN 77:

A Structured Approach

ASAD KHAILANY

Eastern Michigan University

PRENTICE-HALL, INC., Englewood Cliffs, New Jersey 07632

Library of Congress Cataloging in Publication Data

Khailany, Asad S
   Business programming in FORTRAN IV and ANSI FORTRAN.

   1. FORTRAN (Computer program language) 2. Struc-
tured programming. I. Title.
HF5548.5.F2K48   001.64'24   80-25819
ISBN 0-13-107607-8

Editorial production/supervision by
Maureen Wilson and Maria McKinnon
Interior design by Maureen Wilson
Page layout by Jeanette Markus
Cover design by Wanda Lubelska
Manufacturing buyer: Ed O'Dougherty

Printed in the United States of America

10 9 8 7 6 5 4 3 2 1

PRENTICE-HALL INTERNATIONAL, INC., *London*
PRENTICE-HALL OF AUSTRALIA PTY. LIMITED, *Sydney*
PRENTICE-HALL OF CANADA, LTD., *Toronto*
PRENTICE-HALL OF INDIA PRIVATE LIMITED, *New Delhi*
PRENTICE-HALL OF JAPAN, INC., *Tokyo*
PRENTICE-HALL OF SOUTHEAST ASIA PTE. LTD., *Singapore*
WHITEHALL BOOKS LIMITED, *Wellington, New Zealand*

To my people: Iraqi and Kurds

CONTENTS

PREFACE

Currently there is a large quantity of programming material in the FOR-TRAN language. The majority of this material is geared toward engineering, mathematics, or science students. Many FORTRAN text books do not contain descriptions of such important topics as file organizations, modular programming, structured programming, and structured design tools. Understanding these topics is important in today's modern programming environment.

This book is primarily designed for students in business schools taking an introductory programming course in the FORTRAN language. Such a course is either one of the core courses of an under graduate business curriculum or a required programming course for MBA students. The text orientation also makes it appropriate for students in humanities, social science, and education.

The combination of the following features makes this text book distinguishable from others in the field.

Many colleges and universities assign two texts for an introductory course in programming: one is a data processing text book and the other a FORTRAN text book. This text, however, eliminates the need for two books since it contains basic material on data processing and computer organization along with indepth coverage of FORTRAN programming. Chapter 1 presents up-to-date material on computer organization, input/output and storage devices, central processing units, different types of memory, operating systems, the computer industry, careers in the computer field, the capabilities and limitations of computer systems, and the impact of computers on business, government and society.

The material in Chapter 1, along with Chapter 2's discussion of design tools including the ANSI flowchart and pseudo codes, make it easier for students to learn programming and system design as presented in the remaining chapters of the text.

This book covers both FORTRAN IV and ANSI FORTRAN 77. Throughout the text the differences between ANSI FORTRAN 77 and FORTRAN IV are explained. A summary of both languages is given in the appendices.

With the exception of a few programs in chapter 16, all programs were tested and run on the computer.

There are extensive examples and exercises in the text. Learning FORTRAN and programming techniques is greatly facilitated by numerous, carefully designed examples and exercises. Coverage of programming starts with simple programs and proceeds to more difficult programs. Students run complete programs by the end of Chapter 3. In each chapter there is at least one complete example accompanied by a flowchart diagram, pseudo code, input data, and the output generated by the program after it is run.

Structured programming is emphasized. Programming style, meaningful variable names, and readability of the programs are given the highest priority. The theoretical concepts of differently structured programming and design techniques are presented in Chapter 12. The discussion ranges from the basic constructs of structured programming to differently structured programming and design tools such as top-down programming, Nassi-Schneiderman charts, HIPO diagrams, and Warnier diagrams.

All programs are well documented. Documentation problems such as over, not sufficient, and no documentations are discussed in Chapter 12.

Modular programming is so important that nonmodular programs are generally neither flexible nor economically desirable.

Modular programming techniques along with FUNCTION and SUBROUTINE subprograms are discussed in Chapters 13 and 14.

Chapter 15 discusses examples, sample programs, and several storing, sorting, and searching techniques.

Chapter 16 discusses both sequential and random file organization through examples and sample programs in ANSI FORTRAN and FORTRAN IV on the IBM system 370 and the DECSYSTEM-10.

At the end of every chapter is a summary of the material presented in that chapter. The end of chapter exercises, designed to motivate students, are drawn from practical problems in business, economic, and other sectors. Each exercise set also contains exercises which are intended to challenge the better student.

There is an instruction manual which contains the solutions and programs for all exercises in the text. The manual also has three samples of each of the following: a first exam, a midterm exam, and a final exam. Also in the manual are three samples of course syllabi which list references, course outlines, grading system, and homework assignments. The material in Chapter 1 can be assigned as a reading assignment to those instructors who do not want to cover the subjects presented.

All programs are stored on the DECSYSTEM-10. Inquire about them from the author to get all programs on a DEC tape.

I wish to express my deep appreciation to those who have contributed to this project: to our reviewers, Professor Robert Chenoweth, County College of Morris, Dover, New Jersey; Professor Jean Longhurst, William Rainey Harper College, Palatine, Illinois; Professor Larry Mazlack, University of Cincinnati, Cincinnati, Ohio; Professor Henry Etlinger, Rochester Institute of Technology, Rochester, New York; and Professor Seymour V. Pollack, Washington University, St. Louis, Missouri. I also wish to thank my wife, Laura, a senior system analyst, who offered numerous suggestions and continous encouragement for the project; and finally the rest of my family, Brucek Kurdo, Sheilan Kurdistan, Raygar Nuri, Nashwan Abdul Kareem, and Nariman Abdul Kareem, who had to spend many hours without me.

Asad Khailany
Ypsilanti, Michigan

Business Programming
in FORTRAN IV
and
ANSI FORTRAN 77:
A Structured Approach

1 COMPUTERS:
Hardware, Software, Industry, and Career

1.1 INTRODUCTION

The main activities of any computer system fall into three categories: input, processing, and output. Feeding information into the computer is

an *input operation*, and retrieving information from the computer is an *output operation*. The *processing* activity includes all calculations and manipulations that are performed to produce the desired output or to accomplish a specific task.

The term *hardware* is used for all physical devices that make the system capable of performing these three activities. In other words, the hardware is all the machinery and physical equipment that make up the computer system. Any such equipment belongs to one of the following four categories of hardware devices:

1. *Input devices.* These are used to feed information into the computer. Card readers, terminal units, disk drives, and tape drives are examples of input devices.
2. *Output devices.* These are used to receive information from the computer. Line printers, terminal units, CRTs (cathode-ray tubes), and disk and tape drives are all output devices.
3. *CPU (central processing unit).* The CPU performs the processing activity.
4. *Storage devices.* These are required to store (hold) data and instructions, temporarily or permanently. Main memory, disk packs, diskettes, and magnetic tapes are examples of storage devices.

The hardware capability of a computer system is determined by four factors: (1) processing speed, (2) access time, (3) transfer rate, and (4) storage capacity. Some of the time units that measure the processing speed, the access time, and the transfer rate are:

Millisecond: One-thousandth of a second
Microsecond: One-millionth of a second
Nanosecond: One-billionth of a second

Processing speed is the time required to perform one computer operation, such as adding two numbers. Some computers perform one addition in less than ten microseconds. You can appreciate such speed if you realize that these computers can perform 10,000,000 additions during the time a human being blinks his eyes once (approximately one-tenth of a second).

Access time is the time needed to locate and to obtain a data item from a storage location. A typical memory access time is one microsecond; disk unit access time is longer than memory access time. Some disk units have access time of less than fifty milliseconds.

Transfer rate is the number of characters that are transferred (between storage locations) within a time unit. Some card readers, for example, read 2,000 cards (160,000 characters) per minute. A transfer rate of 80,000 characters/ second for a magnetic tape drive is common. Some disk-unit drives transfer more than 800,000 characters/second. The transfer rate in the main memory is much higher than that of disk units and other devices.

Storage capacity is the amount of information that can be stored in a storage unit. During the last few years, the capacity of storage units has increased tremendously. Today, a bubble memory module (explained later) the size of a U.S. quarter dollar can store 20,000 characters.

Storage size is measured in Ks, where one K = 1,024. When we say that a storage device is 96K byte (explained later), we mean that its size is 96 × 1,024 = 98,304 bytes.

In addition to the hardware component, we must have some means of instructing the computer to perform the three activities of input, processing, and output. The means that have been developed to communicate with computers are called *computer languages*. They come in three general categories: higher-level languages, assembly languages, and machine languages. *Higher-level languages* have more resemblance to natural languages (such as English) than do *assembly languages. Machine languages* have no resemblance to natural languages. FORTRAN (*For*mula *Tran*slation), BASIC (*B*eginner's *A*ll-Purpose *S*ymbolic *I*nstruction *C*ode), COBOL (*C*ommon *B*usiness *O*riented *L*anguage), and PL/1 (*P*rogramming *L*anguage 1) are all examples of higher-level computer languages. Every computer has its own machine and assembly language, but higher-level languages tend to be machine-independent.

A *computer program* is a set of commands (instructions) written in a computer language to perform a specific task or to solve a certain problem. The person who writes the computer program is known as a *computer programmer.*

A *computer program package* is a set of interrelated programs. For example, a financial package may contain payroll, accounts-payable, accounts-receivable, invoicing, billing, and general-ledger programs.

Software is all computer programs, packages, and computer languages that are used to communicate with computer systems.

1.2   INTERNAL DATA REPRESENTATION

As mentioned above, we communicate with computer systems through computer languages. Any language, whether it is a natural or a computer language, must have its own characters, with syntactic and semantic rules for constructing different structures in that language. The word *character* means either a letter (a, b, c), a digit (0, 1, 2), or a special character (=, -, *).

The combination of on and off states is used to represent characters inside computers. We denote the on state as 1 and the off state as 0. Then two different characters can be represented by using a single light bulb, and four different characters when two light bulbs are used. Let us arbitrarily choose the following four characters to be represented by the associated states:

CHARACTER	1st LIGHT BULB	2nd LIGHT BULB	CODE IN TERMS OF 1 and 0
A	on	on	11
B	on	off	10
C	off	on	01
D	off	off	00

Thus, the string 011110 is the word *CAB*. Representation of the word *BAD* in terms of 0 and 1 is 101100. Like the light bulb, any entity that can have only two different states—like a magnetized spot, or the place for a hole in a punched card—can be used in a group to represent a character by a combination of their on and off states. Indeed, storage devices such as disks, magnetic tapes, and computer memories are constructed from thousands of small spots that can be set in two different states.

The language that uses only two characters, 0 and 1, is called *machine language* or *binary language*. Note that a binary digit can only be either 0 or 1 (see Appendix I). The amount of information indicated by a binary digit is called a *bit*. Thus, a bit can be either 1 or 0. A collection of bits that is used to represent a character is called a *byte*. The byte in the light-bulb example was constructed of two bits. A collection of a fixed number of bytes is called a *computer word*. Note that a computer word can hold more than one character, but a byte holds only one character.

A *field* consists of one or several bytes, or characters, in length and may or may not coincide with computer-word boundaries. A *record* is a collection of related fields, and a *file* is a collection of records. For example, a file of employees contains employees' records, and each record may have several fields, such as employee's number, name, address, and salary.

1.2.1 Codes for Internal Representation of Characters

The three best-known codes for the internal representation of data are:

1. BCD (Binary Code Decimal)
2. EBCDIC (Extended Binary Coded Decimal Interchange Code)
3. ASCII (American Standard Code For Information Interchange)

Table 1.1 shows BCD, in which each character is represented by a byte six bits long. The BCD code can have up to 64 different characters. Table 1.2 shows both EBCDIC and ASCII codes, both of which use a byte eight bits long to

TABLE 1.1   BCD (Binary Coded Decimal) for representing characters as six-bit string

CHARACTER	BCD CODE	CHARACTER	BCD CODE	CHARACTER	BCD CODE
Blank	000000	L	100011	*	101100
0	001010	M	100100	)	101101
1	000001	N	100101	;	101110
2	000010	O	100110	Δ	101111
3	000011	P	100111	−	100000
4	000100	Q	101000	/	010001
5	000101	R	101001	.	011011
6	000110	‡	011010	%	011100
7	000111	S	010010	=	011101
8	001000	T	010011	'	011110
9	001001	U	010100	"	011111
A	110001	V	010101	¢	010000
B	110010	W	010110	#	001011
C	110011	X	010111	@	001100
D	110100	Y	011000	:	001101
E	110101	Z	011001	>	001110
F	110110	.	111011	√	001111
G	110111	□	111100	?	111010
H	111000	(	111101		
I	111001	<	111110		
J	100001	‡	111111		
K	100010	&	110000		
		!	101010		
		$	101011		

TABLE 1.2 ASCII and EBCDIC representations of characters as eight-bit string

SYMBOL	ASCII REPRESENTATION	EBCDIC REPRESENTATION
blank	01000000	01000000
0	01010000	11110000
1	01010001	11110001
2	01010010	11110010
3	01010011	11110011
4	01010100	11110100
5	01010101	11110101
6	01010110	11110110
7	01010111	11110111
8	01011000	11111000
9	01011001	11111001
A	10100001	11000001
B	10100010	11000010
C	10100011	11000011
D	10100100	11000100
E	10100101	11000101
F	10100110	11000110
G	10100111	11000111
H	10101000	11001000
I	10101001	11001001
J	10101010	11010001
K	10101011	11010010
L	10101100	11010011
M	10101101	11010100
N	10101110	11010101
O	10101111	11010110
P	10110000	11010111
Q	10110001	11011000
R	10110010	11011001
S	10110011	11100010
T	10110100	11100011
U	10110101	11100100
V	10110110	11100101
W	10110111	11100110
X	10111000	11100111
Y	10111001	11101000
Z	10111010	11101001
a	11100001	10000001
b	11100010	10000010
c	11100011	10000011
d	11100100	10000100
e	11100101	10000101
f	11100110	10000110
g	11100111	10000111
h	11101000	10001000
i	11101001	10001001
j	11101010	10010001
k	11101011	10010010
l	11101100	10010011
m	11101101	10010100
n	11101110	10010101
o	11101111	10010110
p	11110000	10010111
q	11110001	10011000
r	11110010	10011001
s	11110011	10100010
t	11110100	10100011
u	11110101	10100100
v	11110110	10100101
w	11110111	10100110
x	11111000	10100111
y	11111001	10101000
z	11111010	10101001
!	01000001	01011010
"	01000010	01111111
#	01000011	01111011
$	01000100	01011011
%	01000101	01101100
&	01000110	01010000
'	01000111	01111101
(	01001000	01001101
)	01001001	01011101
*	01001010	01011100
+	01001011	01001110
,	01001100	01101011
-	01001101	01100000
.	01001110	01001011
/	01001111	01100001
:	01011010	01111010
;	01011011	01011110
<	01011100	01001100
=	01011101	01111110
>	01011110	01101110
?	10100000	01101111
@	10111100	01111100

represent a character and can have up to 256 different characters. Note that ASCII has some short forms that use six- or seven-bit bytes.

1.3   DATA-RECORDING DEVICES

In addition to input, processing, output, and storage devices, we must have some equipment to prepare information in machine-acceptable form. Such equipment is known as *data-recording devices*. Card keypunch, key to magnetic tape, key to disk, terminal units, and the like are all data-recording devices.

Before discussing some data-recording devices, let us examine the card-punch format.

1.3.1   Card-Punch Format

Figure 1.1 shows the familiar IBM card. The card is designed to accommodate up to 80 characters. There are twelve rows for punching holes in each column. Each character is represented by a unique combination of one or more holes in a column. Digits 0 through 9 are represented by a single hole in row 0 through 9 respectively. Each of the letters A through Z is represented by two holes. For letters A through I, the first hole is always in row 12; the second hole is in row 1 through 9 respectively. The first hole for the letters J through R is always in row 11, with the second hole in row 1 through 9 respectively. The letters S through Z have the first hole in row 0 and the second hole in row 1 through 9 respectively. See Figure 1.1 for the representation of special characters such as =, +, $, *, (, and so on. (This type of code is known as a Hollerith code).

As you can see, the letter A is represented by the string 10010000000, the letter Z by 001000000001, the digit 1 by 00010000000 and the digit 9 by

FIGURE 1.1   80-column punched card

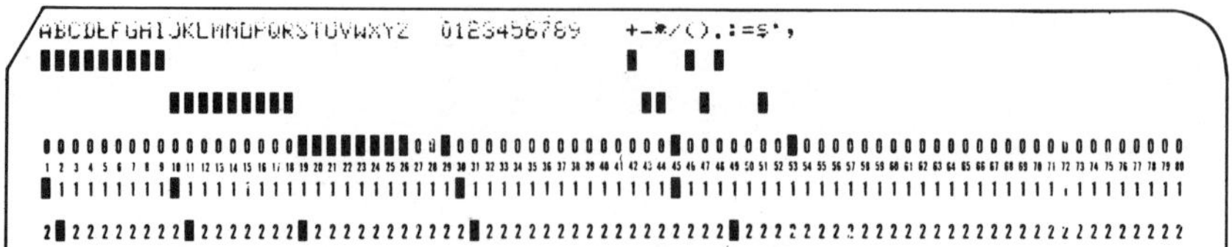

000000000001. You should realize that these formats for character representation are different from BCD, EBCDIC, or ASCII. Since internal processing is done only in either BCD, EBCDIC, or ASCII, once the information is read, it must be converted from card-punch format to one of these formats. Further, the punched-card format above, called BCD card punch, is not the only card-punch format available.

1.3.2   Card Keypunching Machines

These machines are used to prepare punched cards. They are operated like a typewriter. The keypunch operator punches data directly from the keyboard onto cards. Figure 1.2 shows the IBM 029 Keypunch.

There are no small or capital letters on the keypunch machine; its lowercase punches letters (alphabetic mode), and its uppercase punches special characters and numbers (numeric mode). When an incorrect punch has been made on the IBM 029, the card must be released and a new card must be fed to be punched

FIGURE 1.2   IBM 029 Card Keypunch. Courtesy of International Business Machines Corporation.

correctly. Usually, keypunch machines can be programmed to control punching alphabetic or numeric characters, filling in leading zeros, and duplicating or skipping columns. This makes the machine work more efficiently. To program such a machine, a special punched card is prepared, wrapped around a program drum, and inserted into the machine. Keypunch machines are usually rented for $100 to $175 per month, depending on the options selected.

1.3.3   Key-to-Tape Devices

Key-to-tape devices are used to store information directly on magnetic tape. Key-to-tape devices are more acceptable when used with other hardware devices such as cathode-ray tubes (CRT), to display the verification so that the operator can verify the data by sight, reducing the need for key verification.

Further development for keyed data has been made by the use of minireels several hundred feet long, tape cassettes, and cartridge storage. Today, data stations are commonly used. The *data station* is a group of key-to-tape devices that are controlled by a minicomputer. The minicomputer edits, organizes, and recodes data before sending them to the major computer. Various reel-length tapes can be used in the station. In the data station, CRT displays are often used for sight verification.

1.3.4   Key-to-Disk Devices

These devices store data on disks. Disks fall into two categories: diskettes (flexible disks, nicknamed "floppy disks"), and disk platters (explained later).

Diskettes were introduced in 1973. One floppy disk has a storage capacity equivalent to 6,000 punched cards. Its selling price (around $8) is one-tenth that of the traditional disk. Diskettes are reusable and easy to store or mail. Some large computer centers use floppy disks to store some control programs; however, floppy disks are most often used in point-of-sale terminals and with minicomputers. Figure 1.3 shows the Datapoint 1100 Diskette, made by the Datapoint Corporation.

1.4   INPUT DEVICES

Recall that input devices feed information from external storage, such as cards, disks, or tapes, into the computer. In some computer systems, information is read from cards directly into the main memory (explained later), and in others, information is read from cards onto disks or tapes, then later from these into the memory. The reason for this is that card readers have far less

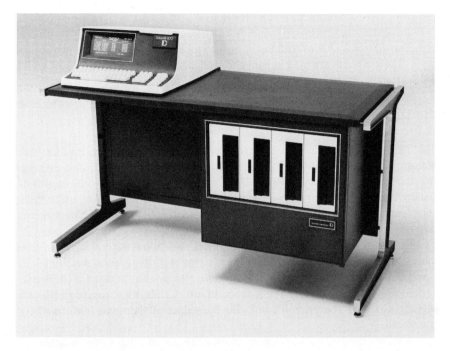

FIGURE 1.3   Datapoint 1100 Diskette. Courtesy of Datapoint Corporation.

speed than disk or magnetic tape. The speed of the central processing unit is far greater than that of the disk or magnetic tape. Following is a discussion of some popular input devices.

1.4.1   Card Reader

The card reader is used to read (transfer) the information from punched cards into the computer. The speed of the card reader varies from 200 to more than 2,000 cards per minute.

There are two types of card readers. The first type uses metal brushes to sense the holes on the card column; the second type is the photoelectric card reader, which uses a light source instead of metal brushes to determine the holes on the card column. This is more reliable than the brush-type card reader, because the metal brushes can be damaged easily.

There are two methods of reading a punched card. One method is to read each row, starting from the first row, until the bottom row (9 edge) has been read. In such an approach, the characters are unknown until all the rows are read. The second approach is to read column by column. In this case, the identification of the character that has been punched in the column is known as soon as the column is read.

9

1.4.2 Magnetic-Ink Character Reader

This device is able to read data printed in magnetic ink on a page in a special style. These devices are used in banks to read account numbers on checks, which are written in magnetic ink.

1.4.3 Optical Character Reader (OCR)

This machine reads data optically, by moving the document into the read station where it is positioned and scanned with a beam of light from a cathode-ray tube. For example, the IBM 1287 Optical Character Reader can read both handwritten and printed data (numbers and special characters from utility bills, telephone bills, cash-register tapes, checks, and so on). This machine can read 550 documents per minute.

Direct sensing, which is a form of OCR, is used in retail stores. A set of lines called the Universal Product Code is printed on each item and is read by a laser beam contained in the input unit, the cash register. The register sends the information to the computer. Then, the computer displays and prints on the cash register not only the price list but also the names of the items that have been purchased.

Another method of direct data entry is by use of a light pen, which has a photocell at its end. The light pen is used in combination with a screen to transmit and receive electronic pulses, enabling the user to draw lines on the screen of the display unit with the pen and to alter or clarify graphs or lines by applying it at the appropriate positions.

1.4.4 Terminals

Terminals and the central processing unit may be located in the same place or in different locations. As a matter of fact, a terminal unit can be thousands of miles away from its parent computer. The terminal units are either hardwired (directly hooked) to the computer or connected to it through telephone lines or by other communication devices. A terminal unit can be an input device or an output device, or both. The output on the terminal unit can be printed lines, information or figures displayed on a CRT, or codes stored on some device at the terminal site. The input to a terminal device can be from the terminal's keyboard, from punched cards, or from specially printed documents or codes that are generated by sense devices.

Of the various types of terminals, some operate under the control of mini-computers and others are as simple as typewriters. Following are some popular types of terminals:

Console typewriter (printer keyboard). The console typewriter is usually hooked directly to the CPU. The keyboard is similar to the keyboard of the typewriter and is used to type (transfer) data directly into the CPU.

CRT terminal. This type of terminal has a keyboard to feed information and a screen to display the output. Usually, CRT terminals do not produce a printed hard-copy output; however, the user can always direct the computer through the CRT terminal to produce a hard copy of the output on the line printer. Some recent CRT terminals are capable of producing the hard copy (printed or photographed) of the displayed information on the screen immediately. The price of a CRT terminal, depending on the type and options, varies from $500 to $3,000. Figure 1.4 is the ADDS 1700 Terminal Unit.

FIGURE 1.4   ADDS 1700 Terminal Unit. Courtesy of Applied Digital Data Systems, Inc.

Terminal typewriter. This type of terminal operates similarly to the CRT; however, instead of a screen, it is equipped with a device like a typewriter to produce a hard copy. Like the CRT, typewriter terminals permit the user to have access to the computer, and they can retrieve, update, add, or delete their information, data, or programs.

Special terminals. A point-of-sale (POS) terminal is one of the popular special terminals. The salesperson uses the POS terminal to read into the computer the price tag on the item sold, which is coded in the Universal Product Code. This eliminates the added steps of coding transaction data and transporting them to the computer center. Special terminals are used by the industry for many specific purposes—for example, to gather data on traffic lights, help bank tellers, and gather data on oil pipelines.

Intelligent terminals. An intelligent terminal performs, in addition to the input and output operations, other tasks such as input collection, input editing, data validation, data compression, and limited calculations and processing. An intelligent terminal operates under the control of a processor, usually a mini-computer, which is part of the intelligent terminal.

Many times the programmer requires column headings to be printed on his or her output. An intelligent terminal prints these column headings without sending the output to the main computer and receives the data from the main computer to print under the appropriate headings. In other words, the intelligent terminal releases the main computer from many tasks that can be performed at the data collection site.

An intelligent terminal may contain a keyboard, a CRT, one or two low-speed card readers and printers, a minicomputer, and some disk storage devices that may contain files referenced by the minicomputer for verification and processing purposes.

1.5   OUTPUT DEVICES

Recall that output devices are used to transfer information from inside the computer to external storage media such as paper, cards, screen, magnetic tape, or disk. Note that both the magnetic tape and disk are external storage devices. The main memory of the computer is the internal storage.

The term *on-line* means the device is available to the CPU without human interference. The term *off-line* means the device is not directly available to the CPU, but must be loaded or connected.

Following is a discussion of some popular output devices.

1.5.1   Printers

These devices print the computer output, producing what is often referred to as hard copy. There are two classifications of printers, impact and non-impact printers. In impact printing, a mechanical action is used to press the paper against the printing element. Non-impact printers use chemical or photographic techniques in the printing process. The impact printer prints either one character or one line at a time. The two different techniques used for one-character impact printers are wire-matrix printers and printer-keyboards. The printer-keyboard operates like an ordinary typewriter except that it is controlled by a program instead of a person. The wire-matrix printer is also known as a dot-matrix device. The normal size of the dot-matrix is seven rows and five columns. The wire-matrix printer creates a character by forming a particular pattern of dots. Here, for instance, is how the letter K is formed on the dot-matrix:

```
● ○ ○ ○ ○
● ○ ○ ● ○
● ○ ● ○ ○
● ● ○ ○ ○
● ● ○ ○ ○
● ○ ● ○ ○
● ○ ○ ● ○
```

One-line-at-a-time impact printers, more common than one-character printers, print the entire line at once. There are three different types of one-line-at-a-time printers: print-wheel printers, chain printers, and drum printers.

A print-wheel printer usually has 120 wheels, each containing 48 characters. Each wheel corresponds to one print position on the line. The print wheels rotate until the required character moves to its print position. When all the characters have moved to their appropriate positions, a hammer strikes and drives the paper against the wheel; thus, the entire line is printed at once.

A chain printer has one hammer for each column of the paper. The character set is assembled in a chain, which moves horizontally across the paper. Characters are printed when the hammer drives the paper against a piece of type.

A drum printer contains one drum for each print position, and each drum contains the complete character set. Each drum positions itself to the character that is to be printed in that position, and a hammer presses the paper against the ink ribbon and the drum. Because each drum has the complete set of characters, in one revolution of the drum all characters reach their position, which makes it possible to print one line at once.

Drum printers and chain printers are faster than wheel printers. Drum printers typically print 132 characters per line and 1,400 lines per minute. The printing speed of impact printers ranges from 100 to 2,000 lines per minute.

The non-impact printer uses several recent printing principles, such as electrostatic printing, ink-jet printing, and even laser-beam techniques. These printers are much faster than the impact printer. Their speed can reach 25,000 lines per minute. An example is the IBM 3800 Printing System, which uses laser-beam techniques to print at a speed of up to 13,000 lines per minute.

1.5.2 On-Line Card Punch

This device converts the incoming data from the computer into holes on punched cards. Recall that the incoming information is in the form EBCDIC or ASCII; the on-line card punch converts these codes to card-punch form.

1.5.3 Plotters

These devices have the ability to draw lines on paper. Output from plotters can take an almost infinite variety of forms; hence, blood-pressure charts, sales charts, maps, tables, and even some excellent art can emerge. Two types of plotting devices are in common use: electromechanical plotters, and electronic plotters. With the former, lines are produced by the incremental movement of the pen on the surface of the paper. With the electronic plotters, a controlled beam from a CRT writes on a microfilm, which is then used to produce a hard copy of the plot. Electronic plotters produce plots at a much faster rate than electromechanical plotters do. Figure 1.5 shows Calcomp Model 1051 Drum Plotter.

FIGURE 1.5   Calcomp Model 1051 Drum Plotter

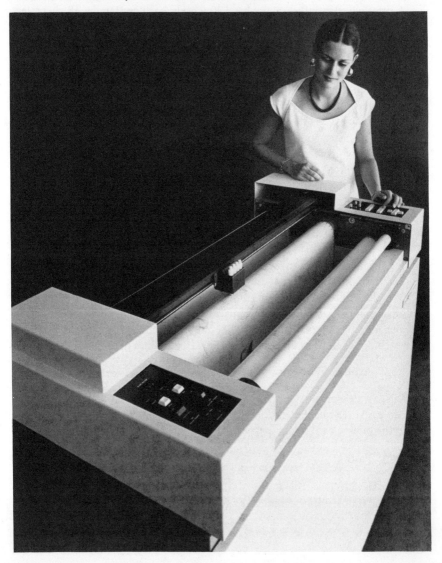

1.5.4 Microfilm Equipment

Microfilm is used to store permanently a large amount of data that is referenced frequently, such as a parts book for an auto manufacturer. To produce microfilm, data must be either written on magnetic tape or displayed on a CRT. Computer-output microfilm requires a large investment. Special equipment is needed to record, develop, duplicate, and read the film. And microfilm output cannot be read again by the computer.

1.6 STORAGE DEVICES

Information in machine-readable form can be stored in many ways—on paper, cards, paper tape, magnetic tape, disk pack, drum, thin films, and so on. The term *secondary storage device* is used for a storage device other than the main memory, and *auxiliary storage* is a storage device that supplements other storage. In general, there are two kinds of storage devices: *sequential-access* and *direct-access*.

Recall that the *access* operation is the process of obtaining data from or placing data in a storage location, and the *access time* is the interval between the instant when data is called for from a storage location and the instant that delivery begins—or between the instant when data is requested to be stored and the instant when storage is completed. When the time required to access data is dependent upon the location of the data most recently accessed, the access is called *sequential access*. It is called *direct* or *random access* when the time required is independent of the location of the data most recently accessed.

1.6.1 Sequential-Access Storage Devices

On such devices, information can be stored and retrieved only in sequential order. Cards, paper tape, and magnetic tape are strictly sequential-access storage devices.

Magnetic tape and tape drive. A magnetic tape is a storage medium consisting of a continuous strip of plastic tape wound on a reel coated with magnetizable material. A typical tape is 2,400 feet long and $\frac{1}{2}$ inch wide, but there are other widths and lengths, such as 1,200-, 600-, and 200-foot reels. Information is recorded on the surface of the tape in patterns of magnetized spots using BCD, EBCDIC, or ASCII codes. Each magnetic spot represents one bit. If the spot is magnetized, the bit is 1; otherwise, the bit is 0. *Tape density* is the number of bits per inch, which varies from 100 bits/inch to 6,250 bits/inch, depending on the type and model of the tape.

Two common types of tapes are seven-track and nine-track (also called seven-channel and nine-channel) tapes. The seven-channel tape uses six bits (such as BCD code) to represent a character; the nine-channel tape uses eight bits (such as EBCDIC or ASCII code). In both seven-channel and nine-channel tapes, the extra bit is called a *parity bit* and is used for machine-check errors. Figure 1.6 shows how data are stored on seven-channel and nine-channel tapes.

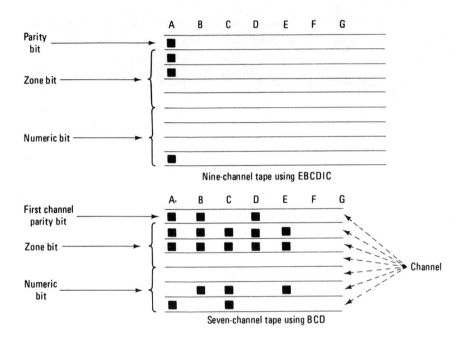

FIGURE 1.6   Nine-channel and seven-channel magnetic tapes

The magnetic-tape drive reads and writes the information on the magnetic tape. The speed of tape drives ranges from 5,000 to 400,000 characters/second. Their price ranges from $11,000 to $30,000, depending on the manufacturer and the model.

Before a tape is read or written, a reel must first be mounted on the tape drive. Read/write heads are used to read/write data. Tape drives are designed to read/write data at a constant speed. Individual records on the tape are separated by *inner-record gaps* (IRGs; see Figure 1.7). The tape drive stops read/write scanning of data when the end of the record, the IRG, is detected. The remainder of the IRG allows the tape drive to regain its speed in order to read/write the next record. The size of the IRG is 0.6 inch on nine-track tapes and 0.75 inch on seven-track tapes. This space is enough to hold 960 characters on nine-track tapes with a density of 1,600 bits/inch, and 1,200 characters on nine-track tapes with a density of 1,600 bits/inch. In many applications, the record size is

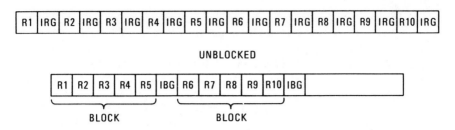

FIGURE 1.7 Blocked records

less than 1,200 or 960 characters; thus, the IRG will be much larger than the record itself.

In addition to wasting storage, too many IRGs increase transfer time, because each start and stop requires some time (a typical start/stop time is 0.008 second, or eight milliseconds). The way to optimize storage usage and to decrease transfer time is to decrease the number of inner-record gaps. This is achieved by using the blocking technique. A *block* is a collection of records. The programmer can specify the number of records that should be in a block. The blocks will be separated by *inner-block gaps* (IBGs). The tape drive reads/writes the whole block at each read/write operation. The computer separates the records of a block while the block is read into the main memory. This operation is called *deblocking*. Likewise, records are blocked in the main memory before being written on the tape. Figure 1.7 shows blocks with five records each.

Magnetic-tape cassettes. Magnetic-tape cassettes, which run on cassette tape recorders, have been developed for small computers. Usually, small computers do not require large amounts of storage. Magnetic-tape cassettes are similar to audio recording tapes; however, they are suitable for high-density digital recording, and their quality is better than that of audio recording tapes. The common length of the tape cassettes is between 150 and 200 feet, and their density ranges from 125 to 200 characters/inch. The low cost and convenience of tape cassettes has increased their usage greatly as an input/output storage medium for small computers.

1.6.2 Direct-Access Storage Devices

On these devices, also called random-access storage devices, information can be accessed in either direct or sequential order. Disk and drum are commonly used direct (random) storage.

Disk pack and disk drive. Disks record data on platters in a manner somewhat similar to phonograph records in a stack. Each platter (disk) has two sides (surfaces) to record information. Each side is divided into concentric circles called *tracks*. In turn, the tracks are divided into *sectors*. Each sector can hold a certain number of characters and has its own unique address to identify it. (See Figure 1.8.)

The disk pack consists of several disks permanently stacked on a central spindle (Figure 1.9). The number of recording surfaces and number of tracks of each surface of the disk pack varies, depending on the type of disk units. All disks are organized like either the IBM 3330 or the Burroughs B9372 Disk Drive. The IBM 3330, a disk unit used with IBM 370 Computer, has ten disks per pack. The disk pack has 19 recording surfaces (the top surface of the first disk is not used), each containing 411 tracks.

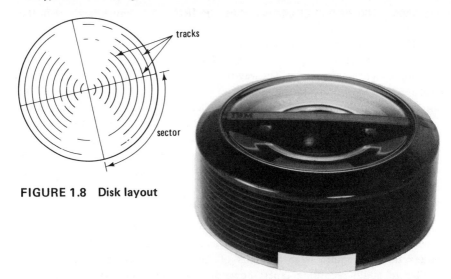

FIGURE 1.8   Disk layout

FIGURE 1.9   IBM 3336 Disk Pack. Courtesy of International Business Machines Corporation.

In most disk units, the read/write heads are assembled on access arms. These arms move in unison to position the heads at any track on the recording surfaces. Once the access arms are fixed in a position, each head can read/write data on one track on each recording surface. The collection of tracks accessible by one move of the access arms is called a *cylinder*. Therefore, the IBM 3330 has 411 cylinders, and each cylinder has 19 tracks.

The time required to transfer data to or from a disk is the sum of access time, rotational delay time, and data transfer time. The *access time*, also called *access motion time*, is the time required for the physical movement of the access arms to position read/write heads to the desired cylinder. The *rotational delay time* is the time required for the desired data on the track to revolve under the read/write head. The *data transfer time* is the time required to transfer data

TABLE 1.3 Performance of some direct-access devices

DEVICE	CAPACITY, MILLION BYTES	TRANSFER RATE, MILLISECONDS PER BYTE	AVERAGE ROTATIONAL DELAY, MILLISECONDS	ACCESS TIME, MILLISECONDS
Burroughs B9372	10	0.0048	20	None
IBM 3330 Disk Unit	100	0.0012	8.4	{ 10 one cylinder 30 average 55 maximum
IBM 2303 Drum	3.9	0.0032	8.6	None

from the device (disk) to the main memory or from main memory to the device. (See Table 1.3.)

Note that read/write heads are activated electronically, and only one of them can be activated at a time. Because the access time is the most time-consuming, efforts have been spent to eliminate it. Computer manufacturers have developed a disk unit with stationary read/write heads for every track of the surfaces. This has eliminated the need for access arms; therefore, the access time has been eliminated. The Burroughs B9372 Disk Drive was first; it is a typical disk unit with stationary read/write heads. IBM Disk Units 3344 and 3350 also have stationary read/write heads, with the same result.

The Burroughs B9372 Disk Drive consists of one to five disk drives. Each drive consists of nonremovable disks called *disk modules*. Each module has four disk platters, and data can be recorded on both sides of each platter. There are several models of the B9372. The surface of Model 1 is divided into 125 tracks, each consisting of 100-byte (eight-bit byte) segments. Thus, eight surfaces of the Model 1 unit have the capacity of 10 million bytes. One of the outstanding features of the B9372 is that there is one read/write head for each track.

During the last few years, there have been dramatic increases in the capacity of direct-access devices and reductions in their costs. (See Figure 1.10.) For

FIGURE 1.10 Data Cartridge/Disk Pack. Each data cartridge stores 50 million characters. Courtesy of International Business Machines Corporation.

example, IBM has increased the capacity of its direct-access storage by almost 1,100 percent and reduced its cost per million bytes by 90 percent. The IBM 2314 Disk Unit is being replaced by newer models in the 3300 series. Table 1.4 shows the different IBM disk units with capacities and costs.

TABLE 1.4 IBM disk units

DEVICE	IBM 2314	IBM 3330	IBM 3344	IBM 3350
Cost per million bytes	$25	$7.50	$2.90	$2.25
Capacity, in million bytes	29	100	280	317

FIGURE 1.11 IBM 2303 Drum Storage Device. Courtesy of International Business Machines Corporation.

Magnetic drum. A magnetic drum is a metal cylinder whose outer surface is coated with magnetic material. The drum rotates at a speed of about 3,500 revolutions per minute. The information is stored (recorded) on the surface of the drum, which is divided into channels or tracks, and retrieved from it by means of read/write heads. The drums are faster than disks; however, their storage capacity is less than that of disks. Figure 1.11 shows the IBM 2303 Drum Storage Device, which has a storage capacity of 3.9 million bytes.

Mass storage devices. Drums and disks are less expensive and slower than the main memory, whose speed is limited only by the speed of the electricity. Nevertheless, these direct-access storage devices are inappropriate alternatives from a cost standpoint for storing a large amount of data. Cheaper are mass storage devices for bulk file storage, large files, backup files, and infrequent-use files. These devices are direct-storage devices. Their main disadvantage is that they all require physical movement of access mechanisms to access data. Thus, mass storage devices are slower, but they have much more storage capacity than disk units or drums.

Modern mass storage devices. Magnetic-strip storage devices, such as IBM's Data Cell and NCR's CRAM, (Card Random Access Memory) have been rendered obsolete by newer devices that use cartridge-oriented techniques.

There are two types of cartridge-oriented techniques. The first uses as the storage medium a cartridge tape, similar to the cassette tape. It has a high density and requires only 10 percent of the space needed for an ordinary magnetic tape. Generally, the cartridge-oriented system contains a control unit, a reel selection mechanism, a reel mounting mechanism, and a tape-drive unit. When a particular set of data is needed, the computer commands the control unit to make the data available; the control unit signals the selection mechanism to select the cartridge tape that contains the data; then the reel mounting mechanism mounts the cartridge on the tape drive, where the data is read/written. A similar mechanism is used to dismount the cartridge and store it back in its original place. An equivalent of 8,000 tapes can be housed in such a mass storage system.

In the second approach of cartridge-oriented mass storage devices, a slightly different technique is used. Small magnetic tapes (1,100 to 2,000 inches each) in cartridges are organized in spools. The cartridges are stored in a group of cells that resembles a honeycomb (Figure 1.12). When a particular set of data is requested, the tape that contains the data is identified, removed from the storage cell, and moved to the read/write station. In this station, the tape is removed from the cartridge and wrapped around a drum to read/write the data. After the completion of the read/write, the tape is rewound, placed back in the cartridge, and moved to its original place in the storage cell. For example, the IBM 3850 Mass Storage System stores data in fist-size tape cartridges, each with a capacity

FIGURE 1.12   IBM 3850 Mass Storage System, which can store up to 472
billion characters. Courtesy of International Business Machines
Corporation.

of 50 million bytes. An organization such as this can make up to 472 billion
characters available for the system immediately.

1.6.3   Main Memory

The main memory (also called main storage, primary storage, or addressable
memory) can be imagined as a series of mailboxes. Every mailbox has a unique
number, called an *address*, to identify it. Likewise, every memory location has a
unique number, called an *absolute address*, to identify it. The content of a
memory location, as is the case with mailboxes, is completely separate from the
address of the location. To clarify this more, the address of a mailbox is a number written on the face of it; however, its contents can be anything from a bill
to a paycheck or newspaper.

However, here the analogy breaks down, because, first of all, the content of
a memory location can be only one type of data at one time—either letters *or*
numbers *or* some special characters. Thus it is unlike the mailbox, which can
contain different kinds of items at one time. Second, the memory location is
never empty; if some values have not been assigned to it, that location will contain unknown data, usually called "garbage."

In some systems, known as *word-oriented computers*, a computer word is
the smallest addressable piece of memory. An example of such a system is the
Honeywell 6060. On the other hand, a byte-oriented computer, such as the IBM
370, can address a byte as well as a word. (Recall that a byte is smaller than a
word.) It should be emphasized that a byte-oriented machine allows the whole
computer word to be addressed, and a word-oriented computer can be made to

behave like a byte-oriented machine through software techniques. Figure 1.13 shows the DECSystem 10, which is word-oriented from the hardware standpoint. However, through software manipulation, the DECSystem 10 behaves like a byte-oriented machine, accepting bytes of either six or seven or eight bits.

FIGURE 1.13   DECSystem 10. Courtesy of Digital Equipment Corporation.

RAM (random-access memory) and *ROM (read-only memory)* are the two general categories of the main memory. In the RAM memory, information can be read or written, much like recording and playing back on a home tape recorder. The ROM memory does not permit writing. It is made and wired in such a way that only reading is allowed, like home phonograph records, which can be played (read out) but not altered. The ROM memory is used to store important instructions, routines, or programs that are frequently needed, such as control programs, and mathematical routines, like a routine for calculating square roots. The memory of the pocket calculator that stores some routines, such as square root or logarithms, is ROM memory.

A *special-purpose computer*, which is made for one specific purpose, has ROM memory. A *general-purpose computer* requires RAM memory, and it will be more efficient if it is supplied with ROM as well. Almost all computers have both ROM and RAM memory.

Whether RAM or ROM, the three currently popular types of memories are *magnetic-core memory, semiconductor memory*, and *bubble memory.*

Magnetic-core memory. The core storage is constructed from thousands of tiny metal doughnut-shaped rings, each of which can be magnetized in two different directions. One direction denotes a 1 bit and the other a 0 bit. The magnetic core needs a restore cycle to restore itself to its original state after a

FIGURE 1.14   64K bytes of memory of NCR Century Series. Courtesy of NCR Corporation.

read operation; otherwise, the read will be a destructive read. Figure 1.14 shows 64 K bytes of memory in National Cash Register (NCR) Century series computers.

Semiconductor memory.   In the early 1970s, the integration of the faster MOS (metal oxide semiconductor) micro-miniaturized integrated-circuit memory was introduced. The semiconductor utilizes circuitry on a silicon chip. It is

FIGURE 1.15   NCR's Microprocessor Chip. Courtesy of NCR Corporation.

smaller and significantly faster than the magnetic-core memory. The semiconductor's state is on when it carries an electrical current and off when it does not. Unlike magnetic-core memory, the semiconductor memory requires a constant power supply, and it cannot retain its content if the electric power is cut. Therefore, there must be an emergency backup system and an emergency procedure to refresh the memory. There is no need for a restore cycle, because the semiconductor memory automatically has nondestructive read capabilities. Currently, semiconductor memory costs more than magnetic-core memory. Figure 1.15 shows a circuit board which includes a powerful microprocessor chip.

Bubble memory.   Bubble memory is made of a thin film of semiconductor material with magnetized spots called bubbles on it (Figure 1.16). Bubbles are microscopic spots with polarity opposite to the material on which they are set. Data are stored on the thin film by shifting bubbles on the semiconductor

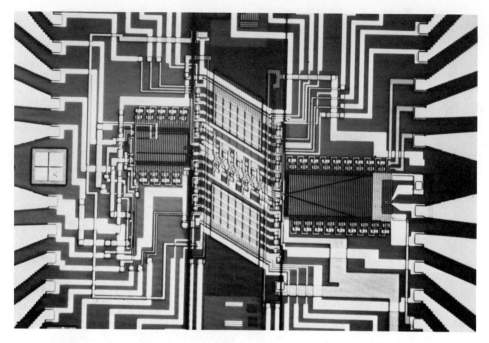

**FIGURE 1.16   1K-bit demonstrates storage functions of bubble lattice.
Courtesy of International Business Machines Corporation.**

material. The presence of a bubble in a specific position represents binary 1; when the bubble is absent from that specific position, it is binary 0. Since bubbles are much smaller than magnetic cores, more data can be stored in a smaller area. For example, 20,000 characters can be stored in a bubble memory module the size of a U.S. quarter. This is one of its main advantages. Also, like magnetic core, bubble memory has the ability to retain its content in case of electric power failure. Bubble memories are more expensive than both semiconductor and magnetic-core memory.

One of the newest experimental devices being considered is the laser memory. This technique employs the polarization of light similar to the way the magnetic core employs magnetic polarization. It is expected to be ten times faster than the existing average access speed, with less than 1 percent of the current cost of storing data and with the primary storage (within the CPU) around 1 trillion characters.

Since 1960, computer manufacturers have dramatically decreased the physical size of main memory while increasing its capacity and, at the same time, have reduced its price by almost 90 percent. Figure 1.17 shows IBM's price reduction for the main memory.

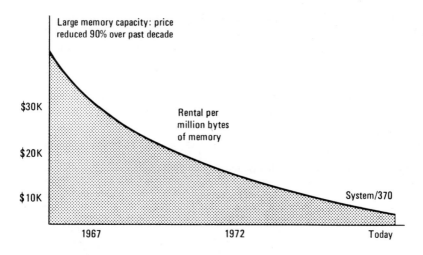

FIGURE 1.17   IBM price for the main memory

The standard definition of the central processing unit limits the CPU to that part of the computer that interprets and executes instructions. Since the interpretation and execution of instructions are performed by the control unit and arithmetic/logical section, the definition implies that the CPU consists of these two sections only. We will follow this standard definition; but keep in mind that many use the term CPU to mean the entire computer (excluding I/O devices) and consider the CPU to contain, besides the control unit and arithmetic/logical section, the main memory and registers.

The activities of a computer system are controlled and coordinated by the *control section*. This component is responsible for recognizing instructions as opposed to data and for providing temporary locations for answers and partial results during calculations.

In executing an instruction, the control section performs the following actions:

1. Selects the instruction to be executed
2. Interprets the instruction and determines the operation that should be performed by the instruction
3. Determines if any data are needed and, if so, their addresses
4. Provides the address where a result should be stored
5. Provides the address of the next instruction that should be executed

The four arithmetic operations (addition, subtraction, multiplication, and division) and all tests are performed in the second component of the CPU, the *arithmetic/logical section*. This section also has the ability to receive data from main memory to a register. Then the control unit interprets the instruction that a register (explained later), and alter the sequence of instructions as a result of testing for the existence of a condition encountered during processing. Since 1960, developments in electronic technology have improved processing performance significantly. Table 1.5 demonstrates the 90 percent reduction in processing time and 92 percent reduction in processing cost in this short period of time.

TABLE 1.5   Processing performance since 1960

YEAR	PROCESSING TIME, SAME TASK	PROCESSING COST, SAME TASK
1960	47 seconds	$2.48
1965	37 seconds	$0.47
Today	5 seconds	$0.20

To realize the scope of developments in the electronics field, compare the Univac I, one of the very first commercial computers, which was introduced by Sperry Rand Corporation in 1952, with some of today's computers. Univac I's memory capacity was 12,000 characters, its speed was 4,000 characters/second, it weighed about four tons, it occupied 575 square feet, and it cost $2 million. Today, one can buy a briefcase computer, with memory capacity around 40 K and able to execute 1 million instructions/second, for less than $20,000.

1.8   REGISTERS

Registers are small storage units that serve as pathways or conduits connecting the CPU and the main memory.

The main memory (see Figure 1.18) contains the program and data. On most computers, the data and instructions get to the CPU from the main memory through the registers. An instruction or a piece of data is first moved from the main memory to a register. Then the control unit interprets the instruction that is in the register and tells the arithmetic/logical section to perform the required task. Usually, the result of each calculation and processing is first stored temporarily in the register before it is stored in the main memory.

Registers exist in many different forms. Some are used by the control section, others by the arithmetic section, and some others are used as temporary storage. On some computers, they are considered parts of the main memory; in others, they are parts of the CPU; and still others consider them to lie between

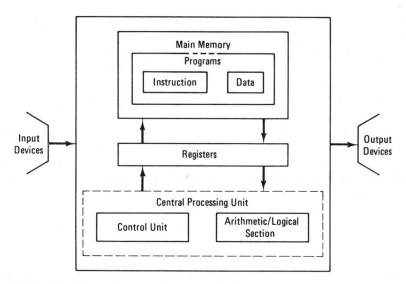

FIGURE 1.18 The entire computer, with I/O devices

the CPU and the main memory. The number and the size of registers differ from one computer manufacturer to another. Some common sizes of registers are 16, 24, 32, and 36 bits. Registers can be accessed as fast as or faster than the main memory.

1.9 MULTIPROCESSING SYSTEMS

A multiprocessing system is a system that has more than one arithmetic/logical section or more than one CPU. Such systems are capable of executing more than one program at a time. The number of programs that can be executed simultaneously depends on the number of CPUs and arithmetic/logical sections in the system.

1.10 CHANNELS

As we have seen, the processor is much faster than input/output devices, such as the card reader, line printer, terminal, and even disk and tape drives. Therefore, it is not economical to tie the performance of the processor to the performance of the input/output devices. Channel devices are used to connect the CPU to the I/O devices. Several I/O devices can be hooked to a channel. Channels work under the control of the operating system (explained later). Once a channel is activated, it has the capability to execute its own specific programs to perform I/O functions. Therefore, channels themselves can be considered small computers designed to execute I/O programs.

Whenever an I/O operation is requested, the operating system checks to see whether the specific channel and device are available. If both are available, then the operating system orders the channel to perform the requested I/O operation. Once the channel starts, no CPU usage is required. This means that the CPU becomes free to perform other tasks, such as calculations or execution of different programs. These CPU activities can occur at the same time that channels are performing I/O functions.

There are two types of channels, multiplexor and selector. The *multiplexor channel* is able to work on more than one device at a time. It transfers a character of each device in turn. For instance, assume that five card readers, all of which can work simultaneously, are attached to a multiplexor channel. The multiplexor channel transfers the first character of the first card reader, then the first character of the second card reader, and so on through the fifth. Then it returns to the first card reader and transfers the second character from it, then the second character from the second card reader, and so on. Since these characters must definitely not be mixed, the multiplexor channel has the capability to store the information of each card reader in a separate place. The slower input/output devices, such as card reader .and line printer, are hooked to the multiplexor channel. One multiplexor channel can have both input and output devices.

More than one device can also be hooked to the *selector channel*, but the selector channel works only on one device at a time. It is used with high-speed I/O devices such as magnetic tape, disk, or drum unit, transferring the information in burst mode. Many channels can be hooked to the CPU by means of channel control units, one of which can serve different channels.

1.11   OPERATING SYSTEMS

Operating systems are also known as monitor systems. The operating system is a collection of programs provided by the manufacturer of the computer to monitor the operations of all programs in the system and to enable computer resources to be shared by different users. The computer system operates under the direction of the operating system.

The *executive program* is the heart of the operating system. The executive itself is a collection of programs and has many components. Functions such as job scheduling, resource allocation, program loading, event monitoring, program termination processing, input/output control, system startup, and processing support are performed by various components of the executive program. The operating system also contains many other programs for system-management functions and data-manipulation functions.

1.11.1 Types of Operating Systems

In general, there are four kinds of operating systems:

1. Batch-processing system
2. Time-sharing system
3. Real-time system
4. Multiprogramming system

In the *batch-processing* environment, the programs (jobs) are executed in a sequential manner, and the programmers do not interact with the system during the processing of their jobs. In the *time-sharing* environment, the programmers have access to the CPU through terminals, and they can interact with the system while their jobs are in process. In the *real-time* environment, the on-line input data determine the type of job or the program that should be processed. The role of the terminal users in the real-time system is nothing more than clerical. For example, airline checkers or bank tellers cannot write their own programming; all they do is feed data. The data fed cause a particular program or job to be processed. In the *multiprogramming* environment, more than one program can be in memory at one time; however, it is not necessary that the system be able to execute more than one program at a time. If it does, then the system is a multiprocessing system as well.

1.11.2 Compilers

Recall that computers obey only commands (instructions) that are in machine-language form. Therefore, programs written in any other language, such as FORTRAN, COBOL, BASIC, or PL/1, must be translated to machine lan-

FIGURE 1.19 **The compiler translates the source program into the object program.**

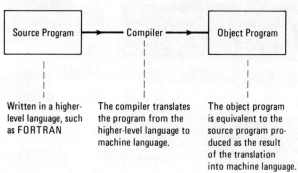

Source Program	Compiler	Object Program
Written in a higher-level language, such as FORTRAN	The compiler translates the program from the higher-level language to machine language.	The object program is equivalent to the source program produced as the result of the translation into machine language.

guage. The computer program that translates the program written in a higher-level language (called *source* program) into the program written in machine language (called *object* program) is called the *compiler*. Thus, compilers are complicated programs written to translate the source program into the object program. (See Figure 1.19.)

When the source program is written in assembly language, the assembler, not the compiler, translates it into the object program. Like the compiler, the assembler is a translator and a part of the operating system. The main difference is that the assembler produces a single machine instruction for every instruction in the source program, but the compiler may generate more than one.

1.12 CLASSES OF COMPUTERS

1.12.1 Microcomputer

The development of LSI (large-scale integrated) circuitry has made the miniaturization of computers possible. An LSI density-packed circuit can contain more than 10,000 transistors. The microcomputer can be set on an area of less than 60 square inches; its circuitry can be held in one hand, but it has all the attributes of a full-size computer. The microprocessor, the heart of the microcomputer, fits on a single silicon chip the size of a nailhead. It contains a control unit and an arithmetic/logical section that is equivalent to the CPU of a full-size

FIGURE 1.20   Radio Shack complete TRS-80 business computer system, sold for less than $4000. Courtesy of Radio Shack, A Division of Tandy Corporation.

Radio Shack TRS-80 Microcomputer System

computer. The microcomputer has the necessary circuitry for its connection to I/O devices such as paper-tape reader, cassette tape units, and terminals.

Microcomputers have been effectively used in both industrial and non-industrial fields. For example, microcomputers are used to control traffic, assembly lines, and electronic cash registers, and to monitor performance of automobile engines and microwave ovens. Usually, ROM memory is used in the microcomputer to perform one specific task, such as one of those mentioned above.

Because of limited storage capabilities, the microcomputer has not greatly attracted the interest of large businesses. However, because of its inexpensive price (usually less than $900), a great number of students, lawyers, doctors, and housewives have become increasingly interested in the microcomputer. Today, more than 50 companies produce microcomputers. Some have predicted that in the 1980s, the price of a microcomputer will be around $10, and that there will be 10-15 million microcomputers by 1985. Figure 1.20 shows Radio Shack Business Computer System configuration, containing a microcomputer.

1.12.2   Minicomputer

In the mid-1960s, Digital Equipment Corporation introduced the first mini-computer, the PDP-8. Since then, more than 50 computer manufacturers have started producing minicomputers. Today, 60 percent of installed computers are minicomputers, and it is estimated that there will be over 2 million installed by 1985. Minicomputers have been accepted widely because of their low prices compared to their processing power. They have comparatively small memories, slow input/output devices and limited compilers and programming languages. Minicomputers are physically small; many models weigh less than 50 pounds. Like the full-size computer, the minicomputer has a CPU, and virtually all I/O devices can be connected to it.

Minicomputers have been used effectively in many sections of industry, business, government, and the educational and scientific fields. Both large and small companies have found many applications for them. Using ROM memory, a minicomputer can be programmed to do some specific tasks very efficiently. Some are used, for example, in intelligent terminals, to monitor a group of I/O devices, to control an industrial process, and to control a chemical process, as well as in other applications by small businesses, engineering and scientific companies, and the medical and communication fields. They are widely used in the network and distributing data-processing organizations.

Some popular minicomputers are Digital Equipment Corporation's PDP-8 and PDP-11, Burroughs's 700 Series and B80, IBM's 5100 Series, Hewlett-Packard's 2000 and 3000 Series, Honeywell's Level 61 and 62, Varian's 620, Micro 800 of Microdata, Texas Instruments' 900, Raytheon's 700, NOVA, and the Eclipse Series of Data General.

1.12.3 Small Computer Systems

Small computers were intended to be used by small businesses, industries, or engineering companies. They are also used by many educational, medical, and government organizations. Small computers are characterized by their moderate price, which such small organizations can afford. Bigger than minicomputers and smaller than medium-size computers, they are usually supplied with an operating system to perform memory, CPU, and data and file management. They also include utilities and built-in routines, text editors, linkages, and even some software packages. Usually, a small computer has most higher-level language compilers, such as FORTRAN, COBOL, RPG, and BASIC. Examples of small computers are Burroughs B80, B800, B1700, and B1800; NCR Century 50; IBM System/3; some models of Hewlett-Packard 3000; and some models of PDP-11 or PDP-16.

1.12.4 Medium-Size and Large Computers

Both medium-size and large computers support ranges of peripheral devices. For example, these systems may have several dozens of disk and magnetic-tape drives, card readers, and line printers, and more than 50 terminals for medium-size and more than 100 terminals for large computers. They are supported by

FIGURE 1.21   Medium-size computer, Honeywell 66DPS. Courtesy of Honeywell Information Systems.

powerful, complicated operating systems, and these systems support all varieties of computer languages and software packages. Some typical medium-size computers are IBM's 370/Model 125, 135, and 145; DECSystem's 10; Burroughs's B1800, B2800, B3800, and B4800; NCR's N-8350; Honeywell's Level 64; and Univac's 1100/20. Some typical large computers are Burroughs's B4800 and B6800; DECSystem's 20; IBM's 370/Models 148 and 155; Honeywell's Level 66; and NCR's 8560.

Figure 1.21 shows a medium-size computer, Honeywell 66 DPS, one of the Honeywell Series 66 computers. It has MOS memory. It can execute 1 million instructions per second. The system runs under Honeywell's General Comprehensive Operating System (GCOS).

Figure 1.22 shows a Univac 1100/40, which is a typical large computer. The

FIGURE 1.22   Large computer, Univac 1100/40. Courtesy of Sperry Univac, A division of Sperry Corp.

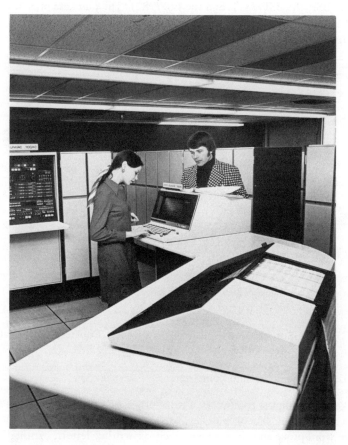

Univac 1100/40 can be a single or multiprocessor. It runs under the Univac 1100 operating system. Its main memory is constructed from semiconductors, and its capacity can be expanded to 1 billion bytes. The CPU cycle of Univac 1100/40 is about 100 nanoseconds; in other words, it can execute about 10 million instructions per second.

1.12.5 Supercomputers

The supercomputers are faster, bigger in size, and more expensive than large computers. Their memory capacity may be more than 10 million bytes. Some examples of supercomputers are Burroughs's B7800; Univac's 1100/80; Honeywell's Level 68; Amdahl's 470V/7; Cyber's 170; IBM's 168, 168MP, and 168AP; and Itel's AS/5-1MP and AS/5-3MP.

Figure 1.23 shows Burroughs's B7800 general-purpose system, which can perform up to 50 million operations per second. The three models of BSP are the basic BSP, the BSP/7811, and the BSP/7821. The purchase price ranges from $3,885,520 to $6,164,520, depending on the system size and auxiliary configuration. The lease rate ranges from $128,523 to $174,633 per month.

FIGURE 1.23   Supercomputer, Burroughs's B7800. Courtesy of Burroughs Corporation.

1.12.6 Word-Processing Computers

Like regular digital computers, a word-processing computer has a CPU, main memory, and input and output devices. However, this computer is dedicated only to word-processing operations, such as writing letters, writing contract forms, text editing, reproducing forms, and other typical business and non-business communication activities.

Word-processing operations are sequential and syntactical functions performed on words. A word-processing computer allows a typist, using a terminal instead of a typewriter, to change or correct material that has been stored (written) or is being typed. The user sees the system as a complete publishing facility using computer technology. The word-processing computer is utilized for input, editing, and output of information and writing of documents. Some have estimated that a secretary using a word-processing system can produce ten times more than without one.

1.13   THE COMPUTER INDUSTRY

The revenue generated in the computer industry in 1977 was around $40 billion; it is estimated that the amount will be $64 billion by 1981. In 1978, computer-related spending was 3.2 percent of the gross national product. A study by the American Federation of Information Processing Societies in 1977 predicted that spending on computer services and products would become 8.3 percent of the GNP by 1985. The same study showed total shipments of $15.9 billion in 1975 and predicted them as $30.5 billion by 1981.

American computer equipment makes up 87 percent of the world's computer market, but it is predicted that it will decrease to 81 percent by 1981. The United States derives 50 percent of its computer revenue from overseas sales. This resulted in a $2.8 billion trade surplus in 1977. The U.S. government is the biggest user of the computer. The number of computers it leased and owned in 1971 was 5,900; in 1977, this number was between 11,000 and 15,000.

There are many different computer companies and corporations. *Computerworld*, a weekly computer newspaper, lists the companies on the stock market in five different categories: computer systems manufacturers, leasing companies, software and EDP services, peripherals and subsystems, and supplies and accessories companies. IBM, Burroughs, Honeywell, Univac, CDC, NCR, Amdahl, Digital Equipment, Data General, and Hewlett-Packard are well-known computer systems manufacturers. Of the leasing companies, Itel, Leasco, Leaspac, U.S. Leasing, and Boothe Courier Corporation are the leaders. EDS, Comshare, On-Line System Incorporated, Automatic Data Processing, LOGICOM, Tymshare Incorporated, and Computer Service Network are well-known software and EDP service companies. Some in the peripheral and service area are Calcomp, Ampex, Centronic, Tektronix Incorporated, Data 100, Hazeltine, Harris, Intel, and Storage Technology. Standard Register, Wallace Business Forms, Nashua Corporation, 3M Company, Tab Product Company, and Wabash Magnetic are examples of supplies and accessories companies.

1.14 CAREERS IN THE COMPUTER FIELD

Following are brief definitions of computer-related careers.

1.14.1 Programmer

Programmers are responsible for design, documenting, coding, debugging, testing, and implementation of programs. They may also be asked to write program specifications.

There are several levels of programming careers, such as programmer I, II, or III, or senior programmer or programmer analyst. Programmers can be either commercial or scientific. Most commercial programmers are COBOL programmers; common among the scientific are FORTRAN and PL/1 programmers.

1.14.2 Systems Programmer

Systems programmers are responsible for creating, updating, or maintaining compilers, assemblers, utility programs, and other components of the operating system. They also write ·necessary software programs to support application programs, maintain and modify existing vendor software packages, and create and tailor software packages according to the needs of their company.

1.14.3 Systems Analyst

Systems analysts are responsible for systems analysis, systems design, systems specifications, and liaison with the user. Systems analysts in some places are even responsible for program specifications and some programming as well. They may also supervise implementation of systems and programs and may design systems test data and testing strategy. Systems analysts are also responsible for determining the definition of the systems problems at hand. There are different levels of systems analysts; the highest level is the senior systems analyst, who leads a group of analysts or a project team.

1.14.4 Technical Service Manager

The responsibilities of technical service managers include supervision and leadership of the staff responsible for operating systems software, maintenance of software packages, and hardware/software planning and evaluation. Often they have some additional responsibilities related to computer operations and internal technical education.

1.14.5 Systems and Programming Manager

A systems and programming manager, in small organizations, usually directs and supervises the efforts of a group of analysts or programmers. In a large organization, he or she has the responsibility for the development and implementation of information systems for a functional area or areas.

1.14.6 Computer or Data Center Manager

A person in this position is responsible for the operation, scheduling, and management of all computers, peripheral equipment, data entry equipment, data control, and quality control of the equipment in the computer center. Supervision of the software systems, and applications, maintenance, and programming are also included in the responsibilities.

1.14.7 Information Systems Director

The information systems director is responsible for overall management—directing the information and computer systems operations and activities—and generally reports to a top-level executive.

1.14.8 Computer Industry Marketing
Representative

The computer industry marketing representative sells computers, peripherals, and services.

1.14.9 Computer Industry Marketing Manager

Management and administration of marketing representatives are the responsibilities of the computer industry marketing manager.

1.15 SUMMARY

Input, processing, and output are the three main activities of the computer system. The hardware component of the computer system includes input, output, processing, storage, and data-recording devices. The software component consists of all programs and computer languages, including computer program packages, operating system programs, compilers, application programs, and the like. The CPU is composed of a control and an arithmetic section. The disk and drum are direct-access storage devices; magnetic tape is a sequential-access device. The main memory is the fastest direct-access storage device. BCD, EBCDIC, and ASCII are the three best-known codes for the internal representation of data.

1.16   REVIEW QUESTIONS AND SUGGESTED PROBLEMS

1. What are the main activities of the computer system?

2. Feeding information into the computer is _____ .

3. A set of instructions (or commands) written in a computer language to accomplish a task is called_____ .

4. The person who writes the computer program is called the _____.

5. Give three examples of higher-level computer languages.

6. *True or False. Character set* means the set of all letters, digits, and special characters such as $, *,), (, etc.

7. *True or False.* The byte is used to represent a character.

8. What is the relation between a bit, a byte, and a computer word?

9. Give three examples of some well-known codes for internal data representation.

10. Using EBCDIC, convert your first name into machine language.

11. Using ASCII, convert your last name into machine language.

12. *True or False.* Once the card reader reads the information from the punched card, that information must be translated into either BCD, EBCDIC, or ASCII to be suitable for processing.

13. *True or False.* In output operations, the information is retrieved from inside the computer to the outside media.

14. *True or False.* The tape drive and disk drive are used for input/output operations.

15. Give an example of an output device that cannot be used as an input device.

16. *True or False.* Testing, calculating, and all other processing are performed in the CPU.

17. What is a microsecond?

18. What is the hardware component?

19. What is a data station?

20. What is a floppy disk?

21. What is a key-to-tape device?

22. For what is the CRT used with keying devices?

23. For what are minicomputers used in input operations?

24. List some disadvantages of keypunched input.

25. *True or False.* Data can be punched directly onto the tape or the diskette.

26. What is meant by POS?

27. In general, there are two kinds of storage devices. Name them.

28. What are mass storage devices?

29. What are secondary storage devices?

30. Arrange the following storage devices in decreasing order with respect to storage capacity: disk pack, main memory, drum.

31. Arrange the devices of question 30 in order with the fastest device first.

32. What is the magnetic-tape drive?

33. Is the magnetic-tape drive an input, output, or input/output device?

34. Is the disk drive an input, output, or input/output device?

35. Another popular name for the direct-access storage device is _____.

36. Can information from magnetic tape be retrieved randomly?

37. Can information from the disk or drum be accessed randomly?

38. Can information from random-access storage devices be accessed sequentially?

39. Which takes less time, reading from cards or from magnetic tape into the computer?

40. Is there a device that is able to read magnetic-ink characters? If so, name it.

41. What is the input device that can read data optically?

42. What does CRT stand for? Is it an input or an output device?

43. Can a terminal unit be used for both input and output operations?

44. Name four output devices.

45. Can the information in main memory be accessed sequentially, randomly, or both?

46. What is meant by transfer rate?

47. The surface of the disk is divided into _____.

48. What is meant by access operation?

49. What is access time?

50. What does sequential access mean?

51. What does random access mean?

52. What are auxiliary storage devices?

53. Compare the advantages and disadvantages of magnetic tape and punched cards.

54. Define:
    a. The cylinder
    b. Rotational delay time
    c. Access motion time
    d. Transfer time rate
    e. Block of records

55. What are different types of terminals?

56. What is an intelligent terminal?

57. What is meant by the term *processing*?

58. Define *central processing unit*.

59. What are the two components of the CPU?

60. What is the purpose of the main memory?

61. What are the functions of the control section?

62. What is a register?

63. Which is faster, bubble memory or semiconductor memory?

64. Which is faster, semiconductor memory or magnetic-core memory?

65. Can information from the main memory be accessed randomly?

66. Can information from the main memory be accessed sequentially?

67. A system that is able to have more than one program in the main memory at one time is called _____.

68. What are the functions of the arithmetic/logical unit?

69. The component of the CPU that recognizes instructions as opposed to data is _____.

70. The system with two or more arithmetic/logical sections is called _____ _____.

71. *True or False.* The multiprocessing system has the ability to execute more than one program at a time.

72. *True or False.* A system can be multiprogramming and multiprocessing at the same time.

73. *True or False.* A multiprogramming system does not necessarily have the ability to execute more than one program at a time.

74. What is the main advantage of bubble memory?

75. Which has more storage capacity, bubble memory or semiconductor memory?

76. *True or False.* For a program to be executed, the program must be in the main memory.

77. For what are registers used?

78. What is K?

79. Can more than one channel be hooked to a channel control unit?

80. Describe both selector and multiplexor channels.

81. Can more than one device be attached to a multiplexor channel? a selector channel?

82. What are the differences between RAM and ROM memories?

83. What is a FORTRAN compiler?

84. In general, computer languages are classified into three categories. What are these categories?

85. What are the different categories of computers?

86. What are the five different categories of computer companies?

87. Name some computer-related careers.

88. Make a survey and write a paper to classify computers.

89. Write a paper about a typical microcomputer.

90. Write a paper about a typical minicomputer.

91. Write a paper about a typical small computer.

92. Write a paper about a typical supercomputer.

93. Write a paper about microcomputer manufacturers.

94. Write a paper about mainframe computer manufacturers.

95. Write a paper about minicomputer manufacturers.

96. Write a paper about the usage of minicomputers in business.

97. Write a paper about the personnel-type computer market.

98. Write a paper about small computer usage in business.

99. If you have to choose a computer, what characteristics should you look for?

100. Make a survey of salaries of the data-processing professionals in your area or state.

101. Make a survey about different types of computer-related careers in your area or state.

102. Write a paper about the responsibilities of a:
   a. Systems analyst
   b. Programmer
   c. Data-processing manager
   d. Systems programmer

103. Write a paper about computer leasing companies.

104. Write a paper about software and EDP services companies.

105. Write a paper about peripheral and subsystems companies.

106. Write a paper about supplies and accessories companies.

2 PROBLEM-SOLVING TOOLS

A large part of the solution of any problem lies in knowing the objectives of the problem. An adequate statement and definition of the problem is the most important part of the framework for problem solving. This is particularly true with computer problem solving. Because the computer permits no ambiguity, the definition of the problem must be clear and complete, and must contain no ambiguity whatsoever.

2.2   ALGORITHMS

Once the problem has been defined, the next task is to determine a strategy to solve it. One of the best approaches to finding and expressing the solution for a given problem is a stepwise approach. A set of directions or instructions for performing these stepwise operations designed to lead to the solution of a problem or the accomplishment of a task is called an *algorithm*, a word that comes from the name of the ninth-century Persian mathematician, al-Khuwarizmi. Examples of algorithms are the formulas and steps in computing depreciation, turnover rate, compound interest, service charge for a stock transaction, or a recipe for cooking.

Any computer-based algorithm should have three characteristics: (1) finiteness, (2) unambiguity, and (3) generality.

Finiteness means that the algorithm must have an internal control to be terminated after a finite number of steps and iterations, which should give a desired result.

A computer-based algorithm allows *no ambiguity*. A statement such as, "Find the depreciation rate per year using the straight-line method," is ambiguous. You must spell out *how* to calculate the depreciation rate using the straight-line method, such as:

Yearly depreciation rate = (Cost − Scrap value)/Number of expected years of useful life of the asset

Also considered ambiguous are statements like, "Forecast the sale for the coming period," "Find the charge per amount of stock transaction," or, "Find the compound interest." You must outline the exact formulas and the steps for their calculation. In the recipe algorithm to bake a cake, a statement like, "Mix flour, milk, and salt together," is ambiguous. You must specify what proportions of these materials should be mixed.

Generality is the third characteristic of the computer-based algorithm. It is better for the algorithm to be general; otherwise, it works only for the specific case it is designed for. The example below will help you comprehend these concepts.

Example 2.1: Car-Rental Problem

To rent a car from the Modern Car Rental Agency, you must pay a fee of $10 per day plus 10 cents for each mile you drive. Write an algorithm for instructing the computer to read a card file of customer data, and to calculate and print the rental charge. One possible stepwise solution (algorithm) is:

1. Start.
2. Read number of days, old mileage, new mileage.
3. Charge = (Number of days × 10) + [0.10 × (New mileage − Old mileage)] .
4. Write charge.
5. Stop.

The algorithm above is not general, because if the Modern Car Rental Agency decides to charge $12 instead of $10 per day, the algorithm—specifically, step 3—must be modified. This is the case with the mileage charge as well (10 cents per mile). To generalize this algorithm, these rates should be read from an external medium, adding the task to step 2. In addition, once the steps of the algorithm are initiated, it calculates only the charge for one customer; to find the charge for the next customer, we have to start again from scratch. The deficiency in this algorithm can be understood if you imagine that you are going to make five identical products on a machine. How inefficient it would be if you turned the machine on and off to produce these five products! To overcome this deficiency in the algorithm, a step following step 2 is implemented: The number of days is checked. If it is zero, the operation is stopped; otherwise, the operation in the step following step 2 is performed. Thus, the algorithm becomes:

1. Start.
2. Read number of days, rate per day, rate per mile, new mileage, old mileage.
3. If number of days = 0, stop.
4. Charge = (Number of days × Rate per day) + [Rate per mile × (New mileage − Old mileage)] .
5. Write charge.
6. Go to 2.

In this algorithm, the signal to stop the operation is number of days. In step 3, this flag is tested. If it is zero, the operation is stopped.

The computer will always go to the next step except when told explicitly to go to a different step. Because the instruction of step 6 always sends the control back to step 2—that is, to another Read, you must be sure that the number of days in the last data card is zero; otherwise, the operations will continue and never end.

2.3   HOW TO EXPRESS ALGORITHMS

There is a variety of methods to express algorithms. Pseudo code and flowcharts are explained below, several others in Chapter 12.

2.3.1   Pseudo Code

Pseudo code is an informal method used to represent program logic in a structured narrative form resembling English sentences. The text is similar to some high-level computer languages, such as FORTRAN or COBOL or PL/1. However, the text does not impose the strict rules that must be obeyed when the actual program is written. As a matter of fact, the algorithm for the car-rental problem in the previous section was expressed in pseudo code form. Other ways to express the algorithm of example 2.1 are shown below.

1. Start.
2. Do steps 3 through 5 until end of data.
3. Read DAYS, RATDAY, RATMIL, NEWMIL, OLDMIL.
4. CHARGE = DAYS × RATDAY + RATMIL × (NEWMIL − OLDMIL).
5. Write CHARGE.
6. Stop.

Or:
Start

DOWHILE not end of data

    Read DAYS, RATDAY, RATMIL, NEWMIL, OLDMIL

    CHARGE = DAYS x RATDAY + RATMIL x (NEWMIL — OLDMIL)

    Write CHARGE

End DOWHILE

Stop

Or:

1. Start.
2. Repeat step 3 through 4.
3. Read DAYS, RATDAY, RATMIL, NEWMIL, OLDMIL.
4. IF DAYS = 0 Stop
    Else CHARGE = DAYS x RATDAY + RATMIL x (NEWMIL – OLDMIL)
        Write CHARGE
   End IF.

Note that the abbreviated words DAYS, RATDAY, RATMIL, NEWMIL, and OLDMIL are used for number of days, rate per day, rate per mile, new mileage, and old mileage respectively.

2.3.2   Flowcharts

Flowcharting language is a graphic language for depicting and expressing algorithms. In this language, geometrical shapes (figures) are used to represent commands (instructions) to a computer and the discrete operations of a computer. The programmer expresses his program in a series of boxes (diagrams) connected by arrows that indicate the order of the operations. In other words, the flowchart diagram presents the components of the problem pictorially, expresses each operation, and demonstrates the logical relationships between the various operations and their effect on the overall system. There are two sets of flowcharting symbols: program flowcharting symbols and system flowcharting symbols.

2.3.2.1   PROGRAM FLOWCHART

The program flowchart is a micro flowchart—in other words, a detailed flowchart expressing in detail all operations that must be performed in the program. Figure 2.1 shows the American National Standards Institute's recommendations for the use of flowcharting symbols in program flowcharting. Below is a more detailed description of the usage of some of these symbols.

1. Start, exit, or stop symbol:

This symbol is used to indicate the initiation of a program or procedure when the word *Start* is written inside:

Start

and to indicate the termination of a program or procedure when the word *Stop* or *Exit* is written inside:

Stop

2. Input/output symbol:

The parallelogram is used to express an input or output operation—that is, to read or write the values of *variables*. A *variable* is a name representing a memory location whose content varies. (Chapter 3 discusses the rules for creating variable names.) For example:

Read NUMDAY, RATDAY, RATEML,
NEWML, OLDML

indicates that the value for the variables NUMDAY, RATDAY, RATEML, NEWML, and OLDML should be read into the computer. But

Write CHARGE

indicates that the value of the variable CHARGE is written onto an outside medium (such as paper or magnetic tape) from inside the computer.

3. Processing symbol:

The rectangle is used to express a processing operation such as arithmetic calculation or data manipulation. Thus:

INTRST = AMOUNT * RATE

indicates that the result of multiplying AMOUNT by RATE will become the value of INTRST. (Note that in the computer language, * and / are used for multiplication and division symbols respectively.)

4. Decision symbol:

The diamond-shaped box is used for testing a condition. The condition should be clearly written inside the box. If the result of testing the condition is true,

Symbol	Symbol Name	Meaning
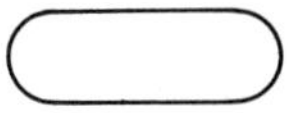	Start or Terminal	Start or end a sequence of operations
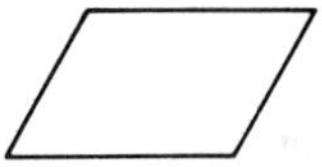	Input/Output	Input/output operations
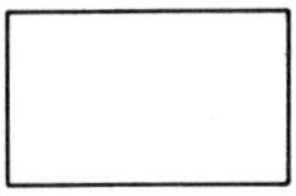	Process	Processing functions
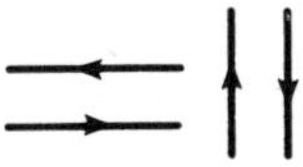	Direction of Flow	The direction of flow of processing is indicated by arrows
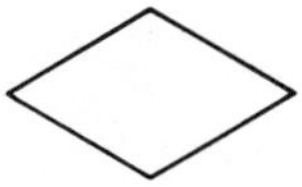	Decision	A logical decision
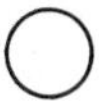	Connector	Connections between parts of the flow chart in the same page
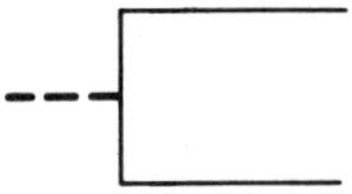	Annotation	Explanatory comments
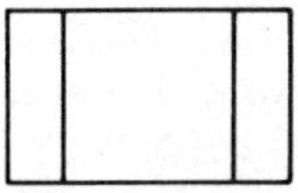	Predefined Process	For predefined functions or processes
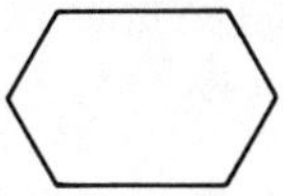	Preparation	For preparations of field or instructions
	Off page Connector	Connection between parts of the flowchart in different pages

FIGURE 2.1   ANSI symbols for program flowcharting

control takes one direction; otherwise, it follows the other direction. Usually, the direction to be taken if the result of the test is true is marked by *Yes* (or simply *Y*) or *True* (or simply *T*), and the direction if the result of the test is false is marked by *No* (or simply *N*) or *False* (or simply *F*). For example, in Figure 2.2, in Box 1, the condition whether the value of AMOUNT is less than 100 is tested. The result of this test determines which instruction should be executed next. If the result of the test is true—that the value of AMOUNT is less than 100—the processor executes the instruction in Box 2 and then the instruction in Box 4. However, if the value of AMOUNT is not less than 100 (the result of the test is false), the instruction in Box 3 will be executed, followed by the instruction in Box 4.

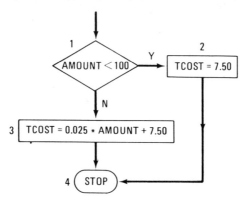

FIGURE 2.2   Use of flowchart diagram

The diamond figure may have more than two exits. This version of it will be discussed in Chapter 8, in conjunction with the computed GO TO statement.

Figure 2.3 shows the flowchart for the Modern Car Rental Agency program. For convenience, the algorithm is repeated in the figure. Note that meaningful shorter names are used instead of longer names—for example, NUMDAY in place of "number of days"—because most computer languages limit variable names to a certain number of characters. (Chapter 3 explains in detail how to choose variable names.) The variable names used in Figure 2.3 are these:

NUMDAY: Number of days
RATDAY: Rate per day
RATEML: Rate per mile
NEWML: New mileage
OLDML: Old mileage
CHARGE: Charge

Pseudo Code Form

1. Start.
2. Read number of days, rate per day, rate per mile, new mileage, old mileage.
3. If number of days = 0, stop.
4. Charge = Number of days x Rate per day + Rate per mile x (New mileage — Old mileage)
5. Write charge.
6. Go to 2.

Program Flowchart

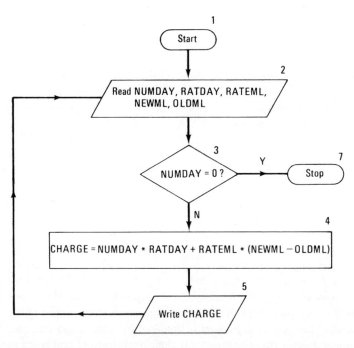

FIGURE 2.3 Pseudo code form and program flowchart for car-rental problem

The instructions in boxes 1, 2, 4, and 5 of the flowchart in Figure 2.3 represent steps 1, 2, 4, and 5 of the algorithm. Step 3 of the algorithm corresponds to both boxes 3 and 7. Step 6 (GO TO 2) of the algorithm is represented by the line (with the direction of flow indicated by arrows) that joins box 5 to box 2 of the flowchart.

The program flowchart indicates that the execution of the instructions begins from box 1. Then the instruction of box 2 is executed, followed by the execution of the instruction of box 3. The result of the test that is performed by the instruction of box 3 determines which instruction should be executed next. If the result of the test is true—if the value of NUMDAY is zero—then the instruction in box 7, Stop, will be executed. However if the value of NUMDAY is not zero, the condition is false; then the instruction of box 4 is executed and then the instruction of box 5. From box 5, control is returned to box 2.

The instructions from box 2 through box 5 are an example of a *loop*—a subprocedure to execute a set of instructions a number of times.

2.3.2.2 SYSTEM FLOWCHART

The system flowchart is the macro flowchart. In other words, it is not concerned with the details but gives an overall picture of the system. Figure 2.4 is the system flowchart for an information system that has one program to read input data from cards and to generate a report onto a line printer. Note that Figure 2.4 is indeed the system flowchart for example 2.1.

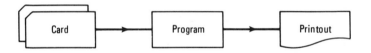

FIGURE 2.4   System flowchart to generate a report from input data cards

Figure 2.5 shows the system-flowcharting symbols that are recommended by the American National Standards Institute.

A system flowchart may have more than one program. Figure 2.6 shows a system flowchart for a payroll system that has three programs: The edit program has an input card file (a file is a collection of records) and produces the edit report (output file) on the line printer and the transaction file on the disk. The register program has two input and two output files. The check and journal program has an input file from the disk and produces three output files.

Usually, the system flowchart is prepared by either a systems analyst or a programmer analyst (see Chapter 1 for their qualifications and responsibilities). The programmer makes the flowcharts and writes the programs that are identified in the system flowchart.

The system flowcharts of all the systems described in this text (with the exception of those in Chapters 15 and 16) are the same as the one in Figure 2.4, so the flowcharts of those systems will not be presented.

Note that a programming flowchart is actually the expression of the algorithm. For this reason, it will be sufficient to present the flowchart only to express a solution to a problem.

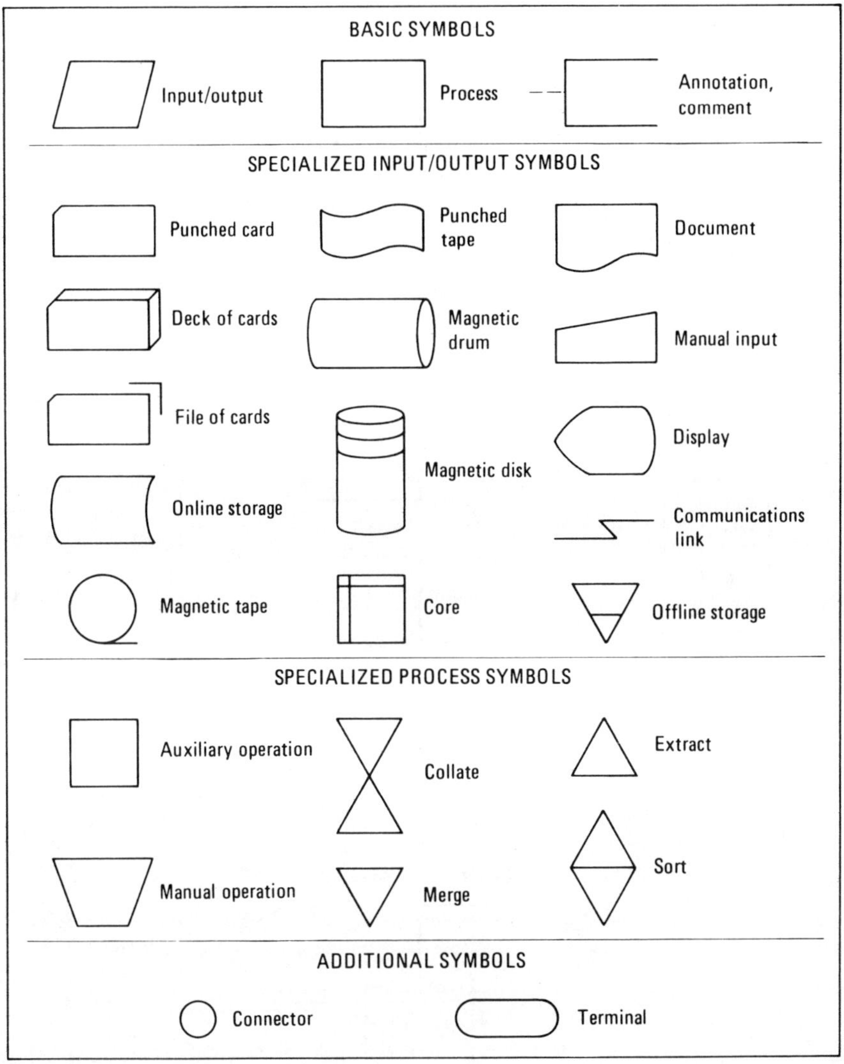

BASIC SYMBOLS

Input/output | Process | — — Annotation, comment

SPECIALIZED INPUT/OUTPUT SYMBOLS

Punched card | Punched tape | Document

Deck of cards | Magnetic drum | Manual input

File of cards | |

Online storage | Magnetic disk | Display

Magnetic tape | Core | Communications link

| | Offline storage

SPECIALIZED PROCESS SYMBOLS

Auxiliary operation | Collate | Extract

Manual operation | Merge | Sort

ADDITIONAL SYMBOLS

Connector | Terminal

FIGURE 2.5   Standard flowcharting symbols for system flowcharts

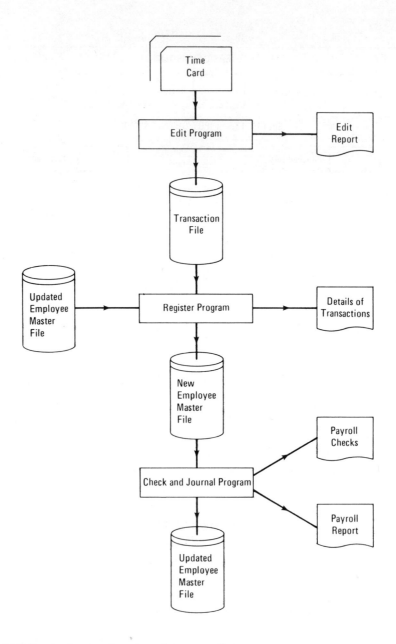

FIGURE 2.6   System flowchart for a payroll system

Example 2.2: **Stock Transaction Service Charge**

Draw a program flowchart and write pseudo codes for a program to read the transaction amount for 20 customers of Best Stock Dealer Corporation, to calculate and print their service cost per transaction. The BSDC regulations for the transaction service charge are:

$ AMOUNT OF TRANSACTION	$ SERVICE CHARGE
Less than $100	$8.50
$100 or more but less than $800	$8.50 + 2.4% of the amount
$800 or more but less than $2,500	$15 + 1.5% of the amount
$2,500 or more but less than $5,000	$26 + 1.1% of the amount
$5,000 or more but less than $20,000	$28 + 1.1% of the amount
$20,000 or more	$48 + 1.0% of the amount

The variable names used are:

AMOUNT: Transaction amount
COUNT: Counter
SCHRG: Service charge per transaction

Figure 2.7 is the flowchart called for.
One way to express the algorithm for this problem in pseudo code form is:

1. Start.
2. Do steps 3 through 4 twenty times.
3. Read AMOUNT
    If AMOUNT < 100 then SCHRG = 8.50
      ELSE IF AMOUNT < 800 then SCHRG = 0.024 * AMOUNT + 8.50
        ELSE IF AMOUNT < 2500 then SCHRG = 0.015 * AMOUNT + 15
          ELSE IF AMOUNT < 5000 then SCHRG = 0.011 * AMOUNT + 26
            ELSE IF AMOUNT < 20000 then SCHRG = 0.011 * AMOUNT + 28
            ELSE SCHRG = 0.01 * AMOUNT + 48
4. Write SCHRG
5. Stop

Before going to the next example, let us clarify the concepts of field, record, and file. The *file* is a collection of records, and the *record* is composed of *fields*. The field contains a piece of data. For example, an asset record may comprise four fields; the first field holds an asset number, the second holds asset cost, the third holds the estimated useful life of the asset, and the fourth field holds the estimated scrap value of the asset at the end of its useful life. An example of such a record is:

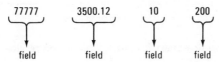

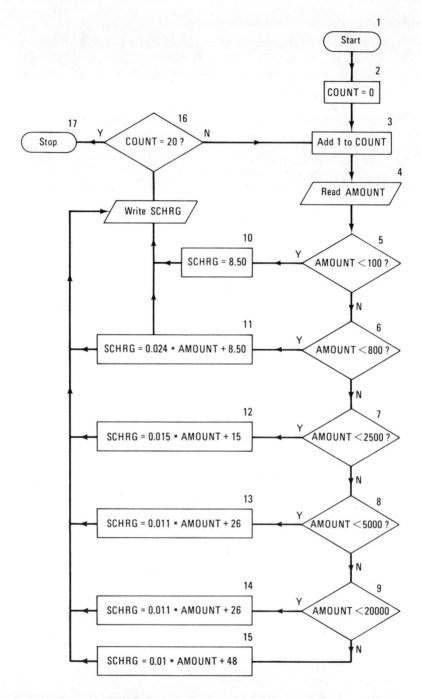

FIGURE 2.7 Program flowchart for stock transaction service

In this record, the asset number is 77777, its cost is $3500.12, its useful life is ten years, and its estimated scrap value after ten years is $200. The records of all assets in a company make up a file of assets. Another example would be a students file, a collection of student records each containing the student's number, name, grade point average, and academic rank.

Example 2.3: **Calculating Depreciation Using the Straight-Line Method**

Figure 2.8 shows the pseudo code and the flowchart for a program that reads the records of an unknown number of assets and calculates and prints their

Pseudo Code Form

```
DOWHILE not end of data
        Read NASST, COST, USEL, SVAL
        DEPYR = (COST — SVAL)/USEL
        Write NASST, COST, USEL, SVAL, DEPYR
End DOWHILE
Stop
```

Flowchart Diagram

FIGURE 2.8   Pseudo code and flowchart diagram for calculating depreciation using the straight-line method

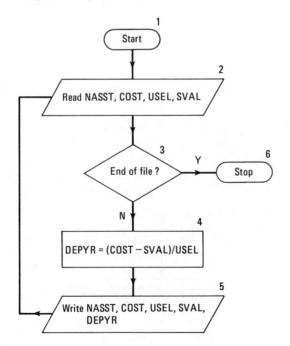

yearly depreciation. Each record contains asset number, cost, useful life, and estimated scrap value. The variable names used are:

NASST: Asset number

COST: Asset cost

USEL: Useful life

SVAL: Estimated scrap value

DEPYR: Yearly depreciation

In the flowchart of Figure 2.8, execution starts in box 1. In box 2, data are read. In box 3, the processor tests to see whether the end of the file is encount-

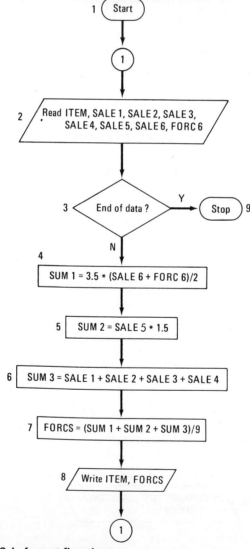

FIGURE 2.9 Sale forcast flowchart

ered. If it is, the program is terminated; otherwise, the instruction of box 4 is executed, followed by the execution of the instruction of box 5. Finally, control returns to execute again the instruction of box 2. Thus, the whole process is repeated until the end of the file is found.

Example 2.4: Sales Forecasting for the Coming Month

The Best Deal Store uses a weighted-average procedure to find the sales forecast for the coming month. The procedure used to find the sales forecast for a commodity is:

1. Multiply the average of last month's sales price and forecast by 3.5.
2. Multiply the sale price for month before last month by 1.5.
3. Find the sales forecast by adding the sum of the oldest four months to the results of steps 1 and 2, then divide the new sum by 9.

Figure 2.9 shows the flowchart diagram and the pseudo code for a program to find the sales forecast for the Best Deal Store. Note that eight data items should be read. These are the sales of each of the last six months, the forecast of the last month, and the item number. The variable names used are:

ITEM: Item number
SALE6: Sales price for the last month
SALE5: Sales price for month before last
SALE1, SALE2, SALE3, SALE4: Sales prices for the oldest 4 months, respectively
FORC6: Sales forecast for the last month
SUM1, SUM2, SUM3: Variable names used to hold results temporarily
FORCS: Forecast for the coming month

Note that in the flowchart, the connector ○ is used. After the Write statement, the arrow points to ①. This indicates that control will go back to connector ① just before the Read instruction. The connector is used instead of joining boxes 8 and 2 with a line carrying an arrow pointing toward box 2.

Another observation about the flowchart in Figure 2.9 is that three variables—SUM1, SUM2, and SUM3—are used to hold intermediate results. Boxes 4, 5, 6, and 7 can be replaced by a single instruction, as shown in the following box:

$$FORCS = (3.5*(SALE6 + FORC6)/2 + SALE5 * 1.5 + SALE1 + SALE2 + SALE3 + SALE4)/9$$

In such a setup, there is no need for variables to hold intermediate results. It is advantageous, however, to break down a long and complicated formula into smaller pieces, because it becomes easier to understand and there is less chance

I.

```
1.  Start

2.  Read ITEM, SALE1, SALE2, SALE3, SALE4, SALE5, SALE6, FORCS6

3.  If end of data, then stop.

        Else   SUM1 = 3.5 * (SALE6 + FORCS6)

               SUM2 = SALE5 * 1.5

               SUM3 = SALE1 + SALE2 + SALE3 + SALE4

               FORCS = (SUM1 + SUM2 + SUM3)/9

               Write ITEM, FORCS

    END IF

4.  Repeat steps 2 and 3.
```

II.

```
Start

DOWHILE not end of data

   Read ITEM, SALE1, SALE2, SALE3, SALE4, SALE5, SALE6, FORCS6

   SUM1 = 3.5 * (SALE6 + FORCS6)/2

   SUM2 = SALE5 * 1.5

   SUM3 = SALE1 + SALE2 + SALE3

   FORCS = (SUM1 + SUM2 + SUM3)/9

   WRITE ITEM, FORCS

END DOWHILE

STOP
```

FIGURE 2.10

of error. Figure 2.10 shows different pseudo code forms for sales forecasting problem.

2.4   SUMMARY

An essential part of the solution of any problem lies in understanding the objectives of the problem. After problem identification, algorithms and flowcharts should be used to solve computer-oriented problems. An algorithm is a set of instructions for performing stepwise operations to accomplish a task or to solve a problem. Any computer-based algorithm should be finite, general, and free of ambiguities.

Flowcharting language uses geometrical figures to represent instructions (operations). The program flowchart is a micro flowchart, which represents program instructions and their order of execution in detail. The system flowchart is a macro flowchart, which is not concerned with details but gives an overall picture of the system. A loop is a set of instructions that will be executed a number of times. A file is a collection of records. A record is made up of fields, and the fields contain the data items.

2.5   REVIEW QUESTIONS AND
SUGGESTED PROBLEMS

1. A record is a collection of _____.
2. A file is a collection of _____ .
3. A field contains_____ .
4. What is an algorithm?
5. Every computer-based algorithm should be _____ , _____ , and _____ .
6. Give three examples of algorithms.
7. What is a program flowchart? What is pseudo code?
8. Is the program flowchart a micro or macro flowchart?
9. What is meant by a loop?
10. What is a system flowchart?
11. Modify Figure 2.7 to test COUNT immediately after the Read instruction.
12. Modify Figure 2.7 to make the initial value of COUNT equal 20 in box 2, instead of zero.
13. Modify Figure 2.7 to make it general, to read and process the data for an unknown number of customers.

14. Identify each of the following symbols:

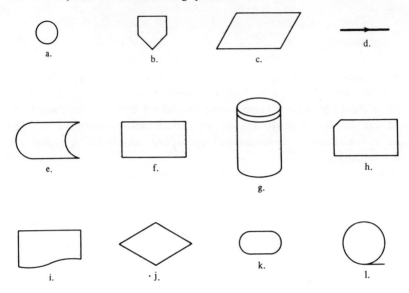

15. *Inventory System*. One way to find an economical order quantity for an item in an inventory control system is:

$$EOR = \sqrt{\frac{2 \times D \times S}{C \times h}}$$

where:

> EOR = the economic order quantity
> D = the demand
> S = the cost of placing an order
> C = the unit cost
> h = the carrying cost (a percentage of C)

Draw a flowchart diagram for a program to read demand, ordering cost, unit cost, and carrying cost, and to calculate and print *EOR* for more than one item. Then redo the problem using pseudo code form.

16. *Loan Amortization Schedule*. Draw a flowchart diagram for a program to read the principal amount of the loan, number of payments to be made, annual rate of interest, and number of payments per year, and to calculate and print the amount of each payment for more than one loan. Note that the amount of each payment is:

$$P = A * RP * \frac{(1 + RP)^N}{(1 + RP)^N - 1}$$

where $RP = I/NY$ and:

A = the principle amount of the loan
I = the annual rate of interest
RP = the rate of interest per payment period
NY = the number of payments in a year
N = the number of payments

17. *Breakeven Analysis*. The breakeven point is the smallest quantity of a product that must be sold so that the firm's revenue equals the total cost of producing that product. Draw a flowchart diagram for a program to read the product code, the fixed operation cost to produce that product, the variable cost per unit, and the sales price per unit. Then the program should calculate and print the breakeven point and the profit (or loss) per unit, along with the product code. The breakeven point and the profit (or loss) per unit are found by the following formulas:

$$\text{Quantity to be produced} = Q = \frac{F}{S - V}$$

$$\text{Total cost} = C = F + V * Q$$

$$\text{Profit (loss) per unit} = S - \frac{C}{Q}$$

where:

F = the fixed operating cost
V = the variable unit cost
S = the sale price per unit
C = the total cost
Q = the quantity to be produced

18. *Arithmetic Mean and Standard Deviation of a Sample of Size 5.* Draw a flowchart diagram to find the arithmetic mean and standard deviation of a sample of five numbers. The arithmetic mean for a sample of size n is:

$$\bar{X} = \frac{1}{n} \sum_{i=1}^{n} X_i = \frac{1}{n} (X_1 + X_2 + \ldots + X_n)$$

where $X_1, X_2, \ldots, X_n$ are observations, and the standard deviation is:

$$\sqrt{\frac{\sum_{i=1}^{n} (X_i - \bar{X})^2}{n - 1}}$$

19. *Finding the Maximum and Minimum of a Set of 20 Numbers.* Draw a flowchart diagram for a program to read 20 numbers and to find and print the largest and the smallest values of these numbers.

20. *Weekly-Payroll Problem.* Draw a flowchart diagram for a program to read employee number, number of prime hours, rate per prime hour, and number of overtime hours. The program should calculate and print the net pay, federal tax, state tax, and FICA, along with the employee name and number. Use the following formulas to calculate these quantities:

$$
\begin{aligned}
GR &= (PH + 2 * OH) * RH \\
FT &= GR * 0.18 \\
ST &= (GR - FT) * 0.03 \\
FICA &= (GR - FT - ST) * 0.025 \\
NETP &= GR - FT - ST - FICA
\end{aligned}
$$

where:

GR	= gross pay
PH	= number of prime hours
OH	= number of overtime hours
RH	= rate per hour; the rate for overtime is twice the ordinary rate
FT	= federal tax
ST	= state tax
FICA	= Social Security tax
NETP	= net pay

21. Draw a flowchart diagram for a program to find the sum of all prime numbers between 1 and 100.

22. *Property Tax.* Draw a flowchart for a program to read the value of a home and to calculate the homeowner's real estate tax according to the percentages in the following table:

HOUSE VALUE	TAX RATE (IN PERCENT)
Less than $10,000	0.003
Between $10,000 and $20,000	0.006
Between $20,001 and $35,000	0.01
Between $35,001 and $50,000	0.02
Between $50,001 and $100,000	0.045
More than $100,000	0.055

23. *Stock Turnover Rate.* Draw a flowchart diagram for a program to read a company's total retail sales and the dollar amount of the inventory in the last twelve months, and to calculate and print the rate of stock turnover. Use the following formula for these calculations:

Rate of stock turnover = Net retail sale/Average stock value

where the average stock value is the average monthly inventory value.

24. *Compound Interest*. Denote the compound amount of $1 by $A_1 = 1 + r$, where r is the rate of interest and $A_t = A_{t-1}(1 + r)$ for $t = 2, 3, \ldots, n$ is the compound amount after t years. Draw a flowchart diagram for a program to read the customer account number, invested amount, rate of interest, and number of years of the investment; to calculate the compound amount; and to print the customer account number, original investment, number of years of the investment, rate of interest, and the compound amount. The program should be capable of processing data for more than one customer.

25. Redo problems 16 through 24, this time using pseudo code forms instead of flowchart diagrams.

3 INTRODUCTION TO FORTRAN

A computer program is a set of instructions organized by the programmer to direct the computer to the solution of a problem. Each instruction is constructed according to the rules of the language in which the program is written. The language we will discuss is FORTRAN—an acronym that stands for *Formula Translation*.

3.1   THE FORTRAN LANGUAGE

In Chapter 1, it was explained that FORTRAN is a high-level language—a language that resembles a natural language, such as English. Recall that the compiler translates the source program into the object program. As a FORTRAN programmer, you ask the system to use the FORTRAN compiler to translate your FORTRAN program into the object program.

FORTRAN as a language has its own character set, keywords, and rules for creating names, expressions, and statements. Like any language, it has syntactical rules for the construction of grammatically correct statements and expressions.

During the translation of the source program into the machine language, the FORTRAN compiler checks every statement for violations of FORTRAN language rules. If any violation is encountered, an error called *compiler time error* is said to have occurred. A message describing the violation is generated, and the resulting object program is defective; therefore, the FORTRAN program cannot be executed properly.

FORTRAN IV, ANSI (American National Standards Institute) FORTRAN, WATFOR (WATERLOO FORTRAN), and WATFIV (WATERLOO FORTRAN

IV) are the popular versions of FORTRAN compilers. ANSI FORTRAN is supposed to be machine-independent; that is, no changes are required when you run the program on different computers. WATFOR and WATFIV do not require as much memory space as the FORTRAN IV compiler, and they also take less time to compile.

Example 3.1

Write a FORTRAN program to read two numbers punched on a single card, compute their average, and print the result. The input card is organized as follows:

CC (CARD COLUMN)	FIELD
1–3	First number
4–6	Second number

Note that each column on the card can hold only one character. A group of adjacent columns (characters) is called a *field*, and a collection of related fields is called a *record*. Thus, in this example, we have one input record made up of two fields; the length of each field is three characters. Moreover, each record is punched on one card. An example of our input record is shown in Figure 3.1.

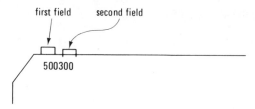

FIGURE 3.1   Input record

FIGURE 3.2   Flowchart to find the average of two numbers

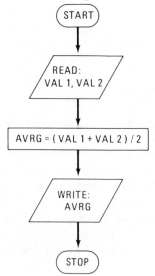

Figure 3.2 is the flowchart diagram, and Figure 3.3 is the FORTRAN program for the problem above. The variables used:

VAL1: The first number
VAL2: The second number
AVRG: Average of the numbers

```
C    THIS IS YOUR FIRST FORTRAN PROGRAM

C

C    THE PROGRAM READS TWO NUMBER AND FINDS THEIR AVERAGE

C

     READ (5,10) VAL1,  VAL2
10   FORMAT (F3.0, F3.0)
     AVRG = (VAL1 + VAL2) / 2.0
     WRITE (6,20) AVRG
20   FORMAT (6X, F6.2)
     STOP
     END
```

FIGURE 3.3   FORTRAN program

When you glance at the FORTRAN program of Figure 3.3, you see the words READ, FORMAT, WRITE, STOP, and END. These are FORTRAN command words. You can see now why FORTRAN is considered a high-level language; although you have not yet learned how to construct FORTRAN statements, you are able to understand the following brief discussion of the functions of the program above because of FORTRAN's similarity to English.

3.2   THE FORTRAN PROGRAM

Each line of the program is called a *statement*. Any line that has a letter C in the first column (position) is considered to be a *comment*. The comment line does not affect the execution or the compilation of the program; it is used for documentation and to help anyone reading the program to understand it. The READ statement instructs the computer to read in two numbers according to the specifications given in the first FORMAT statement and store these numbers in the memory locations identified by the names VAL1 and VAL2. VAL1 and VAL2 are called *variable names*, or simply *variables*, and they are the choice of the programmer. (A detailed discussion of how to create variable names will be presented later.) The 5 in the parentheses following READ specifies that the data value came from a card reader. This is called the *logical unit number*. Each computer installation has its own logical unit number. For example, the logical unit number for the card reader is 5 on IBM/370 and 2 for DECSystem 10. Note that the installation can change these numbers. The 10 in parentheses refers to the statement number of the associated FORMAT statement.

The statement AVRG = (VAL1 + VAL2)/2.0 adds the values of the variables VAL1 and VAL2, divides the result by 2.0, and assigns the results as the value of the variable AVRG. FORTRAN uses the slash (/) to denote division, the asterisk (*) for multiplication, the plus (+) for addition, and the minus (–) for subtraction. Statements such as AVRG = (VAL1 +VAL2)/2.0 are called arithmetic assignment statements. The WRITE statement is a command to print the value of AVRG on the line printer according to the specifications given in the associated FORMAT statement. The 6 in the parentheses of the WRITE statement is the code for the line printer, and the 20 references the associated FORMAT statement.

The STOP statement stops the execution of the program, and the END statement is the signal to the compiler indicating the end of the FORTRAN source program. All FORTRAN programs must have END as the last statement.

3.3   THE FORTRAN STATEMENT

The elements of any FORTRAN statement are FORTRAN command keywords, special characters, variable names, and constants. Before discussing these terms, let us first consider the following examples.

Example 3.2

The following FORTRAN statement contains all the elements named above:

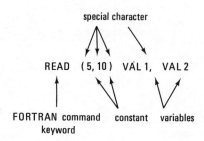

The following FORTRAN statements contain only FORTRAN command keywords: STOP ◄——— FORTRAN Command Keyword

END ◄——— FORTRAN Command Keyword

The following FORTRAN statement contains variable names and special characters:

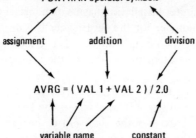

Any FORTRAN statement (instruction) is constructed from two parts: statement number (which is optional) and the command. The general form for any FORTRAN statement is:

statement number   Command

'The statement number is optional

Example 3.3

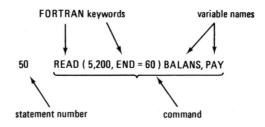

Note that 5, 200, and 60 are constants, and the equals sign, parentheses, and comma are special characters.

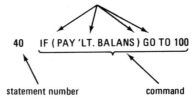

3.4   CHARACTER SET

Here are the characters that are used in the FORTRAN IV language:

Letter: A B C D E F G H I J K L M N O P Q R S T U V W X Y Z
Digits: 0 1 2 3 4 5 6 7 8 9
Special characters: = − / * ! " ' # $ % & ( ) . : ; = ? @ ,

Thus, a character can be any letter from A to Z, any digit from 0 to 9, or any special character.

3.5   STATEMENT NUMBER

The statement number makes up the first part of the FORTRAN statement and is used as the label to identify the statement. It may be any number with five digits or less. Every statement number should be unique; however, the statement numbers may be in any order. (Below, a procedure is recommended for assigning statement numbers.) The statement number is optional, but a statement without a statement number cannot be referenced from other places within the program. Thus, if a statement needs to be referenced, it must have a statement number.

The command part of the FORTRAN statement is constructed from FORTRAN keywords, variable names, and/or special characters. Henceforth, the words *command* and *statement* are used interchangeably.

Example 3.4

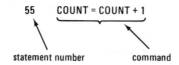

```
55    COUNT = COUNT + 1
```

statement number   command

Example 3.5

```
10 READ (5,20, END=40) AMOUNT
   RINTR = AMOUNT * 0.055
   WRITE (6,30) RINTR
   GO TO 10
20 FORMAT (F7.2)
30 FORMAT (6X,F8.2)
40 STOP
   END
```

In the FORTRAN program of Example 3.5, the first statement needs a statement number (10) because it is referenced by the fourth statement. Since the first statement refers to both the fifth (a FORMAT statement) and seventh statement (STOP statement), both the FORMAT and STOP statements need statement numbers. Thus, 20 and 40 are assigned as the labels for these two statements. The second FORMAT (sixth) statement needs a statement number because it is referenced by the WRITE (third) statement. The second, third, fourth, and END statements do not need statement numbers.

To make your program more readable and easier to follow, use a consistent procedure to assign statement numbers. For example, you might assign 10 as the first statement number, 20 for the second, and so on, making each larger than the preceding one by 10. Here, the number 10 was arbitrarily chosen; you can choose any other number as the increment, but be consistent.

3.6   CONSTANTS IN FORTRAN

Constants are fixed values. In FORTRAN, five different constants are recognized:

1. Integer constant
2. Real constant
3. Literal constant
4. Logical constant
5. Complex constant

Since the complex constant is not of interest for business students, it is not discussed in this text. The literal and logical constants are discussed in the next chapter. Sometimes literal constants are referred to as character constants.

3.6.1   Integer Constants

Integer constants are fixed values (numbers) with no fractions. More precisely, a number without a decimal point is called an integer constant, or, frequently, a *fixed-point constant.*

Example 3.6

Valid integer constants: 25, 68, 1,000, −200,500, 1, 20
Invalid integer constants: 20.5   No fraction is allowed.
                             20.0   No fraction is allowed even if zero.
                             20.   No decimal point is allowed.

In Chapter 1, it was pointed out that a computer word is a memory location, and because the data are stored in these locations, the largest and the smallest integer constant that can be accepted by a computer are determined by the word size of that computer. If the size of the computer word is n bits, then the largest positive integer is $2^{n-1} - 1$, and the smallest negative integer is $-2^{n-1} + 1$. Thus, in the IBM 360/370, which has a word size of 32 bits, the largest integer can be 2, 147, 483, 647 (that is, $2^{31} - 1$); in the DECSystem 10, which has a word size of 36 bits, the largest integer can be no more than $2^{35} - 1$, or 34, 359, 738, 365.

3.6.2   Real Constants

Numbers that contain a decimal point are called *real constants*. A real constant may or may not have a fraction; however, it always has a decimal point.

Example 3.7

The following are valid real constants: 62., −5., 1567.253, 0.197, 58.0.

Note that although both 62. and −5. do not have fractions and 58.0 has the fraction 0, all are valid real constants. Another popular name for a real constant is *floating-point constant*.

Scientific notation (exponent decimal point) of two different forms, E (exponent single precision) and D (exponent double precision), is allowed to represent real constants. See Section 6.4.2 and Appendix III.

3.7   VARIABLES

In Chapter 2, variables were briefly defined, and many variable names— such as AMOUNT, TCOST, NUMDAY, CHARGE, DEPTR, COST, and USEL—were used. We will now discuss variables in detail.

A *variable* is a name chosen by the programmer to be assigned by the computer as the symbolic name of a memory location (whose contents can be varied). Therefore, a variable denotes a memory location whose content is varied.

There are three items related to a memory location. These are:

1. *Absolute address:* An absolute address is a unique number assigned by the computer manufacturer to identify a memory location.
2. *Variable names* (symbolic addresses): These names are chosen by the programmer, and the computer makes a cross-reference table between the variable name and its absolute address. Usually, the cross-reference table is called a *symbol table*.
3. *Content of the location:* The content of the location is the value of the variable.

3.7.1   Rules for Creating Variable Names in FORTRAN

FORTRAN variable names are constructed from a combination of from one to six letters and/or digits, according to the following two rules: (1) The name must start with a letter; (2) it must contain no special characters.

Note: Although some FORTRAN compilers allow the dollar sign ($) to be used as an alphabetic (letter) character, to make your program more general, do not use it.

Example 3.8

Valid variable names: AMOUNT, SALES, FORCST, PAY, INTRST, CROSS7, X, SD, XX, JOB5, X125

Invalid variable names:

INTEREST	Too many characters. The number of characters cannot exceed 6.
9PAY	A variable name must start with a letter.
B.15	Contains a special character (a period).
N BAL	Contains a space (blank), which is a special character.
#DOLLAR	Starts with a special character (#) and has more than 6 characters.

Note that X, XX, and X25X are all valid variable names. The use of meaningful variable names makes the program more readable and easier to understand. For example, to convert the algebraic equation

Amount of interest = Rate of interest ∗ Capital invested

to a FORTRAN statement, you have to choose valid variable names for amount of interest, rate of interest, and capital invested. You are free to choose any names you wish as long as the names satisfy the rules for variable names. For example, you might choose AINTRS, RINTRS, and CAPITAL to denote amount of interest, rate of interest, and capital invested, respectively. Hence, the equation above in the FORTRAN language becomes

AINTRS = RINTRS ∗ CAPITAL

If the programmer had chosen X, Y, and Z to denote amount of interest, rate of interest, and capital, respectively, then the equation in the FORTRAN language would be $X = Y * Z$, which is as valid a statement as the previous one. It should be clear, however, that AINTRS = RINTRS ∗ CAPITAL is more readable and meaningful to the human.

Be careful to choose meaningful variable names. This is an important part of program documentation, not only in business data processing but in the scientific environment as well.

3.7.2 Variable Types

As with constants, there are five different variables in FORTRAN. These are:

1. Integer variable
2. Real variable
3. Character variable (a variable whose content can be any FORTRAN character)
4. Logical variable
5. Complex variable

The discussion of the complex variable is omitted; the third and fourth variables are discussed in Chapters 5 and 6 respectively.

An *integer variable* is a variable whose value must be an integer constant. A *real variable*'s value must be a real constant.

There are three ways to declare a variable to be integer or real—by predefined rule, by implicit declaration, or by explicit declaration (that is, using the specification statements INTEGER and REAL). The last two methods are discussed in Chapter 6.

3.7.2.1 DECLARATION BY PREDEFINED RULE

The FORTRAN compiler considers a variable to be:

1. An integer variable if the first character of the variable name is I, J, K, L, M, or N.
2. A real variable if the first character of the variable name is a letter other than I, J, K, L, M, or N.

Therefore, by the predefined rule, the first character of its name determines whether the variable is integer or real.

Example 3.9

INTEGER VARIABLES	REAL VARIABLES
INTRST	XINTRS
JCOST	COST
K	PAY
KK	AMOUNT
MROOT	ROOT

3.8 CODING FORTRAN STATEMENTS

The rules that govern punching FORTRAN statements on cards (or submitting FORTRAN statements through a terminal) are these:

1. Columns 1 through 5 may contain a statement number. Blanks and leading zeroes are ignored.
2. Column 6 is used for continuation. (See rule 4 below.)
3. Columns 7 through 72 are used for FORTRAN statements.
4. Each FORTRAN statement is written on one line—i.e., punched on one 80-card column card. If a statement is too long for one card, it may be continued on as many as 19 successive cards by placing a character other than zero or blank in column 6. In other words, if column 6 is a character other than a blank or zero, this card contains a part of the previous statement.
5. Columns 73 through 80 are not significant to the FORTRAN compiler. A skilled programmer uses these columns for program identification, sequencing of statements, etc.

Figure 3.4 shows a punch card with the FORTRAN designated fields.

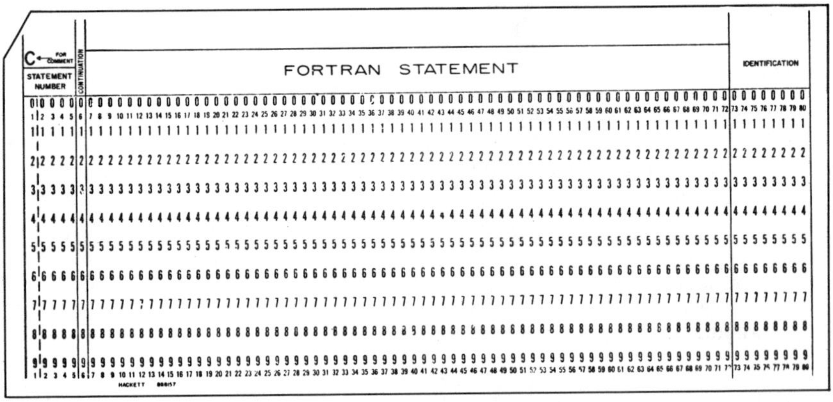

FIGURE 3.4   Punch card with FORTRAN fields

3.9   PROGRAM SETUP

The FORTRAN program must be preceded by a few statements that direct the computer system to translate the FORTRAN program (source program) into the object program—that is, compile the source program—or to compile the source program and execute the object program as well. These statements are usually called JCL (job control statements) or job control cards. Each computer system has its own job control statements. Figure 3.5 is the

IBM System/360 Basic Assembler Long Coding Form

| PROGRAM | FIRST FORTRAN PROGRAM | | PUNCHING INSTRUCTIONS | GRAPHIC | | | PAGE | OF |
| PROGRAMMER | Asad Khailany | DATE Jan. 20, 1978 | | PUNCH | | | CARD ELECTRO NUMBER | |

```
//SAMPL1 JOB (5700,34),KHAILANY,CLASS=A   These statements are job control statements.
//   EXEC FORTRAN
//FORT.SYSIN DD  *
C
CTHIS IS YOUR FIRST FORTRAN PROGRAM
C
CTHE PROGRAM READS TWO NUMBERS AND FINDS THEIR AVERAGE
C
      READ(5,10)VAL1, VAL2                      Fortran Program
10    FORMAT(F3.0,F3.0)
      AVRG=(VAL1 + VAL2)/2.0
      WRITE(6,20)AVRG
20    FORMAT(6X,F6.2)
      STOP
      END
/*                This statement signals the end of the program
//GO.SYSIN DD  *   This statement causes the execution of the program
500300               Input data
/*              Last job control card
```

These statements are job control statements.

This statement signals the end of the program

This statement causes the execution of the program

Last job control card

job control cards

FIGURE 3.5 FORTRAN program for IBM/370

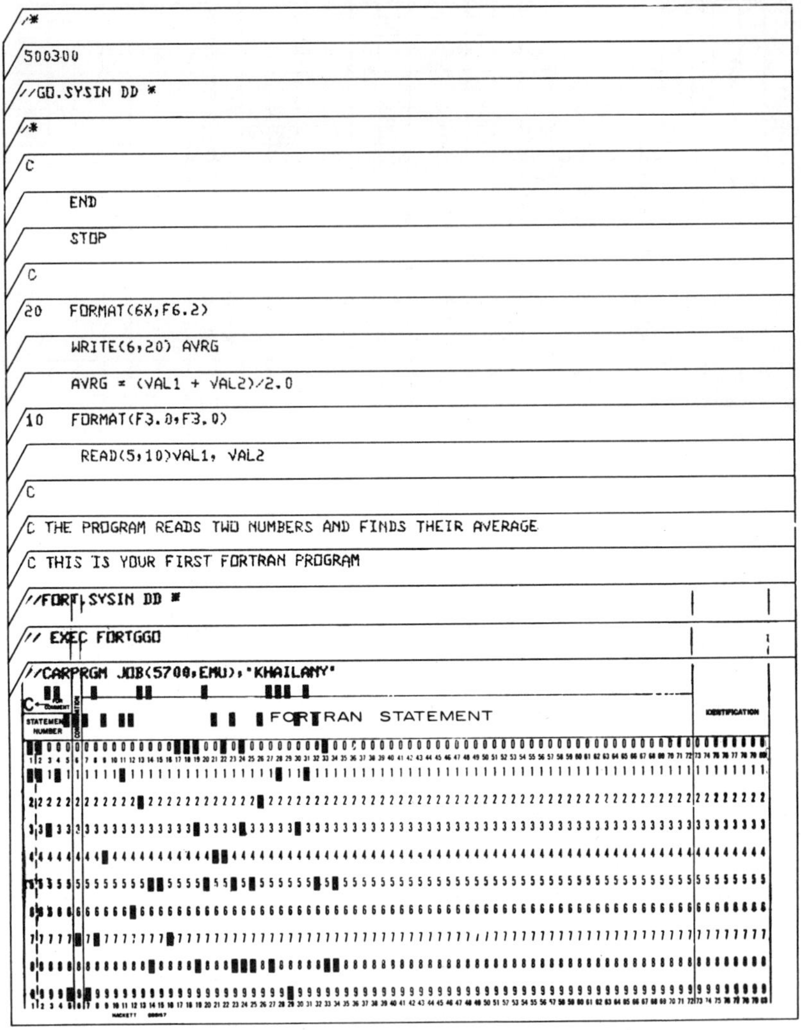

```
/*
500300
//GO.SYSIN DD *
/*
C
      END
      STOP
C
20    FORMAT(6X,F6.2)
      WRITE(6,20) AVRG
      AVRG = (VAL1 + VAL2)/2.0
10    FORMAT(F3.0,F3.0)
      READ(5,10)VAL1, VAL2
C
C THE PROGRAM READS TWO NUMBERS AND FINDS THEIR AVERAGE
C THIS IS YOUR FIRST FORTRAN PROGRAM
//FORT.SYSIN DD *
// EXEC FORTGGO
//CARPRGM JOB(5700,EMU),'KHAILANY'
```

FIGURE 3.6   FORTRAN program punched on the cards ready to be run on IBM/370

FIGURE 3.7   Source program listing and the output on IBM/370 computer

```
C THIS THIS YOUR FIRST PEROGRAM
C
C THE PROGRAM READS TWO NUMBERS AND FINDS THEIR AVERAGE
C
        READ(5,10) VAL1,VAL2
10      FORMAT (F3.0,F3.0)
        AVRG = (VAL1 + VAL2) / 2.0
        WRITE (6, 20) AVRG
20      FORMAT (6X,F6.2)
        STOP
        END


    400.00
```

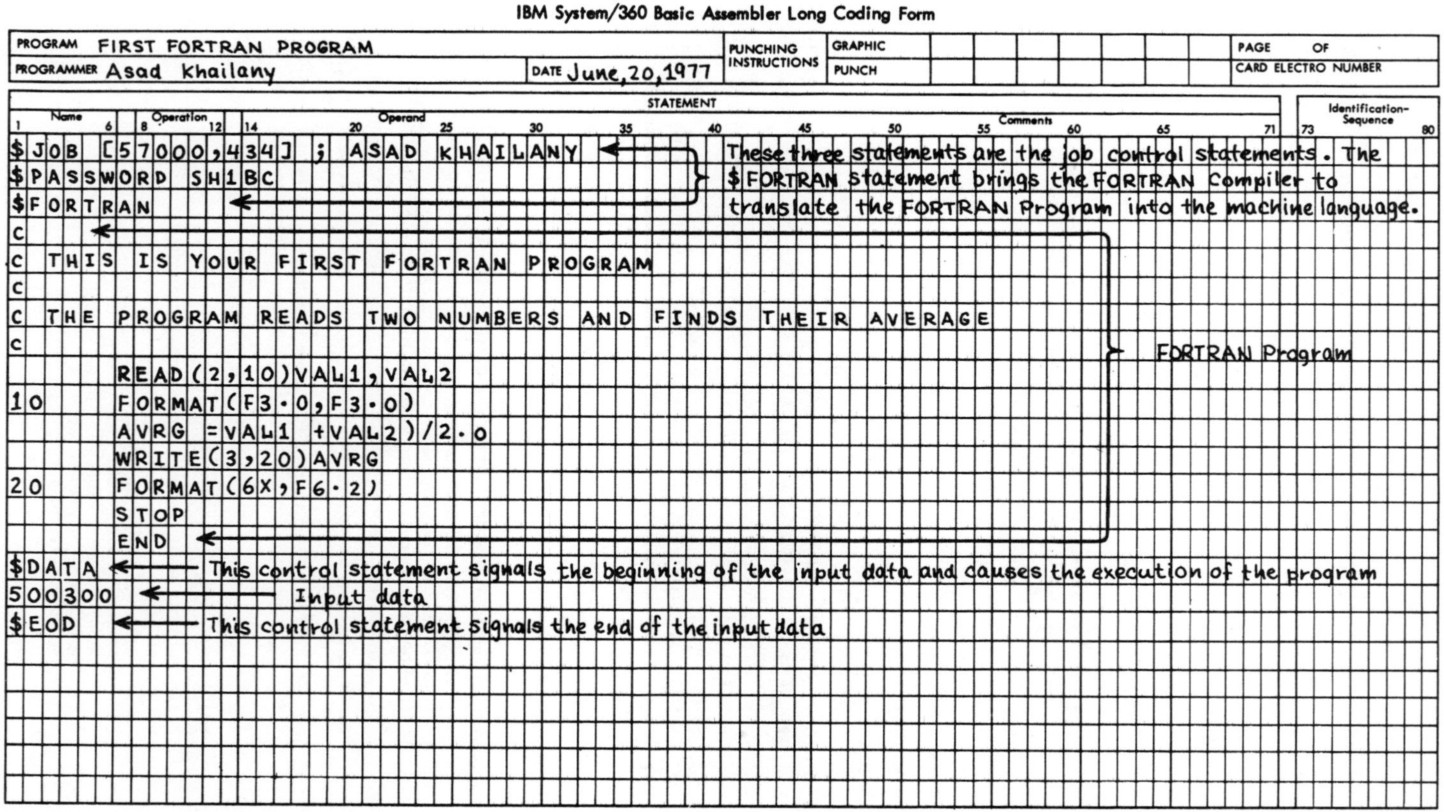

IBM System/360 Basic Assembler Long Coding Form

PROGRAM	FIRST FORTRAN PROGRAM			PUNCHING INSTRUCTIONS	GRAPHIC		PAGE	OF	
PROGRAMMER	Asad Khailany	DATE June,20,1977			PUNCH		CARD ELECTRO NUMBER		

Coding form contents (columns by Name / Operation / Operand / Comments):

```
$JOB  [5700,2434]; ASAD KHAILANY      These three statements are the job control statements. The
$PASSWORD SH1BC                        $FORTRAN statement brings the FORTRAN compiler to
$FORTRAN                               translate the FORTRAN Program into the machine language.
C
C  THIS IS YOUR FIRST FORTRAN PROGRAM
C
C  THE PROGRAM READS TWO NUMBERS AND FINDS THEIR AVERAGE
C
      READ(2,10)VAL1,VAL2                              FORTRAN Program
10    FORMAT(F3.0,F3.0)
      AVRG =(VAL1 +VAL2)/2.0
      WRITE(3,20)AVRG
20    FORMAT(6X,F6.2)
      STOP
      END
$DATA ←——— This control statement signals the beginning of the input data and causes the execution of the program
500300 ←—— Input data
$EOD  ←—— This control statement signals the end of the input data
```

FIGURE 3.8 FORTRAN program set up on DECSystem 10

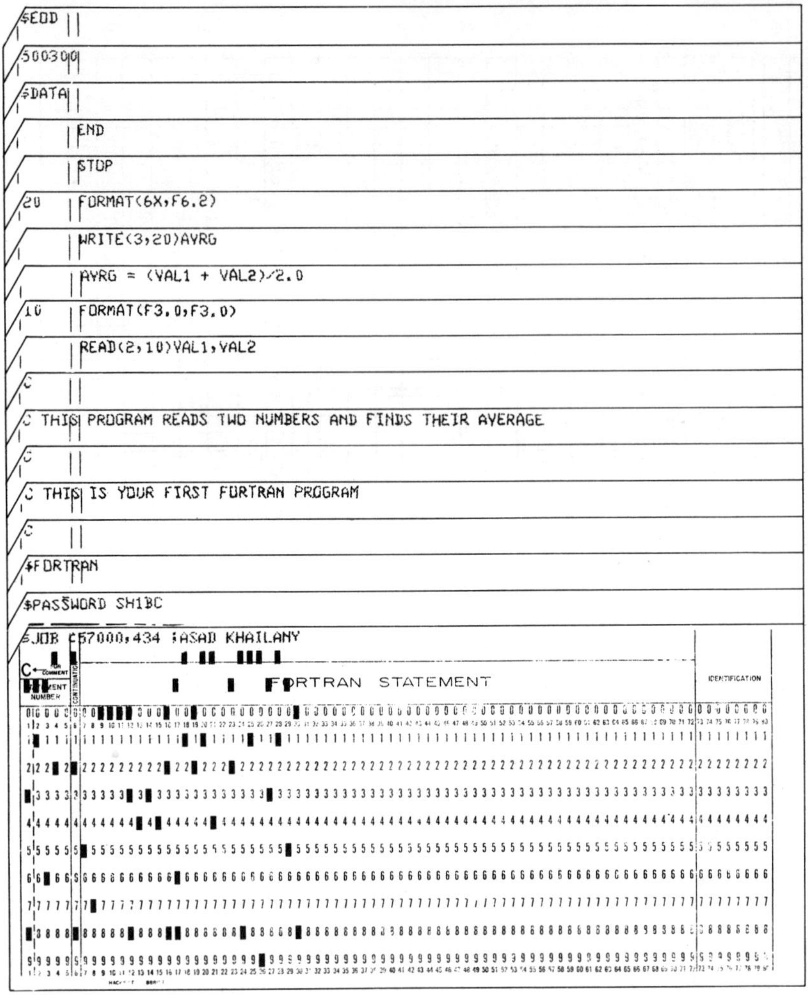

FIGURE 3.9   The program punched on the cards, ready to be run on DECSystem 10 computer

FIGURE 3.10   Source program listing and the output on DECSystem 10 computer

```
Input data

500300


C THIS IS YOUR FIRST FORTRAN PROGRAM
C
C THE PROGRAM READS TWO NUMBERS AND FINDS THEIR AVERAGE
C
      READ (2,10) VAL1,VAL2
   10 FORMAT (F3.0,F3.0)
      AVRG = (VAL1 + VAL2) / 2.0
      WRITE (3, 20) AVRG
   20 FORMAT (6X,F6.2)
      STOP
      END

Output produced by the above program


   400.00
```

80

FORTRAN program of Figure 3.2, along with job control statements for IBM/ 370 written on the IBM FORTRAN coding form. Figure 3.6 shows the same program punched on cards to be run on the IBM/370, and Figure 3.7 is the listing of the source program and the output after running the program on the IBM/370.

For DECSystem 10, the coding of the program, along with JCL statements, is given in Figure 3.8. Figure 3.9 shows the program punched on cards with JCL statements to be run on DECSystem 10, and Figure 3.10 is the listing of the source program and the output after running the program on the DECSystem 10.

Review how to use the keypunch machine (in Chapter 1) and do problems 9 through 19 below. By doing each of these problems, you will learn certain programming rules and "debugging" (removing "bugs" or errors from the program) techniques. These problems do not require any programming experience.

3.10   SUMMARY

An integer constant is a number without a decimal point. A real constant is a number with a decimal point. A variable is a name chosen by the programmer to denote a memory location whose content is varied. A variable name is composed of from one to six characters; it must start with a letter, and it should not contain a special character. If the first letter is I, J, K, L, M, or N, the variable is an integer variable; otherwise, the variable is real.

A FORTRAN program is a set of instructions. Each instruction is constructed from two parts—the statement number, which is optional, and the command. Statement numbers can be from one to five digits long, but they must be unique. When you punch your program, every FORTRAN statement should be punched on a single card. Columns 1 through 5 are reserved for the statement number, and column 6 for continuation. The command part of the FORTRAN statement is punched in columns 7 through 72. Columns 73 through 80 are used for identification purposes and do not affect the compilation or execution of the FORTRAN program. A comment statement is written by punching C in column 1.

3.11   REVIEW QUESTIONS AND
SUGGESTED PROBLEMS

1. Give three examples of (a) integer constants; (b) real constants.

2. A FORTRAN statement that has C in the first column is considered a
_____ .

3. Identify the types of the following constants: 256, −256, 256., 256.0, 218.7, 0., 0.

4. Determine whether the following are valid FORTRAN variable names, and write the reason if they are invalid: JOB, JOB1, INTEREST, BALANCE, PAY, 2PAY, PAY2, X, 3X, X3, DATE, N-BALN, CITY-TAX, CITY TAX, I, COUNT, ICOUNT.

5. Decidè which of the valid variables of problem 4 are real and which are integers by the predefined rule.

6. What are the three items related to every memory location?

7. What is meant by (a) absolute address? (b) symbolic name? (c) contents of a memory location?

8. Why are comments used?

9. The following FORTRAN program prints the column headings EMPLOY-NUMBER, PAY, and HOURS, reads the value of variables NUMB, HOURS, and RATE from punched cards, calculates the payment, and prints the value of the variables NUMB, PAYMN, and HOURS under the appropriate headings. It continues reading the values of the variables, calculating payments, and printing the results until the end of the data is encountered. Punch the program and the data following the program on cards and then run the program.

```
      WRITE (6, 10)
10    FORMAT ('1', 5X, 'EMPLOY-NUMBER', 6X, 'PAY',3X,'HOURS'
      3X, 'RATE')
20    READ (5, 30, END = 50) NUMB, HOURS, RATE
30    FORMAT (I5, F5.2, F5.2)
      PAYMN = HOURS * RATE
      WRITE (6, 40) NUMB, PAYMN, HOURS
40    FORMAT (10X, I5, 6X, F7.2, 3X, F5.2, 3X, F5.2)
      GO TO 20
50    STOP
      END
```

The data (start punching in the first column):

1st card:	1234540.0005.18
2nd card:	8888843.1807.92
3rd card:	2224530.5010.50
4th card:	3333325.4009.25
5th card:	9367240.0004.28

Note that before and after the end of the FORTRAN program, you need several cards to instruct the computer what it should do with your program. Ask your instructor or any employee in the computing center about these job control cards for your particular machine. *Note*: You may have to change the logical unit number for input/output devices (see Chapter 4). Ask your instructor for the logical unit numbers that are associated with READ and WRITE in your particular computing environment.

10. Take both FORMAT statements (10 and 40) of the program of problem 9 and place them at the beginning of the program—i.e., before the WRITE statement. Rerun the program. If you have not made any typing errors, your program should run. Thus, you can conclude from this example that the format statement can be anyplace in the program as long as it is before the END statement.

11. Remove 20, the statement number of the READ statement of the program of problem 9, and run the program. Your program does not run, and you should get an error message indicating that a label (i.e., a statement number) is missing.

12. Remove the END statement of the program of problem 9 and rerun your program. Does your program run? The END statement must be the last statement of every FORTRAN program.

13. Interchange the order of the statements STOP and GO TO 20 of the program of problem 9 and rerun the program. Does your program run? What are the differences between this run and the run of problem 9?

14. Add the following comment cards to the program of problem 9 and run the program:

a. 1st comment card, before the first line:

```
C   THE FOLLOWING WRITE STATEMENT PRINTS
    COLUMN HEADING
```

b. 2nd comment card, before the READ statements:

```
C   READ IN THE VALUE OF EMPLOYEE NUMBER,
    HOURS AND THE RATE
```

c. 3rd comment card, before the arithmetic assignment statement:

```
C   CALCULATE THE PAYMENT
```

d. 4th comment card, before the 2nd WRITE statement:

```
C   PRINT OUT EMPLOYEE NUMBER, PAY AND HOURS
```

e. 5th comment card, before GO TO statement:

```
C   GO BACK TO READ ANOTHER EMPLOYEE RECORD
```

15. Rerun the program of problem 9 with the following modifications:
a. Misspell RATE in the assignment statement; write it as RAT—i.e., the assignment statement should be:

```
PAYMN = HOURS * RAT
```

Note that the variable name RATE still appears in the READ and WRITE statement.

b. Keep the modification in and change the variable name RATE in both the READ and WRITE statements to RAT. Now does your program run?

c. The variable name PAYMN appears both in the arithmetic assignment statement and the second WRITE statement. In only one of these two statements (*not* in both), change PAYMN to PAYMNT. Does your program run? If so, what are the values printed under the heading PAY?

16. In problem 9, add the following statement:

PAYMN = 450.75

and insert it after the arithmetic assignment PAYMN = HOURS * RATE but before the WRITE statement. Rerun your program. (Your program should run.) What are the differences between the output of this program and the output of problem 9? What did the inserted statement do?

17. Again, refer to problem 16, but this time put the statement PAYMN = 450.75 *before* the statement PAYMN = HOURS * RATE instead of after it. Now run the program. Is there any difference between the output of this run and the ones of problem 16 and problem 9?

18. Consider problem 9 and insert the statement HOURS = 10.0 before the READ statement. Run the program. Is there any difference between this output and the output of problem 9?

19. Redo problem 18. However, this time insert the statement HOURS = 10.0 between the READ statement and the statement PAYMN = HOURS * RATE. Run the program. Is there any difference between this run and the run of problem 18 or problem 9? Can you explain why there are differences (or why not)?

4 INPUT/OUTPUT AND FORMAT STATEMENTS

You will recall that input statements are used to transfer data from external storage devices—such as cards, disk, or tape—to main memory, and output statements are used to transfer data from main memory to external storage devices. Usually the input/output statements reference FORMAT statements for description of data fields.

4.1   READ STATEMENT

The READ statement is used to "read in" the value of variables. In other words, the READ statement transfers data from external storage devices to the memory locations that are identified by the variable names *in the list part* of the READ statement. Here is one general form of the READ statement:

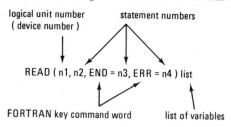

where:

n1 is an integer variable or constant, which designates a logical unit number, as explained below.

n2 is a FORMAT statement number.

n3 and *n4* are statement numbers.

list is a list of valid FORTRAN variables—i.e., *v1, v2* . . .

Both *END* = *n3* and *ERR* = *n4* are optional. If *END* = *n3* is included, then whenever the end of data is encountered, control transfers (jumps) to the statement that has *n3* as its statement number. And if *ERR* = *n4* is included, then control transfers to the statement that has *n4* as its statement number when an error in data is encountered. Compare the following READ statement with the general format presented above:

```
READ (2, 8, END = 70, ERR = 18) AMOUNT, RATE
```

4.2   LOGICAL UNIT NUMBER

In many organizations, every employee has his or her own employee number as identification. Similarly, every device in the computer center has a number used by the computer as the identifier of that device. Such numbers are called *logical unit numbers*. The logical unit number is an integer constant or integer variable used within the input/output statement to identify the external storage medium and the input/output device that is used by the statement. On some computers, such as IBM/370, the data file created on the device identified by the logical unit number is called a *data set*.

Every organization has its own standard logical unit numbers, and any computer center can create its own. Below are the standard logical unit numbers for the card reader and line printer for the IBM/370 and DECSystem 10 computer systems.

	LOGICAL UNIT NUMBERS	
DEVICE	IBM/370/360	DECSystem 10
Card reader	5	2
Line printer	6	3

Other computers may have different standard logical unit numbers. Later, the programmer will learn how to override the standard logical unit numbers and assign his or her own.

Example 4.1

The statement:

```
READ (5, 8, END = 70) AMOUNT, RATE
```

could be used on the IBM/370 to input data from the card reader. The elements of this statement are:

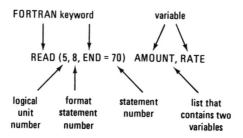

This statement instructs the computer to do the following:

1. Read in the values of AMOUNT and RATE from punched cards. In other words, the card reader will be used as an input device because the logical unit number is 5.
2. From the FORMAT statement that has 8 as its statement number, get information about the type and length of the fields on the punched card that contains the values of the variables AMOUNT and RATE in the list part of the READ statement.
3. END = 70 tells the computer to transfer to statement number 70 when the end of data is encountered.

If we were writing the READ statement for the DECSystem 10, we would have to write:

```
READ (2, 8, END = 70) AMOUNT, RATE
```

As you see, the only change is in the logical unit number.

The logical unit number that appears in the input/output statement can be an integer variable as long as it has a value indicating the correct input/output device. Thus, instead of writing

```
READ (5, 8, END = 70) AMOUNT, RATE
```

you can write the following two statements:

```
ICARD = 5
READ (ICARD, 8, END = 70) AMOUNT, RATE
```

The first statement assigns 5 as the value for the integer variable ICARD. This setup is preferred to the previous one because if you decided to run your program on a computer other than the IBM/370, such as the DECSystem 10, you would not have to change all the READ statements in your program (there may be many). Instead, you would need to change only one statement: ICARD = 2 in place of ICARD = 5. Another advantage is that the program becomes more readable, because one can better associate ICARD with a data set punched on the cards, than the numbers such as 2 or 5.

4.3   WRITE STATEMENT

The WRITE statement is used to transfer data from memory locations to external storage devices. The general form for the WRITE statement is:

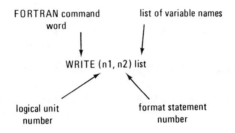

where:

$n1$ is an integer variable or constant representing the logical unit number.
$n2$ is the FORMAT statement number.
list is a list of variables. Note that the list is optional; if only messages or column headings are to be printed, then the list is not required.

Example 4.2

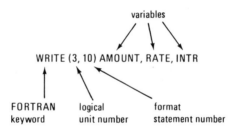

On DECSystem 10 computers, this statement tells the computer to write the value of the variables AMOUNT, RATE, and INTRS on the line printer. Furthermore, the computer is told that the FORMAT statement with statement number 10 contains the specifications and details on how these values should be printed on the printed page.

4.4   FORMAT STATEMENT

The FORMAT statements are used to specify the fields of the records in conjunction with the input/output statement. Each FORMAT statement should be referenced by at least one input/output statement. The FORMAT statements are not executed but merely supply information to the object program. They may be placed anywhere in the source program as long as they precede the END statement. The general form of the FORMAT statement is:

n   <u>FORMAT</u> (e1, e2, . . . ,, ej)

where:

> *n* is the statement number that has been used in the input/output statement to reference this FORMAT statement.
>
> *e1, e2,..., ej* are format codes. These are the entries within the parentheses.

The following are the general forms for the format codes and their functions that are used within the FORMAT statement. Note that a capitalized underlined word means the word is a FORTRAN command word.

FORMAT CODE	FUNCTION
a<u>I</u>n	Describes an integer field of *n* digits length.
n<u>X</u>	Skip (bypass) *n* characters (columns).
a<u>F</u>w.d	Describes a real field with a total of *w* digits. Of these, the rightmost *d* digits are considered decimal places.
<u>E</u>n.d	Describes a single precision real field. The *n* is the size of the field and *d* is the number of digits to the right of the decimal point in the precision field.
<u>D</u>n.d	Describes a double precision real field. The *n* is the size of the field and *d* is the number of digits to the right of decimal point in the precision field.
n<u>H</u>string	Transmit a literal constant.
'string'	Transmit a literal constant.
<u>T</u>n	Specifies the position in the FORTRAN record where transfer I/O should start.
a(<u>/</u>)	Skip a record.
a<u>A</u>w	Describes a character field of length *w*.
a<u>L</u>w	Describes a logical field of length *w*.
a<u>G</u>w.d	Describes an integer, real, or logical data field.

Note that in many of the format codes above, an integer constant *a* may precede the format code to indicate the number of times the code is repeated. Thus, 5I2 can be written instead of I2, I2, I2, I2, I2; 3F4.2 instead of F4.2, F4.2, F4.2; 5(/) instead of /////; and so on. Therefore, for simplicity, we omit *a* in the general form in the following discussion. In this chapter, I-, X-, and F-Format codes are discussed.

4.4.1 I-Format Code

The general form of I-Format code is:

The I-Format code is used to transmit integer data. Leading, embedded, and trailing blanks in the input are treated as zeros. In the output, leading zeros are suppressed.

4.4.2 X-Format Code

The general format for the X-Format code is:

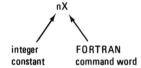

The X-Format is used to skip n characters or columns.

Example 4.3

Suppose that the input card

is read by the statements:

```
    READ (5, 12) ICONT, NUM, ITEM
12  FORMAT (I2, I5, 2X, I3)
```

The READ statement tells the computer to read from the punched card the values of the variables ICONT, NUM, and ITEM according to the specifications given in the FORMAT statement whose statement number is 12. Note that by predetermined rule, all three variables—ICONT, NUM, and ITEM—are integer variables.

The FORMAT statement that corresponds to this READ statement contains four format codes within its parentheses. The first format code (entry) corresponds to the first variable in the READ list, the second format code to the second variable in the READ list, and so on.

However, there are some format codes—such as the X-Format, T-Format, slash (/), and literal format (explained in later chapters)—that do not correspond to any variable in the list of the READ or WRITE statements. Thus I2, I5, and I3 format codes correspond to the variables ICONT, NUM, and ITEM respectively. The format code 2X does not correspond to any variable in the list part of the READ statement.

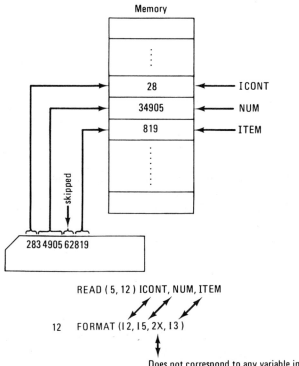

READ (5, 12) ICONT, NUM, ITEM

12   FORMAT (I 2, I 5, 2X, I 3)

Does not correspond to any variable in the list

FIGURE 4.1   Reading in the values of the variables

The *I* in I2 indicates that the corresponding variable is an integer, and the 2 indicates that two columns (digits) should be read. Thus, 28 is read as the value for ICONT (See Figure 4.1.) The second format code is I5, which corresponds to NUM. The *I* indicates the corresponding variable is an integer, and the 5 tells it to read the next five digits. Therefore, 34905 is read as the value for NUM. The next format code within the parentheses is 2X. The X Format does not correspond to any variable and is used to skip columns. The 2 in the 2X indicates that two columns should be skipped. Hence, the next two columns on the input data cards are skipped. (These two columns contain 6 and 2.) The format code I3 corresponds to the variable ITEM. The 3 indicates that the next three columns should be read. Thus, the value of ITEM becomes 819.

4.4.3　F-Format Code

This format code is used in conjunction with real variables—that is, to transmit real data. The general form of the F-Format code is Fw.d, where w is an integer constant and specifies the number of characters (columns) in the field (its width), and d is also an integer constant and specifies the number of decimal places to the right of the decimal point.

Example 4.4

Suppose that the input data card and the READ statement that processes it are as follows:

| input card | 12345 | 5817921 | 22 | 185172 |

```
READ (5, 10) NASST, COST, LIFE, SVAL
```

If the FORMAT statement that corresponds to the READ above is:

```
10  FORMAT (I5, F7.2, I2, F6.2)
```

then the value of NASST is 12345; COST is 58179.21; LIFE is 22; and SVAL is 1851.72.

Let us explain how these values are transmitted. The first entry, I5, of the FORMAT statement corresponds to the first variable, NASST, of the READ statement. The I5 indicates transmission of five digits (columns) starting from the beginning of the data card and storing it as the value for the corresponding variable. Thus, 12345 is assigned as the value for NASST. The second entry, F7.2, of the FORMAT statement corresponds to the second variable, COST, of the READ statement. Note that by predefined rule, COST is a real variable. The F7.2 indicates the transmission of the data in the seven columns following the previous field (note that the previous field was 12345). The last two columns become the fraction; hence, the value assigned to the variable COST is 58179.21. The different parts of F7.2 contain different information. The F says the number is real, 7 says to transfer seven columns, and 2 says that the rightmost two digits are decimals (fraction). As you see, although no decimal point was punched, we were able to tell the system where the decimal point should be placed.

The third entry of the FORMAT statement is I2. This entry causes the next two digits to be transferred as an integer value for its corresponding variable LIFE of the READ statement. Hence, 22 is assigned as the value of the variable LIFE.

The last entry of the FORMAT statement is F6.2, which transmits the next six columns as a real number with the rightmost two columns as decimals, giving the value 1851.72 for the corresponding variable SVAL. In other words, 1851.72 is read as the value of SVAL. Thus, the FORMAT statement determines the length and the type of the transmitted data.

If we were using the FORMAT statement

```
10   FORMAT (I3, F5.2, I2, 2X, F4.1)
```

then NASST would be 123, COST would be 455.81, LIFE would be 79, and SVAL would be 221.8. Do not forget that because of 2X, two characters (21) after the third field were skipped.

Now, you should be able to explain why the following values are assigned to the variables if the same input card is processed by the same READ statement in conjunction with the different FORMAT statements. For convenience, we repeat the input record and the READ statement.

input record ⌐ 12345581792122185172

```
READ (5, 10) NASST, COST, LIFE, SVAL
```

	VARIABLES			
	NASST	COST	LIFE	SVAL
10 FORMAT (I1, F3.3, I5, F2.1)	1	0.234	55817	9.2
10 FORMAT (I3, F3.3, I5, F2.2)	123	.455	81792	.12
10 FORMAT (I3, F3.5, I5, F2.0)	123	.00455	81792	12.0
10 FORMAT (I3, F3.4, I4, F1.2)	123	.0455	8179	.02
10 FORMAT (2X, I3, F3.1, 2X, I2, F5.1)	345	58.1	21	2218.5

Further rules regulating transmitting data are these:

1. Punching the decimal point is optional. However, when it is punched, the decimal point overrides the format code specification.
2. A sign is required for negative numbers, but it is optional with positive numbers. The sign may appear anywhere in the field prior to the first punched number.
3. If an input value exceeds the precision limit of a processor, then the processor truncates (drops) the least significant digits in order to fit the value within the procession limit.

The rules above are further clarified in the following example.

Example 4.5

Suppose that the input data card and the READ statement that processes it are as follows:

Input card:

15.267	152.67	15267.	+152.6	− ƀ52.6	ƀ − 52.6	1234567890

```
    READ (5, 10) VAL1, VAL2, VAL3, VAL4, VAL5, VAL6, VAL7
10  FORMAT (F6.3, F6.3, F6.3, F6.3, F6.3, F6.3, F10.2)
```

Then the stored values of the variables are:

VAL1	VAL2	VAL3	VAL4	VAL5	VAL6	VAL7
15.267	152.67	15256.	+152.6	−52.6	−52.6	1234567.

Explanation: The decimal point in the input field overrides the format code specification. For example, 15267. is in the corresponding field for VAL3. Although the corresponding format code for VAL3 is F6.3, this format code is ignored and 15267. is stored as the value for VAL3. Similar arguments can be made for VAL1, VAL2, VAL4, VAL5, and VAL6. Assuming that this computer has seven precision digits (see section 6.4.2), then for a real variable with the F-Format code, there is room for only seven significant digits. Thus, the last three digits are dropped, and the value 1234567. is stored for VAL7.

The FORMAT statement used in conjunction with the WRITE statement is the same as those with the READ statement. However, in the case of the WRITE statement, one print position for the decimal point should be counted; otherwise, asterisks will be printed instead of the value. This indicates an error in which there are not enough places reserved for the actual value.

Example 4.6

Suppose that the values contained in the memory locations (which are indicated below), referenced by their corresponding variable names, are to be printed on the line printer by the following WRITE statement.

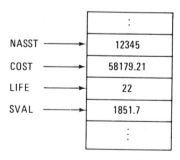

```
    WRITE (6, 12) NASST, COST, LIFE, SVAL
12  FORMAT (4X, I5, 2X, F8.2, 3X, I2, 2X, F6.2)
```

This causes the following line to be printed. (*Note:* ⊅ is used to visualize a blank—that is, a space.)

⊅⊅⊅12345⊅⊅58179.21⊅⊅⊅22⊅⊅1851.7

The first entry of the FORMAT statement caused three spaces to be skipped on the line printer. Whenever a FORMAT statement is referenced by a WRITE statement to PRINT on the line printer, the first character of the first format code is used for carriage control—that is, to control the movement of the paper or the line printer. (See section 5.5.) The second entry (I5), corresponding to NASST, causes the five-digit value of NASST to be printed. Thus, 12345 was printed. The third entry (2X) of the FORMAT statement specifies that two spaces should precede the next field. F8.2 corresponds to the variable COST, and indicates that the value of COST is real (because of the *F*) and occupies eight columns, the last two of which are decimal. Indeed, 58179.21 needs all eight columns.

Every character including the period occupies a column (position) on the printed page. Thus, in the case of the WRITE statement, a position for the decimal point should be reserved. If F7.2 instead of F8.2 were used, then the value of COST would not be printed; rather seven asterisks (*******) would be printed to indicate an overflow error. The 3X following F8.2 directs that after the value of COST is printed, three spaces should be skipped. I2, the fifth entry of the FORMAT statement, causes the value of the corresponding variable LIFE to be printed. Thus, 22 is printed. This is followed by two spaces because of 2X, and the final entry (F6.2) of the FORMAT statement causes 1851.7, the value of SVAL, to be printed.

```
    WRITE (6, 12) LIFE, COST, NASST, SVAL
12  FORMAT (3X, I2, 2X, F8.2, 2X, I5, 2X, F6.2)
```

These statements cause the following line to be printed:

⊅⊅22⊅⊅58179.21⊅⊅12345⊅⊅1851.7

Note that the order of the printed values is determined by the order of the variables in the WRITE list.

```
    WRITE (6, 12) LIFE, COST, NASST, SVAL
12  FORMAT (3X, I2, 2X, F8.2, 2X, I4, 2X, F4.2)
```

These statements cause the following line to be printed:

⊅⊅22⊅⊅58179.21⊅⊅****⊅⊅****

The asterisks indicate an overflow error. The first group of asterisks is the third printed field. This means that the format code that corresponds to the third variable in the list of the WRITE statement did not reserve enough columns (positions). The format code I4 of the FORMAT statement corresponds to the third variable, NASST, of the WRITE list. And you can see that the value of NASST is 12345, which requires five columns. Hence, the cure for this overflow error is to change I4 to I5.

The second group of asterisks in the output is the fourth printed field. Therefore, the format code that corresponds to SVAL (fourth variable in the WRITE list) needs to be modified. This overflow error can be corrected by changing F4.2 to F6.2, because 1851.7 needs six positions.

```
WRITE (6, 12) LIFE, COST, NASST, SVAL
12  FORMAT (3X, I4, 2X, F10.2, 2X, I7, 2X, F6.2)
```

causes the following line to be printed:

ᴅᴅᴅᴅ22ᴅᴅᴅᴅ58179.21ᴅᴅᴅᴅ12345ᴅᴅ1851.7

Note that no errors result if a format code reserves more column characters than the maximum value a variable needs. In such cases, the leftmost unneeded columns are replaced with blanks. The following shows how the line above was printed:

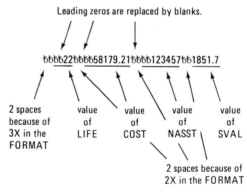

In example 2.3, a brief description of the straight-line method for calculating yearly depreciation, and a flowchart for a program using this method, were given. In the following example, a FORTRAN program is written to calculate yearly depreciation using the straight-line method.

Example 4.7: Calculating Depreciation Using Straight-Line Method

Write a FORTRAN program to read the records of all assets in ABC Company and print their yearly depreciation. Each asset's record is punched on the card in the following manner:

CC	FIELD DESCRIPTION
1–5	Asset number
6–13	Original cost
14–15	Estimated useful life (years) of the asset
16–23	Estimated scrap value of the asset

The depreciation per year using the straight-line method is fixed (constant) for every year and is calculated by the following formula:

Depreciation per year = (Cost − Scrap value) ÷ Useful life (in years) of the asset

The program should produce the output on the line printed, and each output line should be printed in the following manner:

PC (PAGE COLUMN)	FIELD DESCRIPTION
11–15	Asset number
16–20	Blank
21–29	Original cost
30–34	Blank
35–43	Depreciation per year

Most line printers allow up to 132 characters (columns) per line. Our input record has four fields; therefore, we need four variables in the list portion of the READ statement to accept the value of these fields. In the program, we choose the names NASST, COST, USEL, and SVAL for the corresponding fields of the input records. The output record contains the values of NASST, COST, and

FIGURE 4.2   Flowchart diagram to calculate depreciation

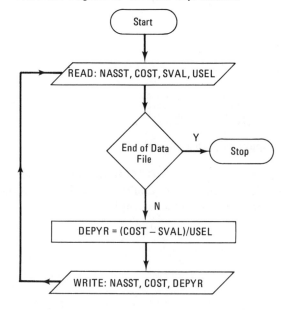

DEPYR. Therefore, there are only three variables in the list portion of the WRITE statement.

Figure 4.2 is the flowchart diagram for the problem above. Figure 4.3 shows the input data, the FORTRAN program, and the output produced by the program. The variable names used are:

NASST: Asset values

COST: Original asset value

USEL: Useful year life of the asset

SVAL: Estimated scrap value

DEPYR: Depreciation per year

```
Input data:


4444400500.000200050.00
3333320900.002507000.00
2222212500.501001500.00
1111106000.000600500.00

C
C CALCULATING DEPRECIATION PER YEAR USING STRAIGHT LINE METHOD
C
          ICARD = 5
          LINE = 6
C
C THE FOLLOWING STATEMENT READS ASSET'S ID,ORIGIONAL COST,
C USEFUL LIFE AND SCRAP VALUE
C
 10       READ (ICARD, 20, END = 40) NASST, COST, USEL, SVAL
 20       FORMAT(I5, F8.2, F2.0, F8.2)
C
C CALCULATE  DEPRECIATIN PER YEAR
          DEPYR = (COST - SVAL)/USEL
C PRINT THE OUTPUT
          WRITE (LINE, 30) NASST, COST, DEPYR
 30       FORMAT (11X, I5, 5X, F9.2, 5X, F9.2)
          GO TO 10
 40       STOP
          END


Output produced by the above program:


          44444         500.00         225.00
          33333       20900.00         556.00
          22222       12500.50        1100.05
          11111        6000.00         916.67
```

FIGURE 4.3 Input data, program, and output

In the program, the statement GO TO 10 transfers control to the statement labeled with 10. This is called an unconditional GO TO statement. The general form for an unconditional GO TO statement is:

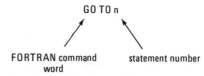

When this statement is encountered, control transfers to the statement with statement number *n*.

Although statements such as GOTO 20 or GOTO50 are valid, you should avoid writing them in such a manner because the program becomes less readable. Instead, write these statements as GO TO 20 and GO TO 50.

4.5   SUMMARY

The READ statement is used to read in the value of variables. The WRITE statement is used to write the value of variables onto the external storage devices from the memory locations identified by the variables. The general forms for the READ and the WRITE statements are:

```
READ (n1, n2, END = n3, ERR = n4) list
WRITE (n1, n2) list
```

where:

>   *n1* is a logical unit number.
>   *n2, n3,* and *n4* are statement numbers.
>   *list* is the list of variables.

The logical unit number is an integer variable or integer constant used within the input/output statement to identify the data files. Every time the READ or the WRITE statement is executed, a new record will be read or written, respectively.

The FORMAT statement is used to specify the fields of the records in conjunction with the input/output statements. The FORMAT statement is a specification statement, and it can be placed anywhere in the program as long as it precedes the END statement. The general form of the FORMAT statement is:

```
n    FORMAT (e1, e2, . . . , en)
```

where:

>   *n* is the statement number.
>   *e1, e2, . . ., en* are the format codes.

In this chapter, I-, X-, and F-Format codes were discussed. The general forms and the usage of these format codes are:

FORMAT CODE	FUNCTION
In	Describes an integer field of *n* digits.
nX	Skip *n* characters (columns).
Fw.d	Describes a real field with a total of *w* digits, of which *d* digits are to the right of the decimal point.

4.6   REVIEW QUESTIONS AND
             SUGGESTED PROBLEMS

1. *True or False.* Every time an input statement such as READ is executed, a new record is read.

2. *True or False.* Every time an output statement such as WRITE is executed, a new record is written.

3. For what purpose are logical unit numbers used?

4. *True or False.* A logical unit number must be either an integer constant or an integer variable.

5. *True or False.* A FORMAT statement must be referenced by at least one input or output statement.

6. Which set of instructions below is preferable? Why?

a.
```
      READ (5, 10) NUM, PAY, OLDBLN
   10 FORMAT (I5, F7.2, F9.2)
```

b.
```
      READ (ICARD, 10) NUM, PAY, OLDBLN
   10 FORMAT (I5, F7.2, F9.2)
```

7. Identify the elements of the following READ and WRITE statements:

```
a.   READ (5, 20, END = 60, ERR = 100) NUM, PAY, BALNS
b.   READ (ICARD, 30, END = 70) NUM, PAY, BALNS
c.   WRITE (JPRINT, 60) NUM, PAY, BALNS
d.   READ (2, 50, ERR = 70) I, J, R1, R2
e.   WRITE (6, 50)
f.   READ (5, 20) READ, END, IF, LAST
```

8. Explain the actions performed by END = 60 and ERR = 100 in question 7a.

9. One general form of the READ statement is:

$$\text{READ } (n1, n2, \underline{END} = n3, \underline{ERR} = n4) \ v1, v2 \ . \ . \ .$$

where *n1* is an integer variable or constant, *n2, n3* are integer constants, and *v1, v2* . . . are variables. Decide which of the following statements are valid and which are not.

```
a.   25  READ (5, 200) NUM, HOURS, RATE
b.   50  READ (ICARD, 200) NUM, HOURS, RATE
c.   50  READ (CARD, 200) NUM, HOURS, RATE
d.       READ (ICARD, 200, ERR = 60) NUM, HOURS, RATE
```

```
e.      READ (ERR = 60, ICARD, 200) NUM, HOURS, RATE
f.      READ (2, 200, END = 70 ERR = 90) NUM, HOURS, RATE
g.      READ (ICARD, END = 100) NUM, HOURS, RATE
h.      READ (5, 200) NUM, HOURS, RATE
i.      READ (5, 200) NUM, HOURS, RATE
```

10. The general form of the WRITE statement is:

```
WRITE (n1, n2) v1, v2, . . .
```

where $n1$ is an integer variable or constant, $n2$ is an integer constant, and $v1$, $v2$, . . . are variable names. Decide which of the following statements are valid and which are not:

```
a.   50  WRITE (6, 10) NUMBR, HOURS, RATE
b.   50  WRITE (IPRINT, 10) NUMBR, HOURS, RATE
c.       WRITE (JOUT, 12)
d.       WRITE (JOUT, IFORM)
e.       WRITE (6, 13)
f.       WRITE (5, IPR) NUMBR, HOURS, RATE
```

11. Assume the following input data card:

```
8903752508679201450782310
```

Determine the values of the variables in the list of the following READ statements when the input card above is processed by the input/output statements in conjunction with the indicated FORMAT statements.

```
a.       READ (5, 10) INP, X2, VAL1, VAL2
     10  FORMAT (I5, F5.2, F3.2, F5.2)

b.       READ (5, 10) NCST, OLBL, PAY
     10  FORMAT (I6, F6.2, F6.2)

c.       READ (5, 10) J1, J2, R1, R2, R3
     10  FORMAT (2I5, 3F3.2)

d.       READ (5, 10) RATE, AMOUNT
     10  FORMAT (F1.2, F6.2)

e.       READ (5, 10) J1, J2, R1, R2, R3
     10  FORMAT (2X, I2, 2X, I3, 2X, F1.3, F2.3, F5.3)
```

12. *Sales Forecasting.* In Example 2.4, a weighted-average procedure for finding the sales forecast for the coming month was explained. Figure 2.9 is a flowchart diagram for a forecasting program. Write a FORTRAN program to read each record of the commodity file of the Best Deal Store, and to calculate and print

the forecasted sales for the coming month, along with the commodity code. Each input record contains eight fields punched on the card in the following manner:

CC	FIELD	TYPE
1–5	Commodity code	Integer
6–8	Sales for the last month (of the six-month period)	Integer
9–11	Sales for month before last (of the six-month period)	Integer
12–14	Sales for the fourth month (of the six-month period)	Integer
15–17	Sales for the third month (of the six-month period)	Integer
18–20	Sales for the second month (of the six-month period)	Integer
21–23	Sales for the first month (of the six-month period)	Integer
24–26	Sales forecast for the last month	Integer

13. *Breakeven Analysis.* Breakeven analysis was discussed in problem 17 of Chapter 2. You are to design the input file of ABC Company's products where each input record contains four fields. These are the product code, the fixed operation cost (setup cost) to produce the product, the variable cost per unit, and the sales price per unit.

Write a FORTRAN program to read each input record, calculate the breakeven point and total cost, and print the product code, breakeven point, and total cost. Recall that the breakeven point determines the least quantity of a product that must be sold so that the firm's revenue equals the total cost of producing that product. The breakeven point and the total cost are calculated by the following formulas:

$$\text{Quantity to be produced} = Q = \frac{F}{S - V}$$

$$\text{Total cost} \qquad C = F + V * Q$$

where:

F is the fixed cost
V is the variable unit cost
S is the sale price per unit
C is the total cost
Q is the breakeven point (quantity to be produced)

14. *Simple Interest.* Write a FORTRAN program to read each customer record of the Modern Industrial Bank, calculate the interest and the new balance, and

print out account number, old balance, new balance, interest, and rate of interest. Each input record is punched on the card in the following manner:

CC	FIELD	TYPE
1–5	Account number	Integer
6–13	Balance	Real xxxxxx.xx
14–15	Rate of interest	Real 0.0xx

The output record should be:

CC	FIELD	TYPE
1–5	Blank	
6–10	Account number	Integer
11–15	Blank	
16–24	Old balance	Real xxxxxx.xx
25–29	Blank	
30–38	New balance	Real xxxxxx.xx
39–43	Blank	
44–51	Interest	Real xxxxx.xx
52–56	Blank	
57–61	Rate of interest	Real x.xxx

15. *Compound Interest.* Let CAPITL be the initial amount invested and RATE the rate of interest per dollar invested. The balance at the end of the first year is CAPITL $(1 + \text{RATE})$. The balance at the end of n years is CAPITL $(1 + \text{RATE})^n$, and the interest amount for the period of n years is CAPITL $(1 + \text{RATE})^n -$ CAPITL.

Design the input record for the customer of Modern Industrial Bank. Each input record contains the customer account number, initial amount invested, number of years, and rate of interest.

Write a FORTRAN program to read each customer's record, find the balance and the savings amount at the end of the period, and print out the account number, the initial balance, the accumulated savings, the new balance, the number of years invested, and the rate of interest. You should organize and design the output record yourself.

5 PROGRAM DESIGN AND MORE FORMAT CODES

STEPS IN DESIGNING AND IMPLEMENTING COMPUTER PROGRAMS

1. Define the problem to be solved.
2. Identify the desired output and design the output record or records, including page and column headings (if any).
3. Identify the input data. Design the input record or records. This is achieved by identifying all the fields of the input record.
4. Find an algorithm to solve the problem. In other words, identify the steps and procedures required to solve the problem.
5. Draw the flowchart diagram or write pseudo codes. Check the validity of the procedure that is represented by the codes on the diagram.
6. Convert the flowchart or pseudo codes into the FORTRAN program.
7. Prepare the input data according to the specification of the input fields— i.e., according to the format codes of the input statements.
8. Run the program.
9. If the program did not run because of compilation errors (such as mis-spelling FORTRAN command words), then correct the errors and return to step 8.
10. If the program ran but there were execution time errors (such as an unidentified routine, or the program producing wrong and unexpected results), then return to step 4. Correct the errors and make the required changes in steps 4 through 7. Repeat steps 8 through 10.

There are instances in which a programmer must print a message, or a page heading (such as EMPLOYEE LIST FOR JULY 1981), or column headings for a payroll listing—for example:

EMPLOYEE ID   EMPLOYEE NAME   ADDRESS   PAY

In FORTRAN, the H-Format code (the Hollerith format code) and literal data can be used for such purposes. Before going into the discussion of these format codes, we need to know what a literal constant is.

5.2   LITERAL CONSTANTS (CHARACTER CONSTANTS)

A *literal constant* (also called *character constant*) is a string of characters that is organized in one of two ways: Either (1) the string is enclosed in apostrophes (such literal constants are also called *literal data*); or (2) the string is preceded by nH, where n is the number of characters in the string.

Example 5.1

LITERAL CONSTANT	REMARKS
'PRODUCT NAME'	This literal constant has 12 characters created by the first rule.
12 H PRODUCT NAME number H the string of of characters characters	This literal has 12 characters created by the second rule. Note that the 12 before the H indicates that the 12 characters following the H make up the literal constant.
' PRODUCT NAME'	This literal constant contains 13 characters. Do not forget to count the blank character between the apostrophe and P.
13H PRODUCT NAME	Note that the blank character before P is counted.
'STUDENT''S NAME'	A single apostrophe must be replaced by two single apostrophes if rule 1 is used.
14HSTUDENT'S NAME	Equivalent to 'STUDENT''S NAME'.
'25'	This literal constant has two characters, 2 and 5. *It is not the number 25* but contains the characters (symbols) 2 and 5.
2H25	Equivalent to '25'.
'*****'	This literal constant contains 5 asterisks.

More examples of literal constants are '$AMOUNT', 'USA', 'AVERAGE IS:', 3HPAY, and 'KURDISTAN'. The uses of literal constants are in printing page headings, column headings, messages, and the like.

The general form of the H-Format code is:

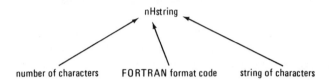

Literal data is what we call a string of characters enclosed in apostrophes.

Both the H-Format code and literal data can appear within the FORMAT statement; they have the same effect. For example, the following two FORMAT statements are equivalent:

```
10   FORMAT(5X, 'EMPLOYEE LIST FOR 1977')

10   FORMAT(5X,22HEMPLOYEE LIST FOR 1977)
```

As with the X-Format code, no variable in the I/O (input/output) list corresponds to the literal data.

5.3.1 Using H-Format Code or Literal Data with Output Statement

The output statement, when it references a FORMAT statement with an H-Format code or literal data, causes the characters following the H or the characters between the apostrophes to be written on the output data set (such as an output file with a line printer).

Example 5.2

```
    WRITE (6,10)

10   FORMAT(10X, 'STUDENT LIST')
```

This causes the line printer to skip nine columns and write the phrase *STUDENT LIST*. The same thing can be accomplished by writing:

```
    WRITE(6,10)

10   FORMAT(10X,12HSTUDENT LIST)
```

Recall that when the FORMAT statement is referenced by a WRITE statement, the first character of the first entry of the FORMAT statement is used as carriage control, to control the movement of the paper on the line printer. The first entry of the FORMAT statement above is 10X (which is equivalent to XXXXXXXXXX). The first X is used for carriage control, and the remaining 9X causes the line printer to skip nine columns. To avoid confusion whenever a FORMAT statement is referenced by a WRITE statement using the line printer, we shall write the carriage control explicitly. Therefore, the following form of the FORMAT statement above is preferable to the previous one.

```
10  FORMAT(1X,9X, 'STUDENT LIST')
```

Suppose that the value of the variable AVR is 258.95; then the statements

```
    WRITE(6,12)AVR
12  FORMAT(1X ,5X, 'AVERAGE IS: ',F6.2)
```

cause the line printer to write:

ƀƀƀƀƀAVERAGE IS:258.95

5.3.2 Using H-Format Code or Literal Data with Input Statement

The input statement that references a FORMAT statement having the H-Format code or literal data causes the information read from the input card to replace the literal data in the FORMAT statement. If the nH format code is used, n characters are read. If apostrophes are used, then the number of characters read equals the number of characters between the apostrophes.

Example 5.3

The READ statement in both

```
    READ(5,10)
10  FORMAT(5X,22HEMPLOYEE LIST FOR 1977)
```

and

```
    READ(5,10)
10  FORMAT(5X, 'EMPLOYEE LIST FOR 1977')
```

causes the computer to skip the first five characters (because of 5X), and then read 22 characters to replace *EMPLOYEE LIST FOR 1977*. Now, if the same FORMAT were referenced by a WRITE statement, then the information just read would be printed.

One can take advantage of this property of the H-Format code and literal data and use it as a trick to read and write character data. This is shown in example 5.4 below. However, a basic principle that the programmer should follow to write good programs is to keep the program simple and readable and avoid using any tricks. Therefore, you are not encouraged to use the H-Format code and literal data with the input statements. A preferred method for reading and writing character data is by means of A-Format code, explained later in this chapter.

Example 5.4

Assume the input data card is:

```
bbbbbGEORGEbRUSSELb52341
```

Then consider:

```
    READ(5,10) NUM
10  FORMAT(5X,14Hbbbbbbbbbbbbbb,I5)
    WRITE(6,10) NUM
```

The READ statement causes the skipping of the first five columns, the next 14 characters are read into the place of those characters that follow the H, and 52341 is read as the value for NUM. The WRITE statement causes the following output:

bbbbbGEORGEbRUSSEL52341

Note that one FORMAT statement can be referenced by several input/output statements.

The following FORTRAN program reads 30 columns after skipping the first column of each punched card and prints them on the line printer.

```
 50 READ(5,100,END= 300)
100 FORMAT(1X,30Hbbbbbbbbbbbbbbbbbbbbbbbbbbbbbb)
    WRITE(3,100)
    GO TO 50
300 STOP
    END
```

The T-Format code indicates the position in the FORTRAN record where transfer should occur.

Example 5.5

```
READ(5,12) NUM,RATE
12   FORMAT(T5,I5,T20,F4.2)
```

This example causes five digits starting from column 5 to be transferred as the value for NUM. The T20 indicates that the next transfer should start in column 20, and the format code F4.2, which corresponds to RATE, causes four digits, with the rightmost two digits being decimal, to be assigned as the value of RATE. Thus, if the following card is processed by the READ statement above, the value of NUM is 25734 and that of RATE is 07.50.

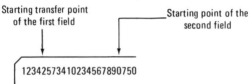

This statement:

```
WRITE(6,18) NUM,RATE
18   FORMAT( T8, 'EMPLOYEE NUMBER IS: ',I5,T32,'RATE IS:',F5.2)
```

causes the following line to be printed;

ƀƀƀƀƀƀEMPLOYEEƀNUMBERƀIS:25734ƀƀRATEƀIS:7.50

The format code T8 is the first entry of the FORMAT statement 18. Because one character (the first) of the first entry of the FORMAT statement is used for carriage control (see section 5.5), the format code T8 causes printing of the next field to start from column 7 instead of 8. However, the format code T32 causes printing of the next field to start in column 32.

5.5   CARRIAGE-CONTROL CHARACTER

When the FORMAT statement is used in conjunction with the WRITE statement, the first character of the first entry will be used for carriage control—to control the movement of the printed paper on the line printer. Therefore, when formatted records are prepared for printing, the first character of the record is not printed. The carriage control can be specified as literal data— that is, either by H Format or by enclosing the character within two single quotations. Below are the carriage-control characters and their meanings.

CHARACTER	MEANING
1	Advance to first line on new page.
0	Skip 2 lines before printing.
Blank	Skip 1 line before printing.
+	No advance—i.e., rewrite on the same line without going to the next line.
Any other character	Considered as blank.

Note that more carriage-control characters can be assigned at the option of the installation. For example, the DECSystem 10, in addition to those above, allows 2 and 3 to be used as carriage controls to advance 1/2 and 1/3 of a page respectively.

Example 5.6

```
    WRITE(6,10)
10  FORMAT('EMPLOYEE LIST')
```

causes *MPLOYEE LIST* to be printed at the beginning of a new line. The *E* (the first character of *EMPLOYEE*) is not printed, because it is used for carriage control.

```
    WRITE(6,10)
10  FORMAT('ɓEMPLOYEE LIST')
```

prints *EMPLOYEE LIST*. As you see, the blank character before *E* is used for carriage control.

```
    WRITE(6,10)
10  FORMAT('1',6X, 'EMPLOYEE LIST')
```

prints *EMPLOYEE LIST* on the first line of a new page after skipping six columns.

```
    WRITE(6,10)
10  FORMAT('+',T90,'PART1')
```

prints *PART1*, starting in column 90 on the same line; no line is skipped.

```
    WRITE(6,10)
10  FORMAT('0',49X, 'EMPLOYEE LIST')
```

prints *EMPLOYEE LIST* starting in column 50 after two lines are skipped.

**5.6   SUCCESSIVE REPETITION OF
         FORMAT CODES**

Recall that any format code can be preceded by an integer constant to indicate the number of the code's repetition. This is a very useful tool for writing fewer entries within the FORMAT statement. Not only can the repetition of a single format code be abbreviated, but the repetition of a group of format codes can be abbreviated as well.

Example 5.7

The following FORMAT statements are equivalent:

```
10   FORMAT(I2,I2,F5.2,F5.2,F5.2,I3,I3,I3,I3)

10   FORMAT(2I2,3F5.2,4I3)
10   FORMAT(2I2,3(F5.2),4(I3))
```

and

```
50   FORMAT(I2,//////,F6.3,F6.3)
```

is equivalent to

```
50   FORMAT(I2,6(/),2F6.3)
```

(See section 5.7 for the slash (/) format.)
The following FORMAT statements are the same:

```
70   FORMAT(I2,F5.3,4X,I2,F5.3,4X,I2,F5.3,4X,F7.2)

70   FORMAT(3(I2,F5.3,4X),F7.2)
```

Note that the group I2, F5.3, 4X was repeated three times successively.

```
100 FORMAT(2X,'XXXXXXXXXX',F4.2,2X,'XXXXXXXXXX',F4.2)
```

is equivalent to

```
100 FORMAT(2(2X,10('X'),F4.2))
```

The slash format code is used to skip the remainder of the current record and start a new record. If the last entry of the FORMAT statement is /, then the / causes the remainder of the record to be skipped. The / format does not need to be preceded or followed by the delimiter comma as the other format codes do. Instead of writing /////, one can write 5(/). This causes five records to be skipped. However, if 5(/) is the last entry within the FORMAT statement, then the remainder of the current record and four other complete records will be skipped.

Example 5.8

Write the necessary FORTRAN statements to accomplish the following:

1. Skip 3 lines at the beginning of a new page.
2. Starting from column 50 of the fourth line, print *ACCOUNTS PAYABLE FOR THE CURRENT PERIOD.*
3. Skip 5 lines, then write the column headings as specified below:

COLUMN START

10	CUSTOMER NUMBER
30	NAME
60	PAY
70	ADDRESS

The following WRITE and FORMAT statements accomplish this:

```
    WRITE(6,200)
200 FORMAT('1',///,T50,'ACCOUNTS PAYABLE FOR THE
    CURRENT PERIOD',6(/))
    WRITE(6,300)
300 FORMAT (T11, 'CUSTOMER NUMBER',T30,'NAME',T60,
    'PAY',T70,'ADDRESS')
```

Explanation: The first entry, '1', is for carriage control and causes a skip to a new page. The /// causes the skipping of three lines, the T50 positions the printer in column 50, the literal 'ACCOUNTS PAYABLE FOR THE CURRENT PERIOD' is printed, and finally the 6(/) causes five complete lines and the remainder of the current one to be skipped.

The function of the second WRITE statement is clear. A single WRITE statement can be written instead of the two WRITE statements above. The following WRITE and FORMAT statements achieve these requirements:

```
WRITE(6,100)
100 FORMAT('1',///,T50,'ACCOUNTS PAYABLE FOR THE CURRENT',
+'PERIOD',5(/),T10,'CUSTOMER NUMBER',T30,'NAME',T60,'PAY',
+T70,'ADDRESS')
```

5.8   A-FORMAT CODE

The A-Format code is used to transmit characters as the values of. their corresponding variables in the I/O list. The general form of the A-Format code is Aw, where w is an integer constant that specifies the number of characters in the field. The maximum number of characters that can be transmitted is limited by the size of the memory locations of the corresponding variable in the I/O list. For example, on the DECSystem 10, the maximum for double precision variables is ten characters (a double-precision variable occupies two computer words, see Section 6.4.2); for all other variables, the maximum is five characters. However, on the IBM/370, the maximum is eight if the variable is declared to be Real–8, or four if standard length is used (two computer words are required for a Real–8 variable and one for standard variables). In this text, the standard five of DECSystem 10 and four of IBM are assumed unless otherwise specified. Other computers have different variable sizes.

Example 5.9

Assume the input data card is:

```
JOHNbSMITHbJR.325.18
```

Then the statements

```
READ(5,10) NAM1,NAM2,NAM3,NAM4,SAL
10  FORMAT(A4,A4,A4,A2,F6.2)
```

cause the variables NAM1, NAM2, NAM3, NAM4, and SAL to have the following values (see Figure 5.1):

NAM1	NAM2	NAM3	NAM4	SAL
JOHN	ƀ SMI	TH ƀJ	R.	325.18

The corresponding format code for each of the variables NAM1, NAM2, and NAM3 is A4. Thus, the first four characters (*JOHN*) are transmitted as the value for NAM1, the second four characters (*ƀSMI*) as the value of NAM2, and the third four characters (*THƀJ*) as the value for NAM3. The corresponding format code for NAM4 is A2; hence, the two characters R. are assigned as the value of NAM4. The variable SAL is real and its value becomes 325.18. Note that in the FORMAT statement, 3A4 can be written instead of writing A4 three times. Therefore, the FORMAT statement above can be written:

```
10   FORMAT(3A4,A2,F6.2)
```

If the number of characters in the A-Format code—that is, *w*—exceeds the maximum number of characters that can be stored in the corresponding variable, *then the leftmost characters are lost on input and replaced with blanks on output.*

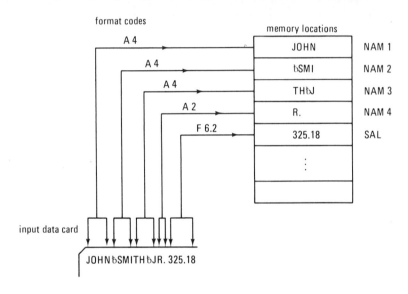

FIGURE 5.1   Reading characters as the value of variables

Example 5.10

Input card:

```
SHEILAN ƀ BROWN ƀ 218 ƀ GREEN ƀ RD.
```

then:

```
      READ(5,10) J1,J2,J3
10   FORMAT(A10,A7,A10)
```

causes J1, J2, and J3 to have the following values;

J1	J2	J3
NØBR	Ø218	ØRD.

Note that the A10 format code corresponds to J1, but J1 can hold only four characters (standard on IBM). Therefore, the leftmost six characters, *SHEILA*, of the ten-character list *SHEILANØBR* are lost, and only the last four characters, *NØBR*, are transmitted as the value for J1. Try to justify why J2 and J3 assumed the values shown above.

Example 5.11

Assume J1, J2, and J3 have the following values:

J1	J2	J3
JOHN	SMIT	H

then the following WRITE statement:

```
   WRITE(3,10) J1,J2,J3
10   FORMAT( 1X,2X,A4,A4,A1)
```

prints:

ØØJOHNSMITH

To insert a space between JOHN and SMITH, insert the format code 1X between the format codes that correspond to J1 and J2. If, instead of the one above, the following FORMAT statement is used:

```
10   FORMAT(1X,2X,A4,1X,A4,A1)
```

then the output becomes:

ØØJOHNØSMITH

Example 5.12: **Student Information System**

Suppose you were asked by the registration office at Eastern Michigan University to write a FORTRAN program to read from the card reader and write on the line printer all student records. After studying the problem, you come up with the following possible design:

Input record: The input record contains five fields, punched on the card in the following manner:

CC	FIELD	FIELD LENGTH	TYPE
1–5	Student number	5	Integer
6–25	Name	20	Character
26–29	Grade point average	4	Real X.XX
30–39	Major	10	Character
40	Sex	1	Character
41–68	Address	28	Character

Typical input card:

12345	RUSSELbJENKINbbbbbbb	2.50	COMPUTERS	bb	M	1428bGREENbDR.bYPSIMI 48197

Output record:

1. Print the title EASTERN MICHIGAN UNIVERSITY starting in column 30 of the third line of a new page.
2. Skip 2 lines after the title, then print the subtitle STUDENT INFORMATION LIST FOR FALL 1982, starting in column 10.
3. Skip 5 lines after printing the subtitle, then print the following column headings:

SPC (STARTING PAGE COLUMN)	COLUMN HEADINGS
3	ID
8	STUDENT NAME
32	GPA
38	SEX
42	MAJOR
53	ADDRESS

4. Print each student's information under the appropriate heading.

Both pseudo code form and flowchart diagram are shown in Figure 5.2 for our FORTRAN program.

Note that in both the input and output records, the contents of the four fields NAME, MAJOR, SEX, and ADDRESS are not numbers but characters. The variable names SN1, SN2, SN3, SN4, SN5 are used to store the information for the field NAME. Each of these variable names will hold only four characters. By the same token, the variables AD1, AD2, AD3, AD4, AD5, AD6, AD7 store the address; MJ1, MJ2, MJ3 store the major; and SEX stores one character (M or F) to identify sex.

(A more efficient scheme for naming this type of variable will be discussed under the topic of subscripted variables. See Chapter 10).

Note: If your compiler does not allow T-Format code, replace the FORMAT statements 30 and 60 by the following:

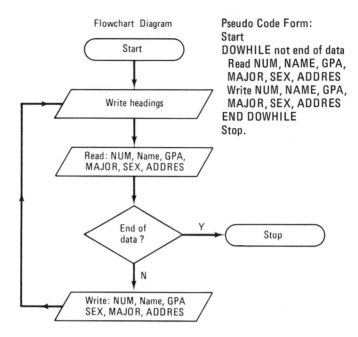

FIGURE 5.2 Flowchart diagram and pseudo code to read and write student records

```
10   FORMAT('1',29X,'EASTERN MICHIGAN UNIVERSITY',5(/))

20   FORMAT(1X,10X,'STUDENT INFORMATION LIST FOR FALL 1982')

30   FORMAT(1X,2X,ID,6X,'STUDENTNAME',11X,'GPA',13X,'SEX',3X,
     'MAJOR',c15X,'ADDRESS')

60   FORMAT(1X,2X,I5,2X,5A4,4X,F4.2,3X,A1,5X,2A4,A2,9X,7A4)
```

5.9 SUMMARY

Literal constants are strings of characters of two types: literal data, in which the string is enclosed in parentheses; and H-Format, where the string is preceded by a figure representing the number of characters in it, and then the letter H. In this chapter, we learned how to use these with input and output statements, and we also discussed T-Format, A-Format, and slash format codes and their uses.

One FORMAT statement can be referenced by many input/output statements. If the FORMAT statement is referenced by a WRITE statement using the

Input data:

```
12345RUSSEL JENKIN        2.50COMPUTER   M11428 GREEN DR. YPSI MI 48197
12345GEORGE BROWN         3.45MATHEMATICM37456 GRAND DENVER COL 45672
65745LINDA OGDEN          2.87HISTORY    F56 PARK ST. LOIUS MO 23451
87652BRUCEK KURDO         3.89COMPUTER   M3729 WATERFALL, TROY, MI 48197
98765SHEILAN KHAILANY     3.87ART        F1456 MAPLE RD. YPSI, MI 34521
```

```
C                 STUDENT INFORMATION SYSTEM
C  PROBLEM NARRATIVE:
C                       THIS PROGRAM READS AND WRITESS STUDENT
C                       INFORMATION RECORDS.
C INPUT FILE: THE INPUT FILE IS PUNCHED ON CARDS
C OUTPUT FILE: THE OUTPUT IS PRINTED ON THE LINE PRINTER
C
C
C VARIABLE NAMES USED IN THE PROBLEM:
C        NUM                      STUDENT NUMBER
C        GPA                      GRADE POINT AVERAGE
C        SN1,SN2,SN3,SN4,SN5      STUDENT NAME
C        MJ1,MJ2,MJ3              MAJOR
C        AD1,AD2,AD3,AD4,AD5,AD6,AD7  ADDRESS
C        SEX                      SEX
C
C
         ICARD = 5
         LINE  = 6
C
C PRINT THE TITLE
C
         WRITE(LINE,10)
10       FORMAT('1',//T30,'EASTERN MICHIGAN UNIVERSITY',3(/))
C
C PRINT THE SUBTITLE
C
         WRITE(LINE,20)
20       FORMAT(1X,T10,'STUDENT INFORMATION LIST FOR FALL 1982',6(/))
C PRINT COLUMN HEADINGS
C
         WRITE(LINE,30)
30       FORMAT(1X,T3,'ID',T8,'STUDENT NAME',T32,'GPA',
      +  T38,'SEX',T42,'MAJOR',T53,'ADDRESS')
C
C
C STARTING LOOP
C
C READ THE INPUT DATA . IF END OF DATA IS FOUND   GO TO 70
C
40       READ(ICARD,50,END =70)NUM,SN1,SN2,SN3,SN4,SN5,GPA,MJ1,MJ2,MJ3,
      +                  SEX,AD1,AD2,AD3,AD4,AD5,AD6,AD7
50       FORMAT(I5,5A4,F4.2,2A4,A2,A1,7A4)
C
C PRINT THE RECORD WHICH JUST READ
         WRITE(LINE,60)NUM,SN1,SN2,SN3,SN4,SN5,GPA,SEX,MJ1,MJ2,MJ3,
      +            AD1,AD2,AD3,AD4,AD5,AD6,AD7
60       FORMAT(1X,T2,I5,T8,5A4,T32,F4.2,T38,A1,T42,2A4,A2,T53,7A4)
         GO TO 40
70       STOP
         END
```

Output produced by the above program:

```
                        EASTERN MICHIGAN UNIVERSITY

        STUDENT INFORMATION LIST FOR FALL 1982

ID    STUDENT NAME        GPA   SEX MAJOR       ADDRESS
12345 RUSSEL JENKIN       2.50   M   COMPUTER    11428 GREEN DR. YPSI MI 4819
12345 GEORGE BROWN        3.45   M   MATHEMATIC  37456 GRAND DENVER COL 45672
65745 LINDA OGDEN         2.87   F   HISTORY     56 PARK ST. LOIUS MO 23451
87652 BRUCEK KURDO        3.89   M   COMPUTER    3729 WATERFALL, TROY, MI 481
98765 SHEILAN KHAILANY    3.87   F   ART         1456 MAPLE RD. YPSI, MI 3452
```

FIGURE 5.3   FORTRAN program for student information system

line printer, then the first character of the first code of the FORMAT statement is used for carriage control, to control the movement of the paper on the line printer. The format codes have to be separated by the delimiter comma or by the slash (/). The repetition of a single code or a group of format codes can be abbreviated.

5.10   REVIEW QUESTIONS AND SUGGESTED PROBLEMS

1. Give three examples of (a) integer constants; (b) real constants; (c) literal constants.

2. Identify the following types of constants: 5H12345, '12345', 12345, 12345., 12345.0, 123.45, '256', 1Hƀ, '1', '0'.

3. Identify the errors (if any) in the following statements:

```
     WRITE(6,10)
a. 10  FORMAT(1,5X,'WEEKLYPAYROLL)
```

```
     WRITE(6,10) TOTAL
b. 10  FORMAT(1H1,T50, TOTALINCOME:,F9.2)
```

```
     WRITE(6,10)
c. 10  FORMAT('1',T20,'ITEMNAME',T5,'ITEMCODE')
```

4. *True or False.* Assume the input card is:

| ƀƀƀ | 1234 | ƀƀƀƀ | EDWARDJOHNSONƀJR. |

Then the statements

```
     READ(5,10) ID
10   FORMAT(3X,I4,4X,18('b'))
     WRITE(6,10) ID
```

produce the following output:

ƀƀ1234ƀƀƀƀEDWARD JOHNSONƀJR.

5. Make a WRITE statement and a FORMAT statement to generate the following column headings:

SPC	HEADING
3	NUMBER
12	EMPLOYEE NAME

6. In the following FORMAT statement, several groups of format codes are repeated. Abbreviate the FORMAT statement.

```
     READ(5,10) J1,R1,N1,J2,R2,N2,R3,R4,R5,
10  FORMAT  2X,I5,1X,F5.2,1X,I2,I5,1X,F5.2,1X,I2,2X,F3.2,
     2X,F3.2,2X,F3.2)
```

7. For what purpose is each of the following format codes used?
   a. I-Format
   b. F-Format
   c. T-Format
   d. X-Format
   e. / format
   f. H-Format
   g. "String" format
   h. A-Format

8. Suppose the value of the variable BIG is 2672.89. Write a WRITE statement and a FORMAT statement to generate the following output on the fourth line of a new page:

ƀƀƀƀƀTHE ƀLARGEST ƀVALUE ƀIS:ƀ2672.89

9. Write one WRITE statement and one FORMAT statement to generate the following output on the line printer:
   a. Start in column 50 of the third line of a new page and print *INVEN-TORY REPORT FOR FEBRUARY 1985.*
   b. Skip 5 lines and print the following column headings:

SPC	HEADING
3	ITEM NUMBER
15	ITEM NAME
30	PRICE
45	ON HAND
65	DEMAND
75	ON ORDER
85	LEAD TIME
100	SUPPLIER

   c. Underline each of the column headings.

10. Redo problem 12 (sales forecasting problem) of Chapter 4. This time, generate appropriate report title and column headings before printing the other output.

11. Redo problem 13 (breakeven analysis) of Chapter 4. Your program should generate appropriate report title and column headings.

12. Determine the values of the variables in the list of the READ statement

when the following input card is processed by the indicated READ and FOR-MAT statements:

12345 LINDA SMITH 1258 GREEN DR. YPSI, MI 48197

```
READ(5,6) NUM, N1, N2, N3, N4, A1, A2, A3, A4, A5, A6, A7
6    FORMAT(I5,3A4,A2,7A4)
```

13. Assume that the variables NUM, N1, N2, N3, N4, A1, A2, A3, A4, A5, A6, and A7 have values as read in problem 12. What will be the output if the following WRITE statements are executed?

```
      WRITE(6,10) NUM,N1,N2,N3,N4,A1,A2,A3,A4,A5,A6,A7
a. 10 FORMAT(4X,I5,4X,3A4,A2,4X,7A4)

      WRITE(6,10) N1,N2,N3,N4,NUM
b. 10 FORMAT(4X,3A4,A2,I5)

      WRITE(6,10) N1,N3,N2,N4
c. 10 FORMAT(4A4)
```

14. Input card:

BRUCE RUSSEL JR. 2576 FOREST ST. LOUIS

```
READ(2,10) J1,J2,J3
10  FORMAT(A10,A7,A10)
```

What are the values of J1, J2, and J3 if the input card above is processed by the indicated READ statement? Assume that each J1, J2, and J3 is standard 4.

15. *Sales Commissions.* Write a FORTRAN program for Brucek Retail Store, Incorporated, to read each salesperson's record, and calculate and print his/her name, number, commission, weekly sales, and commission rate. The input records are designed in the following manner:

CC	FIELD	LENGTH	TYPE
1-5	Account number	5	Integer
6-25	Name	20	Character
26-34	Weekly sales	9	XXXXXX.XX
35-37	Commission rate	3	.XXX

Design the output records. Include appropriate headings in your report.

16. *Sales Analysis.* You have been asked by Smith Corporation to write a FORTRAN program to find the total sales and average daily sales at the end of

each week (five working days). Each input record contains five daily sales totals (in dollars) punched consecutively beginning in column 1; each field is real XXXXXXX.XX. Your program should read the data card, find the average, and print the average and the total sales under the appropriate headings.

6 MORE FORMAT CODES AND FORTRAN STATEMENTS

Before discussing the remaining format codes and format rules, let us first describe the different kinds of statements that are allowed in FORTRAN.

6.1 TYPES OF FORTRAN STATEMENTS

There are ten different types of statements in FORTRAN:

1. *Input/output statements*. These are used to transfer data between internal storage (main memory) and input/output media (such as cards, disk, tape, etc.). READ and WRITE are examples of input/output statements.
2. *FORMAT statements*. The FORMAT statement is used in conjunction with the input/output statement to specify the fields of a record.
3. *Arithmetic statements*. These are used for calculations, such as PAY = 5.6 * HOURS.
4. *Logical statements*. These are used to calculate the value of a logical variable.
5. *Control statements*. These are used to control the flow of the program's execution or to terminate the program. STOP and GO TO are examples of control statements.
6. *Specification statements*. These are used to declare the properties of variables, arrays, and functions (explained later). Also, they can be used to assign initial values to variables and arrays. IMPLICIT, INTEGER, REAL, and DIMENSION are examples of specification statements.

7. *DATA statements.* These can be used to assign initial values to variables and arrays.

8. *NAMELIST statements.* These are explained in Appendix III.

9. *Function statements.* Explained in Chapter 13.

10. *Subprogram statements.* Explained in Chapter 14.

So far, we have studied the READ, WRITE, GO TO, STOP, END, and FORMAT statements (with the majority of the format codes). Two other format codes are allowed in FORTRAN: the L-Format and G-Format codes. The L-Format is used for logical variables, and the G-Format is a generalized format code. Before discussing these, we must introduce the logical constant, logical variable, and some specification statements.

6.2   LOGICAL CONSTANTS AND LOGICAL VARIABLES

Integer, real, and literal constants have been discussed in the previous chapters. The fourth type of constant allowed in FORTRAN is the *logical constant*, which specifies the result of a logical test in terms of true or false. There are two logical values; they are:

.TRUE.   and   .FALSE.

Note that the words TRUE and FALSE must be preceded and followed by a period.

The *logical variable* is a variable name that must be declared to be logical by means of a specification statement (explained below). The logical variable's value must be one of the logical constants.

6.3   SPECIFICATION STATEMENTS

In Chapter 3, the predefined rule for declaring a variable type was explained. Below are the specification statements to declare a variable type implicitly or explicitly. Most compilers require that the specification statements be placed at the beginning of the program, with *no* executable statement placed before any specification statement.

6.3.1   Declaration by IMPLICIT Specification Statement

The IMPLICIT specification statement enables the programmer to declare the type of variable. As you recall, by the predefined rule, the variable type is determined by the first character of the variable name. However, by using the IMPLICIT statement, the programmer has the option of specifying which initial letters determine a particular variable type. The IMPLICIT statement overrides the predefined rule. Except for the character variable in FORTRAN IV, all other types of variables can be specified by the IMPLICIT statement.

The IMPLICIT statement is a specification statement and as such should be written at the beginning of the program. The general form for the IMPLICIT statement is:

$$\text{IMPLICIT REAL} \quad (a_1 - a_2)$$
$$\text{IMPLICIT INTEGER} \ (a_1 - a_2)$$
$$\text{IMPLICIT LOGICAL} \ (a_1 - a_2)$$

where $a_1 - a_2$ is the range of letters, and IMPLICIT, REAL, INTEGER, and LOGICAL are FORTRAN command words.

Example 6.1

$$\text{IMPLICIT INTEGER (A - D)}$$

This statement causes any variable name that starts with A, B, C, or D to be considered an integer variable. Thus, variable names such as AMOUNT, COST, BALNCE, DEPRSH would be all considered integer variables. These variables by the predefined rule would be real, but remember that the IMPLICIT statement overrides the predefined rule. Note that the predefined rule is still in effect for all variable names that start with a character not included in the range of the IMPLICIT statement. Thus JOB, INTRST, and MX would still be integer variables, and ROOT, ZAB, and YOUNT real variables.

The statement IMPLICIT REAL (K − M) causes any variable name starting with K, L, or M to be considered a real variable; the type of variables that start with a letter other than K, L, or M is determined by the predefined rule. The statement IMPLICIT LOGICAL (G − K) makes any variable that starts with G, H, I, J, or K a logical variable.

6.3.2 Explicit Declaration

The explicit specification statement declares the type of a variable by its whole name. In other words, by this rule, the type of a variable will be determined not by the first character of the name but by the whole name. The explicit specification statement overrides both the IMPLICIT specification statement and the predefined rule. A variable can be declared an integer, real, logical, or complex variable by using an explicit specification statement.

The general forms of these specification statements to declare a variable type explicitly are:

INTEGER $v_1, v_2, v_3, \ldots$

REAL $v_1, v_2, v_3, \ldots$

LOGICAL v_1, v_2, v_3

where $v_1, v_2, v_3, \ldots$ are variable names, and INTEGER, REAL, and LOGICAL are FORTRAN command words. See Appendix III for implicit and explicit declarations of character variables in ANSI FORTRAN 77.

Example 6.2

INTEGER   COUNT, TRANS

REAL   INTRS, PAY

In this example, both the variables COUNT and TRANS would be integer variables, whereas INTRS and PAY would be real variables. Note that the whole name is considered for determination of the type of variable, rather than the first character only. Thus, variables such as COST or TRAN are still real by predefined rule. Note that the difference between TRAN and TRANS is only the last character. (This is an excellent method for introducing confusion: having variable names that differ only in the last character. You should avoid such names for your variables!)

Example 6.3

INTEGER   DAYS, YEAR, AGE

REAL   NUM, MODE

LOGICAL   D, EXAM, TEST

IMPLICIT INTEGER (B − D)

From the statements above, you should be able to justify the following:

VARIABLE	TYPE	REASON
DAYS, YEAR, AGE	Integer	Explicit declaration
NUM, MODE	Real	Explicit declaration
D, EXAM, TEST	Logical	Explicit declaration
DAY, BAD, COST, D1	Integer	Implicit declaration
EXAMN, YEARS, T	Real	Predefined rule
NOM, MOD, K, M	Integer	Predefined rule

6.4 MORE FORMAT CODES AND RULES FOR THE FORMAT STATEMENT

6.4.1 L-Format Code

This code is used to transmit the value of a logical variable. The general form of the L-Format code is Lw, where w is an integer indicating the number of characters in the input field. When the L-Format code is used, the computer takes only the first character of the input field. If the character is T, then .TRUE. is assigned as the value for the corresponding logical variable in the I/O list; otherwise, the value .FALSE. is assumed for that variable.

Example 6.4

Input card:

```
LOGICAL TEST1, TEST2,TEST3,TEST4,TEST5,TEST6
    READ(5,10) TEST1,TEST2,TEST3,TEST4,TEST5,TEST6
10  FORMAT(6L4)
```

From the example above, the value of the variables are;

TEST1	TEST2	TEST3	TEST4	TEST5	TEST6
.TRUE.	.TRUE.	.FALSE.	.FALSE.	.FALSE.	.FALSE.

On the output, T or F is inserted into the output record, depending upon whether the value of the logical variable in the I/O list is .TRUE. or .FALSE., respectively.

6.4.2 E- and D-Format Codes

E code. When real numbers are very large, the F-Format code is not sufficient to store the values of such large numbers. Instead, E-Format code and real constants represented in E format may be used. In general, the E-code form is used to represent:

1. A real constant number such as 25.4E02, which is equal to 2540.
2. An input format code such as E10.3
3. An output format code such as E15.4

E-code form is also known as *scientific notation* or *exponential form.*

Real constant represented in the E-code form. The E code is a shorthand method to express real numbers. Each real constant represented by an E-code form is composed of three elements. The first is the precision portion, the second is the letter E (exponential indicator), and the third is the exponent size.

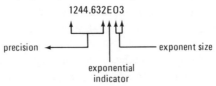

The number 1244.632E03 equals 1244.632×10^3 = 1244632. The letter E stands for "times the power of 10." The precision portion may contain a decimal point. If the decimal point is omitted, it is assumed to be to the right of the rightmost digit of the precision portion. Blanks within the precision portion are treated as zeros. The precision portion may contain a sign (+ or −). Every real constant represented in E-code form must contain the letter E following the precision portion. The letter indicates that the precision portion is to be multiplied by 10 raised to the power of the number following E (the exponent portion). The exponent portion consists of two digits (some processors allow three digits) preceded by an optional sign (+ or −).

The number of significant digits is the number of nonzero digits in the precision portion. For this purpose, imbedded zeros are counted as nonzero digits. In most processors, single precision (F-Format code and E-Format code) has seven significant digits.

REAL CONSTANT IN E-CODE FORM		EQUIVALENT DECIMAL VALUE
254E02	$= 254 \times 10^2 \ =$	25400
254E−02	$= 254 \times 10^{-2} \ =$	2.54
2.54E+02	$= 2.54 \times 10^2 \ =$	254
−2.54E+02	$= -2.54 \times 10^2 =$	−254

When the following statements are executed, the value of R1 becomes 25434.0 and R2 becomes 123456700.00. Note that the last two digits in the precision portion (8 and 9) are lost, because with single precision, only seven significant digits are permitted. The excess digits are replaced by zeros.

R1 = 254.34E02
R2 = 1234567.89E02

E-Format code for input and output. To read in a real constant in the E-code form as a value of a real variable, an E-Format code must be used. The general form of the E-Format code is:

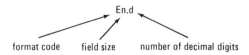

format code   field size   number of decimal digits

where E is the format code, n is the size of the input field (precision, E and the exponent portion) and d is the number of digits to the right of the decimal point in the precision portion. As an example, assume the input card is:

523.61E05 | − 21.3E02 | 28E − 02

Then after the execution of:

```
      READ(5,10)X,Y,Z
10    FORMAT(E9.2,E8.1,E6.0)
```

the values of X, Y, and Z respectively are 523.61E05, −21.3E02, and 28E−02. These values are equivalent to 52361000.0, −2130.0, and 0.28 in their respective order.

The E-Format code for the output is En.d, which is the same as the E-Format code for the input. The precision portion of an output field must have at least three positions. The first position contains a sign (+ or −), the second position contains 0 (zero), and the third position contains the decimal point.

At least four more positions are required for an output field in E-code form. The first of these contains the letter E, the second contains a sign (+ or −), and the third and fourth positions each contain a digit. Therefore, the value of n in E-Format code used in conjunction with an output statement must be at least 7. The printed value when an E-Format code is used is right-justified. Asterisks are printed if n is not large enough to supply all required positions. This is called an overflow error.

In the following example, the stored values of X, Y, Z, and A are in the second column. Their respective format codes, which are in the third column, cause the values of X, Y, Z, and A to be printed as shown in the fourth column. Note that an overflow error occurred, because the value of A, which is 25.46, is +0.2546E+02 in the E-Format code. This occupies eleven positions, not ten as indicated in E10.4, the E-Format code for A.

VARIABLE	STORED VALUE	FORMAT CODE	PRINTED VALUE
X	52361000	E12.5	+0.52361E+08
Y	−2130	E10.3	−0.213E+04
Z	0.28	E9.2	+0.28E+00
A	25.46	E10.4	**********

Double precision. Precision is the number of significant digits in the value of a variable or in the result of an expression. Zeros to the right of most non-zero digits are not counted as significant digits. Each of the numbers 1204567,

1234567, 1000007, 123456700000, and 12345670 has seven significant digits. Every computer has a limitation on the number of digits that can be stored in one memory location. For example, the IBM 370 allows only seven significant digits to be stored in a memory location. This is the case with most computers. When a single memory location is allocated to a variable, then we say that the variable has a single precision. When two memory locations are allocated for a variable, it is called a double-precision variable. In most processors, a double-precision variable may have 16 significant digits. Both double-precision variables and constants are used for real fields.

Double-precision variables. A variable is declared to be a double-precision variable by either one of the following two specification statements:

1. The type statement:

```
DOUBLE PRECISION v1,v2,v3, . . . .
```

where v_1, v_2, v_3, . . . are variable name, array name, array element name, or array declaration.
Example:

```
DOUBLE PRECISION Y(10), X , N(20,10)
```

2. The IMPLICIT statement:

```
IMPLICIT DOUBLE PRECISION (a1, a2, . . .)
```

or

```
IMPLICIT DOUBLE PRECISION (a1 — a2)
```

where each of a_1, a_2, . . . is a single letter.
Example:

```
IMPLICIT DOUBLE PRECISION (A,B,G)
IMPLICIT DOUBLE PRECISION (A — D)
```

The first statement declares that all variables starting with A, B, or G are double-precision real variables, and the second statement declares all variables that start with a letter in the range A to D inclusive to be double-precision real variables.

Double-precision constant. Double-precision constants are similar to real constants that are expressed in E-code form. Example:

$$521.378D+05 = 521.378 \times 10^5 = 52137800$$

Like the real constant in E-code form, each double-precision constant is composed of three portions: the precision portion, letter D, and the exponent portion. The only difference between the E-code form and the D-code form is that the first occupies a single memory location and has seven significant digits, while the second occupies two memory locations and has 16 significant digits.

Example:

```
DOUBLE PRECISION A, B, D, R
A = 25.98D+05
B = 1234567890123.456D+03
C = 1234567890123.456E+03
D =1234567890123.456789D+06
R = 12345D-04
```

After execution of the statements above, the values of A, B, C, D, and R are 2598000.0,   1234567890123456.0,   1234567000000000.0,   1234567890-123456000, and 1.2345 respectively.

D-Format code for input and output. The D-Format code has the same format as E-Format, which is:

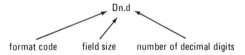

where D is the format code, n is the size of the field, and d is the number of digits to the right of the decimal point in the precision portion. As an example assume the input card is:

| 123.45D+05 | 15645D-03 | 123456789012.3456D+04 |

Then after the execution of:

```
    DOUBLE PRECISION A,B,C
    READ(5,10)A,B,C
10  FORMAT(D10.2,D9.0,D21.4)
```

the values of A, B, C will become 12345000.0, 15.645, and 1234567890123456.0 respectively.

Like the E-Format, the n in the D-Format for an output must be at least 7, otherwise an overflow error occurs. In the following example, X, Y, Z, and A are double-precision real variables. Their stored values, D-Format codes, and printed values are shown in the second, third, and fourth columns respectively.

VARIABLE	STORED VALUES	FORMAT	PRINTED VALUES
X	12345000.0	D12.5	+0.12345D+08
Y	0.0012345	D12.5	+0.12345D−02
Z	1234567890123456	D23.16	+0.1234567890123456D+16
A	1234550	D12.6	***********

6.4.3 G-Format Code

The G-Format is a generalized code used to transmit integer, real, logical, and complex data, depending upon the type of the corresponding variables in the I/O list. The general form of G-Format code is:

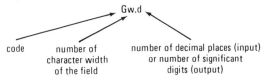

Below are several characteristics of the G-Format code.

1. When the G-Format code corresponds to an input/output variable of the integer or logical mode, the d part of Gw.d is ignored.
2. When the G-Format code corresponds to an output variable of the real mode, then the value of the variable is printed in a format equivalent to the F Format, provided that the value of the variable is in the range 0.1 to 10**d (where d is the number of significant digits in G-Format code). Otherwise, the value of the variable will be printed in E Format.
3. The G-Format code may not be used in conjunction with character variables.

Example 6.5

Input record:

123456	TRUEbb	123456	123	1234567

```
      LOGICAL TEST
      READ(5,10) NUM, TEST,VAL1,VAL2,VAL3
10    FORMAT(3G6.3,G3.6,G7.2)
```

The values of the variables are:

NUM	TEST	VAL1	VAL2	VAL3
123456	.TRUE.	123.456	0.000123	12345.67

Explanation: Since NUM is an integer variable, the 3 of G6.3 was ignored, and the format code considered it to be G6; therefore, six columns are read as the value for NUM. Because TEST was declared to be a logical variable, the 3 of G6.3 is also ignored, and the value of TEST becomes .TRUE. The format code G6.3 is used for the real variable VAL1, hence its value becomes 123.456. The format codes G3.6 and G7.2 are used for the real variables VAL2 and VAL3 respectively. Their values become 0.000123 and 12345.67.

Now consider the following statements:

```
WRITE(6,12) NUM,TEST,VAL1,VAL2,VAL3
12  FORMAT(1X,2(3X,G6.3),3X,G7.3,3X,G9.2,3X,G13.3)
```

These statements print the following line:

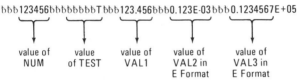

Explanation: Because NUM is an integer and TEST is a logical variable, the 3 of G6.3 is ignored. Since the value of VAL1, 123.456, is within the range 0.1 to 10^3 (3 is the *d* part of the G-Format code), its value is printed in a format equivalent to the F Format. The value of VAL2 is 0.000123, and this is not in the range of 0.1 to 10^2 (note, 2 is the *d* part of G9.2); therefore, its value is printed in a format equivalent to the E Format. Finally, the value of VAL3, 12345.67, is outside the range 0.1 to 10^3 (the 3 of G13.3); therefore, its value is printed in the E Format.

6.4.4 Number of Variables in I/O List Different From Number of Format Codes

The following two rules govern cases where the number of variables in the I/O list is not the same as the number of format codes in the associated FORMAT statements:

1. *Fewer variables in the I/O list than format codes:* If the FORMAT statement contains more format codes than the number of variables in the I/O list, the computer uses as many format codes as are required by the variables, and the extra format codes are ignored (except H or literal format).

Example 6.6

Input: | 12345 | 2893.52

```
    READ(5,10) NUM,PAY
10  FORMAT(I5,F7.2,F8.3,A4,L2,G5.2)
```

Here, the value of NUM is 12345 and of PAY is 2893.52. There are only two variables in the READ list; therefore, only the first two format codes are used, and the extra format codes are ignored.

2. *More variables in the I/O list than format codes:* Whenever the rightmost parenthesis of the FORMAT statement is encountered and there are still more variables in the I/O list, then the system does the following:

a. Skips the current record and brings in a new record (card) or skips a line.

b. To choose the format codes for the remaining variables, the system returns from the *rightmost* parenthesis to the *rightmost left parenthesis* in the FORMAT statement—in other words, it goes backwards from the rightmost parenthesis until it hits the first left parenthesis—and starts using the format codes from that point.

Example 6.7

1. Note that the FORMAT statement below:

```
    READ(5,10) TOTAL,NUM1,COST1,NUM2,COST2,NUMTL
10  FORMAT(F8.2,2(I4,F7.2),I6)
```

is equivalent to:

```
10  FORMAT(F8.2,I4,F7.2,I4,F7.2,I6)
```

As you see, the number of variables in the READ list and the number of format codes are both six. Therefore, the values of the variables are read from one card starting from the first column. If the input card is:

02567.81	0125	0456.72	1250	2111.09	001625

then the values of the variables are:

TOTAL	NUM1	COST1	NUM2	COST2	NUMTL
2567.81	125	456.72	1250	2111.09	1625

2. Change the FORMAT statement to:

```
10  FORMAT(F8.2,2(I4,F7.2)).
```

The number of codes within the FORMAT statement is five, which is less than the number of variables in the READ list. The FORMAT statement above is equivalent to:

10   FORMAT(F8.2,I4,F7.2,I4,F7.2)

Therefore, the computer uses the first code, F8.2, for TOTAL; the second code, I4, for NUM1; the third code, F7.2, for COST1; the fourth code, I4, for NUM2; and the fifth code, F7.2, for COST2. At this time the computer reaches the rightmost parenthesis and there is still one more variable, NUMTL, in the READ list. Hence the current card is skipped; a new card will be brought in and, the value of NUMTL read from this new card with respect to the first format code following the rightmost left parenthesis. As you see, this format code is I4. Thus, the value for NUMTL is read from the second card according to the format code, I4. Note the rightmost and the rightmost left parenthesis of the FORMAT statement below:

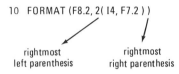

10   FORMAT (F8.2, 2(I4, F7.2))

rightmost   rightmost
left parenthesis   right parenthesis

Assume that the following input cards are processed by the READ of number 1 above and the FORMAT of number 2:

1512	387259

08234.52	1000	6345.25	0512	1889.27	9342	56728

Then the values of the variable are:

TOTAL	NUM1	COST1	NUM2	COST2	NUMTL
8234.52	1000	6345.25	512	1889.27	1512

Note that only five fields from the first card and one field from the second card are read, and the rest are ignored.

3. In this statement:

READ(5,10) TOTAL,NUM1,COST1,NUM2,COST2,NUMTL

10   FORMAT(F8.2,(I4,F7.2))

the value of TOTAL, NUM1, and COST1 are read from the first card. The value of NUM2 and COST2 are read from the second card with the respective format codes I4 and F7.2. The value of NUMTL is read from the third card with format code I4.

4. This statement:

READ(5,10) TOTAL,NUM1,COST1,NUM2,COST2,NUMTL

10   FORMAT(F8.2,I4,F7.2)

causes an execution time error, because an attempt will be made to use F8.2 as the format code for the integer variable NUM2, I4 for the real variable COST2, and F7.2 for the integer variable NUMTL.

5. This statement:

```
READ(5,10) TOTAL,NUM1,COST1,NUM2,COST2,NUMTL
10  FORMAT(2(F7.2,I4),F7.2)
```

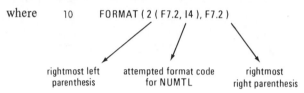

where   10   FORMAT (2 (F7.2, I4), F7.2)

     rightmost left   attempted format code   rightmost
     parenthesis   for NUMTL   right parenthesis

causes an execution time error. The first five fields will be read from the first card, and an attempt will be made to use F7.2 as the format code for the integer variable NUMTL.

6. The statement:

```
READ(5,10) VAL1,VAL2,VAL3,VAL4
10  FORMAT(4(F7.2))
```

reads the values of the variables VAL1, VAL2, VAL3, and VAL4 from one card.

7. The statement:

```
READ(5,10) VAL1,VAL2,VAL3,VAL4
10  FORMAT(F7.2)
```

reads four cards with the value of VAL1 from the first card, VAL2 from the second, VAL3 from the third, and VAL4 from the fourth.

8. The statement:

```
WRITE(6,12) NUMDY,NUMML,COSTDY,COSTML,TOTCST
12  FORMAT(1X,20X,G7.4)
```

causes five lines to be printed. Each value of NUMDY, NUMML, COSTDY, COSTML, and TOTCST will be printed on one line after 20 spaces are skipped. The following FORMAT statement has the same effect:

```
10  FORMAT(5(1X,20X,G7.4,/))
```

Example 6.8: An Investment Problem

The following three possibilities for investing $100,000 have been suggested to the ABC Corporation:

1. Invest cash to earn 10.25% interest compounded annually for 10 years.
2. Invest cash to earn 7.25% interest compounded annually for 15 years.
3. Invest cash to earn 13.35% interest compounded annually for 7 years.

Write a FORTRAN program to compute the total interest that would be earned by each of the options above so that the ABC Corporation can make its decision.

The formula to calculate the compound amount is:

$$A = P(1 + R)^N$$

where:

A is the compound amount after N periods
R is the rate of interest
P is the original (principal) amount invested
N is the period of the investment

First, we should decide on the design of the input and output records, including any options (the title and column headings). The following input and output records seem reasonable:

Input record:

CC	FIELD	LENGTH	TYPE
1–2	Period in years	2	Real XX.
3–6	Interest rate	4	Real .XXXX
7	Option number	1	Integer

Output records:

1. Report title: Start at column 30 of a new page and print ABC COR-PORATION after skipping 5 lines.
2. Subtitle: Start in column 20 and print THE THREE SUGGESTED INVESTMENTS FOR $100,000 after skipping 2 lines.
3. Skip 3 lines, then print the following column headings:

SPC	HEADING
5	OPTION
15	INTEREST RATE
30	YEARS
50	COMPOUND INTEREST

4. Print out the input data and calculated quantities under appropriate headings after skipping 2 lines.

Pseudo Code Form

```
Start

DOWHILE not end of data
        Read YEAR, RATE, TYPE
        AMOUNT = PRNSPL * (1 + RATE) ** YEAR
        INTRST = AMOUNT — PRNSPL
        Write TYPE, RATE, YEAR, INTRST
End DOWHILE
Stop
```

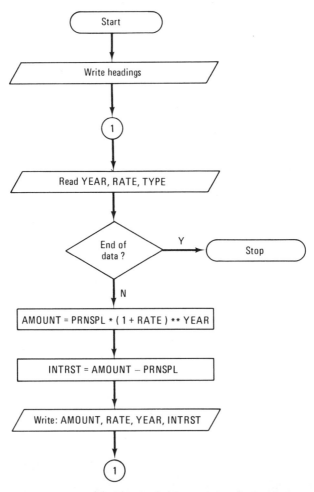

FIGURE 6.1 Pseudo code form and flowchart diagram for the program of investment problem

```
1010251
1507252
0713253


C               INVESTMENT PROBLEM
C PRINCIPLE INVESTMENT IS $100000
C THE INPUT RECORDS ARE ON THE PUNCHED CARDS. EACH RECORD CONTAINS THREE
C FIELDS. THESE ARE YEAR, RATE AND OPTION TYPE. THE OUTPUT IS PRINTED
C ON THE LINE PRINTER.
C
C THE COMPOUND AMOUNT IS CALCULATED BY THE FORMULA:
C AMOUNT = PRNSPL * (1 + RATE) ** YEAR
C VARIABLE NAMES USED:
C       YEAR     THE PERIOD OF THE INVESTMENT
C       RATE     THE RATE OF INTEREST
C       PRNSPL   THE PRINCIPLE AMOUNT
C       TYPE     THE SUGGESTED INVESTMENT
C       AMOUNT   THE COMPOUND AMOUNT
C       INTRST   THE COMPOUND INTEREST
C
C
C
C DECLARE INTRST AS A REAL VARIABLE, TYPE AND CARD AS INTEGER VARIABLES
C
        REAL INTRST
        INTEGER TYPE, CARD
C
        CARD = 5
        LINE = 6
C
C PRINT THE REPORT TITLE
C
        WRITE(LINE,10)
 10     FORMAT('1',5(/),59X,'ABC CORPORATION')
C
C PRINT THE SUBTITLE
C
        WRITE(LINE,20)
 20     FORMAT(1X,2(/),29X,'THE THREE SUGGESTED INVESTMENTS FOR $100,000')

C
C PRINT THE COLUMN HEADINGS
C
        WRITE(LINE,30)
 30     FORMAT(1X,3(/),T5,'OPTION',T15,'INTEREST RATE',T30,'YEARS',
     +  T50,'COMPOUND INTEREST')
C
C ASSIGN $100,000  AS THE VALUE FOR PRNSPL
C
        PRNSPL = 100000.00
C
 40     READ(CARD,50,END=70) YEAR, RATE, TYPE
 50     FORMAT(F2.0,F4.4,I1)
C
C COMPUTE THE COMPOUND AMOUNT
C
        AMOUNT = PRNSPL * (1 + RATE) ** YEAR
C
C COMPUTE THE COMPOUND INTEREST
C
        INTRST = AMOUNT - PRNSPL
C
        WRITE(LINE,60) TYPE, RATE, YEAR, INTRST
 60     FORMAT(1X,T8,I1,T20,F5.2,T30,F4.1,T57,F9.2)
C
        GO TO 40
C
 70     STOP
        END
```

FIGURE 6.2 Program for investment problem

139

```
                    ABC CORPORATION

         THE THREE SUGGESTED INVESTMENTS FOR $100,000

OPTION      INTEREST RATE  YEARS         COMPOUND INTEREST
  1            0.10        10.0              165329.77
  2            0.07        15.0              185732.43
  3            0.13         7.0              138928.24
```

FIGURE 6.3 Output of investment-problem program

Figure 6.1 is the flowchart diagram of the problem, Figure 6.2 is the program itself, and Figure 6.3 is the output generated by the program. The input data are:

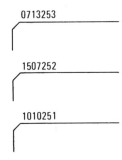

The variable names used are:

YEAR: Number of years
RATE: Rate of interest
TYPE: Type of interest
PRNSPL: Principal amount
AMOUNT: The compound amount
INTRST: The compound interest

6.5   SUMMARY

In FORTRAN, five different types of constant are allowed: integer, real, literal, logical, and complex. Likewise, FORTRAN permits five different variable types: integer, real, logical, complex, and a variable whose value is a FORTRAN character. The type of variable can be declared by predefined rule, by an IMPLICIT specification, or by an explicit specification statement. The IMPLICIT declaration overrides the predefined rule, and the explicit declaration overrides both the IMPLICIT and predefined declarations. All specification statements should be placed at the beginning of the program. Below are the general forms and usage of all format codes and the summary of all the rules for the FORMAT statements (where *a* is an integer indicating occurrences of the format codes).

FORMAT CODE	FUNCTION
a<u>I</u>n	Describes an integer field of n digits.
n<u>X</u>	Skip n characters (columns).
a<u>F</u>w.d	Describes a real field with a total of w digits. Of these, d digits are the fractions.
<u>E</u>n.d	Describes a single precision real field. The n is the size of the field and d is the number of digits to the right of the decimal point in the precision field.
<u>D</u>n.d	Describes a double precision real field. The n is the size of the field and d is the number of digits to the right of the decimal point in the precision field.
n<u>H</u>string	Transmits a literal constant.
'string'	Transmits a literal constant.
<u>T</u>n	Specifies the position in the FORTRAN record where I/O transfer should start.
a(<u>/</u>)	Skip a record.
a<u>A</u>w	Describes a character field of length w.
a<u>L</u>w	Describes a logical field of length w.
a<u>G</u>w.d	Describes an integer, real, or logical data field.

The rules for the FORMAT statement are these:

1. The FORMAT statement is not an executable statement, but it is a specification statement and can be placed anywhere in the program as long as it precedes the END statement.
2. One FORMAT statement can be referenced by many input/output statements.
3. On output, the first character of the first code of the format statement is used for carriage control. (See section 5.5 and example 5.6.)
4. The format codes have to be separated by the delimiter comma or by the /.
5. The repetition of a single format code or group of codes can be abbreviated. (See section 5.6.)
6. If the FORMAT statement contains more format codes than the number of variables in the I/O list, the extra format codes are ignored.
7. If there are more variables in the I/O list than format codes of the referenced FORMAT statement, then the system does the following:
   a. Skips the current record and processes a new record. Every time the

rightmost parenthesis is encountered, the current record is skipped and a new record is processed.

b. The system returns backwards from the rightmost parenthesis until it hits the first left parenthesis and starts using the format codes from that point.

8. On input, punching the decimal point is optional. But when it is punched, the decimal point overrides the format code specification. (See section 4.4.3.)

6.6   REVIEW QUESTIONS AND
SUGGESTED PROBLEMS

1. Give two examples of (a) integer constant; (b) real constant; (c) literal constant; (d) logical constant; (e) single precision real constant; and (f) double precision real constant.

2. Write an IMPLICIT specification statement so that all variables that start with a letter in the range A to K are integer variables.

3. Write IMPLICIT statements so that the variables that start with I, J, K, L, M, or N are real, and variables that start with any other letter are integers.

4. Write a specification statement to declare explicitly the variables COUNT, SUM, and VALUE to be integer.

5. Write an explicit statement to declare TEST, RESULT, and ANSWER logical variables.

6. Write the necessary specification statements to declare any variable starting with the letters C or D to be integers, COST and DINT to be real, and TOTAL and REVNU be real double precision.

7. How many different statements are there in FORTRAN?

8. Write the names of all the different statements in FORTRAN.

9. Give an example of each of the following statements:
   a. Input statement
   b. Output statement
   c. Control statement
   d. FORMAT statement
   e. Arithmetic assignment statement
   f. Specification statement

10. Consider the following specification statements and then decide which of the subsequent variables are integers, real, and logical.

INTEGER	DATE, YEAR, LIFE
REAL	PAY, INTRS, YARD, LOAN
LOGICAL	TEST1, TEST2, EX1, EX2
IMPLICIT	INTEGER (A–E)
IMPLICIT	REAL (L–M)

Variables:

DATE, YERAR, LIFE, PAY, INTRS, YARD, LOAN, TEST1, TEST2, EX1, EX2, EX3, TEST3, EXAM, LAND, MOUNT, MOOR, PRODCT, COST, AMOUNT

11. Identify the errors (if any) in the following FORMAT and input/output statements.

a.
```
    WRITE (6,10)
 10 FORMAT (6X, 'EMPLOYEE LIST)
```

b.
```
    READ (5;10) NUM, PAY, OLDBLN
 10 FORMAT (I6, I6, G6.2)
```

c.
```
    READ (5,10) NUM, PAY, OLDBLN
 10 FORMAT (I6, F7.2)
```

d.
```
    READ (5,10) NUM, PAY, OLDBLN
 10 FORMAT (I6, (F7.2))
```

e.
```
    READ (5,10) NUM, PAY, OLDBLN
 10 FORMAT (G6.3)
```

f.
```
    WRITE (6,10) NUM, PAY, OLDBLN
 10 FORMAT (T6, 'NUMBER IS: ,I6,T8, 'PAYMENT:', F7.2,T2,
    'BALANCE' F7.2)
```

g.
```
    WRITE (6,10)
 10 FORMAT (1H1,11HSTUDENT LIST)
```

h.
```
    READ (6,10) STNM, ADDR
 10 FORMAT (A15,A25)
```

12. What are the values of N, J1, J2, R1, and R2 when the following input cards are read by the following READ statement?

2nd input card:
```
1253TRUE1234
```

1st input card:
```
FAT 7324
```

```
    LOGICAL J1,R1
    READ (5,10) J1,R2,N,R1,J2
 10 FORMAT (L4,F4.2/I4,L4,I4)
```

13. Assume that the stored value of NUM is 2567, of PAY is 450.28, and of BAL is 600.12. How will the output look when the following WRITE statement is executed in conjunction with the following FORMAT statements?

```
WRITE (6,10) NUM, PAY, BAL
```

   a.   `10   FORMAT ('1',2X,I5/(2X,F6.2/))`
   b.   `10   FORMAT ('1',2X,I5/(2X,F6.2))`
   c.   `10   FORMAT ('1',2X,I3,(2X,F5.2/))`
   d.   `10   FORMAT (1H1,3X,I7,T25,F6.2,T50,F6.2)`
   e.   `10   FORMAT (T4,'NUM',T20,'PAY',T50,'BALANCE'//`
                `T4,I6,T20,F6.2,T50,F6.2)`

14. Assume the following input data cards:

4th input data card: `123456789012345678901234567890`

3rd input data card: `123456789012345678901234567890`

2nd input data card: `123456789012345678901234567890`

1st input data card: `123456789012345678901234567890`

What will be the values of VAL1, VAL2, VAL3 when the READ statement:

```
READ (5,20) VAL1, VAL2, VAL3
```

is executed in conjunction with the FORMAT statements indicated below?

   a.   `20   FORMAT (3F4.2)`
   b.   `20   FORMAT (3(F4.2/))`
   c.   `20   FORMAT (F4.2)`
   d.   `20   FORMAT (F4.2,5(F3.2))`
   e.   `20   FORMAT (F4.2,(F3.2))`

15. Assume the input data cards as those of problem 14. What will be the values of J, VAL1, and VAL2 when the following READ statement is executed?

```
      READ (5,20) J, VAL1, VAL2
   20 FORMAT (I2,(F3.2))
```

16. Does the following READ statement cause an execution time error? If so, why?

```
    READ (5,10) J, VAL1, VAL2
10  FORMAT (I2,F3.2)
```

17. **Payroll System.** The employee records of Hendrein Informatic, Inc., are punched on cards in the following manner:

cc	
1–5	Employee number
6–21	Employee name
22–25	Number of prime hours XX.XX
26–29	Rate per prime hour XX.XX
30–33	Number of overtime hours XX.XX
34–37	Rate per overtime hour XX.XX
38–39	Number of dependents
40–63	Address

Write a FORTRAN program to do the following:
- a. Start at column 50 at the top of a new page and print the title *WEEKLY PAYROLL FOR HENDREIN INFORMATIC INC. EMPLOYEES.*
- b. Skip 3 lines from the heading above and print the following column headings:

STARTING COL. #	
2	NUMB
7	NAME
23	PR. HRS.
32	OV. HRS.
41	PR. RATE
50	OV. RATE
59	FED TAX
69	STATE TAX
79	FICA
87	NETPAY
96	GROSS
105	ADDRESS

- c. Read each employee record and calculate the gross pay, federal tax, state tax, FICA, and net pay from the formulas below and print the information under the appropriate headings.

Gross = Prime hours × Rate per prime hour + Overtime hours × Rate per overtime hour

Taxable gross = Gross − (750/52) × Number of dependents

Federal tax = Taxable gross × 0.18

State tax = (Taxable gross − Federal tax)∗0.02

FICA = (Taxable gross − Federal tax − State tax) × 0.025
Net pay = Taxable Gross − Federal tax − State tax − FICA

Make your own data but use realistic numbers.

18. Redo problem 17 with the following modifications: After reading the input card, your program should read another data card that contains the exemptions allowed per dependent and contains another field on the same card showing the sum of all other miscellaneous deductions.

19. **Dividend Computation.** Online Data System, Incorporated, asked you to write a FORTRAN program to read each stockholder record and to compute and print the dividend. Each input record contains the following fields:

FIELD	LENGTH	TYPE
Stockholder account	9	Character
Stockholder name	20	Character
Number of shares held	5	Integer

The dividends are to be computed at a rate of $0.25 per share. Design the output record along with the appropriate headings and run your program.

20. **Using Relative Index Numbers for Adjusting Account Balance.** Write a FORTRAN program for adjusting account balances by relative index numbers. The input record is designed as follows:

CC	FIELD	LENGTH	TYPE
1–5	Current index number	4	Real XXX.X
6–10	Account number	5	Integer
11–19	Original balance	9	Real XXXXXX.XX
20–24	Index number of period in which balance was prepared	5	Real XXX.X

The following formulas can be used in preparing this program:

$$\text{Adjusted balance} = \text{Original balance} \times \frac{\text{Current index}}{\text{Index of the period}}$$

$$\text{Adjusted amount} = \text{Adjusted balance} - \text{Original balance}$$

The output should contain the account number, original balance, adjusted balance, adjusted amount, current index, and the index of the period of the original deposit, along with the appropriate headings.

21. Assume the following input data card:

2E − 02	b + 15E + 6	573321E03	1E − b5	− bb412.53E4	.6723E + 5

Show how the E Format code should be written for each of the six values. Also write the equivalent decimal value of each field shown in the data card.

FIELD	FORMAT CODE	EQUIVALENT DECIMAL VALUE
1	_____	_____
2	_____	_____
3	_____.__	_____
4	_____	_____
5	_____	_____
6	_____	_____

22. Suppose that the values of the variables A, B, C, D and E and their corresponding format codes to print their values are:

VARIABLE	VALUES	FORMAT CODE
A	-0.01	E15.9
B	$.5724317 \times 10^6$	E15.8
C	16.56×10^{-3}	E15.7
D	-415.12×10^5	E15.6
E	890.534	E15.5

Determine how their values would be printed by the following **WRITE** statement:

```
    WRITE (6,10) A,B,C,D,E
10  FORMAT(1X,E15.9/,E15.8/,E15.7/,E15.6/,E15.5)
```

23. The following program calculates the value of AMOUNT and prints the results in both F and D Format forms. RUN the program.

```
    INTEGER YEAR
    DOUBLE PRECISION AMOUNT,PRINSP
    YEAR = 16
    PRINSP = 0.8D07
    RATE = 0.09
    AMOUNT = PRINSP * (1+RATE) ** YEAR
    WRITE (6,10) AMOUNT
10  FORMAT (1X,T10,'DOUBLE PRECISION'///
   +T20, 'F-CODE: COMPOUND AMOUNT;6X,F12.2)
    WRITE (6,20) AMOUNT
20  FORMAT(1X,T20,'D-CODE:COMPOUND AMOUNT'; 6X,D18.10)
    STOP
    END
```

Note that because AMOUNT is declared to be a double precision variable, both D and F Format print the same number of precision digits.

24. Assume the following input data card:

+ 567.281D − 05	1234D − 3	− 1234.62D + 18b	bb − 1834521D03

Show how the D Format code should be written for each of the four fields.

25. Suppose that the values of the double precision variables A, B, C, and D are:

VARIABLE	VALUES
A	−25.98D+05
B	1234567890123.456D+03
C	123.456D−08
D	−.1D−03

```
     WRITE (6,10) A,B,C,D
10   FORMAT(1X,D-,5X,D ,5X,D- ,5X,D-)
```

Complete the FORMAT statement above and show how the values of A, B, C, and D are printed after the execution of the WRITE statement above.

7 ARITHMETIC EXPRESSIONS AND STATEMENTS

In previous chapters, we showed how the programmer can define (or redefine) variables in FORTRAN programs using the READ statement. The arithmetic assignment statement is another way to define (or redefine) variables as the result of an algebraic equation or by a simple replacement statement.

There are two kinds of expressions in FORTRAN, arithmetic and logical expressions. The value of an arithmetic expression is always a number (real or integer or complex). The value of a logical expression is always either .TRUE. or .FALSE. Expressions may appear in assignment statements (see below) and in some control statements.

7.1 ARITHMETIC EXPRESSIONS

A single constant or a variable is an arithmetic expression by itself. For example, AMOUNT, PAY, 267, −457.12, 0, and J are all arithmetic expressions. More complicated arithmetic expressions are constructed by joining two or more arithmetic expressions with an arithmetic operator. The arithmetic operators in FORTRAN are:

ARITHMETIC OPERATORS	MEANINGS
**	Exponentation
*	Multiplication
/	Division
+	Addition
−	Subtraction

An arithmetic expression enclosed between parentheses or preceded by a unary operator (+ or —) is still an arithmetic expression.

Example 7.1

The following are valid arithmetic expressions:

	TYPE OF EXPRESSION
I	Integer
PAY	Real
I + 1	Integer
BALANS — PAY	Real
50	Integer
(BALANS — PAY) * RATE	Real
—B + (B**2. — 4.*A*C)/(2*A)	Real
PAY-INTRST	Mixed
(58.3 + J)*5	Mixed

All the variables and constants of an integer arithmetic expression are integers, and those of a real arithmetic expression are real; but in a mixed arithmetic expression, some are real and some are integers.

7.2   ARITHMETIC ASSIGNMENT STATEMENTS

An arithmetic assignment statement is constructed from a single variable followed by an equals sign and then an arithmetic expression. Thus, the general form of an arithmetic assignment statement is:

Variable = Arithmetic expression

Example 7.2

These are valid arithmetic assignment statements:

```
NBLNS = OLDBLN—PAY+RINTRS
J = 0
ICOUNT = ICOUNT+1
X = —B+((B**2—4.*A*C)/(2*A))**0.5
EOQ = (2*DMND*SCST/(UCST*ACST))**0.5
Q = F/(S—V)
R = 256.28
I = 20
K = —100
```

The following are invalid arithmetic assignment statements, because no more than one variable is allowed to the left of the equals sign.

```
X1+X2 = 20
3X1-5X2 = 50
```

Also, a statement such as 20 =X1+X2 is invalid, because on the left of the equals sign there must be a variable, not a constant.

The examples above point out a very important concept concerning the "equals" sign: It indicates not equality but *replacement*. This means that the result of the arithmetic expression on the right-hand side of the replacement sign is placed into the memory location identified by the variable name on the left side of the sign. For example, I = 20 places 20 into the memory location identified by I. That is, it assigns 20 as the value for the variable I. In the statement I = I+1, the value of I on the right side of the equals sign is called the old value, and the value of I on the left side is called the new value of I. Therefore, the statement I = I+1 adds 1 to the old value of I and puts the new result back in I; hence, the new value of I is one more than its old value. In other words, this statement increases the value of I by 1. The statement M = (M + 1)**2 takes the old value of M, adds 1 to it, squares the result, and the new result is placed back in M. The statement J = J − 1 decreases the value of J by 1.

From the discussion above, it is clear that the computer does not deal with equations but with evaluations of expressions and their replacement. Whenever the arithmetic expression on the right side of the replacement sign is a single constant, the arithmetic assignment statement is called a simple assignment statement. For example, I = 0, R = 25.9, INTRST = 0, RATE = 3.5, and ICOUNT = 20 all are simple assignment statements. They assign the values 0, 25.9, 0, 3.5, and 20 to the variables I, R, INTRST, RATE, and ICOUNT, respectively.

The following example shows how easily algebraic expressions and formulas are translated into FORTRAN expressions and statements.

Example 7.3

Write a separate FORTRAN arithmetic assignment statement for each of the following algebraic relations:

ALGEBRAIC RELATION	FORTRAN STATEMENT
a. $i = (i + 2) \times K + (n + 1)^m$	I = (I + 2) * K + (N + 1)**M
b. $x = \dfrac{-b + \sqrt{b^2 - 4ac}}{2a}$	X = (−B + (B**2−4*A*C)**0.5)/(2*A)
c. $a = (1 + r)^n \times b$	A = ((1 + R)**N)*B
d. $f = a + \dfrac{b^3 + d^3}{2(y + x)}$	F = A + (B**3 + D**3)/(2*(Y + X))

7.3 RULES FOR CONSTRUCTING ARITHMETIC EXPRESSIONS AND STATEMENTS

1. No two arithmetic operators can appear next to each other. For example, the following expressions are invalid:

A*—B, C+/D

The expression A∗—B should be written as A∗(−B).

2. Multiplication signs cannot be omitted as they often are in algebra. The algebraic expression AB should be written as A∗B in FORTRAN, and the expression $20X + 30Y$ should be written as 20∗X + 30∗Y.

3. Both FORTRAN IV and ANSI FORTRAN 77 allow mixed-mode expressions. However, there are smaller FORTRAN compilers that do not permit mixed-mode expressions. For example, OBLN − PAY + INTRST is not permitted. On such systems, this expression can be written as OBLN − PAY + RINTRS, or INTRST can be declared a real variable by explicit declaration.

4. *Order of Computation:* In mathematics, there is a certain order in which operations are performed. Exponentiation is performed before multiplication, and multiplication before addition. The computer is also governed by such an order, called a *hierarchy of operations*. The hierarchy of operations is:

HIERARCHY	OPERATIONS
1st	Evaluation of functions
2nd	Exponentation (∗∗)
3rd	Multiplication and division (∗ and /)
4th	Addition and subtraction (+ and −)

Most computers scan the expression from left to right, and the hierarchy is used to determine which of two consecutive operations is performed first. The first operation is performed if its place in the hierarchy is not lower than that of the second operation. Otherwise, the computer compares the second operator to the third and performs the second operation if its hierarchy place is not lower than that of the third. This process continues until the last operator in the expression is encountered. At this point, depending on the computer's FORTRAN compiler design, some compilers, such as the IBM 370/360 and DECSystem 10, move from right to left and perform the rest of the operations in the expression. Others return to the beginning of the expression and start evaluation from left to right again.

Example 7.4

Assume that the value of A = 6.0, of B = 8.0, of R = 4.0, and of C = 20.0. Then the overall result of the expression $A - B/2.0 + 3.0*R**2 - 2.0*C$ is 10. The expression after replacing the variables by their values becomes:

$$6.0 - 8.0/2.0 + 3.0*4.0**2 - 2.0*20.0$$

On many computers, such as the IBM 370/360 and DECSystem 10, the order of calculation of the expression above is division, subtraction, exponentation, multiplication, addition, multiplication, and subtraction. In detail, the expression is evaluated in the following order:

1. The computer starts from the left side of the expression and moves toward the right.
2. It compares the first operator $(-)$ with the second operator $(/)$. The first operator $(-)$ is not performed because its rank in the hierarchy is lower than that of the second operator, division $(/)$. Now the rank of the second operator $(/)$ is compared with the rank of the third $(+)$. Since the rank of $/$ is greater than that of $+$, the second operation $(B/2.0)$ is performed. At this point, the expression becomes $6.0 - 4.0 + 3.0*4.0**2 - 2.0*20.0$.
3. Since the rank of the first operator $(-)$ is not lower than the rank of $+$, the first operation, subtraction, is performed. The expression becomes $2.0 + 3.0*4.0**2 - 2.0*20.0$.
4. The rank of $+$ is lower than the rank of $*$. Therefore, the addition is not performed, and the rank of $*$ is compared with the rank of exponentation $(**)$. Multiplication is not performed because its rank is lower than that of $**$. Since the rank of $**$ is higher than the rank of the next operator $(-)$, exponentation is performed. Then the expression becomes $2.0 + 3.0*16.0 - 2*20.0$.
5. The operation $3.0*16$ is performed because the rank of $*$ is higher than that of subtraction. Now the expression becomes $2.0 + 48.0 - 2.0*20.0$.
6. $2.0*20.0$ is performed because the rank of $*$ is higher than that of the operator $-$. The expression becomes $2.0 + 48.0 - 40.0$.
7. $48. - 40.$ is performed, and the expression becomes $2.0 + 8.0$.
8. Finally, 2.0 is added to 8, and the overall result is 10.0.

When parentheses are used, the expressions within the parentheses are evaluated first.

Example 7.5

The expression

$$A/(B + C) + D**2$$

is evaluated in the following order:

1. $B + C$ (call the result $T1$). The expression becomes $A/T1 + D**2$.
2. $A/T1$ (call the result $T2$), hence the expression becomes $T2 + D**2$.
3. $D**2$ (call the result $T3$). The expression becomes $T2 + T3$.
4. $T2 + T3$ is the final operation.

On the IBM 370/360, the unary + or − has the same rank as the binary + or −. (Binary + or − means the operations require two operands; for instance, $A + B$ or $C − D$.) Therefore, $−A$ is treated as $0 − A$, $−A + B$ as $(−A) + B$, and $−A*B$ as $−(A*B)$. On the DECSystem 10, the rank of unary + or − is lower than exponentation and higher than * and /.

The CDC 6500 computer essentially makes these three passes to evaluate an expression:

1. Go from left to right and perform all exponentation.
2. Go from left to right and perform all divisions and multiplications in the order in which they appear.
3. Go from left to right and perform all subtractions and additions in the order in which they appear.

5. All FORTRAN compilers allow exponentation to be mixed-mode operations. In FORTRAN compilers that do not permit mixed operations, both real numbers and integers can have integers as exponents, but only real numbers can have real numbers as exponents. The exponent can be an arithmetic expression, a variable, or a constant. Many computers, such as the IBM 370/360 and DEC-System 10, allow an expression such as $A**B**C$. The evaluation of such an expression is from right to left. That is, first $B**C$ is calculated (call the result T), then $A**T$ is calculated.

6. The mode of the two operands involved in the operation determines the mode of the result. Table 7.1 shows the mode of the result based on the mode of the operands where mixed expressions are allowed.

TABLE 7.1 The mode of the result based on the mode of the operands

OPERATION +, −, *, /		TYPE OF THE FIRST OPERAND	
		INTEGER	REAL
Type of second operand	Integer	Integer	Real
	Real	Real	Real

Example 7.6

Assume that the value of I = 5, of J = 10, of K = 4, and of R = 10.0. Then:

1. The result of J/I is 2.
2. The result of J/K is 2. Note that 10/4 is equal to 2.5, but in FORTRAN, when an integer is divided by an integer, the fraction is dropped (no rounding).
3. The result of R/K is 2.5. Note that in this case the result is real because one operand (the variable R) is real. Therefore, the fraction is not lost, as happened in case 2.
4. The result of R/4.0 is 2.5.
5. The results of 9/J and I/J are 0, because J is 10 and 9/10 is 0 in FORTRAN. See case 2.
6. The result of J/I + R/K is 4.5, because R/K is the real number 2.5. Since the result of adding an integer to a real number is a real number, the overall result is 4.5.

7. In the case of an assignment statement, the mode of the overall result of the expression on the right side of the replacement sign (=) is converted to the mode of the variable on the left side of the replacement sign.

An expression such as COUNT = 1 is not allowed in FORTRAN compilers, which do not allow mixed expressions. However, ICOUNT = 1 is allowed. An expression such as COUNT = 1 can be written as COUNT = 1.0 or

```
J = 1
COUNT = J.
```

In compilers that do not allow mixed expressions, the type of expression on the right side of the replacement sign can differ from the type of variable on the left side of the sign. However, if the expression is a single constant, the constant must be in the same mode as the variable on the left side of the replacement sign.

Another way to convert a mixed-mode expression to a single-mode expression is to use built-in functions (explained in Chapter 13). FLOAT, for example, converts an integer variable or constant to real, and IFIX converts from real to integer. Thus, a statement such as COUNT = 1 can be written as COUNT = FLOAT (1) or J = I/IFIX(R) + IFIX(B)*K.

Example 7.7

Convert the following expressions and statements to a single type of expression and statement:

```
1.  R = I*B + 14.8/K
2.  J = RAN*100.0 + 8
```

Answers:

1. `R = FLOAT(I)*B + 14.8/FLOAT(K)`

   or replace the statement above by the following three statements:

   ```
   T1 = I
   T2 = K
   R = T1*B + 14.8/T2
   ```

2. `J = IFIX(RAN*100.0) + 8`

   or

   ```
   N = RAN*100.0
   J = N + 8
   ```

For computers that allow mixed-mode expressions, such as the IBM 370/360 and DECSystem 10, the conversion as indicated in Table 7.1 is performed automatically. To minimize transportability problems when you write your FORTRAN program, make the program least dependent on the specific character of your computer. Transportability problems are those that are involved in writing a program for a given computer and later trying to run it on a different computer. For example, try to avoid using mixed operations, even though your computer may permit them.

Example 7.8

1. $J = 9/10$, then the value of J is 0.
2. $N = 5.75$, then the value of N is 5.
3. If you wish to round, add 0.50 to the quantity. Thus, if you write $N = 5.75 + 0.50$, the value of N is 6.
4. After execution of

$$
\begin{aligned}
I &= 5 \\
R &= 20.8 \\
M &= R - I*2
\end{aligned}
$$

the value of M becomes 10. The statement $M = R - I*2$ is executed in the following manner:

a. $I*2$: the result is integer 10.

b. $R - 10$: the result is real 10.8.

c. Now 10.8 will be converted to the integer 10 because M is an integer variable; hence, the value of M becomes 10.

Example 7.9: **Weekly Payroll System**

Write a FORTRAN program to read employee records of Informatic Consulting Associates, to calculate and print gross pay, net pay, federal taxes, state taxes, and FICA, along with the employee's name and personnel number.

The input records are punched on the card in the following manner:

CC	FIELD	TYPE
1-5	Employee number	Integer
6-25	Employee name	Character
26-29	Number of prime hours	Real XX.XX
30-33	Number of overtime hours	Real XX.XX
34-37	Rate per hour	

The rate for an overtime hour is twice the ordinary rate.

The following formulas are to be used to calculate the required quantities:

$$\text{Gross pay} = (\text{Prime hours} + 2*\text{Overtime hours})*\text{Rate}$$
$$\text{Federal tax} = \text{Gross pay} * 0.18$$
$$\text{State tax} = (\text{Gross pay} - \text{Federal tax})*0.03$$
$$\text{FICA} = (\text{Gross pay} - \text{Federal tax} - \text{State tax})*0.025$$
$$\text{Net pay} = \text{Gross pay} - \text{Federal tax} - \text{State tax} - \text{FICA}$$

The program should generate the following output:

1. Report title: Starting in column 50 of a new page, print *INFORMATIC CONSULTING ASSOCIATES.*
2. Skip 3 lines after the title above, and in column 56 print *WEEKLY PAYROLL FOR THE FIRST WEEK OF NOVEMBER 1981.*
3. Skip 5 lines and print the following column headings:

PAGE COLUMN	COLUMN HEADINGS
1-5	Blank
6-20	EMPLOYEE NUMBER
21-24	Blank
25-28	NAME
29-49	Blank
50-54	GROSS
55-59	Blank
60-66	NET PAY
67-70	Blank
71-75	F. TAX
76-80	Blank
81-86	S. TAX
87-90	Blank
91-94	FICA

Figure 7.1 is the flowchart diagram of this problem, Figure 7.2 is the program itself, and Figure 7.3 is the output generated by the program. The input data are:

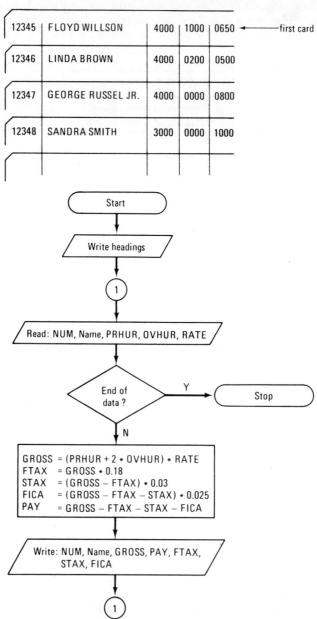

FIGURE 7.1 Flowchart diagram for a payroll program

Input data are:

```
12345FLOYD WILSON        400010000650
12346LINDA BROWN         400002000500
12349GEORGE RUSSEL JR.   400005000500
```

```
C WEEKLY PAYROLL SYSTEM PROGRAM
C THIS PROGRAM CALCULATES WEEKLY PAY AND FEDERAL TAX FOR
C EACH EMPLOYEE.
C INPUT FILE IS PUNCHED ON CARDS. THE OUTPUT FILE IS WRITTEN
C ON THE LINE PRINTER.
C
C
C VARIABLE NAMES USED IN THE PROGRAM :
C       NUM EMPLOYEE NUMBER
C       GROSS GROSS PAY
C       PRHUR PRIME HOUR
C       OVHR  OVERTIME HOURS
C       RATE  RATE PER AN HOUR
C       PAY   NET PAY
C       FTAX  FEERAL TAX
C       STAX  STATE TAX
C       FICA  SOCIAL SECURITY TAX
C
C
C
        ICARD = 5
        LINE = 6
C
C THE FOLLOWING WRITE STATEMENT PRINTS TITLE HEADING AFTER
C ADVANCING TO A NEW PAGE AND SKIPPING THREE LINES.
C
        WRITE (LINE, 10)
  10    FORMAT('1',49X,'INFORMATIC CONSULTING ASSOCIATES',/////)
C
C PRINT THE SECOND HEADING
        WRITE (LINE, 20)
  20    FORMAT(1X,55X,'WEEKLY PAYROLL FOR THE FIRST WEEK OF NOV. 1981',
     +  6(/))
C PRINT THE COLUMN HEADINGS
        WRITE (LINE, 30)
  30    FORMAT(1X,5X,'EMPLOYEE NUMBER',4X,'NAME',21X,'GROSS',
     +  5X,'NET PAY',4X,'F.TAX',5X,'S.TAX',4X,'FICA')
C READ THE DATA CARD : IF THE END OF ATA TRANSFER TO STOP STATEMENT.
C
  40    READ(ICARD,50,END=70)NUM,NAM1,NAM2,NAM3,NAM4,NAM5,PRHUR,OVHUR,RATE
  50    FORMAT(I5,5A4,3F4.2)
C
C CACULATE THE GROSS PAY,FTAX,STAX,FICA, AND PAY
C
        GROSS = (PRHUR + 2 * OVHUR) * RATE
        FTAX = GROSS * 0.18
        STAX = (GROSS - FTAX) * 0.03
        FICA = (GROSS - FTAX - STAX) * 0.025
        PAY = GROSS - FTAX - STAX - FICA
C
C PRINT THE RESULTS
        WRITE(LINE,60)NUM,NAM1,NAM2,NAM3,NAM4,NAM5,GROSS,PAY,FTAX,STAX,
     +  FICA
  60    FORMAT(1X,10X,I5,9X,5A4,5X,F7.2,3X,F7.2,4X,F6.2,4X,F6.2,4X,F6.2)
C
C GO TO READ ANOTHER CARD
        GO TO 40
C
C
  70    STOP
        END
```

FIGURE 7.2 Program for payroll problem

WEEKLY PAYROLL FOR THE FIRST WEEK OF NOV. 1981

EMPLOYEE NUMBER	NAME	GROSS	NET PAY	F.TAX	S.TAX	FICA
12345	FLOYD WILLSON	390.00	302.45	70.20	9.59	7.76
12346	LINDA BROWN	220.00	170.61	39.60	5.41	4.37
12347	GEORGE RUSSEL JR.	320.00	248.16	57.60	7.87	6.36
12348	SANDRA SMITH	300.00	232.65	54.00	7.38	5.97

FIGURE 7.3   Output of payroll-problem program

The variable names used are:

NUM: Employee number
NAM1, NAM2, NAM3, NAM4, NAM5: Employee names
GROSS: Gross pay
FTAX: Federal tax
STAX: State tax
FICA: Social Security tax
PAY: Net pay

7.4   SUMMARY

The arithmetic operators are $+$, $-$, $*$, $/$, and $**$, which represent addition, subtraction, multiplication, division, and exponentation, respectively. The arithmetic expression is constructed from a constant or a variable, or several constants or variables, joined by arithmetic operators with or without parentheses. The general form of an arithmetic assignment statement is:

$$\text{Variable} = \text{Arithmetic expression}$$

The expression is scanned from left to right, and the hierarchy is used to determine which of two consecutive operations is performed first. An operation is performed if its hierarchy is not lower than the immediately following one.

7.5   REVIEW QUESTIONS AND
SUGGESTED PROBLEMS

1. Write a separate FORTRAN arithmetic assignment statement for each of the following algebraic equations:

a. $a = (1 + K)^n$

b. $x = \dfrac{-b + \sqrt{b^2 - 4a \cdot c}}{2^a}$

c. $E = \dfrac{2d \cdot a}{\sqrt{h \cdot c}}$

d. $x = \dfrac{a - b + \dfrac{a^3 + b^3}{a^2 + 2a \cdot b + b^2}}{a^2}$

e. $r = 1 - \left(\dfrac{e}{c}\right)^{1/n}$

f. $A = \pi * r^2$ (Note that $\pi = 3.14159$)

2. Assume that

A = 5.4
B = 16.8
J = 2
I = 10
K = 1

Find the value that will be assigned to the variable by each of the following independent assignment statements:

a. RATE = J/I   , RATE =   _____ .
b. D = J
    R = I
    RATE = D/R   , RATE =   _____ .
c. RATE = J/10   , RATE =   _____ .
d. D = J
    RATE = D/10   , RATE =   _____ .
e. SHARE = B/2.0   , SHARE =   _____ .
f. SHARE = A + B/2.0   , SHARE =   _____ .
g. NUM = I*2 + J   , NUM =   _____ .
h. NUM = I*(2 + J)   , NUM =   _____ .
i. N = I**J + 2   , N =   _____ .
j. N = I**(J + 2)   , N =   _____ .
k. N = (16)**5/1   , N =   _____ .
l. D = I
    N = (16.0)**5.0/D
m. M = (J + K)**2 − K/J*18   , M =   _____ .

3. Determine which of the following assignment statements are invalid, and state why:
    a. OLDBL − PAY = BALANS
    b. BALANS = OLDBL − PAY
    c. RINTRS = (RATE +)** N * AMOUNT
    d. A = B* − D/5
    e. 25 = X1 + X2

4. List the order in which the operations in the following statements will be performed by FORTAN:
    a. STDV = SUMX/N − XBAR**2
    b. EOQ = (2.0* D*S/H*C)** 0.5

   c. $EOQ = (2.0*D*S/(H*C))**0.5$
   d. $A = B + A - R*Y** (3.0*F/2) - 125.0$
   e. $Z = A + B**C**2/y$

5. What is the difference between A*C/B and (A*C)/B?

6. What is the difference between A + B*C/D and (A + B*C)/D?

7. What is the difference between A + B*C/D and (A + B)*C/D?

8. Give the hierarchy of evaluation of arithmetic operators.

9. What is the difference between an arithmetic expression and an arithmetic statement?

10. *True or False.* An arithmetic statement should refer to a FORMAT statement.

11. **Depreciation Using the Declining-Balance Method**. When the declining balance method is used, the depreciation for each year is calculated as:

Depreciation for the year = Depreciation rate*Carrying value

where:

$$\text{Depreciation rate} = 1 - \left(\frac{\text{Estimated scrap value}}{\text{Cost}} \right)^{\frac{1}{\text{Useful life in years}}}$$

and

Carrying value = Cost − Accumulated depreciation up to the current year

Write a FORTRAN program to read each asset record, calculate its depreciation for the year, and print the asset number, asset name, cost, scrap value, estimated useful life, and depreciation for the year. Each input record is punched on a card in the following manner:

CC	FIELD	TYPE
1–4	Asset number	Integer
5–21	Asset name	Character
22–27	Cost	Real XXXX.XX
28–33	Estimated scrap value	Real XXXX.XX
34–35	Estimated use-life	Integer

Your program must also print out appropriate titles, subtitles, and column headings.

12. **Coefficient of Correlation**. The coefficient of correlation, r, is a statistical tool that indicates where there is a linear relationship between two sets of data. The coefficient of correlation may be calculated from the following formula:

$$r = \frac{N\Sigma XY - (\Sigma X)(\Sigma Y)}{\sqrt{[N\Sigma X^2 - (\Sigma X)^2][N\Sigma Y^2 - (\Sigma Y)^2]}}$$

where:

ΣX = the sum of Xs
ΣY = the sum of Ys
ΣX^2 = the sum of X^2
ΣY^2 = the sum of Y^2
$(\Sigma X)^2$ = the square of the sum of X
$(\Sigma Y)^2$ = the square of the sum of Y
ΣXY = the sum of $X \times Y$ for all pairs
N = the number of pairs of X and Y

Prepare 20 pairs of values of X and Y and write a FORTRAN program to find the coefficient of correlation between X and Y.

13. **Inventory Systems.** In inventory control, the economic order quantity for an item is given by:

$$EOQ = \sqrt{\frac{2 * D * S}{c * h}}$$

where:

EOQ = the economic order quantity
D = the demand per period
S = the cost of placing an order
c = the unit cost
h = the carrying cost per period

Design an input record that contains the demand, cost of placing an order, unit cost, and carrying cost. Write a FORTRAN program to read the input record for each item, calculate the economic order quantity, and print the economic order quantity, the demand, the cost of placing an order, the unit cost, and the carrying cost under appropriate column headings. Your program should also print an appropriate title for the inventory report.

14. **Computation of Unit Sales Price.** ABC Company uses the following formula to compute the average sales price:

Nominal sales = Number of units × Sales price per unit
Gross sales = Nominal sales − Packaging cost − Transportation cost −
Insurance cost
Average sales price per unit = Gross sales ÷ Number of units

Design an input record to contain the following fields:

FIELDS	TYPE	LENGTH	
Item code	Integer	5	
Item description	Character	20	
Number unit	Integer	4	
Sales price per unit	Real	5	XX.XX
Packaging cost per order	Real	7	XXXX.XX
Transportation cost per order	Real	8	XXXXX.XX
Insurance cost	Real	7	XXXX.XX

Write a FORTRAN program to print an appropriate title and subtitles, and to read for each item, calculate the gross sales and the average sales, and print the item number, description, gross sales, and average sales price.

15. **Financial Analysis.** One indicator used in financial analysis is the debt/equity ratio. This ratio is calculated by dividing a firm's debt by the total of its debt and stockholders' equity. Flowchart and write a FORTRAN program to compute the debt/equity ratio for Informatic Consulting Associates. The input record is organized in the following manner:

CC	FIELD	TYPE	SIZE
1–10	Firm's debt	Real	10
11–20	Stockholders' equity	Real	10
21–30	Total debt	Real	10

Do not forget to write appropriate headings.

8 LOGICAL EXPRESSION, LOGICAL IF, AND LOGICAL STATEMENT

8.1 RELATIONAL AND LOGICAL EXPRESSIONS

8.1.1 Relational Expressions

Relational expressions are used to test the relationship between two arithmetic expressions. The result of a relational expression is always a logical constant, either .TRUE. or .FALSE.. That is, the relation is either true or false.

The general form of a relational expression is:

$$A1 \text{ .op. } A2$$

where *A1* and *A2* are arithmetic expressions, and *.op.* is a relational operator. The following six relational operators can be used to compare two arithmetic expressions:

OPERATOR	MEANING
.LT.	Less than ($<$)
.LE.	Less than or equal to ($\leq$)
.GT.	Greater than ($>$)
GE.	Greater than or equal to ($\geq$)
.EQ.	Equal to ($=$)
.NE.	Not equal to ($\neq$)

FORTRAN IV for the IBM 370/360, DECSystem 10, and many other computers permit either the symbols above or the mathematical symbols $<$, $<=$, $>$, $>=$, $=$, and $\neq$ (or $\neg =$) to be used in place of .LT., .LE., .GT., .GE., .EQ., and .NE., respectively.

Note that all relational operators are preceded and followed immediately by a period. The relational operators can compare two integer expressions or two real expressions. Both ANSI FORTRAN and FORTRAN IV allow an integer expression to be compared with a real expression (and vice versa). However, to decrease the transferability problems and to save computer time, it is preferable that the expressions be in the same mode.

Example 8.1

1. Valid relational expressions:
A .LT. B + 5.2
J .EQ. K + 2
OBALAN – PAY .GT. 0
A + D .GT. F + B
WITHDR .LE. (BALNS + DEPSIT)
(J + (K/(3∗N)) .NE. (M + 5∗(N/2 – L))
J .LT. 10
I .NE. K

2. Invalid relational expressions:

	Reasons:
A .LT B	Any relational operator must be preceded and followed immediately by a period.
.LT. B	Every relational operator must have two operands.

In a relational expression, only a single relation between two arithmetic expressions is tested. As a matter of fact, a relational expression is a simple condition.

8.1.2 Logical Expressions

Logical expressions are used to test more than one relation in an expression (that is, more than one condition). A simple logical expression is constructed by joining two relational expressions with a logical operator. The logical operators are:

OPERATOR	EXAMPLE	EFFECT
.NOT.	.NOT. A	.NOT. A is true if the value of A is .FALSE.. .NOT. A is .FALSE. if the value of A is .TRUE..
.AND.	A .AND. B	The value of A .AND. B is true if both the values of A and B are .TRUE..
.OR.	A .OR. B	The value of A .OR. B is true if either the values of A or B or both are .TRUE..

Two logical operators may appear next to each other if the second one is the logical operator .NOT.. For example, A .AND. .NOT. B and A .OR. .NOT. B are valid logical expressions.

Some FORTRAN compilers, such as FORTRAN IV for the DECSystem 10, allow two additional logical operators:

OPERATOR	EXAMPLE	EFFECT
.XOR.	A .XOR. B	The value of A .XOR. B is .FALSE. if both A and B are both either .TRUE. or .FALSE.. (This is the exclusive OR.)
.EQV.	A .EQV. B	The value of A .EQV. B is .TRUE. if both A and B are both either true or false.

More complicated logical expressions can be created by joining two or more logical expressions with a logical operator.

Example 8.2

1. Valid logical expressions:
   (A + B .LT. 100.0) .AND. A .NE. 50.0
   (I .NE. 0) .OR. (J .GT. 10) .AND. (J .LT. (K − 5))
   LOGICAL A, B
   (A .EQ. .FALSE.) .AND. .NOT. B .OR. J + 5 .GE. 100
   The last expressions are compound logical expressions.

2. Invalid logical expressions: Reasons:
   I + 5 .AND. J .NE. 6   I + 5 is not allowed. This must be either a relational or a logical variable or expression.

   J .LT. 5 .OR. .AND. J .GT. 0   No two logical operators can appear in sequence, except when the first one is .NOT..

   .NOT. A .OR.   The second operand of .OR. is missing.
   T*(G + 5.0) .LT. 20.0 .OR. Y   This expression is true only if Y is declared to be a logical variable. See preceding item.

8.1.3 Order of Evaluation in Relational and Logical Expressions

The hierarchy of operations in relational and logical expressions is:

HIERARCHY	OPERATION
1st	Evaluation of functions
2nd	Exponentation (**)
3rd	Multiplication (*) and division (/)

HIERARCHY	OPERATION
4th	Addition (+) and subtraction (−)
5th	Relational operators (.LT., .LE., .GT., .GE., .EQ., .NE.)
6th	.NOT.
7th	.AND.
8th	.OR.

The order of evaluation is similar to that of an arithmetic expression (see item 4 in section 7.3)—that is, from left to right, based on the operator's rank within the hierarchy. Where parentheses are used, the expression within the innermost parentheses is evaluated first.

Example 8.3

1. The expression A + B .LT. 100.0 .AND. A .NE. 50.0 is evaluated in the following order:
   a. A + B (call the result T1), addition
   b. T1 .LT. 100.0 (call the result T2), relational operator .LT.
   c. A .NE. 50.0 (call the result T3), relational operator .NE.
   d. T1 .AND. T3, final operation, logical operator .AND.
2. The expression (I .NE. 0 .OR. J .GT. 10) .AND. J .LT. K − 5 is evaluated in the following order:
   a. I .NE. 0 (call the result T1), relational operator .NE.
   b. J .GT. 10 (call the result T2), relational operator .GT.
   c. T1 .OR. T2 (call the result T3), logical operator
   d. K − 5 (call the result T4), subtraction
   e. J .LT. T4 (call the result T5), relational operator .LT.
   f. T3 .AND. T5, final operation, logical operator .AND.

8.2   LOGICAL ASSIGNMENT STATEMENT

The truth value of a relational expression or a logical expression is assigned to a logical variable by the logical assignment statement. The logical assignment statement is composed of a logical variable followed by a replacement sign (=) and a logical expression to the right of the replacement sign. That is, v = expression, where v is a logical variable and the expression is either a relational expression, a logical expression, or a single logical variable. (See section 6.3 for methods of declaring a logical variable, and section 6.4.1 for the format codes used in conjunction with the input statement to read in the truth value of a logical variable.)

Example 8.4

```
1. LOGICAL DEBT
   DEBT = OBLNS .GT. PAY
```

First, the relational expression OBLNS .GT. PAY is evaluated. If this relation is true, then .TRUE. is assigned as the value for the logical variable DEBT; otherwise, the value of DEBT becomes .FALSE..

2. LOGICAL TEST

TEST = J + 5 .LT. 20 .AND. I .NE. 0

If the value of J + 5 is less than 20 and I is not equal to 0, then .TRUE. is assigned as the value of TEST; otherwise, the value of TEST becomes .FALSE..

The logical variable and relational and logical expressions used in conjunction with the logical IF statement are explained below.

Example 8.5

```
LOGICAL Y, X, TEST1, TEST2, TEST3, TEST4
Y = .TRUE.
X = .FALSE.
A = 50.0
B = 20.0
TEST1 = A .GT. B .AND. .NOT. X
TEST2 = A .GT. B .AND. X
TEST3 = A + B .LE. 100 .OR. Y
TEST4 = Y .AND. X .OR. B .EQ. A
```

After execution of the statements above, the value of TEST1 is .TRUE., TEST2 is .FALSE., TEST3 is .TRUE., and TEST4 is .FALSE..

8.3   LOGICAL IF

The general form of the logical IF is:

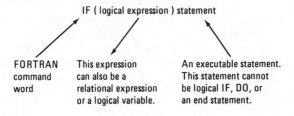

IF (logical expression) statement

| FORTRAN command word | This expression can also be a relational expression or a logical variable. | An executable statement. This statement cannot be logical IF, DO, or an end statement. |

Thus, the logical IF is constructed from the FORTRAN command word IF, followed by a logical expression or a relational expression or a logical variable enclosed in parentheses and ending with an executable statement. This statement cannot be another logical IF or a DO statement (explained later) or an END statement.

The function of the logical IF is very simple. If the logical value of the expression is true, then the statement that follows the parentheses is executed; otherwise, the statement is not executed. When the statement that follows the parentheses is not a GO TO, the statement immediately following the IF statement will be executed next regardless. This case can be flowcharted as in Figure 8.1.

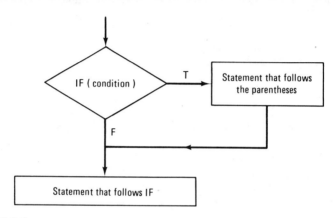

FIGURE 8.1

Example 8.6

```
SCHARG = 0.
BALANS = 250.00
PAY = 100.0
IF(PAY .LT. BALANS) SCHARG = (BALANS − PAY)*0.015
CBLNS = BALANS − PAY + SCHARG
```

After execution of the statements above, the value of CBLNS is 152.25.

Explanation: The first statement assigns 0 to the variable SCHARG, the second statement assigns 250 to BALANS, and the third statement assigns 100 to PAY. When the IF statement is encountered, the value of PAY (100) is less than the value of BALANS (250), so that the condition PAY .LT. BALANS is true. Hence, the statement SCHARG = (BALANS − PAY)*0.015 is executed, and the value of SCHARG becomes 2.25. After that, the statement CBLNS = BALANS − PAY + SCHARG is executed, and the value of CBLNS becomes 152.25. Figure 8.2 is a flowchart of the preceding code.

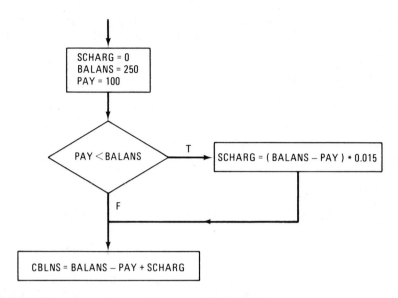

FIGURE 8.2

If the third statement is changed to PAY = 250., then the condition PAY
.LT. BALANS is false, and the statement SCHARG = (BALANS − PAY)*0.015
will not be executed.

Example 8.7

What will be the values of Y and X after the execution of the following
statements?

```
      Y = 0.
      X = 5.5
10    IF(X .LT. Y) X = X + 1.0
      Y = Y + 1.0
      IF(Y .LE. 6.0) GO TO 10
      STOP
```

Answer: The value of X becomes 6.5, and the value of Y becomes 7.

Explanation: The first statement assigns 0 to Y, and the second statement
assigns 5.5 to X. When the first IF is executed, the value of X is not less than Y,
so that the statement X = X + 1 is not executed. Next, Y = Y + 1 is executed,
which makes the value of Y = 1. When the second IF statement is executed, the
value of Y is less than 6, hence the statement GO TO 10 (which sends control
back to the first IF statement) is executed. This procedure is repeated until the
value of Y becomes 7. Since 7 is greater than 6, the statement GO TO 10 is not

executed, so that the statement STOP is executed and the program stops. Knowledge of the logical IF enables us to write reasonably complicated programs.

You should have noticed that the logical IF has two exits on a flowchart. One exit is followed when the condition is false (usually marked by F or N); otherwise, the other exit (usually marked T or Y) is followed. Below are a few more examples. Although they are not direct applications of business techniques, these examples should help you gain insight into solving problems on the computer.

Example 8.8

Write a FORTRAN program to read two numbers and find and print the larger of them.

Input record:

CC	FIELD	TYPE
1–7	First number	Real XXXXX.XX
8–14	Second number	Real XXXXX.XX

Input data:

5679.269437.81

Figure 8.3 is the flowchart diagram for the FORTRAN program in Figure 8.4.

Example 8.9

Suppose we have five statistical observations of students' ages from your class. You are asked to write a FORTRAN program to calculate and print the range of these observations. (The range is equal to the difference between the largest and the smallest observation.) Assume that each data contains a student's age (with no fractions).

The input record:

CC	FIELD	TYPE
1–2	Age	Integer XX

Figure 8.5 is the flowchart and pseudo code for a program to find the range. Before writing the program, it is sessential to understand the flowchart diagram.

Explanation of the flowchart: At box 2, 0 is assigned as the value of COUNT. The variable COUNT is used to control the number of times the instructions in the loop between boxes 5 and 11 should be executed (such a variable is called a counter). At box 3, the first number NUM is read. At box 4, the value of NUM is assigned to both LARG and MIN. At box 5, 1 is added to

Pseudo Codes

```
Read VAL1, VAL2
IF VAL1 < VAL2 Then BIG = VAL2
   ELSE BIG = VAL1
End IF
Write BIG
STOP
```

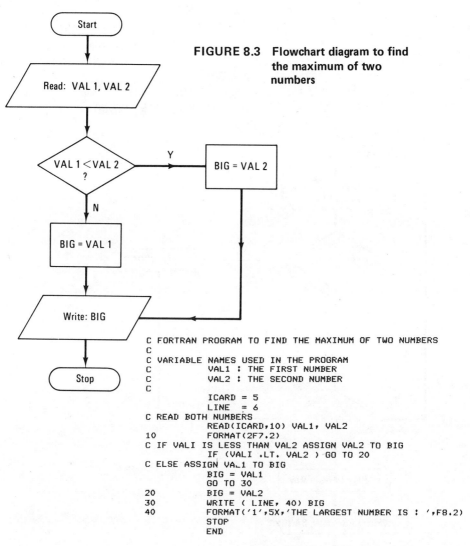

FIGURE 8.3   Flowchart diagram to find the maximum of two numbers

```
C FORTRAN PROGRAM TO FIND THE MAXIMUM OF TWO NUMBERS
C
C VARIABLE NAMES USED IN THE PROGRAM
C          VAL1 : THE FIRST NUMBER
C          VAL2 : THE SECOND NUMBER
C
           ICARD = 5
           LINE  = 6
C READ BOTH NUMBERS
           READ(ICARD,10) VAL1, VAL2
10         FORMAT(2F7.2)
C IF VAL1 IS LESS THAN VAL2 ASSIGN VAL2 TO BIG
           IF (VAL1 .LT. VAL2 ) GO TO 20
C ELSE ASSIGN VAL1 TO BIG
           BIG = VAL1
           GO TO 30
20         BIG = VAL2
30         WRITE ( LINE, 40) BIG
40         FORMAT('1',5X,'THE LARGEST NUMBER IS : ',F8.2)
           STOP
           END

    THE LARGEST NUMBER IS :   9437.81
```

FIGURE 8.4   Program to find the maximum of two numbers

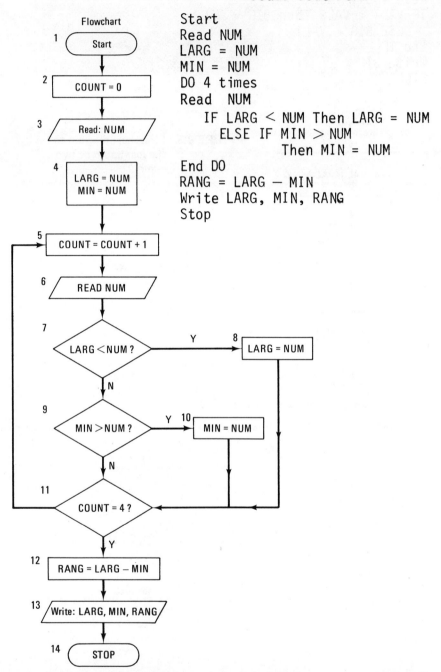

Pseudo Code Form

```
Start
Read NUM
LARG = NUM
MIN = NUM
DO 4 times
Read   NUM
     IF LARG < NUM Then LARG = NUM
       ELSE IF MIN > NUM
                 Then MIN = NUM
End DO
RANG = LARG — MIN
Write LARG, MIN, RANG
Stop
```

FIGURE 8.5   Pseudo code form and flowchart diagram to find the range of five observations

the counter COUNT. At box 6, the next value is read. Box 7 compares the new value of NUM to the value of LARG. If the value of LARG is less than the value of NUM, the instruction of box 8 assigns this new value to LARG (the old value of LARG is destroyed). After box 8, the instruction in box 11 is executed. However, if LARG is equal to or greater than NUM, then after the instruction in box 7, the one in box 9 is executed. At this point, if the value of MIN is greater than that of NUM, the instruction in box 10 is executed; otherwise, it is ignored. Next, the instruction in box 11 is executed. If COUNT is not equal to 4, control returns back to box 5. However, if COUNT = 4, then the instruction in box 12 is executed. By this time, the values of the largest (LARG) and of the smallest (MIN) of the five data cards have been determined, and hence RANG can be calculated. This is followed by execution of the instruction in box 13, and then the process is terminated.

To gain better understanding, assume that the input data cards are:

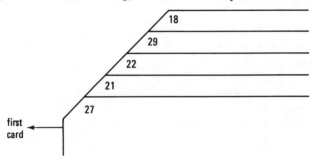

After the execution of the instructions in boxes 1, 2, 3, and 4, we have:

COUNT	NUM	LARGE	MIN
0	27	27	27

The execution of the instruction in box 5 adds 1 to COUNT. At box 6, the second card is read, and the new value for NUM becomes 21. Since the current value of LARG is bigger than the value of NUM, the branch with mark N (for *no*) is taken. At box 9, because the value of MIN is greater than 21 (the value of NUM), the Y (*yes*) branch is taken. Thus, the instruction in box 10 is executed, and the new value of MIN becomes 21. At this point, the values of the variables are (the old values are crossed out):

	COUNT	NUM	LARG	MIN
Old values	~~0~~	~~27~~	27	~~27~~
Current values	1	21	27	21

Since COUNT does not equal 4, control returns to box 5. Now another iteration begins; 1 is added to COUNT, and a new value for NUM is read. The values of the variables at the end of the second iteration are:

	COUNT	NUM	LARG	MIN
	2	22	27	21

At the end of the third and fourth iterations:

	COUNT	NUM	LARG	MIN
Third iteration	3	29	29	21
Fourth iteration	4	18	28	18

At this point, the instruction in box 12 is executed, and the value of RANG becomes 10.

Note that the flowchart above can be used to calculate the range for any number of observations. All you have to do is to change the instruction in box 11. For example, to find the range for 100 observations, change box 11 to COUNT = 99.

Figure 8.6 is the FORTRAN program for this problem, and Figure 8.7 is the output generated by the program.

Input data:

27

21

22

29

18

In Chapter 7, we explained that the result of dividing an integer by an integer is an integer. In the following example, this property is used to determine whether a number is even or odd.

Example 8.10

Write a FORTRAN program to read five numbers and print only the odd numbers. Each number is an integer punched on a card as follows (input record):

CC	FIELD	TYPE	LENGTH
1–4	Number	Integer	4

Figure 8.8 portrays the flowchart and pseudo code for the program of this problem.

```
C FORTRAN PROGRAM TO CALCULATE THE RANGE OF STATISTICAL OBSERVATIONS.
C EACH NUMBER IS PUCHED ON ONE CARD
C
C VARIABLE NAMES USED:
C       LARG      THE LARGEST NUMBER
C       MIN       THE SMALLEST NUMBER
C       NUM       THE OBSERVATION VALUE
C       COUNT     COUNTER
C
C
C PROGRAM NARRATIVE: THIS PROGRAM CALCULATES THE RANGE OF OBSERVATIONS.
C                    THE RANGE IS THE DIFFERENCE BETWEEN THE LARGEST AND
C                    THE SMALLEST OBSERVATIONS.
C
C****************************************************************************
C****************************************************************************
C
C
        INTEGER CARD, COUNT, RANG
C INTIALIZE THE VALUE OF COUNT TO 0
C
        COUNT = 0
        CARD  = 5
        LINE  = 6
C
C READ THE FIRST NUMBER AND ASSIGN IT TO BOTH LARG AND MIN
C
        READ(CARD,10)NUM
10      FORMAT(I2)
        LARG = NUM
        MIN  = NUM
C
C START THE LOOP
C
C ADD 1 TO COUNT
20      COUNT = COUNT + 1
C
C READ THE NEXT NUMBER
C
        READ(CARD,10)NUM
C
C IF THE VALUE OF LARG IS LESS THAN THE NEW NUMBER CHANGE IT TO NEW NUMBER
C
        IF(LARG .LT. NUM) GO TO 30
C
C ELSE IF MIN GREATER THAN NUM, THEN ASSIGN NUM TO MIN
C
        IF(MIN .GT. NUM) GO TO 40
C
C       ELSE DO NOT CHANGE ANY
        GO TO 50
C
30      LARG = NUM
        GO TO 50
C
40      MIN = NUM
C
C IF COUNT IS LESS THAN 4 REPEAT THE LOOP
C
50      IF (COUNT .NE. 4) GO TO 20
C
C ELSE END THE LOOP
C
        RANG = LARG - MIN
        WRITE(LINE,60) LARG, MIN, RANG
60      FORMAT('1',6X,'LARGEST VALUE IS : ',I2,6X,'SMALLEST VALUE IS : ',
     +  I2,6X,'THE RANGE IS : ',I2)
        STOP
        END
```

FIGURE 8.6   Program to find the range of five observations

```
LARGEST VALUE IS : 29     SMALLEST VALUE IS : 18     THE RANGE IS : 11
```

FIGURE 8.7 Output of program to find the range of five observations

Pseudo Codes

```
COUNT = 1
DOWHILE COUNT ≤ 5
   Read NUM
   If the remainder of (NUM/2) NOT
            equal 0 Write NUM
   End IF
   COUNT = COUNT+1
End DOWHILE
STOP
```

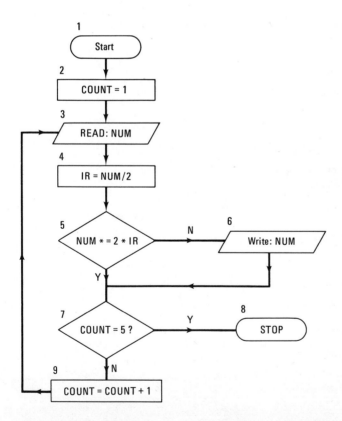

FIGURE 8.8 Flowchart and pseudo codes for a program to find the odd number

Before writing the program, let's check the validity of the flowchart. Assume the following five input data cards:

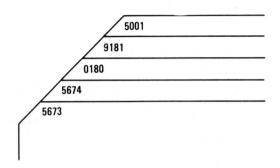

Flowchart explanation: The main ingredient of the flowchart is the instruction IR = NUM/2 in box 4. When NUM is divided by 2, the remainder will be lost because both NUM and 2 are integers. Therefore, after execution of the first four instructions, we have:

COUNT	NUM	IR
1	5673	2836

Note that 5673/2 is equal to 2836 and the remainder is 1. However, the remainder is lost. At box 5, the value of NUM, 5673, does not equal the value of IR (2836) multiplied by 2. Therefore, the *N* branch is taken and NUM is written because it is an odd number. After that, the test in box 7 is performed. Since COUNT does not equal 5, branch *N* is taken, another 1 is added to COUNT, and control returns to box 3. The values of the variables after the remaining four iterations are as follows:

ITERATION	COUNT	NUM	IR	TEST NUM = 2*IR?	NUM PRINTED
2	2	5674	2837	Yes	No
3	3	180	90	Yes	No
4	4	9181	4590	No	Yes
5	5	5001	2500	No	Yes

Figure 8.9 is the program and Figure 8.10 the output generated by it for the problem and data.

8.4   IF-THEN-ELSE STRUCTURE IN ANSI FORTRAN 77

ANSI FORTRAN 77 supports the IF-THEN-ELSE control structure that enables the FORTRAN programmer to write better programs. (See

```
C FORTRAN PROGRAM TO FIND ODD NUMBERS
C VARIABLE NAMES USED IN THE PROGRAM:
C
C        COUNT    : COUNTER
C        NUM      : NUMBER
C        IR       : THE REMAINDER OF NUMBER DIVIDE BY 2
C
C*******************************************************************************
C
C PROGRAM NARRATIVE: THIS PROGRAM READS FIVE NUMBERS AND FINDS AND PRINTS
C THE ODD NUMBERS ONLY, EACH NUMBER IS PUNCHED ON A CARD.
C
C*******************************************************************************
C
         INTEGER CARD, COUNT
C
C INTIALIZE COUNT, CARD AND LINE
C
         COUNT = 1
         CARD = 5
         LINE = 6
C
C START LOOP
C
10       READ(CARD,20) NUM
20       FORMAT(I4)        .
         IR = NUM / 2
C
C IF THE REMAINDER IS NOT ZERO  THE NUMBER IS ODD, THREEFORE PRINT IT.
C
         IF(NUM .NE. IR * 2) WRITE(LINE,30)NUM
C
C ELSE THE NUMBER IS EVEN SKIP PRINTING IT.
C
C IF COUNT EQUAL 5 STOP
         IF(COUNT .EQ. 5) STOP
C
C ELSE INCREMENT THE COUNT AND REPEAT THE LOOP.
C
         COUNT = COUNT + 1
         GO TO 10
C
30       FORMAT('0',6X,I4,' IS AN ODD NUMBER')
         END
```

FIGURE 8.9   Program for finding the odd number

FIGURE 8.10   Output of program for finding the odd number

```
5673 IS AN ODD NUMBER
9181 IS AN ODD NUMBER
5001 IS AN ODD NUMBER
```

section 12.1.) The general form of IF-THEN-ELSE is:

```
IF (condition) THEN e
     ELSE d
END IF
```

where *e* and *d* are blocks of statements. Note that a block may contain one or more statements. If the condition is true, then *e*, which is a block of statements, is executed and the ELSE part is bypassed. However, if the condition is false, then *e* is bypassed and *d* is executed. The IF can be combined with ELSE IF as follows:

```
IF (condition 1) THEN e1
     ELSE IF (condition 2) THEN e2
          ELSE d1
     END IF·
END IF
```

If condition 1 is true, then *e1* is executed and the ELSE IF part is skipped. If condition 1 is false, *e1* is skipped and ELSE IF is executed. Then if condition 2 is true, *e2* is executed, and *d1* is skipped; otherwise, *e2* is skipped and *d1* is executed.

Example 8.11

Consider the following nested IF statement:

```
IF (PAY .LT. BAL) THEN
        INTRST = (BAL — PAY) * 0.01
        NBAL = BAL — PAY + INTRST
    ELSE IF ( PAY .GT. BAL) THEN
             OVRPAY = PAY — BAL
             NBAL = 0
        ELSE
             NBAL = 0
        END IF
END IF
```

After execution of the statements above:

1. If PAY = $100 and BAL = $300, then INTRST will be $2 and NBAL will be $202. In this case, the ELSE IF part is bypassed.

```
      C THIS PROGRAM IS WRITTEN IN ANSI FORTRAN 77
      C FORTRAN PROGRAM TO CALCULATE THE RANGE OF STATISTICAL OBSERVATIONS.
      C EACH NUMBER IS PUCHED ON ONE CARD
      C
      C VARIABLE NAMES USED:
      C      LARG     THE LARGEST NUMBER
      C      MIN      THE SMALLEST NUMBER
      C      NUM      THE OBSERVATION VALUE
      C      COUNT    COUNTER
      C
      C
      C PROGRAM NARRATIVE: THIS PROGRAM CALCULATES THE RANGE OF OBSERVATIONS.
      C                    THE RANGE IS THE DIFFERENCE BETWEEN THE LARGEST AND
      C                    THE SMALLEST OBSERVATIONS.
      C
      C******************************************************************************
      C******************************************************************************
      C
      C
             INTEGER CARD, COUNT, RANG
      C INTIALIZE THE VALUE OF COUNT TO 0
      C
             COUNT = 0
             CARD  = 5
             LINE  = 6
      C
      C READ THE FIRST NUMBER AND ASSIGN IT TO BOTH LARG AND MIN
      C
             READ(CARD,10)NUM
      10     FORMAT(I2)
             LARG = NUM
             MIN  = NUM
      C
      C START THE LOOP
      C
      C ADD 1 TO COUNT
      20     COUNT = COUNT + 1
      C
      C READ THE NEXT NUMBER
      C
             READ(CARD,10)NUM
      C
      C IF THE VALUE OF LARG IS LESS THAN THE NEW NUMBER CHANGE IT TO NEW NUMBER
      C
             IF(LARG .LT.NUM) THEN
                       LARG = NUM
      C IF NOT SEE WHETHER MIN IS GREATER THAN THE NUMBER
             ELSE IF (MIN .GT. NUM) THEN
                     MIN = NUM
                 END IF
             END IF
      C
      C      ELSE DO NOT CHANGE ANY
             CONTINUE
      C
      C
      C IF COUNT IS LESS THAN 4 REPEAT THE LOOP
      C
             IF (COUNT .NE. 4) THEN GO TO 20
      C
      C ELSE END THE LOOP
      C
             ELSE RANG = LARG - MIN
             END IF
      C
             WRITE(LINE,60) LARG, MIN, RANG
      60     FORMAT('1',6X,'LARGEST VALUE IS : ',I2,6X,'SMALLEST VALUE IS : ',
          +  I2,6X,'THE RANGE IS : ',I2)
             STOP
             END
```

FIGURE 8.11 Program to find the range of five observations, rewritten using IF—THEN—ELSE structure

182

2. If PAY = \$400 and BAL = \$300, then the condition (PAY .LT. BAL) is false, and the statements after the first THEN are not executed, but the ELSE IF portion is executed. Since the condition (PAY .GT. BAL) is true, OVRPAY = \$100 and NBAL = 0, and the portion ELSE is skipped. However, if PAY = \$300 and BAL = \$300, then the condition (PAY .GT. BAL) is false; hence, the statements after THEN are skipped and the statement after ELSE is executed, which makes NBAL = 0.

Example 8.12

Rewrite the FORTRAN program of example 8.9 in ANSI FORTRAN 77, using IF-THEN-ELSE control structure.

The program is shown in Figure 8.11.

8.5   SUMMARY

The relational operators are .LT., .LE., .GT., .GE., .EQ. and .NE.— representing less than, less than or equal to, greater than, greater than or equal to, equal to, and not equal to, respectively. The relational expression (a simple condition) is composed of two arithmetic expressions separated by a relational operator.

The logical operators are .NOT., .AND. and .OR.. A simple logical expression is constructed by joining two relational expressions by a logical operator. A more complicated logical expression is constructed from two or more complicated logical expressions (compound condition) joined by logical operators. The overall value of a relational or logical expression is either .TRUE. or .FALSE.. The general form of a logical assignment statement is var = relational or logical expression.

The logical IF is a control statement used to test conditions (complex or simple). It has two exits; its general form is IF (expression) statement, where the expression is a logical variable or a relational expression or a logical expression. At execution time, when the IF statement is encountered, the statement that follows the parentheses is executed only if the logical value of the expression is true.

8.6   REVIEW QUESTIONS AND
SUGGESTED PROBLEMS

1. Find the errors, if any, in the following expressions and statements:
   a. A GT. 5.0
   b. A + B .LT. 25.0 .AND. .NOT. A .LE. 10.0
   c. LOGICAL B
      B = A .LT. 5.0 .AND. D + 6 .GT. 100.0 .OR. R .NE. 50.
   d. STGR .GE. 2.75 .AND. GMAT .GE. 500.0 .OR.
      (TOTAL .GT. 1000.0 .AND. STGR .GE. 2.0)

e. A .OR. .NOT. C
f. A .OR. .AND. B

2. Write a relational or a logical expression that represents each of the following questions:

a. Is a student's grade point less than 2.75?
b. Is a payment less than the balance?
c. Is the inventory level less than the reorder point?
d. Are A and B equal?
e. Is TALLY equal to or greater than A + B?
f. Is the square root of SUM equal to 0?
g. Is A + B less than 10 or does A not equal 0?

3. Determine the order in which the operations in the following statements will be performed by FORTRAN:

a. LOGICAL B

```
B = A + D .LT. 50.0 .OR. A .NE. 0.0 .AND. D .GT. 20.0
```

b. A/2.0 .NE. 0 .AND. B**2 .GT. 20.0 .OR. Z = Y
c. LOGICAL B

```
B = (A + D .LT. 50.0 .OR. A .NE. 0.0) .AND. D .GT. 20.0
```

d. LOGICAL ADMIT

```
ADMIT = STGE .GE. 2.75 .AND. GMAT .GE. 500.0 .OR.
        (TOTAL .GE. 1000 .AND. STGR .GE. 2.0)
```

4. Determine the value of TEST after executing each of the following statements:

LOGICAL TEST, A, B
Y = 30.5
X = 50.0
J = 20
K = 0
I = 18
A = .TRUE.
B = .FALSE.

	VALUE OF TEST
a. TEST = X .GE. Y .AND. A	_____
b. TEST = X .GE. Y .AND. B	_____
c. TEST = X .GE. Y .OR. B	_____
d. TEST = X .GE. Y .AND. B .OR. A	_____
e. TEST = X .GE. Y .AND. (B .OR. A)	_____
f. TEST = J/2 .LT. I .AND. (K .NE. 0 .OR. A)	_____
g. TEST = .NOT. B .AND. A .OR. X + Y .GT. 60.0	_____

5. After execution of the following instructions, the value of J becomes _____, Y becomes _____ and X becomes _____ .

```
       X = 5.5
       Y = 20.0
10     IF (Y .GT. J * X) Y = Y = X
       J = J + 1
       IF (J .GE. 4) STOP
       GO TO 10
```

6. Assume that the following five data cards are input:

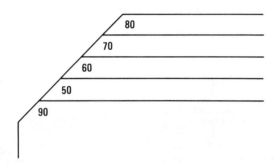

After execution of the following program, the value of AVRG is _____,
SUM IS _____ and J is _____.

```
       REAL NUM
       INTEGER CARD
       CARD = 5
       LINE = 6
       SUM = 0
       J = 1

10     READ(CARD, 20) NUM
20     FORMAT(F2.0)
       SUM = SUM + NUM
       J = J + 1
       IF (J .LT. 5) GO TO 10
       AVRG = SUM/J
       WRITE(LINE, 30) AVRG, SUM
30     FORMAT('1',6X,'AVERAGE IS:',F5.2,6X,'THE SUM IS:')
       STOP
       END
```

7. If the IF statement in problem 6 is changed to IF (J .LT. 4) GO TO 10, after the execution of the program the value of J is _____, SUM is _____ and AVRG is _____.

8. Assume the following three input data cards:

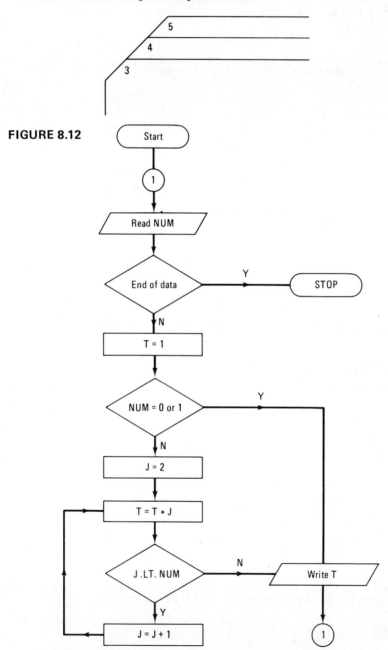

FIGURE 8.12

Trace the flowchart and find the value of T. What does T represent with respect to NUM? Convert the flowchart in Figure 8.12 to a FORTRAN program.

9. **Stock Transaction Service Charge.** Design customers' input and output records for the Best Stock Dealer Corporation. Write a FORTRAN program to read each input record, calculate the service charge, and print the service charge along with the account number, customer name, and amount of the transaction. Each input record contains three fields: account number, customer name, and the amount of the transaction. BSDC's transaction service charges are:

$ AMOUNT OF TRANSACTION	$ SERVICE CHARGE
Less than $100	$8.50
$100 or more but less than $800	$8.50 + 2.4% of the amount
$800 or more but less than $2,500	$15 + 1.5% of the amount
$2,500 or more but less than $5,000	$26 + 1.1% of the amount
$5,000 or more but less than $20,000	$28 + 1.1% of the amount
$20,000 or more	$48 + 1.0% of the amount

10. **Inventory Systems.** The XYZ Company uses the well-known (s, S) inventory policy to maintain its inventory system. The s is the lower critical inventory level and S is the upper critical level. This type of inventory policy requires periodic review of current inventory levels. At review time, if the current inventory level is equal to or above the lower critical number, s, no order is placed; otherwise, an order is placed equal to the upper critical number (S) minus the current inventory level (i.e., S $-$ Current level). Write a FORTRAN program to update the inventory system for XYZ Company. Each input record contains item number, lower critical number, upper critical number, and the current inventory level. The program should print item number, amount of order, lower critical number, upper critical number, and the current inventory level only for those items that should be ordered. The headings and the design of the output are left for you.

11. **Variance and Standard Deviation.** The variance and standard deviation are statistical tools used to measure dispersion of a set of numbers. Denote the numbers by $X_1, X_2, \ldots, X_n$ and denote summation by Σ. Then:

$$\text{Arithmetic mean (AVRG)} = \left(\sum_{i=1}^{N} Xi \right) / N$$

$$\text{Variance} = \left(\sum_{i=1}^{N} Xi^2 \right) / N - (\text{AVRG})^2$$

$$\text{Standard deviation} = \sqrt{\text{Variance}}$$

Write a FORTRAN program to read five numbers (each number punched on one data card) to calculate and print the mean, variance, and standard deviation.

Hint: See problem 6 above and note that $\sqrt{X} = X^{1/2}$.

12. **Customer Discounts.** XYZ Wholesale Corporation uses the following schedule to grant discounts to its customers:

AMOUNT OF SALE	DISCOUNT
Less than $200	0%
$200–$799.99	$5 refund plus 1.5% of sale amount
$800–$1,499.99	$10 plus 3.2% of sale amount
$1,500–$4,999.99	$15 plus 5.1% of sale amount
More than $5,000	$25 plus 6.2% of sale amount

Each input record contains account number, customer name, and amount of sale. Write a FORTRAN program to print each customer name, account number, sale, amount of discount and the applicable discount percentage, and the firm's total sales and discounts.

13. **Editing Payroll System.** Each employee record of the ABC Company is punched on a card in the following manner:

CC	FIELD	TYPE	SIZE
1	Code	Integer	1
2–5	Employee number	Integer	4
6–9	Straight-time hours	Real XX.XX	4
10–13	Rate/hour	Real XX.XX	4
14–17	Overtime hours	Real XX.XX	4
18–25	Salary	Real XXXX.XX	6

If the employee is salaried, then the code field contains the number 1, and the employee record contains only three fields: the code, employee number, and salary. If the employee is paid hourly, then the code field contains a 2 and the record in this case contains all the fields except the salary field.

Write a FORTRAN program to prepare the weekly payroll list. The program should do the following editing:

a. No salaried employee should earn more than $4,000 per run. Generate an error message if a salary of more than $4,000 is encountered.

b. Generate an error message for hourly employees if (1) the number of straight-time hours is more than 80; (2) the number of overtime hours is more than 40; (3) the straight-time rate is more than $10 per hour.

Note that the rate for an overtime hour is $1\frac{1}{2}$ times the straight-time rate.

9 CONTROL STATEMENTS

FORTRAN statements are executed sequentially, beginning with the first executable statement of the program. However, by using control statements, the programmer can alter the normal sequential flow. Control statements have two uses: to allow the programmer to make decisions during the course of execution of the program, and to give the programmer control over the order in which the statements of the program are executed.

The following control statements are available in FORTRAN: GO TO, logical IF, arithmetic IF, STOP, CONTINUE, END, PAUSE, DO, CALL, and RETURN. The logical IF was discussed in the preceding chapter, and the DO statement will be discussed in Chapter 11. The CALL and RETURN are related to subprograms, which are discussed in Chapter 13.

9.1 GO TO STATEMENTS

There are three different types of GO TO statements: unconditional, computed, and assigned. The unconditional GO TO statement was discussed in section 4.4.3, on pages 98 and 99.

Example 9.1

```
     N = 0
10   N = N + 1
     IF(N .GT. 100) STOP
     GO TO 10
```

The GO TO statement above is an unconditional GO TO statement. After the fourth statement, control returns unconditionally to the second statement. Thus, a programmer can unconditionally send control to any part of the program.

Both the second and the third type of GO TO statements are conditional statements.

9.1.1 Computed GO TO Statements

The general form of the computed GO TO statement is:

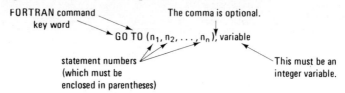

An example of a valid computed GO TO statement is:

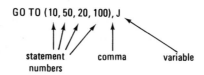

In the form above, the variable must be an integer, nonsubscripted variable. (Chapter 10 explains subscripted variables). The entries $n_1, n_2, \ldots, n_n$ are statement numbers. The comma between the parenthesis and the variable is optional; GO TO is the FORTRAN command word.

The computed GO TO statement transfers control to a statement whose statement number appears within the parentheses. If the value of the variable that follows the comma is 1, control transfers to the first statement enclosed in the parentheses; if the value of the variable is 2, control is transferred to the statement number that is the second entry in the parentheses; and so on. If the value of the variable is outside the previously described range, control transfers to the statement that immediately follows the computed GO TO statement.

Example 9.2

What will be the values of X and INDEX after the execution of the following instructions?

```
      X = 5.0
      INDEX = 4
10    GO TO (20,30,40,50,50),INDEX
20    INDEX = INDEX + 1
      X = X + 2.0
      GO TO 10
```

```
30   X = X − 5.0
     STOP
40   X = X − 7.0
     INDEX = INDEX − 2
     GO TO 10
50   X = X * 2.0
     INDEX = INDEX − 1
     GO TO 10
```

The flowchart in Figure 9.1 portrays the codes above.

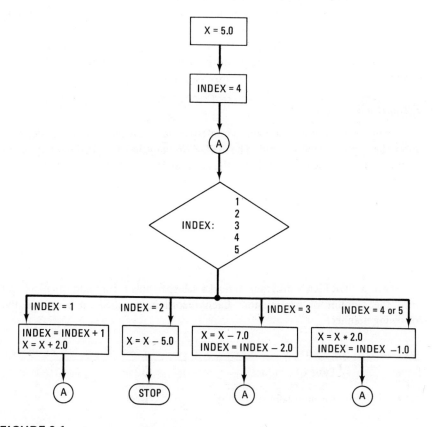

FIGURE 9.1

After execution of the instructions above, the value of X becomes zero and INDEX becomes 2.

Explanation: The first statement assigns 5 as the value for X, and the second statement assigns 4 as the value of INDEX. The third statement is a computed GO TO. Since the current value of INDEX is 4, control transfers to statement 50. (Note that 50 is both the fourth and the fifth entry within the parentheses.) At statement 50, the value of X is multiplied by 2, hence X becomes 10. The next statement subtracts 1 from INDEX, and the value of INDEX becomes 3. After that, control is returned to statement 10. Since the value of INDEX is 3, the computed GO TO sends control to statement 40 (the third entry within the parentheses). At statement 40, the value of X becomes 3. The next statement makes the value of INDEX 1, and then control is returned again to statement 10. Now the computed GO TO transfers control to statement 20, which makes the value of INDEX 2. The next statement makes the value of X 5, after which the control is returned to statement 10. This time, the computed GO TO transfers control to statement 30, which subtracts 5 from X. (So X becomes 0.) The next statement stops execution of the program.

The computed GO TO statement enables the programmer to send control to one of several places, depending upon the value of the variable that follows the parentheses. The following example shows a practical application.

Example 9.3

The percent commission paid to a salesperson of the ABC Company depends upon the type of product sold. The ABC Company has four different types of products. The following table shows the commissions for these products:

TYPE OF PRODUCT	COMMISSION
1	15%
2	10%
3	20%
4	7%

Write a FORTRAN program to read a salesperson's record and calculate and print the amount of commission. Each record is punched on a card in the following manner:

CC	FIELD	TYPE	LENGTH
1	Type of product	Integer	1
2–6	Salesperson's number	Integer	5
7–15	Amount sold (in dollars)	Real	9

The program should first write the appropriate headings and then read a record, calculate the commission based on the type of product, and print the information. Figure 9.2 is the flowchart diagram and the pseudo code for the program, and Figure 9.3 is the Fortran program.

Pseudo Code

```
Start
DOWHILE Not end of data
    Read TYPE,NUM,SALE
    If TYPE=1 Then PERCNT = 0.15
    ELSE IF TYPE=2 Then PERCNT = 0.10
        ELSE IF TYPE=3 Then PERCNT = 0.20
            ELSE IF TYPE=4 Then PERCNT = 0.07
    END IF
    COM=SALE*PERCNT
    WRITE NUM,SALE,COM,TYPE,PERCNT
End DOWHILE
STOP
```

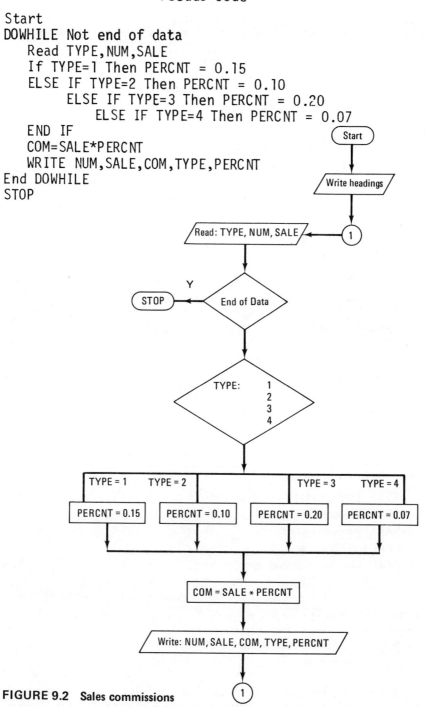

FIGURE 9.2   Sales commissions

```
C FORTRAN PROGRAM TO CALCULATE SALES COMMISSION
C PROGRAM NARRATIVE: THIS PROGRAM READS SALESPERSON'S RECORD, CALCULTES
C THE COMISSION BASED ON THE TYPE OF THE PRODUCT SOLD AND PRNITS THE COMMISSIC
C ALONG WITH OTHER INFORMATION ON EACH SALESPERSON.
C
C        VARIABLE NAMES USED :
C
C                   TYPE    : THE TYPE OF THE PRODUCT
C                   NUM     : SALESPERSON'S ID
C                   SALE    : SALES AMOUNT
C                   PERCNT  : COMMISSION PERCENTAGE
C                   COM     : AMONUT OF COMMISSION
C
C*****************************************************************************
C
           INTEGER TYPE, CARD
C
           CARD = 5
           LINE = 6
C
C PRINT HEADINGS
C
           WRITE(LINE,10)
10         FORMAT('1',T6,'ID NUMBER',T20,'SALE',T35,'COMMISSION',T50,
      +    'PRODUCT-ID',T65,'COMMISSON PERCENTAGE')
C
C START LOOP
20         READ(CARD,30, END=100) TYPE,NUM,SALE
30         FORMAT(I1,I5,F9.2)
           GO TO (40,50,60,70), TYPE
40         PERCNT = 0.15
           GO TO 80
50         PERCNT = 0.10
           GO TO 80
60         PERCNT = 0.20
           GO TO 80
70         PERCNT = 0.07
80         COM = SALE * PERCNT
           WRITE(LINE,90)NUM,SALE,COM,TYPE,PERCNT
90         FORMAT('0',T8,I5,T20,F10.2,T35,F8.2,T54,I1,T70,F4.2)
C
           GO TO 20
100        STOP
           END
```

FIGURE 9.3 Program for calculating sales commissions

The variable names used are:

TYPE: Product's type

NUM: Salesperson ID

SALE: Amount of sale

PERCNT: Commission %

COM: Amount of commission

Note that in the program, the programmer can use four logical IFs rather than the computed GO TO statement.

9.1.2 The ASSIGN and Assigned GO TO Statements

The assigned GO TO statement is another means of implementing a conditional branch. It is available in FORTRAN IV and ANSI FORTRAN. However, many smaller FORTRAN compilers do not support the assigned GO TO statement. Actually, usage of the assigned GO TO requires two statements: the ASSIGN statement and the assigned GO TO statement. The general form of the ASSIGN statement is:

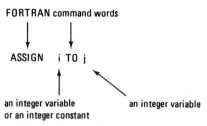

The ASSIGN statement assigns the constant i (or the value of the variable i) to the variable j. The ASSIGN statement must be executed before the execution of assigned GO TO. The general form of the assigned GO TO is:

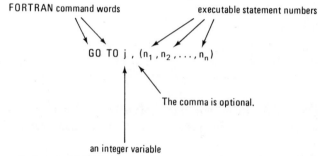

The value of the variable j must be one of the statement numbers that are enclosed within parentheses, and it must have previously been assigned a value by an ASSIGN statement. The variable j should not be subscripted. When the assigned GO TO statement is encountered, control transfers to the statement number enclosed within parentheses, which is the value of the variable j.

Example 9.4

```
    .
    .
    .
ASSIGN 30 TO INDEX
    .
    .
    .
GO TO INDEX,(10,20,30,40,50)
    .
    .
    .
```

The ASSIGN statement assigns 30 to INDEX, and the assigned GO TO transfers control to statement 30.

The variable that is used in an ASSIGN statement must not be used for any other purpose in the program. The order of statement numbers within the parentheses is not significant.

Example 9.5

What will be the value of X and K after the execution of the following statements?

```
      X = 12.5
      J = 30
      ASSIGN J TO K
20    GO TO K , (30,50,70,100)
30    X = X * 2.0
      ASSIGN 70 TO K
      GO TO 20
50    STOP
70    X = X - 5.0
      ASSIGN 100 TO K
      GO TO 20
100   X = X - 10.0
      ASSIGN 50 TO K
      GO TO 20
```

After execution of the statements above, the value of X is 10.0 and of K is 50.

Explanation: The third statement assigns 30 (the value of J) to K. The GO TO statement transfers control to statement 30. (Note that the value of K is 30 and that 30 is a statement number within parentheses.) At statement 30, the value of X becomes 25. The next statement assigns 70 to K; control is then returned to statement 20. Now the GO TO statement transfers control to statement 70, which subtracts 5 from X. The next statement assigns 100 to K, and control is returned to statement 20. At this time, the GO TO statement transfers control to statement 100, which subtracts 10 from X (so that X becomes 10). The next statement assigns 50 to K and then control returns to statement 20. Statement 20 sends control to statement 50, which stops execution.

Use of the assigned GO TO is more complicated than the use of the computed GO TO. Although the assigned GO TO is the fastest method of conditionally branching (which can increase processing efficiency), its use makes a program more complicated and difficult to understand. Therefore, use of the assigned GO TO is not encouraged in the business environment.

9.2   ARITHMETIC IF

The general form of the arithmetic IF statement is:

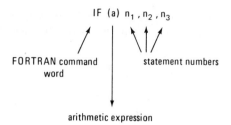

IF (a) n_1, n_2, n_3

FORTRAN command word

statement numbers

arithmetic expression

The arithmetic IF transfers control to one of three statements whose statement number follows the parentheses. Choice of the statement is dependent on the value of the arithmetic expression a. The value of a is compared to zero. If it is less than zero, then control transfers to statement n_1 (the first statement number after the parentheses). If the value of a is equal to zero, control transfers to n_2 (the statement in the second position). And if the value of a is greater than zero, control transfers to n_3 (the last statement number).

Example 9.6

1. IF (X * 2.0 − Y) 10,20,30

   When the value of X * 2.0 − Y is less than 0, control transfers to statement 10. Control transfers to statement 20 when the value of X * 2.0 − Y is equal to 0 and to 30 when the value of X * 2.0 − Y is greater than 0.

2. IF (J) 10,10,20

   Control transfers to statement 10 when the value of J is less than or equal to 0 and to 20 when the value of J is greater than 0.

Example 9.7

What will be the value of X, Y, and Z after execution of the following instructions?

```
       Y = 2.5
       X = 15.0
       Z = 1.0
10     IF (Z * Y − X) 20,30,40
20     Y = Y * 2.0
       Z = Z + 2.0
       GO TO 10
30     Y = X + Y
       GO TO 10
40     STOP
       END
```

197

After execution of the instructions above, the value of X is 15, of Z is 3, and of Y is 20. Try to justify these values. Figure 9.4 is the flowchart for the program above.

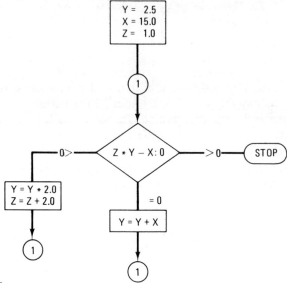

FIGURE 9.4

Note that any statement following an arithmetic IF statement must have a statement number and must be referenced somewhere in the program.

9.3   END, STOP, AND PAUSE STATEMENTS

The END statement indicates to the compiler that the end of the source program has been reached and that compiling should stop. The END statement must be the last statement in the source program. In ANSI FORTRAN, the END statement should not have a statement number.

The STOP statement terminates the execution of the program. There can be more than one STOP statement in a program. If a program does have more than one STOP statement, then each statement that follows a STOP statement must have a statement number (otherwise, that statement could not be reached during execution of the program).

The PAUSE statement temporarily stops execution of the program, displays the PAUSE statement on the operator's console (or the user's terminal), and directs the computer to wait until the operator instructs the computer to resume execution. The general form of the PAUSE statement is:

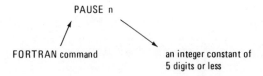

where *n* is the message code. The computer continues with the next statement after a PAUSE when execution is resumed. The PAUSE statement allows the programmer the opportunity to load tapes, terminate execution, examine the content of a storage location, and the like. (The beginning programmer will not have occasion to use the PAUSE statement.)

We have seen many examples of the END and STOP statements. Below is an example of the PAUSE statement.

Example 9.8

Suppose the data for our program are stored on three magnetic tapes and there is only one tape drive available. We can instruct the operator to load the first tape when PAUSE 1 is displayed, the second tape when PAUSE 2 is displayed, and the third tape when PAUSE 3 is displayed. The PAUSE statements are inserted in our program as indicated below.

.
.
.

PAUSE 1

.
.
.

PAUSE 2

.
.
.

PAUSE 3

.
.
.

END

Example 9.9: Sales Analysis

The ABC Firm makes sales in three territories. The firm has a sales quota of $10,000 for each salesperson in each territory. ABC pays 3 percent commission if the salesperson does not meet the sales quota; but in addition to the basic 3 percent commission, the firm pays the following bonuses, depending on the territory, when a salesperson meets or exceeds the sales quota.

TERRITORY	BONUS
1	$250 + 1% of dollar amount in excess of the quota
2	$300 + 1% of dollar amount in excess of the quota
3	$200 + 0.5% of dollar amount in excess of the quota

Write a FORTRAN program to calculate the total sales for each territory and the total sales, total commission, total bonuses, and total pay for the firm. The program should also print each salesperson's number, territory number, amount of sales, bonuses, and total pay in addition to the totals above.

The input records are organized as follows:

CC	FIELD	TYPE	LENGTH
1	Territory	Integer	1
2-6	Salesperson number	Integer	5
7-15	Sales	Real	9

Figure 9.5 is the flowchart and pseudo code and Figure 9.6 the program for this problem.

Pseudo Code Form

```
1.  Start
2.  Initialize TOTLS1,TOTLS2,TOTLS3,TOTBNS,
            TOTCOM and TOTPAY to 0
3.  Do steps 4 through 6 until end of data
4.  PAY = 0
    BONUS = 0
    COM = SALE * 0.03
    IF SALE ≤ 10000 GO TO Step 5
    ELSE IF REGION = 1 Then
            BONUS = 250 + (SALE − 10000) * 0.01
            TOTLS1 = TOTLS1 + SALE
        ELSE IF REGION = 2 Then
                BONUS = 300 + (SALE − 10000) * 0.01
                TOTLS2 = TOTLS2 + SALE
            ELSE IF REGION = 3 Then
                    BONUS = 200 + (SALE − 10000) * 0.005
                    TOTLS3 = TOTLS3 + SALE
    END IF
5.  Add SALE to the SALE
    of Respected Region
6.  TOTBN = TOTBNS + BONUS
    TOTCOM = TOTCOM + COM
    PAY = COM + BONUS
    TOTPAY = TOTPAY + PAY
7.  Write: NUM, REGION, SALE,
            BONUS, COM, PAY
8.  TOTSL = TOTLS1 + TOTSL2 + TOTSL3
    Write: TOTSL, TOTBNS, TOTCOM, TOTPAY
9.  STOP
```

FIGURE 9.5   Flowchart for problem on sales analysis

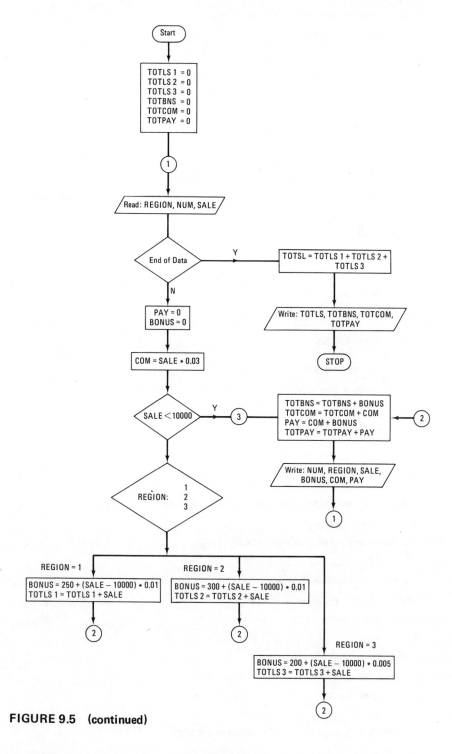

FIGURE 9.5 (continued)

```
C FORTRAN PRROGRAM TO CALCULATE COMPANY'S TOTAL SALES, TOTAL BONUSES,
C TOTAL COMMISSIONS AND TOTAL SALARIES.
C
C        VARIABLE NAMES USED:
C                TOTLS1  : TOTAL SALE FOR REGION 1
C                TOTLS2  : TOTAL SALE FOR REGION 2
C                TOTLS3  : TOTAL SALE FOR REGION 3
C                TOTBNS  : COMPANY'S TOTAL BONUSES
C                TOTCOM  : COMPANY'S TOTAL COMMISSION
C                TOTPAY  : COMPANY'S TOTAL SALARY
C                TOTSL   : COMPANY'S GRAND TOTAL SALE
C                SALE    : SALE AMOUNT
C                PAY     : SALESPERSON'S APY
C                BONUS   : SALESPERSON'S BONUS
C                COM     : SALESPERSON'S COMISSION
C
C
C INPUT RECORDS ARE PUNCHED ON CARDS. EACH RECORD CNTAINS THREE FIELDS:
C REGION ID, SALESPERSON NUMBER AND SALES AMOUNT
C
C***************************************************************************
C
        INTEGER REGION, CARD
        CARD = 5
        LINE = 6
C
C PRINT HEADINGS
C
        WRITE(LINE,10)
10      FORMAT('1',T3,'ID',T13,'REGION',T23,'SALE',T38,'BONUS',T53,
     +  'COMMISSION',T68,'PAY')
C
C INTIALIZE ALL TOTALS TO 0
C
        TOTSL1 = 0.0
        TOTSL2 = 0.0
        TOTSL3 = 0.0
        TOTBNS = 0.0
        TOTCOM = 0.0
        TOTPAY = 0.0
        TOTSL = 0.0
C
C START LOOP
C
20      READ(CARD,30,END=90) REGION, NUM, SALE
30      FORMAT(I1,I5,F9.2)
C
C INTIALIZE PAY AND BONUS FOR NEW PERSON TO 0
C
        PAY = 0.0
        BONUS = 0.0
C
C CALCULATE THE COMMISSION FOR THE SALESPERSOON
C
        COM = SALE * 0.03
C
C IF SALE LESS THAN QUOTA NO BONUS
C
        IF ( SALE .LT. 10000) GO TO 70
C
C ELSE GO TO CALCULATE BONUS
C
        GO TO (40,50,60), REGION
C
C FIRST TERRITORY
C
40      BONUS = 200 + (SALE - 10000.00) * 0.01
        TOTSL1 = TOTSL1 + SALE
        GO TO 78
C
C SECOND TERRITORY
C
50      BONUS = 300 + (SALE - 10000.00) * 0.01
        TOTSL2 = TOTSL2 + SALE
        GO TO 78
```

FIGURE 9.6 Program for sales-analysis problem

```
C
C THIRD TERRITORY
C
60          BONUS = 200 + (SALE - 10000.00) * 0.005
            TOTSL3 = TOTSL3 + SALE
            GO TO 78
C
C CALCULATE PAY AND ADD BONUS, COMMISSION AND PAY TO THEIR
C GRAND TOTALS
C
70          GO TO (72, 74, 76), REGION
72          TOTSL1 = TOTSL1 + SALE
            GO TO 78
74          TOTSL2 = TOTSL2 + SALE
            GO TO 78
76          TOTSL3 = TOTSL3 + SALE
78          PAY = COM + BONUS
            TOTBNS= TOTBNS + BONUS
            TOTCOM = TOTCOM + COM
            TOTPAY = TOTPAY + PAY
C
C PRINT THE SALESPERSON INFORMATION UNDER APPROPIRATE HEADINGS
C
            WRITE(LINE,80) NUM, REGION, SALE, BONUS, COM, PAY
80          FORMAT('0',T3,I6,T13,I1,T23,F10.2,T38,F7.2,T53,F7.2,T65,F8.2)
C
            GO TO 20
C
C CALCULATE THE GRAND TOTAL SALE
90          TOTSL = TOTSL1 + TOTSL2 + TOTSL3
C
C PRINT THE TOTALS
C
            WRITE(LINE,100)TOTSL1,TOTSL2,TOTSL3
100         FORMAT('1',6X,'SALE REGION 1 : ',F12.2//,6X,'SALE REGION 2 : ',
     +      F12.2//,6X,'SALE REGION 3 : ',F12.2)
C
            WRITE(LINE,110)TOTSL, TOTCOM, TOTBNS, TOTPAY
110         FORMAT(5(/),6X,'GRAND TOTAL SALE : ',F14.2//,6X,
     +      'GRAND TOTAL COMMISSION : ', F10.2,///,6X,'GRAND TOTAL BONUS : ',
     +      F10.2//,6X,'GRAND TOTAL PAY : ', F10.2)
            STOP
            END
```

FIGURE 9.6   (continued)

9.4   SUMMARY

There are three different GO TO statements: unconditional, computed, and assigned. The general form of the computed GO TO is:

$$\text{GO TO } (n_1, n_2, \ldots, n_n), j$$

where j is an integer variable and $n_1, n_2, \ldots, n_n$ are statement numbers. The order of these statements is significant. When the computed GO TO is encountered, control transfers conditionally, depending on the value of the variable j, to one of the statement numbers.

The ASSIGN statement is used in conjunction with the assigned GO TO statement. The general forms of the ASSIGN and assigned GO TO statements are:

$$\text{ASSIGN } i \text{ TO } j$$
$$\text{GO TO } j, (n_1, n_2, \ldots, n_n)$$

where $n_1, n_2, \ldots, n_n$ are statement numbers. The value of j must be one of the statement numbers.

The arithmetic IF enables the programmer to branch in three different ways. The general form of the arithmetic IF is:

$$IF\ (a)\ n_1,\ n_2,\ n_3$$

where a is an arithmetic expression. Control transfers to n_1 if a is less than 0, to n_2 if a equals 0, and to n_3 if the value of a is greater than 0.

The STOP statement terminates execution of the program. The END statement signals the end of the source program to the compiler, and the PAUSE statement interrupts execution of the program.

9.5 REVIEW QUESTIONS AND SUGGESTED PROBLEMS

1. Find the errors, if any, in the following FORTRAN statements:

```
a.   IF (BALANS - PAY) ,10,20,30
b.   IF (X) 10,20,30
c.   IF PAY - 1000.00 , 10,10,20
d.   GO TO (10,10,20,30)J
e.   GO TO (10,10,20,30) ,R
f.   GO TO (10,10,20,30) ,IR
g.   ASSIGN 50 TO K
     GO TO K (50,60,70)
h.   ASSIGN 50 TO K
     GO TO K, (40,60,70)
i.   K = 50
     GO TO K, (50,60,70)
```

2. Determine the values of R1, R2, J1, and J2 after execution of the following statements:

```
        J1 = 0
        J2 = 0
        R1 = 50.0
        R2 = 60.0
10      IF (R1 - R2) 20,30,40
20      R1 = R1 + 5.0
        J1 = J1 + 1
        GO TO 10
30      R1 = R1 + R2
        J2 = J2 + 1
        GO TO 10
40      R2 = 0.0
        STOP
        END
```

3. What will be the values of X and J after execution of the following instructions?

```
      X = 10.0
      J = 3
10    GO TO (20,30,40) , J
20    X = X * 2
      J = J + 1
      IF (J .LE. 3) GO TO 10
      STOP
40    X = X + 5.0
      J = J - 2
      IF (X .LE. 2) GO TO 10
      STOP
30    X = 0.0
      J = 0
      STOP
      END
```

4. What will be the values of X, INDEX, and J after execution of the following instructions?

```
      J = 1
10    IF (J - 2) 20,30,40
20    ASSIGN 70 TO INDEX
      GO TO INDEX , (50,60,70)
30    ASSIGN 60 TO INDEX
      GO TO INDEX , (50,60,70)
40    ASSIGN 50 TO INDEX
      GO TO INDEX , (50,60,70)
50    X = X - 5.0
      STOP
60    X = X - 10.0
      J = J + 1
      GO TO 10
70    X = 20.0
      J = J + 1
      GO TO 10
      END
```

5. **Depositors at a Bank.** A bank offers two kinds of services to its customers, savings and checking. Each input card has a field of one-character width; an *S* indicates saving, and a *C* checking. Furthermore, each input card contains the name of the customer, the account number, and amounts of deposits and withdrawals. Arrange the input data and output in any way you wish.

Write a FORTRAN program to read exactly 20 cards and print all information about the customer, including whether he or she has a savings or a checking account. In addition, your program must also print the number of customers with savings accounts and the number with checking accounts.

6. Modify the program in problem 5 so that your program processes as many customers as the bank has.

7. **Property Tax.** Draw a flowchart and write a FORTRAN program to read the values of all homes in Ypsilanti Township and to calculate the homeowners' real estate tax according to the following percentages:

HOUSE ASSESSED VALUE	TAX-RATE PERCENTAGES
Less than $15,000	0.3%
Between $15,000 and $30,000	0.6%
Between $30,001 and $50,000	1.5%
Between $50,001 and $80,000	2.5%
Between $80,001 and $120,000	4%
More than $120,000	5%

Do not forget to include the homeowner's name in the input and output records and write appropriate headings.

8. **Minimum Return on Investment.** Write a FORTRAN program for General Informatic Corporation to read an investment record, analyze the data, and make a decision whether or not to invest. Each input record combines the investment code, the minimum acceptable rate of return on investment, the amount of the investment, the estimated life of the investment, and the expected income during the period of the investment. The output record should contain the investment code, the minimum acceptable rate of return on investment, the average rate of return on investment, and whether or not the decision to invest should be made. The following formulas should be used:

Net income = Expected income from the investment — Cost

$$\text{Average income} = \frac{\text{Net income}}{\text{Life}}$$

$$\text{Average investment} = \frac{\text{Cost}}{2} \quad \text{(when straight-line depreciation with no residual value is assumed)}$$

$$\text{Average rate of return} = \frac{\text{Average net income}}{\text{Average investment}}$$

The investment is acceptable if the average rate of return is greater than the minimum acceptable rate of return on investment.

9. **Promotion and Salary Adjustments.** Draw a flowchart and write a program to promote and adjust the salary of faculty at Kurdistan University. Each faculty input record is punched on a card in the following manner:

CC	FIELD	TYPE	LENGTH
1–5	Faculty number	Integer	5
6–12	Salary	Real	7
13	Rank code	Integer	1
14–15	Number of years in the rank	Integer	2
16	Performance code	Integer	1

The code for the ranks and performances is:

CODE	RANK	CODE	PERFORMANCE
1	Lecturer	1	Below average
2	Instructor	2	Average
3	Assistant professor	3	Good
4	Associate professor	4	Very good
5	Full professor	5	Excellent

Regulations for promotion and salary increases at Kurdistan University are:

RANK	MINIMUM YEARS IN RANK FOR PROMO- TION	PERFORMANCE	MERIT INCREASE	SALARY INCREASE	PROMOTION TO NEXT RANK
1, 2		1	None	2%	No
1, 2	4	2, 3	$200	5%	Yes
1, 2	3	4, 5	$300	6%	Yes
3	—	1	None	3%	No
3	5	2, 3	$350	5%	Yes
3	4	4, 5	$600	7%	Yes
4	—	1	None	4%	Yes
4	5	2, 3	$650	6%	Yes
4	4	4, 5	$950	8%	Yes
5		1	None	5%	
5		2, 3	$1,000	8%	
5		4, 5	$1,500	10%	

Since full professor is the final rank, promotion is disregarded for these faculty. Write the appropriate captions and headings. Note that the formula for new salary is:

New salary = Percent salary increased * Salary + Salary + Merit

10. **Depreciation Using Declining-Balance Method.** When the declining-balance method is used, depreciation per year is found as follows:

$$DPRATE = 1 - \left(\frac{SCRAP}{COST}\right)^{\frac{1}{Life}}$$

$$DEPYR = DPRATE * CARVAL$$

where:

DPRATE is the depreciation rate for the year
SCRAP is the estimated scrap value
COST is the original cost
DEPYR is the depreciation for the year
CARVAL is the carrying value (undepreciated value)
LIFE is the use-life of the asset

Draw a flowchart and write a FORTRAN program to read all the assets for ABC Corporation and print the depreciation for each year starting in 1980 for the duration of use life of the asset. Each input record should contain the asset number, cost, scrap value, and use-life. Print all appropriate captions and headings.

11. **An Econometric System.** In the following model, the variables described in the previous period are called logged variables, and the subscript -1 is used to

denote such variables. The numerical calculation of such a model is to consider time to advance in uniform steps and organize the model in the form of a series of difference equations and use the logged variable (variables in the previous period) to calculate the current variable. One simple mathematical model for the national economy is:

$$I = 2.1 + 0.1 \ Y_{-1}$$
$$T = 0.3 \ Y_{-1}$$
$$Y = C_{-1} + I_{-1} + E_{-1}$$
$$C = 0.8 \ (Y_{-1} - T_{-1}) + 30$$

where all quantities are expressed in billions of dollars and I is the investment, T the taxes, Y the national income, C the consumption, and E the government expenditure. Note that $I = 2.1 + 0.1 \ Y_{-1}$ means the current investment is calculated by multiplying 0.1 by the national income in the previous period (Y_{-1} is the logged variable) and adding 2.1.

Write a FORTRAN program to find the growth in national consumption for five years using the models above. Start the initial national income Y_{-1} to be 100 and assume the government expenditure for five years to be.

YEAR	E
1	35
2	45
3	55
4	65
5	75

12. **Sales Discount.** The ABC Corporation established the following regulations to give discounts to its customers:

TERRITORY	SALES AMOUNT	DISCOUNT
1	Between $500 and $1,000	4%
1	More than $1,000	6%
2	Between $500 and $1,000	6%
2	More than $1,000	8%
3	More than $1,000	7%

Draw a flowchart and write a FORTRAN program to read each customer record and calculate the discount. The input record should contain customer number, amount of sale, and the territory. Your program should calculate the corporation's total sales and total discount and print the appropriate information for each customer and for the corporation under appropriate captions and headings.

13. **Depreciation Using Sum-of-Years'-Digits Method.** Redo problem 10 using the sum-of-years'-digits method. In this method,

$$\text{Depreciation per year} = \frac{p}{q} * (\text{Cost} - \text{Scrap})$$

where

$$q = \frac{\text{Life} * (\text{Life} + 1)}{2}$$

and p is the number of years of life left.

10 ARRAYS AND TABLE HANDLING

10.1 WHAT ARE ARRAYS?

In business and other application-oriented environments, an array is usually referred to as a table. In mathematics, an array is also called a matrix. An array is a group of related data organized in such a manner that the entire group can be referenced by a single name, and an individual element of it by a name and one or more numbers—for example, the third element of the table. The numbers that are used to identify a particular element of an array are called subscripts.

For example, if we let R be the matrix:

$$\begin{pmatrix} 6.20 & 7.30 \\ 8.50 & 5.50 \\ 3.80 & 4.50 \end{pmatrix}$$

then R has six elements, arranged in three rows and two columns. To identify a particular element of R, subscripts are used to designate the row and column of that particular element. (By convention, the first subscript always refers to the row.) Thus, $R_{2,1}$ is the element in the second row (first subscript is 2) and the first column (second subscript is 1). The value of $R_{2,1}$ is 8.50. In general, $R_{i,j}$ is the element in the ith row and jth column.

$$R_{i,j}$$

row   column

Therefore, the value of $R_{3,2}$ is 4.50, and of $R_{1,2}$ is 7.30. What are the values of $R_{2,2}$ and $R_{1,1}$?

In the discussion above, $R_{i,j}$ is said to be a subscripted variable. Since we cannot write subscripts on a punched card as we write them by hand, in FORTRAN a slightly different notation is used to represent subscripted variables. Instead of $R_{2,1}$, we write R(2,1). Similarly, R(1,2) = $R_{1,2}$ = 7.30; R(2,2) = $R_{2,2}$ = 5.50; and so on. Because the array R above is a two-dimensional array (it has rows and columns), each element of it requires two subscripts (row and column) for its identification.

Let's see how we might use arrays in a business environment. Suppose we wish to store the average pay per hour for three different jobs in two districts, as indicated below:

JOB		DISTRICTS	
JOB NAME		1	2
Programmer	1	6.20	7.30
Carpenter	2	8.50	5.50
Cashier	3	3.80	4.50

Denote this array (a table with three rows and two columns) by AVGPAY. Then AVGPAY (1,2) represents the pay for the programmers in the second district, which is $7.30, and the average pay for carpenters in the first district is the value of AVGPAY (2,1), which is $8.50.

Suppose our study required the average wages for these three different jobs in only one district. We therefore do not need a two-dimensional table; a one-dimensional table would suffice. Thus, a table such as:

JOB NAME	DISTRICT
Programmer	6.20
Carpenter	8.50
Cashier	3.80

can be represented as a one-dimensional table:

$$\text{AVGPAY} = \begin{pmatrix} 6.20 \\ 8.50 \\ 3.80 \end{pmatrix}$$

Hence, the average pay for programmers is AVGPAY (1), which is $6.20, the average pay for carpenters is AVGPAY (2) = $8.50, and for cashiers, it is AVGPAY (3) = $3.80.

As another example of a one-dimensional table, consider the following. Suppose we have a class of five students and we wish to represent their scores in a test as an array.

STUDENT NUMBER	GRADE
1	80
2	70
3	90
4	50
5	95

Let the array be called GRADE. Then:

$$
GRADE = \begin{pmatrix} 80 \\ 70 \\ 90 \\ 50 \\ 95 \end{pmatrix}
\begin{matrix} \leftarrow & GRADE\,(1) \\ \leftarrow & GRADE\,(2) \\ \leftarrow & GRADE\,(3) \\ \leftarrow & GRADE\,(4) \\ \leftarrow & GRADE\,(5) \end{matrix}
$$

Because arrays have such widespread application in FORTRAN, understanding them is of paramount importance. You are urged to study this section thoroughly.

10.2 HOW TO CREATE ARRAYS IN FORTRAN

The maximum number of dimensions allowed in FORTRAN is 7. However, since all business applications can be accomplished with one- or two-dimensional arrays, the emphasis in this text is on arrays with few dimensions.

The DIMENSION statement is used to instruct the computer to reserve a set of consecutive memory locations to store the elements of an array. The first element of the array is stored in the first such reserved memory location, the second element of the array in the second memory location, and so on. The name of the array represents the whole set of reserved locations.

The DIMENSION statement is a specification statement. Thus, it has to be placed at the beginning of the program, before all executable statements. The general form of the DIMENSION statement is:

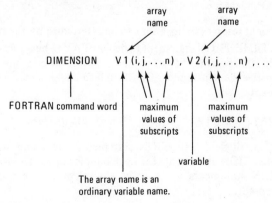

Example 10.1

1. Write a DIMENSION statement to declare GRADE to be a one-dimensional array with five elements.

DIMENSION GRADE(5)

This statement tells the compiler to reserve five consecutive memory locations. The collective name of these locations is GRADE and the individual names of the locations are GRADE(1), GRADE(2), GRADE(3), GRADE(4), and GRADE(5). Figure 10.1 portrays the effects of the DIMENSION statement above.

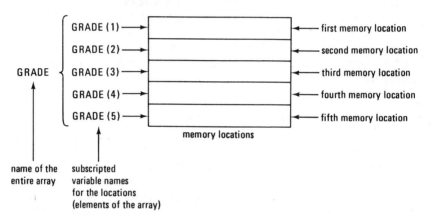

FIGURE 10.1

2. Write a DIMENSION statement to declare RATE to be a two-dimensional array with three rows and two columns.

DIMENSION RATE(3,2)

This statement reserves six locations to be referred to by the name RATE.

3. Write one DIMENSION statement to declare PAY to be a two-dimensional array with 100 rows and twelve columns, NAME to be a one-dimensional array with five elements, and ADDRS to be a one-dimensional array with eight elements.

DIMENSION PAY(100,12) , NAME(5) , ADDRS(8)

Instead of a single DIMENSION statement, one could write two or three DIMENSION statements for the example above. The following two DIMENSION statements are exactly equivalent to the single DIMENSION statement.

```
DIMENSION PAY(100,12) , NAME(5)
DIMENSION ADDRS(8)
```

4. Write a DIMENSION statement to create a table to hold the income of families in 50 states. The study includes 20 counties within each state and five cities within each county.

Thus, FINCOM (3, 1, 5) represents the income for the family in the fifth city in the first county of the third state.

The following rules govern the use of arrays and subscripted variables in FORTRAN:

1. The name of the array must conform to the rules for FORTRAN variable names. That is, the name should be composed of from one to six characters, should start with a letter, and should not contain special characters.

2. A subscripted variable is constructed from the name of the array followed by a left parenthesis, the subscript (or subscripts), and finally a right parenthesis. The subscripted variable that represents the third element of the array GRADE is:

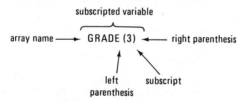

The subscripted variable that represents the element in the third row and second column of the two-dimensional array RATE is:

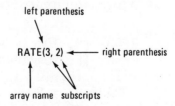

3. A subscript must be either an integer constant, an integer nonsubscripted variable, or an integer arithmetic expression. Only the following seven forms of arithmetic expression can be used as subscripts. (Assume that v refers to an unsigned subscripted integer variable, and c and d are integer constants.)

FORM	MEANING	EXAMPLE
c	One constant	PAY(4)
v	One variable	PAY(J)
$v + c$	One variable + One constant	PAY(J+3)
$v - c$	One variable − One constant	PAY(J−2)
$c * v$	One constant * One variable	PAY(2*K)
$c * v + d$	One constant * One variable + One constant	PAY(3*J+2)
$c * v - d$	One constant * One variable − One constant	PAY(3*J−2)

Note that we need only the first two forms; instead of writing PAY(3∗J−2), we can write N = 3∗J−2, and then refer to PAY(N) (which is the second form). The value of any subscript should be an integer in the range 1 through the maximum value, which is declared in the DIMENSION statement. For example, if we have:

DIMENSION GRADE(5), RATE(5,10)

then in the program, the subscript of GRADE should be an integer between 1 and 5 inclusive. The first subscript of RATE must be an integer in the range 1 through 5, and the second should be in the range 1 through 10.

4. The mode of the array is determined by the mode of the name of the array. For example:

DIMENSION IGRADE(5), RATE(3,2)

defines IGRADE as an integer one-dimensional array of five elements. Note that the array IGRADE is an integer array because IGRADE is an integer variable. Therefore, every element of the array IGRADE will be an integer. On the other hand, RATE will be a real, two-dimensional array with six elements, because RATE is a real variable.

5. Except in input/output, DATA, and type statements, whenever the name of the array appears in the program, it must be followed by the appropriate number of subscripts. For example, if we have:

```
DIMENSION IGRADE(5)

READ   (5, 10) IGRADE (3)
READ   (5, 10) IGRADE
WRITE  (6, 10) IGRADE
IGRADE(2) = 80
```

are all valid statements. The first statement reads only the value for the third element of the array. The second READ statement inputs the values of all elements of the array, the third statement writes the values of all elements of the array, and the fourth statement assigns 80 as the value of the second element of the array. However, the statement:

IGRADE = 0

is invalid, because the array name without subscript cannot appear in arithmetic or logical assignment statements.

6. At most, seven subscripts are allowed in FORTRAN.

Example 10.2

Write a FORTRAN program to read the grades of five students and calculate and print their average. Use an array to hold the grades. Input card:

CC	FIELD	TYPE	LENGTH
1–3	GRADE	Integer	3

Assume the following input data:

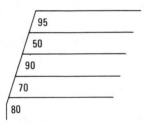

Figure 10.2 is the flowchart and the pseudo code form for averaging the data in a one-dimensional array.

Explanation of the flowchart: The instruction in the second box declares IGRADE to be a one-dimensional array with five elements. In the third box, the values of TOTAL and *I* are initialized to 0. TOTAL will be used as a variable to accumulate the sum of all the elements in the array. The variable *I* will be used as a subscript (index) to identify a particular element of the array. The loop between boxes 4 and 7 will be executed five times. At the first iteration, in box 4, the value of *I* becomes 1. Box 5 instructs the computer to read IGRADE (I). Since the current value of *I* is 1, the instruction in box 5 implies that IGRADE (1) be read. Hence, the first card is read, and 80 is assigned as the value of IGRADE (1). The instruction in box 6 adds the value of IGRADE (1) to the old value of TOTAL. Therefore, the value of TOTAL becomes 80. Since the current value of *I* is 1, which is less than 5, the instruction in box 7 sends control back

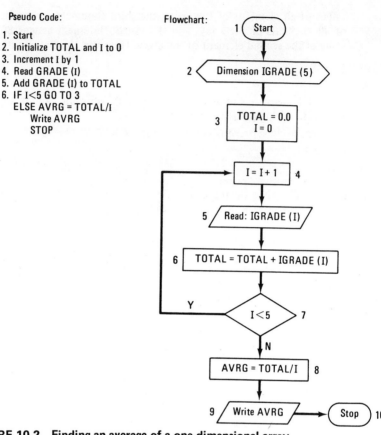

Pseudo Code:

1. Start
2. Initialize TOTAL and I to 0
3. Increment I by 1
4. Read GRADE (I)
5. Add GRADE (I) to TOTAL
6. IF I<5 GO TO 3
   ELSE AVRG = TOTAL/I
     Write AVRG
     STOP

Flowchart:

FIGURE 10.2 Finding an average of a one-dimensional array

to box 4. This is the end of the first iteration. This process can be portrayed as follows:

I	FORMULA BECOMES	TOTAL		
			80	IGRADE (1)
Ø		Ø		IGRADE (2)
1	TOTAL=TOTAL+IGRADE (1)	80		IGRADE (3)
				IGRADE (4)
				IGRADE (5)

As indicated above, only the value of the first element has been read. To read the value of the second element and add it to TOTAL, all that is required is to increase the value of the subscript I to 2 and repeat the read and add instructions. Therefore, the second iteration again starts at box 4, which adds 1 to I (so the value of I becomes 2). Therefore, the instruction in box 5, "Read IGRADE (I)," now means "Read IGRADE (2)." Thus, the second card is read, and 70 is

218

stored in IGRADE (2). At this point, the array IGRADE looks like this:

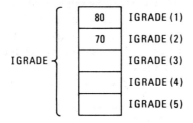

At box 6, IGRADE (I) [which is IGRADE (2)] is added to TOTAL, and the value of TOTAL becomes 150. Since the current value of I is 2, which is less than 5, at box 7 control is transferred back to box 4, and the third iteration starts. The loop between 4 and 7 will be repeated until the value of I becomes 5. This will happen at the end of the fifth iteration. By that time, all the elements of the array will have been read and added to TOTAL. The third, fourth, and fifth iterations can be portrayed as follows:

Array IGRADE

80	IGRADE (1)
70	IGRADE (2)
90	IGRADE (3)

Third iteration

I	FORMULA BECOMES	TOTAL
2̸ 3	TOTAL=TOTAL+IGRADE (3)	240

Array IGRADE

80	IGRADE (1)
70	IGRADE (2)
90	IGRADE (3)
50	IGRADE (4)
	IGRADE (5)

Fourth iteration

I	FORMULA BECOMES	TOTAL
3̸ 4	TOTAL=TOTAL+IGRADE (4)	290

Array IGRADE

80	IGRADE (1)
70	IGRADE (2)
90	IGRADE (3)
50	IGRADE (4)
95	IGRADE (5)

Fifth iteration

I	FORMULA BECOMES	TOTAL
4̸ 5	TOTAL=TOTAL+IGRADE (5)	385

Now the test in box 7 is false, so the instruction at box 8 is executed and the value of AVRG becomes 77. Box 9 causes the value of AVRG to be printed.

The advantages of using arrays should be apparent: With a single name (the name of the array), you can reference any of the elements of the array by changing the value of the subscript. This allows easy manipulation of data and greatly simplifies iterated procedures.

Figure 10.3 is the FORTRAN program for the problem above.

```
C FORTRAN PROGRAM TO CALCULATE THE AVERAGE OF THE
C ELEMENTS OF ONE DIMENSIONAL ARRAY
C
C PROGRAM NARRATIVE:
C       THIS PROGRAM FINDS THE AVERAGE GRADE OF 5 STUDENTS.
C       EACH GRADE IS PUNCHED ON A CARD. THE GRADE IS THEN
C       INTERNALLY STORED IN THE ARRAY IGRADE.
C VARIABLE NAMES USED:
C       TOTAL :  SUM OF THE ELEMENTS OF THE ARRAY
C       I     :  COUNTER
C       IGRADE : ARRAY NAME TO HOLD GRADES
C       AVRG  :  AVERAGE
C
C*****************************************************************************
C
C DECLARE IGRADE TO BE ONE DIMENSIONAL
C ARRAY WITH 5 ELEMENTS
C
        DIMENSION   IGRADE (5)
C
        INTEGER CARD
        CARD = 5
        LINE = 6
C
C
C INITIALIZE TOTAL TO ACCUMULATE THE SUM
C OF THE ELEMENT OF THE ARRAY
C
        TOTAL = 0.0
C
C INITIALIZE THE SUBSCRIPT I
        I = 0
C
C BEGINNING OF THE LOOP
C
C INCREMENT THE SUBSCRIPT BY 1
C
   10   I = I + 1
C
        READ (CARD, 20) IGRADE (I)
   20   FORMAT (I3)
        TOTAL = TOTAL + IGRADE (I)
C IF I IS LESS THAN 5 REPEAT THE LOOP
        IF (I .LT. 5) GO TO 10
C ELSE END OF THE LOOP
C
        AVRG = TOTAL/I
        WRITE (LINE, 30) AVRG
   30   FORMAT ('1', 6X, 'AVERAGE OF THE GRADES IS:', F6.2)
        STOP
        END
```

FIGURE 10.3

Arrays can be used to aid in handling character variables. Recall the inconvenient way that has been used to read or write characters. For example, suppose we had to read a person's name that had, say, 20 characters. We would have had to write a READ statement such as:

```
   READ (5, 10) NAME1, NAME2, NAME3, NAME4,
10  FORMAT (5A4)
```

Such character manipulation becomes quite easy by using arrays. To read 20 characters as a student name, all that is required is to declare a variable to be an array large enough to hold all characters and then use the array name (or the subscripted variables) in all READ and/or WRITE statements. Thus, our previous example becomes:

```
   DIMENSION NAME(5)
   READ (5, 10) NAME
10  FORMAT (5A4)
```

Note that READ (5, 10) NAME is equivalent to READ (5, 10) NAME(1), NAME(2), NAME(3), NAME(4), NAME(5).

If you wanted to have one character per location, then you could write:

```
   DIMENSION NAME(20)
   READ (5, 10) NAME
10  FORMAT (20A1)
```

This READ statement is equivalent to:

READ (5, 10) NAME (1), NAME (2), . . . , NAME (20)

20 subscripted variable names

See Appendix II on how to declare character variables in ANSI 77.

Example 10.3

Write a FORTRAN program to read and write each student record and calculate and print the average grade. The number of students in the class can be at most 60; however, a class may contain fewer than 60 students. One way to accomplish this is to organize the input data so that first we read the number of students in the class. Then the number of student records to be processed has been determined by the previous number read.

Input record:

FIRST INPUT RECORD TYPE

CC	FIELD	TYPE	LENGTH
1–2	Number of students	Integer	2
3–17	Class name	Character	15

CC	FIELD	TYPE	LENGTH
1–3	Grade	Integer	3
4–23	Name	Character	20
24–60	Address	Character	37

Figure 10.4 is the flowchart and the pseudo codes for the program, and Figure 10.5 is the program.

In the previous example, we used the name IGRADE in order to have an integer array. However, we could have used the name GRADE by changing its mode from REAL to INTEGER by means of the INTEGER statement. Thus, the following two statements declare GRADE to be a one-dimensional interger array with 20 elements:

```
INTEGER GRADE
DIMENSION GRADE(20)
```

In ANSI FORTRAN and FORTRAN IV, the order of these two statements is insignificant. However, some compilers consider the order above to be significant.

Pseudo Code Form

```
Start
DOWHILE Not end of data
Read N class
    Write N, class
    Initialize SUM to 0 and J to 1
    DOWHILE J ≤ N
            Read IGRADE(J), NAME, ADDR
            Write IGRADE(J), NAME, ADDR
            Add IGRADE(J) to SUM
            Add 1 to J
    END DOWHILE
    AVRG = SUM/N
    Write AVRG
END DOWHILE
STOP
```

FIGURE 10.4   Using arrays to process one or more class lists

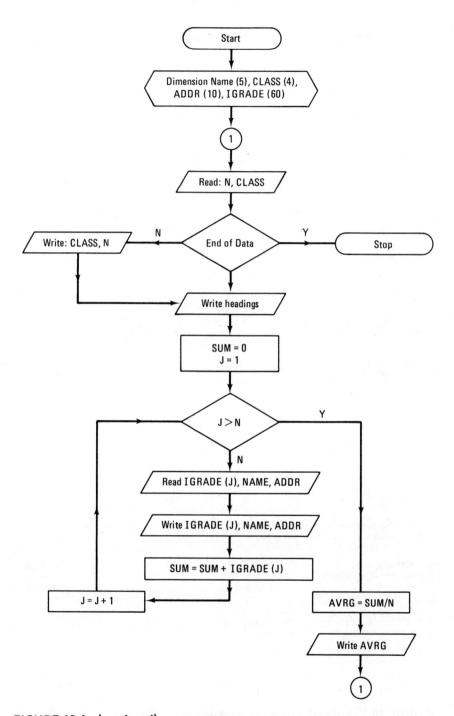

FIGURE 10.4 (continued)

```
C          ADDR   :  STUDENT'S ADDRESS
C          IGRADE :  AN ARRAY FOR STUDENT GRADES IN THE CLASS
C          COURSE :  THE MANE OF THE COURSE
C          N      :  NUMBER OF STUDENTS IN THE CLASS
C          J      :  COUNTER
C          SUM    :  SUM OF GRADES
C
C PROGRAM NARRATIVE:   THERE ARE TWO TYPES OF INPUT RECORDS OF THIS
C PROGRAM.   THE PROGRAM FIRST READS THE FIRST TYPE RECORD WHICH
C CONTAINS NUMBER OF STUDENTS AND THE CLASS NAME.   THEN THE PROGRAM
C READS THE SECOND TYPE INPUT RECORD WHICH HAS STUDENT GRADES,
C NAMES AND ADDRESSES.   THE PROGRAM CLACULATES AND PRINTS THE
C AVERAGE.
C
C************************************************************************
C
C ALLOCATE TABLES FOR GRADES, STUDENT NAME,
C ADDRESS, COURSE TITLE
C
          DIMENSION  NAME(5), ADDRS(10), IGRADE(60), COURSE(4)
          INTEGER   CARD
          CARD = 5
          LINE = 6
C
C READ NUMBER OF STUDENTS FROM THE FIRST CARD
C
  10      READ (CARD, 20, END = 100) N, COURSE
  20      FORMAT (I2, 3A4, A3)
C                          .
C WRITE THE TLTLE OF NEW COURSE AND NUMBER OF STUDENTS
C
          WRITE (LINE, 30) COURSE, N
  30      FORMAT ('1', 4(/), T6, 3A4, A3//, 8X, 'NUMBER',
      +        'OF STUDENTS LISTED IN THE COURSE:', I2)
C
C WRITE COLUMN HEADINGS
          WRITE (LINE, 40)
  40      FORMAT (1X, T6, 'NAME', T30, 'GRADE', T50, 'ADDRESS')
C
C RE-INITIALIZE THE SUM TO 0 AND J TO 1
C
          SUM = 0.0
          J = 1
C
C START THE INNER LOOP
C IF J IS GREATER THAN N END THE LOOP
C
  50      IF (J .GT. N) GO TO 80
C
C ELSE REPEAT LOOP
          READ (CARD, 60) IGRADE(J), NAME, ADDRS
  60      FORMAT (I3, 5A4, 9A4, A1)
          WRITE (LINE, 70) NAME, IGRADE(J), ADDRS
  70      FORMAT (1X, T6, 5A4, T30, I3, T45, 9A4, A1)
          SUM = SUM + IGRADE(J)
C
C INCREMENT THE SUBSCRIPT J. NOTE J ALSO
C USED AS A COUNTER
          J = J + 1
          GO TO 50
  80      AVRG = SUM/FLOAT(N)
          WRITE (LINE, 90) AVRG
  90      FORMAT (3(/), 1X, T6, 'THE AVERAGE GRADE IN THIS CLASS IS:', F6.2)
C GO BACK TO PROCESS ANOTHER CLASS LIST
          GO TO 10
 100      STOP
          END
```

FIGURE 10.5   Program for processing class lists

The first statement declares GRADE to be an integer variable, and the second declares GRADE to be an array. But FORTRAN allows the programmer to write the following single statement with the same effect:

```
INTEGER GRADE(20)
```

Here, one single statement declares GRADE to be an integer array of 20 elements. This approach is preferred, because it is simpler and easier to follow.

By the same token, the specification statements REAL and LOGICAL can also be used to create arrays.

Example 10.4

1. The statement:

```
REAL   INTRST(50), RATE(3, 20), J(100,50)
```

declares a real one-dimensional array INTRST, and two real two-dimensional arrays RATE and J.

The following statements have the same effect:

```
REAL   INTRST, J
DIMENSION   INTRST(50), RATE(3, 20), J(100, 50)
```

2. The statement:

```
LOGICAL   FTST(20, 10), STST(50)
```

declares FTST to be a two-dimensional logical array and also declares STST to be a one-dimensional logical array. The following statements have the same effect:

```
LOGICAL   FTST, STST

DIMENSION   FTST(20,10), STST(50)
```

3. The statement:

```
INTEGER   X(50, 20), RANDOM(100)
```

declares an integer two-dimensional array X and an integer one-dimensional array RANDOM.

Another way to declare an array is by means of the COMMON statement, which is discussed in Chapter 14.

10.3   DATA STATEMENT

The DATA statement is a nonexecutable statement used to initialize values for variables; it may appear anywhere in a program after the specification statement. This initialization is performed during compilation, which makes processing more efficient.

The general form of the DATA statement is:

```
DATA V1, V2,..., Vn/d1, d2,...dn,/,/U1, U2,...,Un/c1, c2, ..., cn/
```

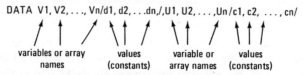

|variables or array names | values (constants) | variable or array names | values (constants) |

The DATA statement assigns $d1$ as the value of $V1$, $d2$ to $V2$, $d3$ to $V3$, and so on. Similarly, $c1$ is assigned as the value of $U1$, $c2$ to $U2$, and so on. The constant must be in the same mode as the variable names.

In many examples, we used the two arithmetic assignment statements:

```
ICARD = 5
```

```
LINE = 6
```

to assign 5 to ICARD and 6 to LINE. The following DATA statement initializes the value of ICARD to 5 and LINE to 6. That is, it has the same effect as the two assignment statements above.

```
DATA ICARD, LINE/5, 6/
```

Note that the order of ICARD, LINE, 5, and 6 is significant.

Example 10.5

1. The DATA statement:

```
DATA ICOUNT, SUM, A, B, LAST/1, 0.0, 5.25, 8., 99/
```

makes the value of ICOUNT 1, of SUM 0, of A 5.25, of B 8.0, and of LAST 99.

Please remember that the values of the variable are assigned according to their order of appearance in the listing, and moreover that the mode of the variable and the associated value must be the same.

The single DATA statement above has the same effect as the following five arithmetic assignment statements:

```
ICOUNT = 1
```

```
SUM = 0.0
```

```
A = 5.25
```

```
B = 8.0
```

```
LAST = 99
```

2. One can write several groups in a DATA statement instead of a single group. The following DATA statement has the same effect as the one in part 1 above:

DATA ICOUNT, SUM/1, 0.0/, A, B, LAST/5.25, 8.0, 99/

↑

mandatory
comma

It can be written like this also:

DATA   ICOUNT/1/,SUM/0.0/,A/5.25/,B/8.0/,LAST/99/

3. As with the specification statements, the effects of the DATA statements are collective. For example, one, two, three, four, or even five DATA statements could be written instead of the single DATA statement in number 1. Thus, the following two DATA statements have the same effect as that one:

DATA   SUM, ICOUNT,   LAST/0.0, 1, 99/

DATA   A/5.25/, B/8.0/

4. The DATA statement can be used to initialize the value of logical variables or to assign characters as the value of variables. The statements:

LOGICAL TEST1, TEST2

DATA I, TEST1, FINSH, TEST2, R/0, .TRUE., 'YES', .FALSE., 50.5/

initialize the value of I to 0, of TEST1 to .TRUE., of FINSH to 'YES', of TEST2 to .FALSE., and of R to 50.50.

5. *Use of the repeator symbol* (∗): When a number of variables are to have the same value, the repeator symbol (an integer followed by an asterisk, followed by the repetitive value) is used. The following two data statements are equivalent:

DATA   I, J, ICOUNT, ISUM/0, 0, 0, 0/

and

DATA I, J, ICOUNT, ISUM/4 ∗ 0/

↗ ↑ ↘

repeator asterisk value
factor

The DATA statement:

DATA   ICOUNT, J, N, A, B, C, D, E/3*1,5*10.20/

assigns 1 as the value for ICOUNT, J, and N, and 10.20 as the value for A, B, C, D, and E.

6. *Initializing the value of arrays:*

INTEGER COUNT(5)

DIMENSION RATE (3), B(4)

DATA COUNT, RATE, B/5*0, 4*5.7, 3*1.0/

The data statement above initializes all five elements of the integer array COUNT to 0, the value of all three elements of the array RATE to 5.7, the first value of the array B (namely, B[1]) to 5.7, and its last three elements (B[2], B[3] and B[4]) to 1.0.

7. To initialize the elements of two dimensional arrays, you must be aware that FORTRAN is column-oriented. In other words, the first column will be filled first, then the second column, and so on. Suppose we want R to be the following two-dimensional array:

$$R = \begin{pmatrix} 0.0 & 1.0 & 1.0 \\ 0.0 & 1.0 & 4.0 \\ 0.0 & 1.0 & 4.0 \\ 1.0 & 1.0 & 4.0 \end{pmatrix}$$

Then the statement:

```
DIMENSION R(4, 3)
DATA R/3*0.0, 6*1.0, 3*4.0/
```

will initialize the elements of R as indicated above. Note that the DATA statement above is equivalent to:

```
DATA R/0.0,0.0,0.0,1.0,1.0,1.0,1.0,1.0,1.0,4.0,4.0,4.0/
```

The following statement initializes all 5,000 elements of the two-dimensional array X to 0:

```
DIMENSION X(50, 100)
DATA  X/5000*0.0/
```

10.4   SUMMARY

An array (table) is a group of related data. The entire array can be referred to by a single name, and an individual element can be referenced by the array name followed by the appropriate subscript. The subscript can be an integer constant or an integer variable or an expression. The value of the subscript must be a positive integer (0 is not allowed). In FORTRAN, arrays of up to seven dimensions are permitted.

A variable can be declared to be an array by means of the specification statements DIMENSION, INTEGER, REAL, or LOGICAL. The DATA statement is used to initialize the value of a variable at compilation time. All the specification statements must be written at the beginning of the program, before any executable statement.

1. Write a DIMENSION statement to declare EXPENS to be a two-dimensional array with 50 rows and 100 columns, and COUNT to be a 200-element one-dimensional array.

2.   `DIMENSION ALPHA(26)`

Write a DATA statement so that the value of ALPHA(1) is the letter A, ALPHA(2) is the letter B, and so on. That is, ALPHA(1), . . ., ALPHA(26) should contain the 26 letters of the English alphabet from A to Z, respectively.

3. How does the FORTRAN compiler recognize a subscripted variable?

4. Can the subscript itself be a subscripted variable?

5. Which of the following arithmetic expressions are not acceptable subscripted forms?

    J + 5
    5 + J
    I − 5
    50 − K
    J * 3 + 2
    3 * J + 2
    9
    K
    R
    5 * N
    N * 5
    2 * J − 3
    2 + 3 * J

6. What happens if the value of a subscript becomes greater than the maximum limit stated in the DIMENSION statement or less than 1?

7. *True or False.* The statements:

    `DIMENSION X(50)`

    `WRITE (6, 10) X`

    `10    FORMAT ('B', F7.2/)`

cause the elements of the array X to be printed on 50 lines, each line containing one element.

8. Write the necessary WRITE and FORMAT statements to print all the

elements of X, five elements per line, with lines separated by four spaces of the following:

```
DIMENSION X(50)
```

9. Write a DIMENSION statement to create the following arrays:
   a. One-dimensional array DEPRMT to hold department names, which can be as long as 20 characters.
   b. One-dimensional array CUSAD to hold customer's address. The maximum allowable length for the customer address is 40 characters.

10. Write a DIMENSION statement to create the following two-dimensional arrays:
   a. The two-dimensional array X with 50 rows and 100 columns. Each element of X must be an integer.
   b. The two-dimensional array PLANTS. Each element of the array can be as large as 35 characters. PLANTS contains the addresses of the branches of the ABC Corporation in its 20 districts. Each district has 30 branches.

11. Suppose we have the following two arrays:

$$X = \begin{pmatrix} 50.5 \\ 79.5 \\ 200.6 \\ 300.4 \end{pmatrix} \qquad K = \begin{pmatrix} 1 & 6 & 0 \\ 5 & 7 & 8 \\ 3 & 2 & 1 \end{pmatrix}$$

What will be the value of X(INDX) in each of the following?

```
a.  INDX = K(2, 2) - K(3,1)

b.  J = K(1,1) + K(3,3)
    N = K(2,3) - K(1,2)
    I = K(2,1) * K(1,3)
    INDX = J + N + I

c.  I = K(3,1)
    INDX = K(3,2) + K(3,3)
    X(INDX) = X(2 * I - 2) - X(INDX)
```

```
12.    DIMENSION X(4), N(6)
       LOGICAL TEST, PASS
       DATA X,R,TEST,TAIL/3*0.0,2*1.0,.TRUE.,'***'/N,K,/
       PASS 7*0,.FALSE./
```

With declaration above:

X(1) =	, X(2) =	, X(3) =	, X(4) =	, R =
TEST =	, TAIL =	, N(1) =	, N(2) =	, N(3) =
N(4) =	, N(5) =	, N(6) =	, K =	, PASS

13.

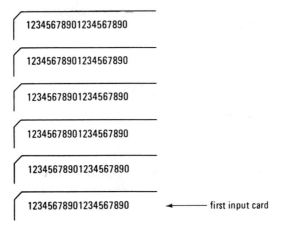

12345678901234567890

12345678901234567890

12345678901234567890

12345678901234567890

12345678901234567890

12345678901234567890   ◄──────── first input card

Assume the input cards above for all parts of this problem.

a. DIMENSION X(6)
    READ (5,10) X
10 FORMAT(6F3.2)

Then:
X(1) =   , X(2) =   , X(3) =   , X(4) =   , X(5) =
X(6) = .

b. DIMENSION X(6)
    READ (5,10) X
10 FORMAT (F3.2)

Then:
X(1) =   , X(2) =   , X(3) =   , X(4) =   , X(5) =
X(6) = .

c. REAL RATE (3,2)

    READ (5, 10) RATE

10 FORMAT (6F3.2)

Then:
RATE(1, 1) =   , RATE(1, 2) =   , RATE(2, 1) =   ,
RATE(2, 2) =   , RATE(3, 1) =   , RATE(3, 2) =   .

14. Write a FORTRAN program to read the arrays BALANS and PAY and calculate from these two a new real array NBLANS. Each of these are 100-

element one-dimensional arrays. The data are punched on 100 cards. Each card is organized as follows:

CC	FIELD	TYPE	LENGTH
1–6	An element of the array BALANS	Real	6
7–12	An element of the array PAY	Real	6

The ith element of NBLANS is calculated as follows:

NBLANS(I) = BALANS(I) − PAY(I) + 3% interest if the new balance is not zero

Your FORTRAN program should also print all three arrays.

15. Redo problem 14; this time, first all elements of BALANS (16 elements per card) are to be read, followed by all elements of PAY (16 elements per card).

16. Suppose we have DIMENSION RATE(30). Write a FORTRAN program to find the largest (maximum) and the smallest (minimum) elements of the array RATE. Your program should also calculate the range (the difference between the maximum and minimum). Print all the element of RATE and the maximum, the minimum, and the RANGE.

17. The commission percentage paid to salespeople at ABC Wholesale Company depends on the type of product sold. ABC sells ten products. Write a FORTRAN program to process an input record, calculate the amount of commission to be paid to each salesperson, the amount sold by each salesperson, the total sales, and the total commission paid. The program should print each salesperson's number, name, address, telephone number, total sales, and commission under appropriate headings and captions. You should use arrays to store the commission percentages, names, and addresses. The input data are organized as follows:

There are three different types of input cards.

    a. Type I data card contains ten fields. Each field is real, of length 4, and represents the commission percentage for each product. There is only one such card per run.

    b. Type II data card:

CC	FIELD	TYPE	LENGTH
1–5	Salesperson's number	Integer	5
6–25	Name	Character	20
26–33	Telephone number	Character	7
34–70	Address	Character	35

    There is one type II data card for each salesperson.

    c. Type III data card:

CC	FIELD	TYPE	LENGTH
1–2	Product type	Integer	2
3–10	Sales amount	Real (XXXX.XX)	6
11	Flag	Character	1

Each type II card is followed by one or more cards of type III, depending upon the number of sales made by the salesperson. The flag field of the last type III card for each salesperson contains *. Thus, if flag equals *, you know that the next card will be a type II card for a new salesperson. *Hint:* The amount of commission paid for sale of product J is Amount * COMIS(J), where COMIS is the commission percentage array.

11 DO STATEMENT, LOOPS, AND TABLE HANDLING

11.1 DO STATEMENT

11.1.1 FORTRAN IV's DO Statement

In many previous programs (such as example 10.2), we used a counter (index) and IF and GO TO statements to control a loop so that it is executed a certain number of times. For example, the following loop adds together the 50 elements of the one-dimensional array X:

```
DIMENSION X(50)
SUM = 0.0
J = 1                    Initial value of the counter J
10   SUM = SUM + X(J)
J = J + 1                        Loop
IF (J .LE. 50) GO TO 10
STOP
```

The flowchart for the loop above is shown in Figure 11.1.

Such processes start by initializing the index to some value (such as 1 above), go through the instructions in the loop, increment the index (1 added to J above), and test the index to see if it has exceeded the limiting value (50 above). If yes, then the loop is terminated.

Because similar procedures for controlling the execution of loops are often needed in many programs, the FORTRAN language has implemented the DO

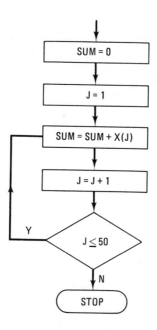

FIGURE 11.1

statement to save the programmer the overhead work of initializing, incrementing, and testing loop indices.

As an example of how the DO statement simplifies loop handling, Figure 11.2 shows the DO statement to accomplish the same task as before—namely, finding the sum of the 50 elements of the one-dimensional array X.

The DO statement during execution produces the following actions:

1. The index J is initialized to 1, the first number after the = sign.
2. The statements in the range of the DO loop (the statements following the DO statement through the statement labeled 20) are executed.
3. When the last statement:

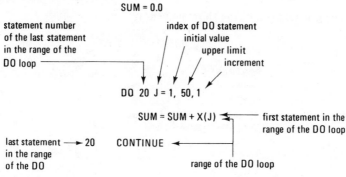

FIGURE 11.2

20   CONTINUE

in the range of the DO loop is encountered, first the value of J is incremented by 1 (the third number after the = sign), and then if the new value of J is less than or equal to the upper limit (50, which is the second number after the = sign), control is transferred back to the first statement in the range of the DO loop—that is, to the statement:

SUM = SUM + X(J)

4. Control exits from the loop if the value of J becomes greater than 50 (upper limit).

The flowcharting preprocessing symbol:

is used for the DO statement. The flowchart for the program above using the DO statement is shown in Figure 11.3. The dotted line indicates that the control returns automatically to the first statement in the range if $J \leq 50$.

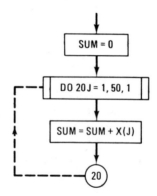

FIGURE 11.3

The general form of the DO statement is:

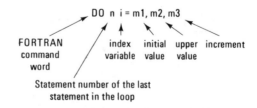

where:

n is the statement number of the last statement in the loop.

i   is the index variable. It must be an unsigned, nonsubscripted integer variable.

m1 is the initial value of the index variable. It is a nonsubscripted integer variable or a positive integer constant.

m2 is the upper limit of the index variable. It is a nonsubscripted variable or a positive integer constant.

m3 is the increment. It is a nonsubscripted integer variable or an integer constant. If *m3* is omitted, 1 is assumed.

The following rules must be observed when DO statements are used:

1. The last statement in the range of the DO loop (labeled *n*) must be an executable statement. It cannot be any of the following statements:

   STOP
   GO TO
   IF
   another DO statement

   The executable statement CONTINUE is often used as the last statement in the range of the DO loop. It can be used to terminate a DO loop if you are unsure whether another statement is valid.

2. Within the range of the DO loop, the variables i, *m1, m2*, and *m3* cannot be redefined.

3. At completion of the DO loop, the value of the index variable *i* becomes undefined.

4. The index variable *i* retains its current value if control is transferred outside the DO loop before completion of the DO loop.

5. When the DO loop is completed (all iterations are performed), then execution proceeds with the first executable statement following the last statement in the range of the DO loop.

6. Many smaller FORTRAN compilers require that $m1 \leq m2$ and *m3* be positive. However, both FORTRAN IV and ANSI FORTRAN 77 permit $m1 > m2$, provided that *m3* (or the value of *m3*) is a negative integer constant. In this case, *m3* represents the decrement, *m2* will be the lower limit, and the process continues until the value of the index variable becomes less than the lower limit (*m2*).

The flowcharts in Figure 11.4 help clarify the behavior of the DO loop in FORTRAN IV. In general, when the DO statement is encountered in FORTRAN IV, the following actions are performed:

1. The value of index variable *i* is initialized to *m1*.

2. All statements in the range of the DO loop are executed. When the last statement is encountered, the following two actions occur:

a. First, the value of the index variable i is changed by the increment $m3$.
b. If the value of the index variable $i \leq m2$, control is transferred back to the first statement in the range of the DO loop. Otherwise, control "falls through" the loop and executes the statement immediately following the last statement in the range of the DO loop.

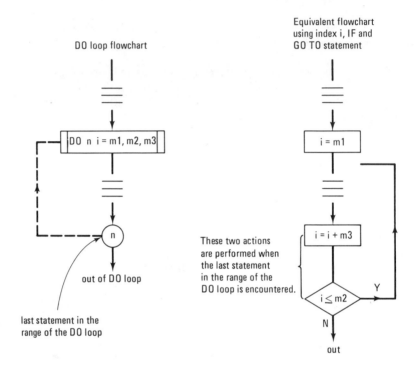

FIGURE 11.4

Because test of the index i is performed after execution of the last statement in the range of the DO loop, whenever the DO statement is encountered, all statements in the range of the DO loop are executed at least once.

11.1.2 ANSI FORTRAN 77's DO
Statement

The DO statement in both FORTRAN IV and ANSI FORTRAN 77 has the same format—namely, DO n i = $m1$, $m2$, $m3$, where n, i, $m1$, $m2$, and $m3$ have the same meanings in both FORTRANs. Recall that the DO statement in FORTRAN IV is a trailing-decision DO (that is, the test is performed at the end of the loop). However, the DO statement of ANSI FORTRAN 77 is a leading-decision DO (tests the condition at the beginning of the DO loop). This means that the statements within the range of the DO loop may never be executed.

This will happen if the initial value of the iteration counter is less than or equal to zero. More specifically, in ANSI FORTRAN 77, when the DO statement is encountered, the following actions are performed:

1. The value of the index i is initialized to $m1$.
2. An iteration counter is established and its value set to $(m2 - m1 + m3)/m3$.
3. If the value of the iteration counter > 0, then all statements in the range of the DO loop are executed. Otherwise, the loop is terminated and control transfers to the statement that follows the last statement in the range of the DO loop.
4. The value of the iteration counter is decreased by 1.
5. The control returns to step 3.

The flowchart in Figure 11.5 will clarify these actions of the DO statement in ANSI FORTRAN 77.

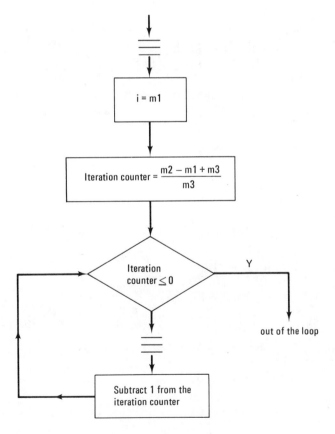

FIGURE 11.5

The CONTINUE statement is an executable statement that instructs the computer to keep on executing statements in sequence. In other words, the CONTINUE statement is a dummy statement and has no effect on execution.

Example 11.1

The results of executing the following two sets of statements are the same:

```
RATE = 5.50                    RATE = 5.50
PAY = HOURS * RATE             CONTINUE
TAX = PAY * 0.15               PAY = HOURS * RATE
NTPAY = PAY — TAX              TAX = PAY * 0.15
                               CONTINUE
                               NTPAY = PAY — TAX
```

The following two programs produce the same results:

```
          DIMENSION X(50)
          SUM = 0.0
          DO 30 .I = 1, 50
              READ (5,10) X(I)
Range  10     FORMAT (F6.2)
of            WRITE (6,20) X(I)
DO     20     FORMAT ('0',6X,F7.2)
Loop   30     SUM = SUM + X(I)
          AVRG = SUM/50.
          WRITE (6,40) AVRG
       40 FORMAT ('1',6X,'AVERAGE IS:',F7.2)
          STOP
          END
```

```
          DIMENSION X(50)
          SUM = 0.0
          DO 30 I = 1, 50
              READ (5,10) X(I)
       10     FORMAT (F6.2)
              WRITE (6,20) X(I)
       20     FORMAT ('0',6X,F7.2)
              SUM = SUM + X(I)
       30 CONTINUE
          AVRG = SUM/50.
          WRITE (6,40) AVRG
       40 FORMAT ('1',6X,'AVERAGE IS:',F7.2)
          STOP
          END
```

Example 11.2

After the execution of the following statements:

```
    N = 50
    DO 10 J = 1, 20, 3
    IF (J * 10 .GE. N) GO TO 20
10  CONTINUE
20  R = (N + J)/2.0
    STOP
```

the value of J is 7 and R = 28.5. The statements in the range of the DO loop are executed three times.

If the statement N = 50 is changed to N = 500, then the loop will be completed when the value of J becomes 22. However, the value of J becomes undefined outside the range of the DO loop.

In the example above, we have to use the CONTINUE statement, because the last statement in the range of the DO loop is an IF statement.

Example 11.3

Suppose X, Y, and Z are each 100-element, one-dimensional arrays. Write a program using DO loops to create the array *Z* from the arrays X and Y in the following manner.

The odd elements of the array Z (such as Z(1), Z(3), Z(5), . . ., Z(99)) are calculated by multiplying the corresponding odd element of X by 7 and adding it to the corresponding odd elements of Y. That is, if I is odd:

$$Z(I) = 7 * X(I) + Y(I)$$

The even elements of Z (Z(2), Z(4), . . ., Z(100)) are calculated from the relationship:

$$Z(I) = X(I) - Y(I) * 2 + 10$$

when I is even.

Figure 11.6 is the flowchart for the program for this problem.

Flowchart explanation: The key to solving the problem above is that when the odd elements are involved, we can start the index I with the odd number 1 and keep it odd by making the increment 2. Hence, the values of the index I will be 1, 3, 5, and so on. This is accomplished by the DO statement:

$$DO\ 20\ I = 1,\ 100,\ 2$$

in box 4. The DO statement in box 7 maintains an even index for the even · elements of Z.

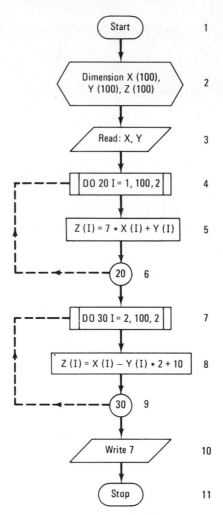

FIGURE 11.6 Manipulation of arrays using DO loops

TABLE 11.1 The first DO loop

ITERATION NUMBER (CYCLE)	INDEX I	INITIAL VALUE	UPPER LIMIT	INCRE-MENT	Z(I)	TEST I ≤ UPPER LIMIT
1	1	1	100	2	$Z(1) = 7*X(1)+Y(1)$	Yes
2	3				$Z(3) = 7*X(3)+Y(3)$	Yes
3	5				$Z(5) = 7*X(5)+Y(5)$	Yes
•	•				•	•
•	•				•	•
•	•				•	•
•	•					
50	99				$Z(99) = 7*X(99)+$ $Y(99)$	Yes
	101					NO

242

Table 11.1 goes through the instructions in the first DO loop (boxes 4, 5, and 6) to demonstrate a technique that is helpful in checking DO loops. At the end of each cycle, the value of I is increased by 2. When cycle 50 is completed, the value of I becomes 101, which is bigger than the upper limit, so that control exits from the DO loop and executes the next instruction (which is in box 7). Below is the FORTRAN program for the problem above.

```
        DIMENSION X(100), Y(100), Z(100)
        READ (5,10) X,Y
10      FORMAT (200 F7.2)
C CALCULATE THE ODD ELEMENTS OF Z
        DO 20 I = 1, 100, 2
            Z(I) = 7 * X(I) + Y(I)
20      CONTINUE
C CALCULATE THE EVEN ELEMENTS OF Z
        DO 30 I = 2, 100, 2
            Z(I) = X(I) - Y(I) * 2 + 10
30      CONTINUE
        WRITE (6,40) Z
40      FORMAT ('0', 6X, F8.2)
        STOP
        END
```

Example 11.4

Write a DO loop to find the sum of all integers between 1 and 30 that are evenly divisible by 7.

```
    INTEGER SUM
    SUM = 0
    DO 10 K = 7, 28, 7
        SUM = SUM + K
10  CONTINUE
```

ITERATION	INDEX K	INITIAL	UPPER	INCREMENT	SUM	TEST K ≤ 28
		7	28	7	0.0	
1	7				7	
2	14				21	Yes
3	21				42	Yes
4	28				70	Yes
	35					No

Example 11.5

Suppose our FORTRAN compiler allows $m1 > m2$. Then we can do example 11.4, but this time we start with a large initial value and decrease the index variable in every iteration.

```
      INTEGER SUM
      SUM = 0
      DO 10 K = 28, 7, -7
          SUM = SUM + K
10    CONTINUE
```

ITERATION	INDEX K	INITIAL	LOWER	DECREMENT	SUM	TEST K ≥ 7
		28	7	-7	0	
1	28				28	
2	21				49	Yes
3	14				63	Yes
4	7				70	Yes
	0					No

Example 11.6

There are many ways to do any problem. For example, here are some other ways to do example 11.4:

```
1. INTEGER SUM
      N = 7
      SUM = 0.0
      DO 10 K = 1,4
          SUM = SUM + N
          N = N + 7
10    CONTINUE
```

```
2. INTEGER SUM
      N = 7
      SUM = 0.0
      DO 10 K = 1,100
          SUM = SUM + N
          N = N + 7
          IF (N .GT. 28) STOP
10    CONTINUE
```

```
3.   INTEGER SUM
     N = 28
     SUM = 0.0
     DO 10 K = 1, 200
         SUM = SUM + N
         N = N - 7
         IF (N .LT. 7) STOP
10   CONTINUE
```

Example 11.7

The following statements are not valid.

```
DO 10 I = 1, 10, 0.5
```

Neither index variable nor upper value nor the increment can be a real variable or a real constant. The real number 0.5 is not allowed to be an increment.

```
DO 10 I = 1, M(N), J
```

Neither the initial nor the upper limit nor the increment can be a subscripted variable. The DO statement above can be written as:

```
L = M(N)
DO 10 I = 1, L, J
```

11.3   RULES FOR TRANSFER OF CONTROL IN DO LOOP

1. Control can be transferred between any two points within the range of the DO loop. This can be portrayed as:

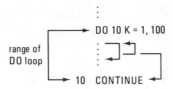

For example, the following GO TO statements are permitted:

```
    DO 20 K = 1, 100
          IF (K .EQ. (K/2) * 2) GO TO 10
          GO TO 20
10        SUMEV = SUMEV + K
20  CONTINUE
```

2. Control can be transferred from any point within the range of the DO loop to outside the range of the DO loop:

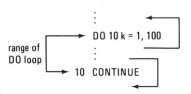

The transfers caused by the IF statement in the following are valid:

```
        DIMENSION X(50)
        SUM = 0.0
        DO 20 J = 1, 50
              READ (5, 10) X(J)
              IF (X(J)) 30, 30, 10
10            SUM = SUM + X(J)
20      CONTINUE
30      AVRG = SUM/(J − 1)
        .
        .
```

3. Transfer of control is not permitted from a point outside the range of a DO loop to a point inside the range of the loop. The following transfers are not allowed:

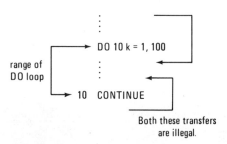

The following GO TO is not permitted:

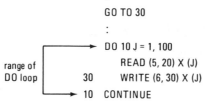

```
                         :
                 GO TO 30
                         :
                ┌────► DO 10 J = 1, 100
  range of      │           READ (5, 20) X (J)
  DO loop       │   30      WRITE (6, 30) X (J)
                └────► 10  CONTINUE
```

4. Control can be transferred from a point outside the range of the DO loop to the DO statement itself. This process initializes the DO loop. The following is permissible:

```
         •
         •
    GO TO 10
         •
         •
         •
10   DO 20 J = 1, 50
         •
         •
         •
20   CONTINUE
         •
         •
    IF (SIGNL .NE. '*') GO TO 10
```

11.4   NESTED DO LOOPS

When a DO loop is placed inside another DO loop, the inner loop is said to be "nested." Nesting may be carried out to any desired extent as long as the following organizational conditions are met:

1. The inner loop must be completely contained in the outer loop. The following arrangement shows one such organization:

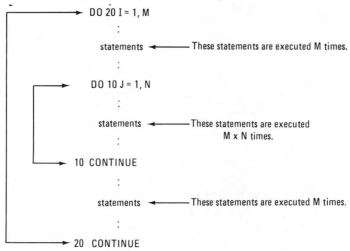

An example of this type of arrangement is:

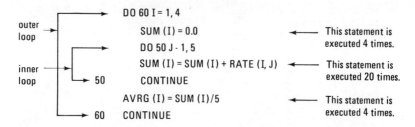

In the example above, each of the four cycles of the outer loop includes five cycles of the inner loop. Some other possibilities include:

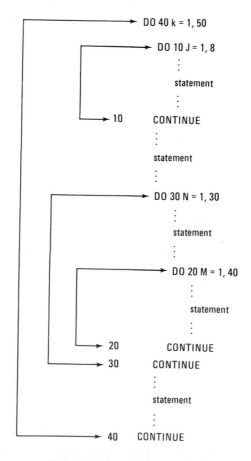

The following example is invalid, because the DO loops overlap:

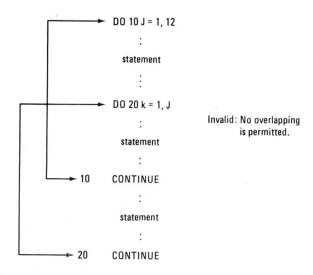

2. Nested DO loops may end at the same statement. The following is a valid example:

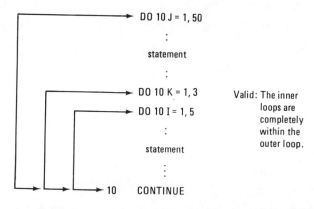

3. The same variable cannot be used as an index variable for both the inner and outer loops in the same nest. The following is an invalid nested DO loop:

```
    DO 10 J = 1, 50      Invalid: The same index
    DO 10 J = 1, 20      variable cannot be used
          X(J) = 0.0     for the inner and outer
10  CONTINUE             loops.
```

4. An inner DO loop must not change the value of the parameters of the outer loop:

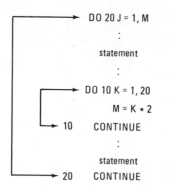

Invalid: This statement changes the value of M, which is the upper limit of the outer DO loop.

5. The index of an outer DO loop is available to the inner one as a starting or limiting value or as an internal value. The following is valid:

```
DO  20  J = 1,  20
        .
        .
        .
    statement
        .
        .
        .
DO  10  K = J,  20
        .
        .
        .
IF (J * 3 .GE.  100) STOP
        .
        .
        .
10  CONTINUE
        .
        .
        .
    statement
        .
        .
        .
20  CONTINUE
```

6. The rules for transferring control in DO loops (section 11.3) must be observed. Examples of valid transfer with nested DO loops are:

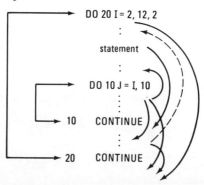

The following are invalid branches:

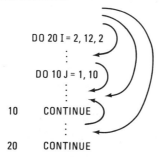

11.5   IMPLIED DO LOOPS

In Chapter 10, we learned how to instruct the computer to read the values of all elements in an array. For example, the following causes the values of all elements of the array IGRADE to be read at once:

```
DIMENSION IGRADE(6)
READ (5, 10) IGRADE
10  FORMAT (6, I3)
```

Note that the FORTRAN statement controls the number of cards that should be read. As explained in section 10.2, this READ statement is equivalent to:

```
READ (5, 10) IGRADE(1), IGRADE(2), IGRADE(3),
IGRADE(4), IGRADE(5), IGRADE(6)
```

Another way to input (or output) arrays is by using what is known as the implied DO loop. The READ statement using the implied DO that is equivalent to the two READ statements above is:

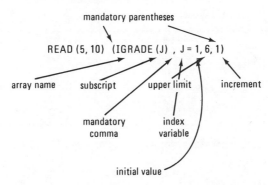

Usually, the increment is omitted if it is 1. Thus, the READ above can be written as:

```
READ (5, 10) (IGRADE(J) , J = 1, 6)
```

The (IGRADE (J), J = 1, 6) implies that the value of the subscript J is to be varied automatically starting from 1 and incremented by 1 until J becomes greater than 6.

The general format for the READ statement using the implied DO loop is:

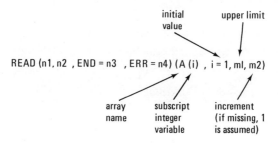

In the example above, the increment *m2* was missing; therefore, 1 was assumed. The statement:

```
READ (5, 10) (IGRADE(J) , J = 1, 60, 2)
```

is equivalent to:

```
READ (5, 10) IGRADE(1), IGRADE(3), IGRADE(5), . . ., IGRADE(59)
```

30 subscripted variables

which reads the value of all odd elements of the array. Note that the increment here is 2.

Thus, using the implied DO, we can read all or any part of an array. Implied DO loops can also be nested.

Example 11.8

Suppose we have the following data, consisting of wages paid per hour for different jobs in various districts:

JOB	DISTRICT 1	DISTRICT 2	DISTRICT 3
Computer operator	$ 4.25	$ 4.50	$ 4.75
Keypuncher	5.00	5.50	5.40
Programmer	7.00	8.50	7.50
Programmer analyst	8.00	9.50	10.50
Systems analyst	10.50	11.00	11.50

We create a two-dimensional array with the name WAGE to store the data in the table above as follows:

```
DIMENSION WAGE (5, 3)
```

Thus, the rows represent the job type and the columns the district.

The statement:

```
READ (5, 10) WAGE
10  FORMAT (15F5.2)
```

reads all the elements of the array WAGE. Because FORTRAN is *column*-oriented (that is, the first column is filled first, then the second column, and so on), the data must be punched first column first, then second column, and so on. More precisely, the data above must be punched as follows:

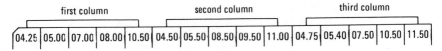

Using the implied DO loop, an equivalent to the READ above is:

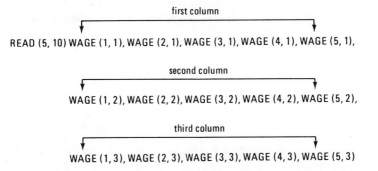

Note that for each cycle of J, the value of I varies five times. The READ above is equivalent to:

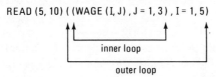

first column

READ (5, 10) WAGE (1, 1), WAGE (2, 1), WAGE (3, 1), WAGE (4, 1), WAGE (5, 1),

second column

WAGE (1, 2), WAGE (2, 2), WAGE (3, 2), WAGE (4, 2), WAGE (5, 2),

third column

WAGE (1, 3), WAGE (2, 3), WAGE (3, 3), WAGE (4, 3), WAGE (5, 3)

As shown, the first subscript varies more rapidly than the second subscript. In other words, the first subscript completes its cycles for each change in the second subscript.

The following READ statement reads the data row by row:

READ (5, 10) ((WAGE (I, J) , J = 1, 3) , I = 1, 5)

inner loop

outer loop

Note that the position of I = 1,5 and J = 1,3 have been reversed from the preceding form. This time, the second subscript varies more rapidly, so that the READ above is equivalent to:

1st row

```
        ┌──────────────┴──────────────┐
READ (5, 10) WAGE (1, 1), WAGE (1, 2), WAGE (1, 3),
```

2nd row

```
     ┌────────────┴────────────┐
WAGE (2, 1), WAGE (2, 2), WAGE (2, 3),
```

3rd row

```
     ┌────────────┴────────────┐
WAGE (3, 1), WAGE (3, 2), WAGE (3, 3),
```

4th row

```
     ┌────────────┴────────────┐
WAGE (4, 1), WAGE (4, 2), WAGE (4, 3),
```

5th row

```
     ┌────────────┴────────────┐
WAGE (5, 1), WAGE (5, 2), WAGE (5, 3)
```

The following READ statement reads only the second and the fourth rows. Note the increment for the first subscript.

```
READ (5, 10) ((WAGE(I, J) , J = 1, 3) , I = 2, 5, 2)
```

The following READ statement reads only the first and the third columns:

```
READ(5,10) ((WAGE(I,J), I = 1,5), J = 1,3,2)
```

Example 11.9

Consider the wage table of example 11.8. Write a FORTRAN program to find the average pay for all jobs in each district and the average pay for each computer-related job in all districts. (In other words, the program requires the average for each row and for each column.) Figure 11.7 is the flowchart diagram for the FORTRAN program for this problem, and a pseudo code for such a program is:

```
Start
Read WAGE
Initialize I to 1
DOWHILE I ≤ 5
        SUM = 0
        Initialize J to 1
        DOWHILE J ≤ 3

            SUM = SUM + WAGE (I,J)
            Add 1 to J
        END DOWHILE
        ROWAVG(I) = SUM/3
        Add 1 to I
END DOWHILE
Write ROWAVG
Initialize J to 1
DOWHILE J ≤ 3
        SUM = 0
        Initialize I to 1
        DOWHILE I ≤ 5
            SUM = SUM + WAGE (I, J)
            Add 1 to I
        END DOWHILE
        COLAVG(J) = SUM/5
        Write J, COLAVG(J)
END DOWHILE
STOP
```

Explanation of the flowchart: The instructions in boxes 5 through 11 are executed in the following manner: At box 5, the first iteration of the outer loop starts:

	ITERATION	INDEX I	INITIAL	UPPER	SUM	TEST I ≤ 5
Outer loop	1	1	1	5	0	

Now, at box 7, the inner loop is encountered. Therefore, all the iterations of the inner loop must be completed before the outer loop repeats. Assuming the data of example 11.8 for the array WAGE, the iterations of the inner loop will be as follows:

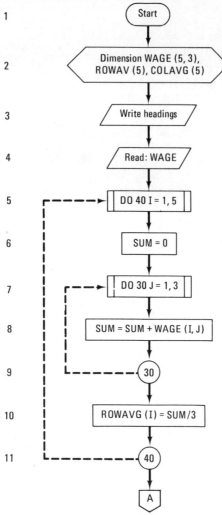

FIGURE 11.7 Flowchart diagram to find the average of each row and each column of a two-dimensional array

	ITER-ATION	INDEX J	INITIAL	UPPER	FORMULA BECOMES	SUM	TEST J ≤ 3
Inner	1	1	1	3	SUM = SUM + WAGE(1,1)	4.25	Yes
loop	2	2			SUM = SUM + WAGE(1,2)	8.75	Yes
in	3	3			SUM = SUM + WAGE(1,3)	13.50	Yes
box 7		4					No

Now the inner loop is completed. Note that in all three iterations, the value of the index variable I of the outer loop (which is the first subscript in WAGE (I, J)) remains 1 (unchanged).

After completion of the inner loop, the instruction in box 10 is executed.

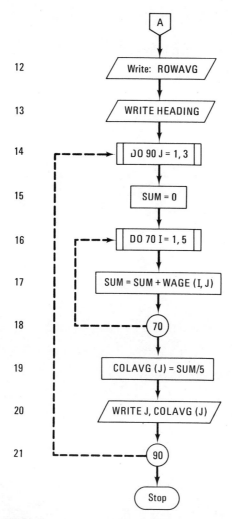

FIGURE 11.7 (Continued)

At this point, the instruction becomes ROWAVG(1) = SUM/3. Thus the average of the first row is calculated. Next, the instruction in box 11 is executed, so that the value of I becomes 2, which is less than 5. Hence, control returns to box 6 and the inner loop will be reinitialized and executed.

The results of the second execution of the inner loop are shown below:

ITER-ATION	INDEX J	INITIAL	UPPER	FORMULA BECOMES	SUM	TEST J ≤ 3
1	1	1	3	SUM = SUM + WAGE(2,1)	5.0	
2	2			SUM = SUM + WAGE(2,2)	10.50	Yes
3	3			SUM = SUM + WAGE(2,3)	15.90	Yes
	4					No

The whole process is repeated until I > 5. The program is shown in Figure 11.8.

```
C FORTRAN PROGRAM TO FIND THE AVERAGE OF EACH ROW AND EACH
C COLUMN OF A TWO DIMENSION ARRAY
C
C THE ARRAY ROWAVG CONTAINS THE AVERAGES FOR ROWS AND COLAVG
C CONTAINS THE AVERAGE FOR COLUMNS
C
          DIMENSION WAGE (5, 3), ROWAVG (5), COLAVG(3)
          INTEGER CARD
          DATA CARD , LINE /5, 6/
C WRITE HEADINGS
C
          WRITE (LINE, 10)
   10     FORMAT ('1', 'THE AVERAGE WAGE PAID FOR DIFFERENT JOB' 5(/))
          WRITE (LINE, 20)
   20     FORMAT('0',T3,'COMUTER',T18,'KEY',T30,'PROGRAMMER',T45,
         + !'PROGRAMMER',T60,'SYSTEM'/,T3,'OPERATOR',T18,'PUNCHER',
         + T45,'ANALYST',T60,'ANALYST'/)
C
C READ THE VALUES OF THE ELEMENTS OF TABLE WAGE
C
          READ(CARD,25) WAGE
   25     FORMAT(15F5.2)
C
C FIND THE AVERAGE OF EACH ROW
C
          DO 40 I = 1, 5
             SUM = 0.0
             DO 30 J = 1, 3
                SUM = SUM + WAGE(I,J)
   30        CONTINUE
          ROWAVG(I) = SUM/3'
   40     CONTINUE
C
          WRITE (LINE, 50) ROWAVG
   50     FORMAT ('0', T3, F5.2, T18, F5.2, T30, F5.2, T45,
         +         F5.2, T60, F5.2)
C
C
C WRITE THE SECOND HEADING
          WRITE (LINE, 60)
   60     FORMAT (5(/), 10X, 'AVERAGE WAGE BY DISTRICT',5(/))
C
C FIND THE AVERAGE OF EACH COLUMN
          DO 90 J = 1, 3
             SUM = 0.0
             DO 70 I = 1, 5
                SUM = SUM + WAGE(I,J)
   70        CONTINUE
          COLAVG(J) = SUM/5
          WRITE (LINE, 80) J, COLAVG(J)
   80     FORMAT ('0', 'AVERAGE WAGE IN DISTRICT -', I1, ' IS: ', F5.2//)
   90     CONTINUE
          STOP
          END
```

FIGURE 11.8 Program to find the average pay for jobs

11.6 SUMMARY

The general form of the DO statement is:

$$DO\ n\ i = m1,\ m2,\ m3$$

where n is the statement number of the last statement in the loop, i the index variable, $m1$ the initial value of the index, $m2$ the upper limit, and $m3$ the increment. Each of $m1$, $m2$, and $m3$ must be a nonsubscripted integer variable or an integer constant. The index i must be a nonsubscripted integer variable. The value 1 is assumed if $m3$ is omitted.

These rules should be observed when using DO loops:

1. The last statement of a DO loop cannot be a STOP, a GO TO, an IF, or another DO statement.
2. The variables i, $m1$, $m2$, and $m3$ cannot be redefined within the range of the DO loop.
3. At the end of completion of a DO loop, the value of the index variable becomes undefined (unavailable). However, the index variable retains its current value if control is transferred outside the range of the DO loop before the completion of all iterations.
4. After the completion of a DO loop, execution proceeds with the first executable statement following the last statement in the range of the DO loop.
5. Control can be transferred between any two points within the range of a DO loop, or from a point within the range of a DO loop to a point outside the range of the DO loop.
6. No transfer is permitted from outside the range of a DO loop to a point within its range.
7. When nested DO loops are used, no overlapping of loops is permitted, and no inner DO loop may change the value of the parameters of an outer loop.
8. The index of an outer DO loop is available to an inner loop as a starting or limiting value for the index of the inner loop or as a value that can be used in calculations.

Implied DO loops are used in conjunction with input/output statements.

The executable statement CONTINUE has no effect on the execution of the program and is often used as the last statement in the range of a DO loop.

11.7 REVIEW QUESTIONS AND SUGGESTED PROBLEMS

Determine the errors, if any, in the following statements:

```
1.    DO 10 I = 5, 20, 0.5
2.    DO 10 I = 5, up, 3
3.    DO 10 R = 5, 10, 3
4.    DO 10 IR = 5, 10, 3
5.    DO 10 IR = 5, 10
```

```
6.        DO 10 IR = 10, 5
7.        DO 50 J = 1, 5
          DO 40 K = 1, 10
          IF (X(J, K) .EQ. 0) IC = IC + 1
   50   CONTINUE
          WRITE (6, 10) X(I, J)
   40   CONTINUE
8.        DO 40 I = 1, M
          J = I + 1
          DO 40 K = J, 100
          IF (I * 10 .GE. 50) M = M - 1
   40   CONTINUE
9.        X = 25.0
          IF (X * 3 .GE. 50) GO TO 10
          DO 20 J = 1, 5
              Y = Y + 1
   10         X = X - Y
   20   CONTINUE
10.       DO 20 K = 1, 100
              Y = Y + 1
   20   IF (Y * K .GT. 500.0) STOP
```

11. In the following nested DO loop, how many times is the statement $N = J + 1$ executed, and how many times are the statements between the second DO and the CONTINUE statement executed?


```
          DO 20 J = 1, 4
          N = J + 1
          DO 20 K = N, 5
          IF (X(J) .LE. X(K)) TO GO 20
          TEM = X(J)
          X(J) = X(K)
          X(K) = TEMP
   20   CONTINUE
```

12. After execution of the following statements, the value of Y is _____, of X is _____ and of I is _____.

```
    Y = 5.5
    X = 8.0
    DO 10 I = 1, 7, 2
    IF (I * 7 .LE. 13) X = X + 5
    Y = Y + X
10  CONTINUE
```

13. After execution of the following statements, the value of Y is _____, of X is _____, and of I is _____.

```
    Y = 5.5
    X = 8.0
    DO I = 1, 7, 2
        IF (I * 7 .GE. 13) GO TO 20
        Y = Y + X
10  CONTINUE
20  STOP
```

14. Given a one-dimensional array

$$X = \begin{pmatrix} 10.0 \\ 20.0 \\ 30.0 \\ 10.0 \\ 30.0 \end{pmatrix}$$

determine the value of A and the elements of X after execution of these instructions:

```
    T = 0.0
    DO 10 J = 1, 5
        T = T + X(J)
        X(J) = X(J) * 2.0
10  CONTINUE
    A = T/5.0
    STOP
```

15. After execution of the following instructions, the value of Y is _____ and of I is _____ .

```
    Y = 0.0
    X = 10.0
    DO 10 J = 10, 5, 2
        Y = Y + X
        X = X - 10.0
10  CONTINUE
    STOP
```

16. Assume the one-dimensional array

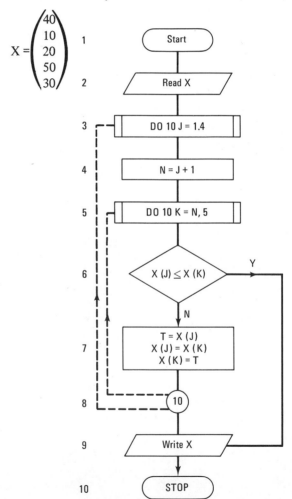

Determine the new values for the element of the array X after execution of the instructions in the preceding flowchart.

17. What will be the values of the elements of X if the instruction in box 6 of the flowchart of problem 16 is changed to:

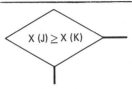

18. Convert the flowchart of problem 16 to a FORTRAN program and run it.

***

In problems 19 through 25, assume the specification statement:

```
DIMENSION X(5), Y(2, 3)
```

and the following input cards for each problem:

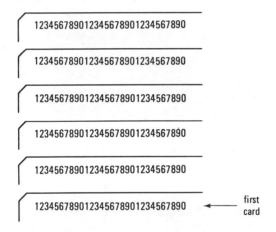

19. After execution of:

```
      READ (5, 10) (X(J) , J = 1, 5, 2)
      READ (5, 10) (X(J) , J = 2, 4, 2)
10    FORMAT (5F4.2)
```

find the values of: X(1) =   ; X(2) =   ; X(3) =   ;
X(4) =   ; X(5) =
20. After execution of:

```
      READ (5, 10) Y
10    FORMAT (6F4.2)
```

find the values of: Y(1, 1) =   ; Y(1, 2) =   ; Y(1, 3) =   ;
Y(2, 1) =   ; Y(2, 2) =   ; (2, 3) =   .

21. After execution of:

```
     READ (5, 10) (Y(I,J) , J = 1, 3) , I = 1, 2)
10   FORMAT (6F4.2)
```

find the values of: Y(1, 1) =   ; Y(1, 2) =   ; Y(1, 3) =   ;
Y(2, 1) =   ; Y(2, 2) =   ; Y(2, 3) =   .

22. After execution of:

```
     READ (5, 10) Y(I,J) , I = 1, 2) , J = 1, 3)
10   FORMAT (6F4.2)
```

find the values of: Y(1, 1) =   ; Y(1, 2) =   ; Y(1, 3) =   ;
Y(2, 1) =   ; Y(2, 2) =   ; Y(2, 3) =   .

23. If the FORMAT statement in problem 22 is changed to:

```
10   FORMAT (3F4.2)
```

find the values of: Y(1, 1) =   ; Y(1, 2) =   ; Y(1, 3) =   ;
Y(2, 1) =   ; Y(2, 2) =   ; Y(2, 3) =   .

24. If the FORMAT statement of problem 22 is changed to:

```
10   FORMAT (F4.2)
```

find the values of: Y(1, 1) =   ; Y(1, 2) =   ; Y(1, 3) =   ;
Y(2, 1) =   ; Y(2, 2) =   ; Y(2, 3) =   .

25. If the FORMAT statement of problem 22 is changed to:

```
10   FORMAT (F4.2)
```

find the values of: Y(1, 1) =   ; Y(1, 2) =   ; Y(1, 3) =   ;
Y(2, 1) =   ; Y(2, 2) =   ; Y(2, 3) =   .

26. Assume X is a 50-element, one-dimensional array. Write a FORTRAN program to read the values of the elements of X and create from it another array Y in the following manner:

   a. If an even element of X is 0 then the corresponding even element of Y should be 5.
   b. If an odd element of X is 0, then the corresponding element of Y should equal the value of the next odd element of X, unless the index would exceed 50, in which case the value of the odd element of Y should be equal to the 50th element of X.

27. **Production Management.** The ABC Corporation produces four products. The raw material, overhead, and labor cost per unit of each product are:

PRODUCT TYPE	MATERIAL	OVERHEAD	LABOR
1	$5.50	$2.00	$3.00
2	4.50	3.00	4.00
3	3.75	4.00	5.00
4	5.00	2.00	4.50

The company has four possible methods of producing each product. These are:

PRODUCT	OPTIONS			
	1	2	3	4
1	5,000	8,000	10,000	12,000
2	4,000	7,000	8,000	10,000
3	1,000	3,000	5,000	8,000
4	3,000	5,000	8,000	11,000

Prepare a flowchart and write a program to find:
  a. The cost of producing each product under each option
  b. The total cost of each option
  c. The option (mixed options) that costs the least.
Your program should produce appropriate titles and captions.

28. Suppose that A is a (3,4) matrix (that is, has 3 rows and 4 columns), and B is a (4,5) matrix. Then the matrix C = A × B is the matrix product of the matrices A and B; C will be a matrix with 3 rows and 5 columns. Note that if we denote an element of C by c_{ij}, an element of B by b_{ij}, and an element of A by a_{ij}, then:

$$c_{ij} = \sum_{k=1}^{4} a_{ik} b_{kj}$$

for $i = 1, 2, 3$ and $j = 1, \ldots, 5$. (The product A × B is defined only if the number of columns of A is equal to the number of rows of B). Write a FORTRAN program to read both A and B and to calculate the matrix C and print out all three matrices.

29. **Parts Explosion Problem.** Write a FORTRAN program for the following problem. A manufacturer produces three products: A, B, and C. Each of these products requires subassemblies 1, 2, 3, and 4. Each subassembly requires parts a, b, c, d, and e. Given a production order for the three products, determine the number of each part required and the total cost of the order.

This problem can be handled conveniently by using matrix multiplication. Assume the following input data:

PRODUCT	NUMBER OF SUBASSEMBLIES REQUIRED			
	1	2	3	4
A	4	2	6	1
B	2	3	5	4
C	3	1	2	6

SUBASSEMBLY	NUMBER OF PARTS REQUIRED				
	a	b	c	d	e
1	2	3	5	7	8
2	5	2	4	6	9
3	3	8	1	2	7
4	4	5	6	1	2

The cost per part is:

PART	C
a	$1.00
b	.50
c	1.50
d	2.00
e	1.75

Hint: Note that $N = S \times P$, where S is the subassembly matrix, P is the part matrix, and N is an array whose first element will be the total number of part *a* required, whose second element will be the total number of part *b* required, and so on. The total cost is a scalar $T = N \times C$ when *c* is the cost array per unit.

30. **Input–Output Analysis.** The input–output concept was invented by Wassily Leontief about 45 years ago. Input–output analysis is an important tool in economic forecasting in which the basic tool is a table. The rows show sales (called outputs) and the columns show purchases (called inputs). There are two additional columns: The first represents final demand, which includes such items as purchases by households, exports, government, and accumulation to inventory; the other represents total output.

Consider the following table, which assumes an economy of three industries— cars, steel, and rubber.

PURCHASES (INPUT)
IN MILLIONS OF $

		INDUSTRIES			FINAL DEMAND	TOTAL OUTPUT
		CARS	STEEL	RUBBER		
Sales (output)	Cars	4,000	1,500	500	44	50,000
in millions	Steel	20,000	3,000	50	17,500	30,000
of $	Rubber	15,000	60	100	4,850	20,000

Reading across row 1, we see that the car industry has a total output (sales) of $50 billion. This is accounted for as intraindustry sales of $4 billion, sales of $1.5 billion to the steel industry, sales of $500 million to the rubber industry, and sales of $44 billion to others. Column 1 shows the purchases by the car industry. There was $4 billion intraindustry purchased (input), $20 billion purchased from the steel industry, and $15 billion from the rubber industry.

The "technological coefficient" is the amount of input required from each industry to produce one dollar's worth of the output of a given industry. The technological coefficient matrix is formed from the original table by dividing all the elements in each industry's column by the total output of that industry. The technological coefficient matrix of the table above is:

	CARS	STEEL	RUBBER
Cars	0.08	0.05	0.025
Steel	0.40	0.10	0.0025
Rubber	0.30	0.002	0.05

This table can be interpreted as follows: Each dollar's worth of production in the car industry will require:

Intraindustry purchase	$0.08
Purchase from steel industry	$0.40
Purchase from rubber industry	$0.30

Write a FORTRAN program to read the sales of each of these three industries, including the final demand. The program should calculate the input–output analysis table and the coefficient matrix, and print both these tables.

31. Input–Output Analysis (Forecasting). The main goal of input–output analysis is the determination of the new output levels required in all industries to meet the change in final demand.

Let A represent the technological coefficient matrix, d the array of final demands, I the identity matrix (i.e., a square matrix with 1s on the diagonal and zeros elsewhere), and X the total output as a one-dimensional array. Then:

$$X = (I - A)^{-1} \times d$$

Note, in this case:

$$I = \begin{pmatrix} 1 & 0 & 0 \\ 0 & 1 & 0 \\ 0 & 0 & 1 \end{pmatrix}$$

and $I - A$ is the difference between the matrix I and A, and $(I - A)^{-1}$ is the inverse of $(I - A)$.

Suppose that a decrease from $50,000 to $45,000 occurs in the car industry, an increase from $20,000 to $21,000 occurs in the rubber industry, and the final demand for the steel industry remains constant. Write a FORTRAN program to calculate the required total output for all industries under new circumstances. *Hint:* Calculate X from the formula above.

12 PROGRAM AND SYSTEM DESIGN AND DOCUMENTATION

The ultimate goals of any program are to perform anticipated tasks correctly and to produce correct and desirable output. Therefore, a program must be correct, must operate correctly on correct data, and must detect incorrect data. Let us call such a program a proper program. There are many programming, designing, and documenting techniques that help one to write proper programs. Many of these techniques and recommendations have been implied throughout our discussion without being named. In this chapter, we will discuss these techniques briefly.

12.1 PROGRAMMING TECHNIQUES

The three popular programming approaches are (1) structured programming, (2) top-down programming, and (3) modular programming. Modular programming is discussed in Chapter 14. These three techniques go hand in hand with each other.

12.1.1 Structured Programming

The structured programming technique employs three control structures—sequence, a binary decision, and a loop mechanism—and certain programming disciplines to code and organize programs that make them easier to understand, debug, and update. A structured program has one entry point and one exit, employs the basic control structures (explained later), and uses GO TO statements in a responsible manner.

The work of Prof. E.W. Dijkstra of the Netherlands and of Bohm and Jacobini have contributed significantly to the development of structured programming. As early as 1965, Professor Dijkstra advocated that programs be written without GO TO statements. In 1968, in his now famous "GO TO Letter" published in *Communications of the ACM*, he pointed out that blatant use of GO TO statements results in unnecessarily complex logic and makes programs harder to debug. Bohm and Jacobini, in their paper, "Structured Theorem," first published in Italy in 1965 and republished in English in May 1966 in *Communications of the ACM*, proved that any algorithm can be expressed using only three basic structures: (1) process structure, (2) a binary decision mechanism, and (3) a looping mechanism.

Since then, many have worked to improve the structured programming technique. We would like to point out that structured programming does not necessarily mean programming without the use of GO TO. However, the programmer should avoid careless use of GO TO statements. Two guidelines to follow are:

1. Do not use GO TO to send control outside the module.
2. If it is possible, try not to use a backwards GO TO. However, do not sacrifice the simplicity and the readability of the program to avoid backwards GO TO statements.

A program that contains many careless GO TO statements is usually known as a "spaghetti-type" program.

12.1.1.1 THREE BASIC CONTROL STRUCTURES

Figure 12.1 demonstrates the three basic patterns of structured programming: simple sequence, IF-THEN-ELSE, and a loop mechanism, such as DOWHILE.

In simple sequence, these statements are executed in the order in which they appear, with control passing from one statement to the next. READ, WRITE, and arithmetic statements are all examples of simple-sequence statements.

The structure of IF-THEN-ELSE is:

If c THEN s ELSE d

where c is a condition and both s and d are blocks of statements. A block may contain one or more statements. If condition c is true, then block s is executed and block d is bypassed. If condition c is false, s is skipped and d is executed.

The structure of DOWHILE is:

DO e WHILE c

where c is a condition and e represents the statements within the range of DO. Condition c is tested. If the result is true, then all the statements in the range of the DO loop are executed and the control returns back to test the condition again. If condition c is false, then no statement in the range of DO is executed,

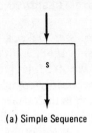

(a) Simple Sequence

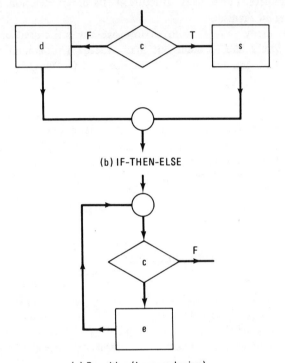

(b) IF-THEN-ELSE

(c) Repetition (Loop mechanism)

FIGURE 12.1 **Three basic control structures**

but control transfers to the statement that immediately follows the last statement in the range of DO.

The DOWHILE tests the condition at the beginning—that is, immediately upon entering the loop. The statements within the range of the DO loop are executed only if the result of the test is true. This means that the statements within the DO loop may never be executed.

12.1.1.2 *ADDITIONAL COMBINED STRUCTURES*

Two combinations of the basic patterns that have proved useful are DOUNTIL and the logical case.

The structure of DOUNTIL is:

DO *e* UNTIL *c*

The statements *e* in the range of DO are executed UNTIL the condition *c* becomes true. In contrast to DOWHILE, which is a leading-decision loop, the DOUNTIL control structure tests the condition at the end of the loop; in other words, DOUNTIL sets up a trailing-decision loop. A DOUNTIL control structure can be constructed from the combination of a simple sequence and DOWHILE.

Figure 12.2(a) shows the DOUNTIL structure. The statements *e* in the range of DOUNTIL are executed at least once, and the condition is tested at the end of the loop. Figure 12.2(b) is the combination of a simple sequence and a DOWHILE, which has the same effect as DOUNTIL. Note that the DOWHILE in Figure 12.2(b) tests the inverse condition *c*.

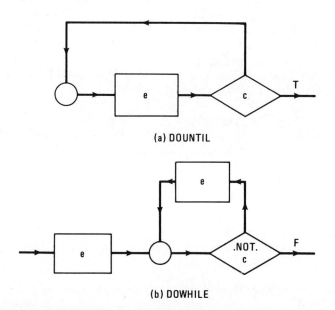

(a) DOUNTIL

(b) DOWHILE

FIGURE 12.2   DOUNTIL control structure

The logical-case control structure is used to replace the nested IF-THEN-ELSE structures. We have discussed computed GO TO in FORTRAN. A structure such as computed GO TO is the logical-case control structure that can replace the IF-THEN-ELSE nested structure.

12.1.2   FORTRAN and Structured Programming

Recall that a block can consist of a single statement or a sequence of statements. Furthermore, a block may contain other blocks that in turn contain other blocks as part of their structure.

12.1.2.1 *FORTRAN IV*

For the reasons outlined below, the current FORTRAN IV is not well suited to structured programming:

1. There is no concept of block structuring in FORTRAN IV. If we wish to simulate blocks, we have to use GO TO statements to jump around a group of statements.
2. There is no IF-THEN-ELSE structure in FORTRAN IV. The two IF statements, logical IF and arithmetic IF, that are supported by FORTRAN IV do not allow nested control structures or consecutive nested IF structures. Recall that the only basis for the test in arithmetic IF is whether the value of the expression is less than, equal to, or greater than zero. Logical IF permits a single statement to be executed or skipped. The fact that this single statement can be a GO TO statement allows the simulation of IF-THEN-ELSE. However, as cited above, no nested control structures or consecutive nested IF statements are permitted.
3. The FORTRAN IV DO loop is a trailing-decision loop. FORTRAN IV DO is not entirely analogous to the DOUNTIL control structure, because the only condition that can be tested in FORTRAN DO is whether or not the index of DO has a particular value.

In spite of this, the basic control structures can be simulated and, hence, structured programs can be written in FORTRAN IV. Following are the basic control structures and simulated basic control structures in FORTRAN IV.

Simple sequence. FORTRAN IV supports simple-sequence statements. Examples of simple-sequence statements are I/O statements and arithmetic assignment statements.

IF-THEN-ELSE. This pattern cannot be represented directly. However, it can be simulated as shown below by using inverse (not condition) logic:

```
IF (.NOT. CONDITION) GO TO 100
   statement
      .
      .
      .
      .
   GO TO 110
```

This is the THEN operand if we
were testing the true condition,
not its inverse.

```
100     statement  ⎫          The ELSE operand if the
         .         ⎬ ◄─────── true condition, not its
         .         ⎭          inverse, is tested.
         .
110 CONTINUE
```

For example, the following IF-THEN-ELSE:

```
IF PAY < BAL THEN INTRST = BAL—PAY
                  NBAL = BAL—PAY+INTRST
   ELSE NBAL = 0
```

can be written in FORTRAN as:

```
    IF (PAY.GE.BAL) GO TO 100
       INTRST = BAL—PAY
       NBAL = BAL—PAY+INTRST
       GO TO 200
100 NBAL = 0
200 CONTINUE
```

Note that the FORTRAN IF above is equivalent to IF (PAY.NOT. .LT. BAL) GO TO 100, which tests the inverse condition.

DOWHILE. To simulate DOWHILE, use inverse condition in the logical IF statement along with an unconditional GO TO statement:

```
100 IF (.NOT. CONDITION) GO TO 200
       statement
         .
         .
         .
       GO TO 100
200 CONTINUE
```

Simulation of DOUNTIL. The DOUNTIL is simulated by using inverse condition in the logical IF statement:

```
           e
100 CONTINUE
       e  IF (.NOT. CONDITION) GO TO 100
```

Where e is a block of statements

Logical case. Computed GO TO is supplied by FORTRAN IV. In the following simple example, simulation of DOWHILE and IF-THEN-ELSE are used to write a structured program in FORTRAN IV.

Example 12.1

Write a FORTRAN program to read employee records and calculate and print the weekly pay for active employees only. The input records are punched on cards in the following manner:

CC	FIELD	TYPE
1–5	Employee number	Integer
6	Status	Integer
7–10	Hours	Real XX.XX
11–13	.Rate/hour	Real XX.XX

If the employee is active, the status field contains 1; otherwise, the status field contains 0. Place a blank card at the end of data and process the data until the employee number becomes 0. Figure 12.3 is the structured flowchart, and Figure 12.4 is the FORTRAN program for our problem.

12.1.2.2 ANSI FORTRAN 77

The inclusion of the IF-THEN-ELSE contruct in ANSI FORTRAN 77 makes structured programming in ANSI FORTRAN easier than in FORTRAN IV. Following are the basic control structures of structured programming in ANSI FORTRAN 77:

1. ANSI FORTRAN 77 supports simple sequence.
2. ANSI FORTRAN 77 supports a new block IF, ELSE IF, ELSE, and END IF, which enable the programmer to construct different forms of IF-THEN-ELSE, such as the following two forms:

```
(a)  IF c THEN e
        ELSE d
     END IF
```

```
(b)  IF c1 THEN e1
        ELSE IF c2 THEN e2
           ELSE d
           END IF
     END IF
```

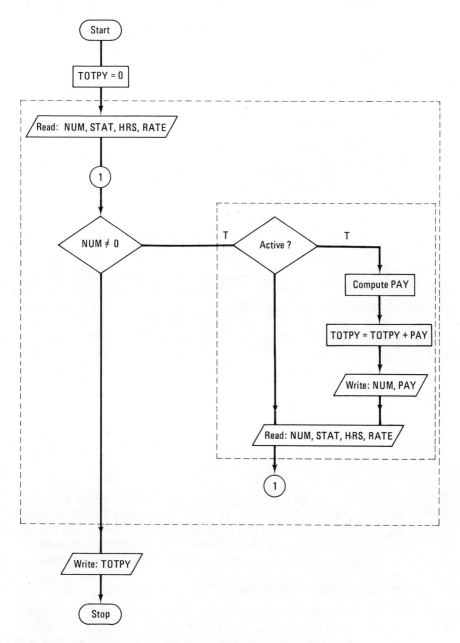

FIGURE 12.3 Structured flowchart for the payroll system

```
C WEEKLY PAYROLL SYSTEM
C
C
C SIMULATING STRUCTURED PROGRAMMING IN FORTAN IV
C
C VARIABLE NAMES USED
C   NUM     EMPLOYEE-NUMBER
C   STAT    EMPLOYEE-STATUS.  1 IF ACTIVE AND 0 IF NOT ACTIVE
C
C   HRS     NUMBER OF HOURS WORKED
C   RATE    RATE PER HOUR
C   TOTPY   TOTAL PAY IN THE RUN
C
          INTEGER CARDS,  STAT
          DATA CARDS, LINE /5, 6/
          TOTPY = 0.0
C
C DOWHILE NUM NOT EQUAL 0
   20        READ (CARDS, 10) NUM, STAT, HRS, RATE
   10        FORMAT (I5, I1, 2F4.2)
          IF (NUM.EQ.0) GO TO 50
C IF-THEN-ELSE
              IF (STAT.NE.1) GO TO 40
              PAY = HRS * RATE
              TOTPY = TOTPY + PAY
              WRITE (LINE, 30) NUM, PAY
   30         FORMAT (1X, T10, I5, F7.2)
C END IF-THEN-ELSE
   40         CONTINUE
              READ (CARDS, 10) NUM, STAT, HRS, RATE
              GO TO 20
C END DOWHILE
   50         CONTINUE
              WRITE (LINE, 60) TOTPY
   60         FORMAT (1X, T30, 'TOTAL PAY IS: ', F8.2)
              STOP
              END
```

FIGURE 12.4 **Simulated structured programming in FORTRAN**

where c, $c1$, and $c2$ are conditions, and e, d, $e1$, and $e2$ are blocks of statements. The IF-THEN-ELSE of part (a) above is the familiar one that has been discussed. In part (b), if condition $c1$ is true, then the block of statements $e1$ is executed and the entire ELSE IF portion is bypassed. If condition $c1$ is false, then the portion ELSE IF is executed. If condition $c2$ in the ELSE IF is true, then $e2$ is executed and d is bypassed. Otherwise, $e2$ is bypassed and d is executed.

3. DOWHILE. ANSI FORTRAN 77 DO is a leading-decision loop. However, this is not entirely analogous to DOWHILE either, because the only condition that can be tested in ANSI FORTRAN 77 DO is whether the iteration counter is less or equal to zero.

   The simulation of DOWHILE is simple and is done by testing the condition (not the inverse condition) as follows:

```
100   IF (CONDITION) THEN
                statement
                    .
                    .
                    .
                statement
                GO TO 100
        END IF
```

4. DOUNTIL. In ANSI FORTRAN 77, DOUNTIL is simulated by testing the inverse condition of IF-THEN-ELSE as follows:

```
      e
100   IF (.NOT.CONDITION) THEN
                statement
                    .
                    .
                    .
                statement
                GO TO 100
        END IF
```

Where e is the same block of statements which are between IF and END IF.

5. ANSI FORTRAN 77 supports the computed GO TO statement.

Example 12.2

Convert the structured program (which was written in FORTRAN IV) of example 12.1 into ANSI FORTRAN 77. Figure 12.5 shows the result.

The main purpose of structured programming is to make programs more readable and better organized, so that they will be easier to understand, debug, and update. Since structured programs in FORTRAN IV must be simulated, it is not clear to what extent such simulation improves the readability and the quality of the programs. It is true that ANSI FORTRAN 77 supports the IF-THEN-ELSE construct, but the other basic constructs must be simulated. ANSI FORTRAN 77 has yet to be implemented, and we shall have to wait and see how widely it will be accepted by business, industry, government, universities, and other FORTRAN users. We should also point out that currently there are some precompiler translators that allow the FORTRAN programmer to use the basic control structures. So far, these precompiler translators have not been

```
C                      WEEKLY PAYROLL SYSTEM
C
C STRUCTURED PROGRAMMING IN ANSI FORTRAN 77
C
C VARIABLE NAMES USED
C   NUM     EMPLOYEE-NUMBER
C   STAT    EMPLOYEE-STATUS. 1 IF ACTIVE AND 0 IF NOT ACTIVE
C
C   HRS     NUMBER OF HRS WORKED
C   RATE    RATE PER HOUR
C   TOTPY   TOTAL PAY IN THE RUN
C
            INTEGER CARDS, STAT
            DATA CARDS, LINE /5, 6/
            TOTPY = 0.0
C DOWHILE NUM NOT EQUAL 0
   20       READ (CARDS, 10) NUM, STAT, HRS, RATE
   10       FORMAT (I5, I1, 2F4.2)
   20       IF (NUM.NOT.0) THEN
                    IF (STAT.EQ.1) THEN
                        PAY = HRS * RATE
                        TOTPY = TOTPY + PAY
                        WRITE (LINE, 30) NUM, PAY
   30                   FORMAT (1X, T10, I5, T30, F7.2)
                    END IF
                READ (CARDS, 10) NUM, STAT, HRS, RATE
                GO TO 20
            END IF
C END DOWHILE
            WRITE (LINE, 40) TOTPY
   40       FORMAT (1X, T30, 'TOTAL PAY IS: ', F8.2)
            STOP
            END
```

FIGURE 12.5   Program for payroll problem in ANSI FORTRAN 77

widely accepted. Therefore, our approach has been to write readable, understandable, and better-documented programs rather than insisting on using only
the basic control constructs of structured programming.

12.1.3   Top-Down Program Design

Top-down programming is the reverse of building with blocks. To design a
top-down program, start with a single process box. Break that process into lower
levels of structures. Continue to break these lower levels into still lower-level
structures until the level of basic building blocks—simple sequence, IF-THEN-
ELSE, or looping—is reached. Figure 12.6 demonstrates the three stages of top-
down design for the program of example 12.1.

12.2   SYSTEM DESIGN, PROGRAM DESIGN,
AND FLOWCHARTING

So far, we have used the ANSI flowchart and pseudo code to represent
systems and program design. There is currently a wide difference of
opinion regarding the use of ANSI or other flowcharting as design techniques.
Some advocate that ANSI flowcharting symbols are not adequate for structured
programming; therefore, other techniques such as pseudo code or other flowcharting techniques should be used. There are even those who feel that because

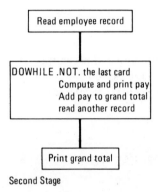

Compute and print pay
for active employees
and grand total

First Stage

Read employee record

DOWHILE .NOT. the last card
　　　　　　Compute and print pay
　　　　　　Add pay to grand total
　　　　　　read another record

Print grand total

Second Stage

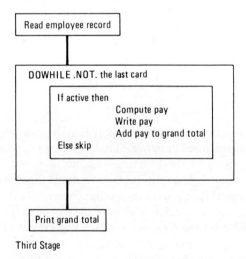

Read employee record

DOWHILE .NOT. the last card

　　If active then
　　　　　　Compute pay
　　　　　　Write pay
　　　　　　Add pay to grand total
　　Else skip

Print grand total

Third Stage

FIGURE 12.6　Top-down design

structured programming is self-explanatory, there is no need for flowcharting at all. They point out that the flowchart usually fails to represent the current status of the program or the system. Nevertheless, in the last few years, a wide variety of structured flowcharting symbols and techniques have been proposed as structured design tools for designing programs and systems. Among these are:

1. Pseudo code
2. Structured box diagrams (Nassi-Shneiderman charts)
3. Structured flowcharting, using ANSI flowchart
4. HIPO diagrams
5. Warnier diagrams

We have already discussed structured flowcharting using ANSI flowchart and pseudo code form. Following is the pseudo code for the program of example 12.1 and a very brief discussion of the other techniques:

```
START
DOWHILE EMPLOY—NUM NOT EQUAL TO 0
        READ
        IF ACTIVE THEN
                    COMPUTE PAY
                    WRITE PAY
                    ADD PAY TO TOTAL
            ELSE SKIP
END DOWHILE
WRITE TOTAL PAY
STOP
```

The structured box diagram (Nassi-Shneiderman chart) uses graphical symbols with a structured narrative. Simple lines are placed around the indented portions. Each piece of the structured diagram is nested within the other to reflect the important logical relationships. To many, this chart presents an overall picture of one logical function within another. Figure 12.7 is a Nassi-Shneiderman chart for a program to calculate and print the pay of each active employee, and to calculate and print the total pay for each department of each company and the grand total of departments in the company.

The drawback of Nassi-Shneiderman charts is that the method has the tendency to obscure logical hierarchy, and it is hard to change or expand the system once it is designed.

The HIPO (Hierarchical-Input-Process-Output chart) was developed and refined by IBM. HIPO is primarily an analytical model, which is used to break

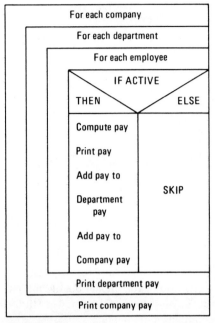

FIGURE 12.7 Nassi-Shneiderman chart

down the problem in a strictly hierarchical manner. A typical HIPO package has the following three components:

1. The visual table of contents, which is constructed in the following manner:

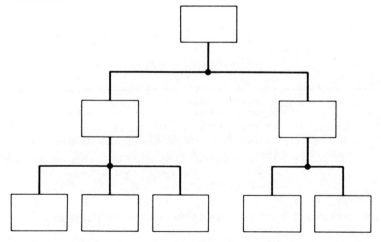

2. The overview IPO (*I*nput-*P*rocess-*O*utput) diagram
3. The detail HIPO diagram

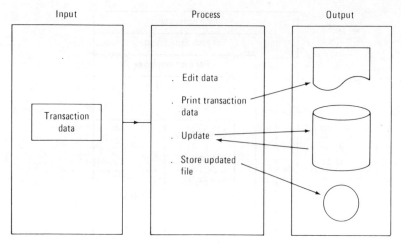

FIGURE 12.8   IPO chart

Figure 12.8 is an overview IPO chart for a system to read transaction data, edit data, print the transaction data, update the old master file, and store a copy of the updated master file on the tape. The detailed HIPO diagram is the same as the IPO diagram but contains more detail.

The Warnier diagram was first developed by Jean Dominique Warnier of France, who used a systematic hierarchical logical approach to design systems and programs. Fundamentally, a Warnier diagram is made up of a series of brackets and a small number of other symbols to portray the system, the program, or the data structure of the program. The sequence of activities in any Warnier diagram is presumed to be from left to right and top to bottom.

Figure 12.9 is a Warnier diagram for the same problem that was represented by the Nassi-Shneiderman chart. The diagram contains all the symbols that are used by Warnier diagrams:

SYMBOL	MEANING
(D)	Execute D times.
(E)	Execute E times.
(1)	Execute 1 time.
(0,1)	Execute 0 or 1 time, depending on the condition.
Active	The complement. Note active and $\overline{\text{active}}$ are mutually exclusive, and only one of them is executed at a time.
⊕	Exclusive symbol.

The advocates of Warnier diagrams point out that the diagrams:

1. Are easy to expand
2. Concentrate on the logical requirements of the problem rather than on the physical ones

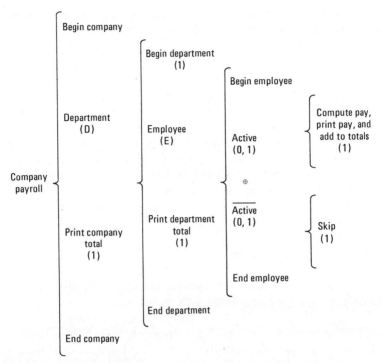

FIGURE 12.9 Warnier diagram

3. Clearly represent the hierarchical relationships between different modules
4. Can represent and describe the structure of the data, as well as program and systems structure

Note that in the design process, the Warnier diagram stresses starting from the output first (the leftmost part of the diagram) and, from the requirements of the output, deriving the input. This approach makes a lot of sense, and it is practical. If you compare this process with the construction of a building, you will realize its logical approach. To construct a building, one must decide first on the type of building (the output). The next step is to define the process and the material (input) that make such a building.

12.3 DOCUMENTATION

Documentation includes all the information about style and procedure techniques that make systems and programs easier to debug, modify, and enhance. Well-documented systems and programs are easier to debug, modify, and enhance because they are more readable and easier to understand.

Not only do many undocumented computer systems and programs become obsolete as soon as their designer and implementer have left the installation. In addition, in many circumstances the original designer of an undocumented computer system or program cannot remember or follow his or her own logic. This happens because he or she has failed to document the significant roles of many critical variables and the functions that are performed by the various parts of the system and its component programs.

Documentation does not affect the execution of the program. However, as pointed out above, it is vital for computer professionals, computer users, and the company itself.

Our brief discussion here will deal with minimum program documentation, both within the program and accompanying the program. The comment statement (a statement with the character C in the first column) is used in FORTRAN to write documentation within the program; but besides this documentation, the programmer must follow certain procedures to make the program easier to read and be understood by other programmers.

12.3.1 Readable Programs

It is essential to make the program as readable as possible. Here are some guidelines to writing readable FORTRAN programs:

1. Meaningful data names. The programmer should select variable names that in some way identify or remind the programmer of their usage and what they represent. Names such as BAL, BALNS, BALANS, and BLANCE are all reasonable to represent *balance.*

2. Writing comments. The programmer should write short, precise, and understandable comments to explain the functions of important statements and loops. The statements or loops should immediately follow the comment line or lines.

3. Statement numbers. Use a consistent procedure to assign statement numbers, such as in increments of 10, as discussed in section 3.5.

4. Using variables for logical unit numbers. Instead of using logical unit numbers, use variable names, and assign the logical unit as the value for the variable. This makes the program more transferable. See section 4.2.

5. Write *1X* explicitly as the first character of any FORMAT statement associated with a line-printer statement. This eliminates confusion regarding usage of the first character of the WRITE statement's FORMAT for carriage control.

6. Use the same variable names in COMMON (explained in Chapter 14) statements in the main program and all subprograms that share the same COMMON area.

7. The EQUIVALENCE statement (see Chapter 14) saves storage space. Careless usage of the EQUIVALENCE may make the program harder to read, understand, and debug. Unless the case is critical, the readability of a program should not be sacrificed for the optimization of storage requirements.

8. Blank spaces. In FORTRAN, blanks are insignificant. Blanks should be used to make the statements more readable. Both the following statements are valid; however, the second one is more readable and is therefore preferable.

```
DO10J=1,50,3                          DO 10 J = 1, 50, 3
```

9. Blank lines. Surround crucial statements, a group of statements, or a loop by one or more blank lines to make them more visible.
10. Indentation. One way to make programs easier to read is to use indentation. Following are some indentation guidelines:
   a. All statements, except those that are mentioned in part *c* below, should start at the same column, such as column 7 for non-comment statements and column 3 for comment statements.
   b. Always use the same character for a continuation card—such as @, *, +, $, or C. The continuing statement should always start in a certain column, such as column 9.
   c. The first and last statements of a loop should start in the same column. The starting position of the other statements of the loop must be to the right of the starting point of the first and the last statements of the loop. For example, the first and last statements of the loop may start in column 7 and the remaining statements start in column 10.

Following are three examples of indentation. In examples 12.3 and 12.4, the first loop is indented.

Example 12.3

First loop:

```
DO 50 J = 1,100
    SUMX = SUMX + X(J)
    SSQX = SSQX + X(J)**2
    WRITE (LINE, 20)X(J)
50  CONTINUE
```

Second DO loop:

```
DO 50 J = 1,100
SUMX = SUMX + X(J)
SSQX = SSRX + X(J)**2
WRITE (LINE, 20)X(J)
50  CONTINUE
```

Example 12.4

First loop:

```
      J = 1
10    IF (J .GT. 100) GO TO 50
C     ELSE
         SUMX = SUMX + X(J)
         SSQX = SSQX + X(J)**2
         WRITE (LINE,20)X(J)
         J = J = 1
         GO TO 10
50    CONTINUE
```

Second loop:

```
      J = 1
10    IF, (J .GT. 100) GO TO 50
      SUMX = SUMX + X(J)
      SSQX + SSQX + X(J)**2
      WRITE (LINE,20)X(J)
      J = J + 1
      GO TO 10
50    CONTINUE
```

Example 12.5

The following nested loop is indented:

```
      DO 50 J = 1, N - 1
         M = J + 1
         DO 40 K = M, N
            IF (X(J) . LE . X(K)) GO TO 40
C           ELSE
               TEMP = X(J)
               X(J) = X(K)
               X(K) = TEMP
C           END IF
40       CONTINUE
         SUM = SUM + X(J)
50    CONTINUE
```

12.3.2 Minimum Desirable System and Program Documentation

12.3.2.1 SYSTEM AND SUBSYSTEMS DOCUMENTATION

Usually, a computer information system is made up of several subsystems. For example, a general accounting system may contain a payroll system, an accounts receivable system, an accounts payable system, an invoicing system, and a checkwriting and check-reconciliation system. Each of these subsystems may consist of several programs. As an example, a payroll system may contain an edit program to edit the input data, a registration program to update the master file and to print the register detail, a check program to print the payroll checks and statements, and a journal program to print the journal summary report.

You can see that such a system can be large and complicated. Therefore, it is essential to keep documentation about the system, the subsystem, and the programs in the system. The following are minimum desirable system documentations:

1. *System abstract.* In this section of the documentation, the overall task or tasks that are performed by the system and subsystems should be briefly described. The system abstract should also contain the following items:
   System name: the name of the system
   System designer: the name of the designer of the system
   Design dates: the starting and ending dates of the design phase
   System implementer: the name of the individuals who have implemented the system
   Implementation dates: starting and ending dates of the implementation
   Source of test data
   System or project manager: the name of the system or project manager
2. *Subsystem directory.* A cross-reference list of subsystem names and their functions. The description of the task or tasks performed by a subsystem should not be more than one line.
3. *System flowchart.* The overall system chart.
4. *Environment. Hardware environment:* A short description of the hardware environment required for the system, including the memory space, secondary storage space, and all other peripheral devices required by the system. *Software environment:* The names of the operating system and all other routines and software packages and compilers required for the system.
5. *Report and other user output.* The names of the outputs that are generated by the system, including samples of the reports.
6. *User's manual.* The system should be accompanied by a user's manual that describes how the system should be run and output distributed.
7. *Other technical items.* Items such as future updating and expansion of the system that are not covered in the previous items.

The documentation of each subsystem should contain the following items:

1. *Subsystem abstract.* Contains all items that are explained in the system abstract section and, in addition, the name of the system that the subsystem belongs to.
2. *Program directory.* Contains a cross-reference table of the names of all programs in the system and the tasks performed by them.
3. *Subsystem flowchart.* The system flowchart for the subsystem.
4. *Environment.* Both the hardware and software environment required by the subsystem should be briefly described.
5. *Report and other user output.* The names of the different outputs generated by the subsystem, including samples of the reports.
6. *User's manual of the subsystem.*
7. *Other technical items.* This contains similar information to that for the system.

12.3.2.2 PROGRAM DOCUMENTATION

Items 1 through 4 of the following program documentation items are written within the program; the remaining items accompany the program.

1. *Program abstract.* The task or tasks performed by the program are briefly described in this section. Furthermore, the program abstract should also contain the following items:

    System name: the name of the system or subsystem that the program belongs to

    Program name: the identification of the program

    Author: the author of the program

    Date written: the date the program was written

    Date implemented: the date the program was implemented

    Environment: the hardware and software environment required by the program

    Process: brief discussion of the processing of the program

    Input file: for each input file, the file name, medium, and the type of record format

    Output file: for each output file, the file name, medium, and the type of record format

    Scientific routine names: the names of any scientific routines used in the program

2. *Problem narrative*. A short description of the problem to be solved by the program.

3. *Section and subprogram directory*. A cross-reference directory for subprograms and important sections of the program and their functions.

4. *Data dictionary*. A cross-reference table for the variable names and their representation. In this section, all the flags and counters must be listed in groups and briefly described by no more than one line.

5. *File format*. The description and the layout of the records of files and the valid contents of each field. See Figure 12.10.

6. *Report format*. The description of the format of all reports produced by the program. See Figures 12.11, 12.12, and 12.13.

7. *Program flowchart*. A rough program flowchart; this can be pseudo code or other diagram.

The other side of the documentation problem is overdocumentation. Many programs and systems have been so overdocumented that they lose their readability. For example, many are accompanied by pages and pages of detailed flowcharting, descriptions of the system, and other such materials. Because overdocumentation makes the system and the programs harder to read and comprehend, it is just as bad as no documentation or insufficient documentation.

For many organizations, the minimum documentation listed above, along with some other information regarding the run schedule, input data, report distribution, security procedures, and budget considerations, makes an adequate amount.

12.4   SUMMARY

Documentation and good program style make systems and programs easier to understand and debug. Documentation does not affect the execution of the program; however, undocumented programs and systems soon become obsolete, because it is hard to remember the functions of their parts and their relation to each other.

Structured programming improves the readability of the program. The three basic structure controls are simple sequence, IF-THEN-ELSE, and a loop mechanism. Top-down design starts with a single process box and breaks it into smaller structures. The decomposition continues until the basic control structures are reached. Some suggested programming and systems design flowcharts and techniques are pseudo code, structured flowchart using ANSI symbols, Nassi-Shneiderman chart, HIPO, and Warnier diagrams.

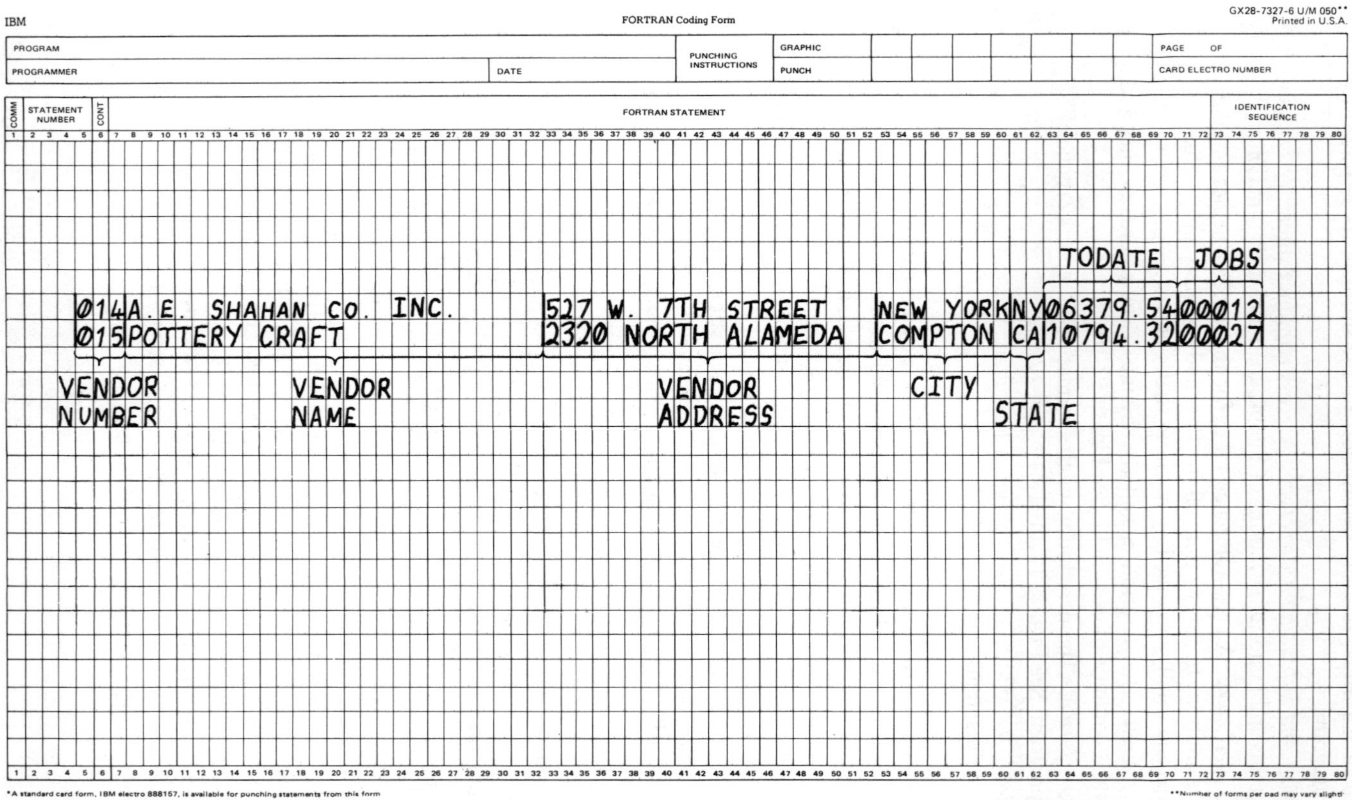
IBM
FORTRAN Coding Form
GX28-7327-6 U/M 050**
Printed in U.S.A.
PROGRAM
PROGRAMMER
DATE
PUNCHING INSTRUCTIONS
GRAPHIC
PUNCH
PAGE OF
CARD ELECTRO NUMBER
COMM
STATEMENT NUMBER
CONT
FORTRAN STATEMENT
IDENTIFICATION SEQUENCE
TODATE JOBS
Ø14A.E. SHAHAN CO. INC. 527 W. 7TH STREET NEW YORKNY06379.5400012
Ø15POTTERY CRAFT 2320 NORTH ALAMEDA COMPTON CA10794.3200027
VENDOR NUMBER
VENDOR NAME
VENDOR ADDRESS
CITY
STATE
*A standard card form, IBM electro 888157, is available for punching statements from this form
**Number of forms per pad may vary slightly

FIGURE 12.10 File layout for VENDOR.DAT. This is a random file organized on the vendor number. VENDOR.DAT is divided into two sections. The first contains the vendor number, name, and address and is used to verify incoming data. The second contains TODATE and JOBS. TODATE is a cumulative total of all purchases from the vendor; JOBS is simply a count of the number of transactions with the vendor.

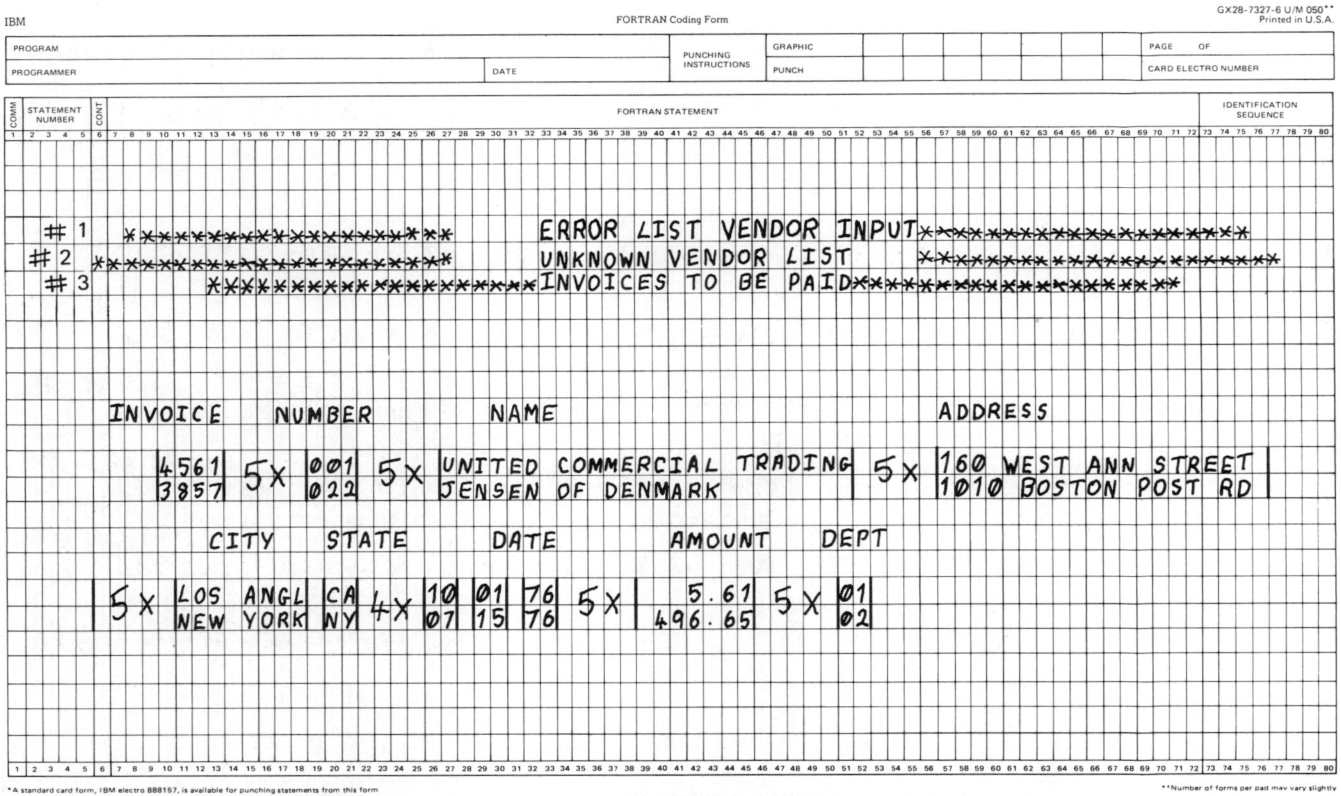

FIGURE 12.11 Layout for ERROR LISTS and TRANSACTION LIST. The appropriate heading is written at the top of the listings. The listings are identical in form and vary only in the actual data listed and the heading used on top. The column headings are identical on all the lists. The data listed under heading #1 are the errors detected in the EDIT program; under #2, the errors detected in the ACTION program; under #3, only the verified invoices to be paid. (The material in the bottom half here, shown divided into two lines, is printed on one line on the line printer.)

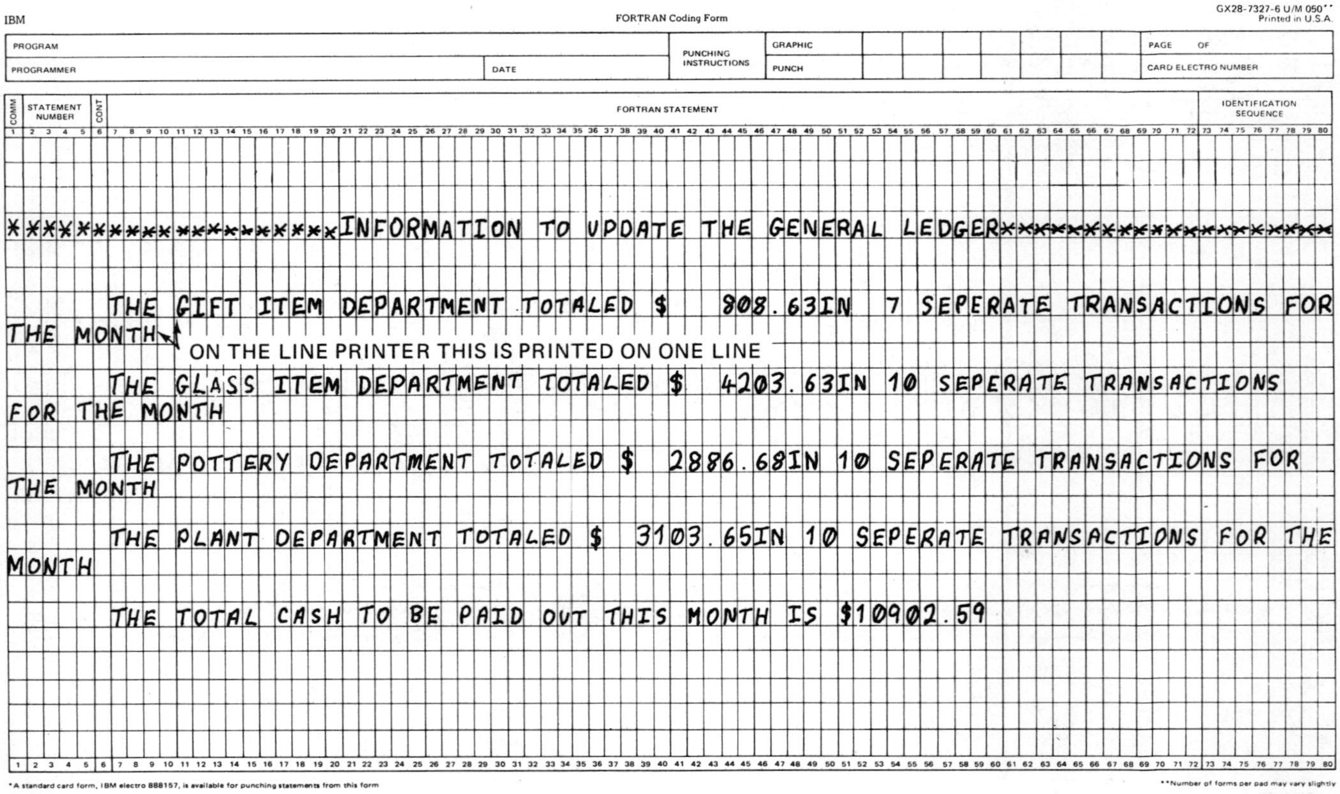
IBM
FORTRAN Coding Form
GX28-7327-6 U/M 050**
Printed in U.S.A.
PROGRAM
PROGRAMMER
DATE
PUNCHING INSTRUCTIONS
GRAPHIC
PUNCH
PAGE OF
CARD ELECTRO NUMBER
COMM
STATEMENT NUMBER
CONT
FORTRAN STATEMENT
IDENTIFICATION SEQUENCE
*******************INFORMATION TO UPDATE THE GENERAL LEDGER*******************
THE GIFT ITEM DEPARTMENT TOTALED $ 808.63IN 7 SEPERATE TRANSACTIONS FOR
THE MONTH
ON THE LINE PRINTER THIS IS PRINTED ON ONE LINE
THE GLASS ITEM DEPARTMENT TOTALED $ 4203.63IN 10 SEPERATE TRANSACTIONS
FOR THE MONTH
THE POTTERY DEPARTMENT TOTALED $ 2886.68IN 10 SEPERATE TRANSACTIONS FOR
THE MONTH
THE PLANT DEPARTMENT TOTALED $ 3103.65IN 10 SEPERATE TRANSACTIONS FOR THE
MONTH
THE TOTAL CASH TO BE PAID OUT THIS MONTH IS $10902.59
*A standard card form, IBM electro 888157, is available for punching statements from this form
**Number of forms per pad may vary slightly

FIGURE 12.12 Layout for journal summary

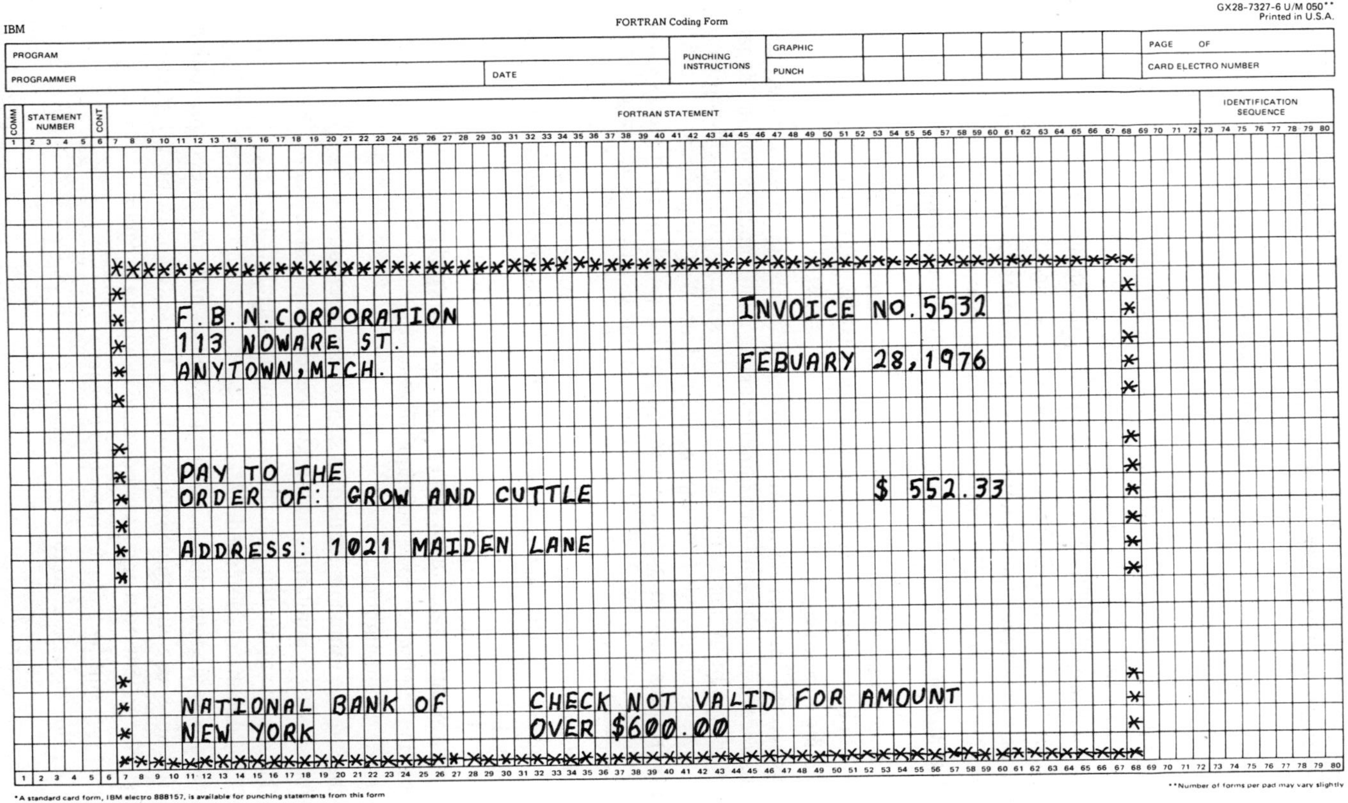

FIGURE 12.13 Line printer layout for checks. The variable INV contains the invoice number.

1. *True or False.* A structured program has one entry and one exit.

2. *True or False.* Structured programming improves the readability of the program.

3. *True or False.* DOWHILE is a leading-decision loop.

4. *True or False.* DOUNTIL is a trailing-decision loop.

5. *True or False.* FORTRAN IV DO is a trailing-decision loop.

6. *True or False.* ANSI FORTRAN 77 DO is a leading-decision loop.

7. What are the three basic structures used in structured programming?

8. What are the characteristics of a structured program?

9. What are the guidelines for using GO TO statements in structured programming?

10. Write the simulation of the following structures in FORTRAN IV and ANSI FORTRAN: (a) IF-THEN-ELSE, (b) DOWHILE, (c) DOUNTIL.

11. Describe top-down structured design.

12. Express the program for the following problem in pseudo code: Each student's record has the student's number, name, major, address, school, department, grade point average, and status field. The student status field contains 1 for an active student and 0 for an inactive student. Write a program to read all students' records and to generate a probation list (a list of all students whose grade point average is less than 2) for active students only and for each department and each school.

13. Express the program of problem 12 in a Nassi-Shneiderman chart.

14. Use ANSI flowcharting symbols and draw a structured flowchart for the program of problem 12.

15. Draw a HIPO diagram for the program of problem 12.

16. Draw a Warnier diagram for the program of problem 12.

17. Describe the pseudo code technique in general.

18. What is documentation?

19. What are the minimum items of system documentation?

20. What are the minimum items for documenting subsystems?

21. What are the minimum items of program documentation?

22. Why is documentation needed?

23. Why is overdocumenting a program as bad as little or no documentation?

24. Write down as many guidelines as you can for writing readable programs.

25. Describe indentation and its importance in writing programs.

26. What is meant by a block structured language?

27. Describe a system abstract.

28. Describe a program abstract.

29. What is a data dictionary in program documentation?

30. Make a survey about the usage of structured programming in your local data-processing installations.

31. Make a survey about the usage of structured programming in FORTRAN.

13 SUBPROGRAMS:
Function Subprograms

WHAT ARE SUBPROGRAMS AND WHY DO WE USE THEM?

Every program we have studied thus far is composed of one unit: the program itself. However, in the writing of a larger program, it is easier to divide the overall task of the program into smaller units and program these units (subtasks) separately. These smaller programs are called *subprograms*, and the program that coordinates and controls their execution is called the *mainline* or *main program*.

Another reason for having subprograms is to avoid programming the same routine more than once. For example, a routine to find the square root of a quantity may be used several times in one program or by many different programs. It is more efficient to program the routine once, store it, and refer to it whenever it is needed, rather than rewrite the instruction for it over and over again.

Figure 13.1 is a schematic diagram for a main program that invokes three types of subprograms (discussed later). The first is an arithmetic function (defined within the main program), which adds two real numbers; the second is the FUNCTION subprogram; and the third is the subroutine subprogram. Both FUNCTION subprograms and subroutine programs are defined outside the main program. Figure 13.2 shows the actual main program along with the subprograms of Figure 13.1.

The advantage of writing subprograms are these:

1. They provide the programmer with the ability to write modularized programs (discussed in Chapter 14).

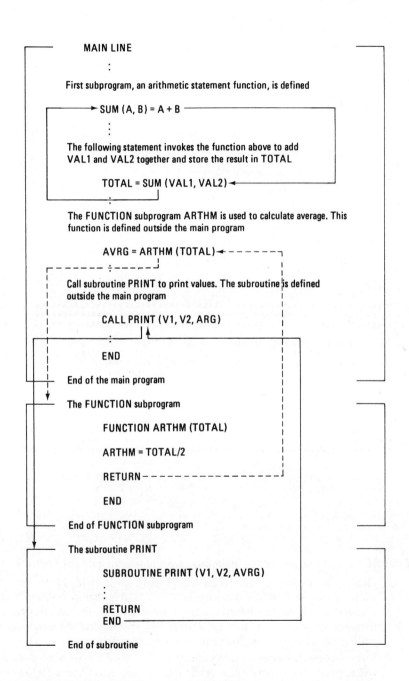

MAIN LINE

. :

First subprogram, an arithmetic statement function, is defined

→ SUM (A, B) = A + B

. :

The following statement invokes the function above to add
VAL1 and VAL2 together and store the result in TOTAL

TOTAL = SUM (VAL1, VAL2) ◄

. :

The FUNCTION subprogram ARTHM is used to calculate average. This
function is defined outside the main program

AVRG = ARTHM (TOTAL) ◄ – – – – – –

. :

Call subroutine PRINT to print values. The subroutine is defined
outside the main program

CALL PRINT (V1, V2, ARG)

. :

END

End of the main program

The FUNCTION subprogram

FUNCTION ARTHM (TOTAL)

ARTHM = TOTAL/2

RETURN – – – – – – – – – – – – – – –

END

End of FUNCTION subprogram

The subroutine PRINT

SUBROUTINE PRINT (V1, V2, AVRG)

. :

RETURN
END

End of subroutine

FIGURE 13.1 Schematic diagram of a main program and subprograms

```
C MAINLINE PROGRAM
C
C THE FOLLOWING STATEMENTS DEFINES A SUBPROGRAM; THE
C FUNCTION STATEMENT SUM WITHIN THE MAIN PROGRAM
C
        SUM(A,B) = A + B
C PRINT HEADINGS
        WRITE(6,10)
   10   FORMAT(6X,'VALUE-1',9X,'VALUE-2'10X,'AVERAGE')
C READ BOTH VALUES
   20   READ(5,30, END=40) VAL1, VAL2
   30   FORMAT(2F5.2)
C
C
C THE NEXT STATEMENT USES DEFINED FUNCTION SUM TO ADD VAL1 AND VAL2
C
        TOTAL = SUM(VAL1,VAL2)
C
C USE THE FUNCTION SUBPROGRAM ARTHM TO DIVIDE TOTAL BY 2
C
        AVRG = ARTHM(TOTAL)
C
C CALL THE SUBROUTINE PRINT TO PRINT THE VALUE OF VAL1, VAL2, AND TOTAL
C
C NOTE THAT PRINT IS THE NAME OF THE SUBROUTINE. CALL STATEMENT SENDS
C CONTROL TO THE SUBROUTINE PRINT.
C
        CALL PRINT(VAL1,VAL2,AVRG)
C AT THIS POINT CONTROL IS BACK FROM THE SUBROUTINE.
        GO TO 20
   40   STOP
        END
C**********************************************************************
C**********      SUBPROGRAM ARTHM          ***************************
C**********************************************************************
C
        FUNCTION ARTHM(TOTAL)
        ARTHM = TOTAL/2
C THE CALCULATED VALUE IS PLACED IN THE FUNTION NAME
C THE FOLLOWING STATEMENT RETURNS CONTROL TO THE MAIN PROGRAM
C
        RETURN
        END
C
C
C**********************************************************************
C********** SUBPROGRAM PRINT              ***************************
C**********************************************************************
C
        SUBROUTINE PRINT (V1,V2,AVRG)
C THE FOLLOWING STATEMENTS PRINT THE VALUES UNDER APPROPRIATE
C HEADINGS WHICH WERE PRINTED IN THE MAIN LINE PROGRAM
C
        WRITE (6,10) V1,V2,AVRG
   10   FORMAT (3(10X,F6.2))
C RETURN TO THE MAIN PROGRAM
        RETURN
        END
```

FIGURE 13.2   Program for the main program and subprograms of Figure 13.1

2. They save memory space. When a large program is divided into smaller subprograms, only one subprogram may be added in memory at one time. The rest can be in secondary storage devices (such as disk). Subprograms that are on secondary storage devices are automatically brought into main memory and linked to the main program whenever referenced.

3. They reduce coding and programming effort. A subprogram needs to be written and stored only once. After that, it can be referenced whenever needed.

4. The possibilities of programming and keypunching errors are reduced, because the routine is written only once.

13.2   TYPES OF SUBPROGRAMS

The following types of subprograms are recognized in FORTRAN:

1. Functions
2. FUNCTION subprograms
3. SUBROUTINE subprograms

In the remainder of this chapter, we will discuss functions. The other two types of subprograms (FUNCTION and SUBROUTINE subprograms) will be discussed in Chapter 14.

13.3   FUNCTIONS

FORTRAN allows three types of functions: (1) open (built-in) functions, (2) closed (library) functions, and (3) arithmetic statement functions. The first two types are supplied by the computer system itself; arithmetic statement functions are written by the programmer. In ANSI FORTRAN, both open and closed functions are called *intrinsic functions.*

13.3.1   Open (Built-in) Functions

In Chapter 7, we used the built-in functions FLOAT—to convert the mode of an integer variable to real—and IFIX—to convert the mode of a real variable to integer. Both FLOAT and IFIX are *built-in* or *open* functions, that specify the compiler's technique for inserting these functions in the object program. Each time a built-in function is encountered, the compiler will insert the function's instruction in the object program.

The programmer can use a built-in function in his or her program by merely referencing its name. For example, the built-in function

is used to determine the remainder when dividing argument *a1* by argument *a2*. Thus, if we write:

$$J = MOD(12,5)$$

the MOD function returns 2, which is the remainder when dividing 12 by 5. Therefore, the value of *J* becomes 2.

TABLE 13.1　FORTRAN built-in (open) functions

NAME OF THE FUNCTION IN FORTRAN	FUNCTION MEANING	NUMBER OF ARGUMENTS	TYPE OF ARGUMENT	TYPE OF VALUE RETURNED
ABS	Determine the absolute value of the argument	1	Real	Real
IABS	Determine the absolute value of the argument	1	Integer	Integer
DIM	The returned value is 0 if argument 1 $\leq$ argument 2; otherwise, the returned value is argument 1 − argument 2.	2	Real	Real
IDIM	The returned value is 0 if argument 1 $\leq$ argument 2; otherwise, the returned value is argument 1 − argument 2.	2	Integer	Integer
FLOAT	Convert an integer value to real value	1	Integer	Real
IFIX	Convert a real value to an integer	1	Real	Integer
SIGN	Assign the sign of argument 2 to argument 1	2	Real	Real
ISIGN	Assign the sign of argument 2 to argument 1	2	Integer	Integer
MOD	Find the remainder when dividing argument 1 by argument 2	2	Integer	Integer
AMOD	Find the remainder when dividing argument 1 by argument 2	2	Real	Real

The built-in functions that are supplied by the computer have standard names. Table 13.1 contains some built-in functions that are of interest to business students.

13.3.2　Closed (Library) Functions

These functions are also supplied by the compiler. In contrast to the case with open functions, the compiler inserts only a single copy of this type of function. References are made to this single copy for any other usage of the function in the program. In general, the procedures for closed functions are much larger than those for open functions. For this reason, the compiler inserts only one copy of a closed function into the object program.

Table 13.2 contains some library functions that are of interest to business students.

TABLE 13.2   FORTRAN library (closed) functions

NAME OF THE FUNCTION IN FORTRAN	FUNCTION MEANING	NUMBER OF ARGUMENTS	TYPE OF ARGUMENT	TYPE OF VALUE RETURNED
ALOG	Calculate the natural logarithm of the argument	1	Real	Real
ALOG1Ø	Calculate the common logarithm (base 10) of the argument	1	Real	Real
EXP	Calculate the antinatural logarithm (base e) of the argument; i.e., e_{**} argument	1	Real	Real
SQRT	Calculate the square root of the argument	1	Real	Real
AMAXØ	Determine the maximum	Two or more	Integer	Real
AMAX1	value of all arguments		Real	Real
MAXØ	in the parentheses		Integer	Integer
MAX1			Real	Integer
AMINØ	Determine the minimum	Two or more	Integer	Real
AMIN1	value of the arguments		Real	Real
MINØ	in the parentheses		Integer	Integer
MIN1			Real	Integer

13.3.3   How to Use Computer-Supplied Functions

To use either open or closed functions, the programmer should observe the following points:

1. Be sure to use the correct name of the function. These names are standard and any misspelling causes errors—for example, writing AMAXO instead of AMAXØ. Note that the latter ends with digit zero, not the letter O.
2. The function name should be followed by parentheses. The argument or arguments are written within the parentheses. Number, type, and mode of arguments must be exactly as indicated in Table 13.1 or 13.2. For example, each of the functions SQRT(16.0) and SQRT(16.) is valid and returns the value 4.0, but the function SQRT(16) is invalid, because the argument of SQRT must be real.
3. A function cannot be placed to the left of an equals (=) sign. However, a function may be used to the right of the sign.
4. One value is returned when the function is called.
5. The function name determines the mode of the returned value.
6. These functions are compiled within the main program.

Example 13.1

    1. The statement

Y = ABS(−5.20)

       causes the value of Y to be 5.20.

    2. The statement

F = IABS(7) * 5

       makes the value of F 35.0.

    3. The statement

X = 5.2
Z1 = DIM(X,1∅.5)

       makes the value of $Z1$ 0.0, since the first argument, X, is less than the second argument.

    4. The statement

X = 20.0
Z2 = DIM(X,1∅.5)

       makes the value of $Z2$ 9.5, which is the difference between the first argument, X, and the second argument, 10.5.

    5. After execution of the following statements:

Y = 5.0
X = 20.0
J = 10
I = 30
R1 = AMAX∅(J,I,40,1)*5
R2 = AMAX1(Y,X,R1,100.0)
R3 = MAX∅(J,I)
R4 = MAX1(R3,X,50.0)

       the value of $R1$ is 200.0, $R2$ is 200.0, $R3$ is 30.0, and $R4$ is 50.0.

    6. Note that e (base of the natural logarithm system) is approximately 2.7182. Suppose we want to find e^3 —that is, $(2.718)^3$. All we need do is use the built-in function EXP:

Y = EXP(3.0)

       so that the value of Y becomes 20.085.

7. To find the natural logarithm of 100 (base *e*), we simply write ALOG (1∅∅.). Thus, the statement

```
Z = ALOG(1∅∅.)
```

assigns 4.6051 (which is the natural logarithm of 100 to base *e*) as the value of *Z*.

8. After execution of the statement

```
K = ALOGI∅   (1∅∅)
```

the value of K becomes 2, because the function ALOG1∅(1∅∅) finds the logarithm of 100 for base 10, which is 2.

Example 13.2

The following are invalid:

EXAMPLE	REASON
SQRT(I)	The argument must be real.
MAX∅(R1,I,J,5.∅)	All arguments of MAX∅ must be integers.
MODE(12,7)	There is no such function as MODE, but there is MOD function.
FLOAT(I,J)	Only one argument is allowed with FLOAT function.

13.3.4   Arithmetic Statement Functions

The arithmetic statement function is referenced by its name and specifies some operations to be performed whenever it appears in other statements in the same program unit; it returns only one result. Unlike built-in and library functions, the arithmetic statement function must be written by the programmer. It is constructed from one statement and must be placed at the beginning of the programming, preceding all executable statements.

Example 13.3

Suppose we want to create an arithmetic statement function to calculate weekly gross pay by adding the regular pay to the overtime pay. The rate for an overtime hour is $1\frac{1}{2}$ times the regular wage. The required arithmetic statement function can be written:

PAY (HRS, OT, RATE) = HRS * RATE + 1.5 * OT * RATE

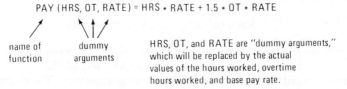

name of function   dummy arguments   HRS, OT, and RATE are "dummy arguments," which will be replaced by the actual values of the hours worked, overtime hours worked, and base pay rate.

Note that we could also define PAY by writing P(X,Y,R) = X*R + 1.5*Y*R with exactly the same results.

Then, within the same program in which PAY is defined, the statement

GROSS = PAY(4Ø.Ø,1Ø.Ø,5.Ø)

causes the value of GROSS to become 275. Here is how the value of GROSS is calculated:

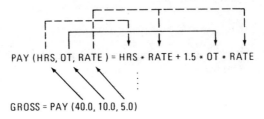

PAY (HRS, OT, RATE) = HRS * RATE + 1.5 * OT * RATE

GROSS = PAY (40.0, 10.0, 5.0)

The execution of the statement GROSS = PAY(40.0,10.0,5.0) invokes the execution of the arithmetic statement PAY(HRS,OT,RATE). At this point, the value of the dummy argument HRS becomes 40.0, OT becomes 10.0, and RATE becomes 5.0. Therefore, the arithmetic statement function becomes:

PAY(4Ø.Ø,1Ø.Ø,5.Ø) = 4Ø.Ø * 5.0 + 1.5 *1Ø.Ø * 5.Ø

which assigns 275 as the value of PAY(40.0,10.0,5.0).

It is important to note that the mode and the order of dummy and actual argument must be the same. To show how arithmetic statement functions are actually used in a program, we will write a FORTRAN program to calculate the total weekly gross paid by a company using the arithmetic statement function above to calculate weekly pay for each employee. Suppose the input record is organized as follows:

cc	
1–4	Regular hours XX.XX
5–8	Overtime hours XX.XX
9–12	Rate per regular hour XX.XX

Then the flowchart is as in Figure 13.3, and the program as in Figure 13.4.

13.3.4.1   RULES FOR USING THE ARITHMETIC STATEMENT FUNCTION

1. The general form of the arithmetic statement function is:

$$Name(a1, a2, \ldots, an) = Expression$$

where *name* is the function name chosen by the programmer according to the rules of variable names in FORTRAN, and *a1, a2, . . ., an* are simple variable names, which are the dummy arguments. The expression

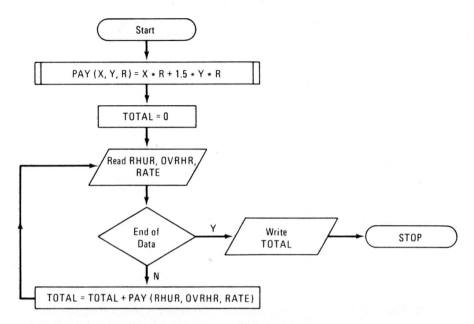

FIGURE 13.3   Flowchart for program to calculate total weekly gross

```
C FIRST DEFINE THE ARITHMETIC STATEMENT BEFORE ANY EXECUTABLE STATEMENT
C
         PAY(HRS,OT,RATE) = HRS * RATE + 1.5 * OT * RATE
C
C NOTE THAT HRS, OT AND RATE ARE DUMMY ARGUMENTS.
C
         TOTAL = 0.0
C
10       READ(5,20,END=30) RHUR, OVRHUR, RATE
20       FORMAT(3F4.2)
C
C USE THE ARITHMETIC FUNCTION PAY TO CALCULATE PAY
C
         TOTAL = TOTAL + PAY(RHUR, OVRHUR, RATE)
C
C NOTE THAT RHUR, OVRHUR AND RATE ARE REAL ARGUMENTS.
C
         GO TO 10
C
30       WRITE(6,40) TOTAL
40       FORMAT(6X,F9.2)
         STOP
         END
```

FIGURE 13.4   Program to calculate total weekly gross

     must be a FORTRAN expression that contains no subscripted variable; however, it may contain a reference to a FORTRAN-supplied function or to a previously defined statement function.

2. The arithmetic statement is constructed of a single statement as shown in rule 1.

3. No executable statement can precede the arithmetic statement function.

4. Whenever the arithmetic statement function is referenced, the actual arguments must agree in number, order, and mode with dummy arguments. For example, define the arithmetic statement function

$$T(N,C,B,F) = N * (C + B) + F$$

to calculate total cost, where N is the number of units, C is the raw-material cost/unit, B is the labor cost/unit, and F is the fixed amount cost (that is, the setup cost).

     Then TOTAL = T(UNITS, CST, WAGE, STUP) is *invalid*, because the first actual argument, UNITS, is real, whereas the corresponding dummy argument N is an integer variable. TOTAL = T(NUM,CST,WAGE) is also invalid, because the number of arguments in the T function must be four as defined originally.

5. The arithmetic statement function is compiled within a program; therefore, it cannot be referenced by any other program except the one that contains it.

6. The arithmetic statement returns only one result.

7. The mode of the result returned by the arithmetic statement is determined by the mode of the name of the arithmetic statement function. Thus, if a real variable name is chosen as the name of the arithmetic statement, then the returned result is real; if the name of the arithmetic statement is an integer variable, the result is an integer; and so on.

13.4   SUMMARY

     FORTRAN permits three types of subprograms: functions, FUNCTION subprograms, and SUBROUTINE subprograms. The three types of functions are open (built-in), closed (library), and arithmetic statement function. Both built-in and library functions are supplied by the computer. The arithmetic statement function is constructed of one statement written by the programmer and must be placed before all executable statements in the program.

     Some characteristics of functions are these:

1. They return one result.

2. The mode of the result is determined by the mode of the name of the function.

3. They are compiled within the main program.

4. They are referenced by name.

1. *True or False.* Functions are compiled within the main program.

2. *True or False.* When a function is referenced, one or more values can be returned.

3. *True or False.* When a function is referenced, the mode of the function's name determines the mode of the result.

4. *True or False.* The statement

```
Y = AMAXØ(5,1Ø)
```

causes the value of Y to equal 10.

5. *True or False.* The statement

```
Y = AMAX1(5,1Ø)
```

assigns 10. as the value of Y.

6. *True or False.* The statement

```
J = MOD(17,5)
```

assigns 2 as the value of J.

7. *True or False.* The statement

```
Y = AMOD(17,5)
```

assigns 2 as the value of Y.

8. After execution of the following statements:

```
N = 5
M = 2Ø
K = MAX(M,21,N)
L = MOD(K,1Ø)
R = AMINØ(K,L,2)
```

the value of K is _____, L is _____, and R is _____.

9. *True or False.* The arithmetic statement function is constructed of a single lined statement.

10. *True or False.* No executable statement can precede the arithmetic statement.

11. *True or False.* A specification statement such as a FORMAT statement can be placed before an arithmetic statement function.

12. *True or False.* When the arithmetic statement function is referenced, the dummy and actual argument must have the same names.

13. *True or False.* The corresponding dummy and actual arguments when an arithmetic statement function is referenced must agree in the same mode.

14. *True or False.* An arithmetic statement function that is defined in one program can be referenced by a different program or programmer.

15. *True or False.* An arithmetic statement function can return more than one result.

16. *True or False.* The mode of the name of the arithmetic function determines the mode of the result.

17. Write a FORTRAN program and use an arithmetic statement function to find the present value of a given amount in order to calculate simple discount. The present and simple discount are calculated as follows:

$$P = \frac{S}{1 + rn} \qquad \text{and} \qquad I = S - P$$

where P is the present value, S is the total amount due after n years, r is the interest rate, and I is the simple discount. Prepare the input record to contain S, r, and n. Your program should print the present value, total amount, rate of interest, and the period length, along with simple discount, under appropriate headings. The program should process more than one set of input data.

18. *Effective Rate of Interest.* Frequently, the effective rate is used as a device to compare one interest rate with another rate compounded over different time intervals. The manager of the ABC Company wishes to borrow from the source that has the lowest effective rate and invest in one having the highest effective rate for investments. The effective rate of interest is calculated by the formula:

$$f = \left(1 + \frac{j}{n}\right)^n - 1$$

where:

    f is the effective rate.
    n is the number of conversion periods for one year.
    j is the nominal rate.

Create an arithmetic statement function and write a FORTRAN program to compare the effective rates for several banks. Each input record should give the name of the bank and the rate of interest offered by the bank.

14 SUBPROGRAMS AND MODULAR PROGRAMMING

In the preceding chapter, it was pointed out that the arithmetic statement function is used to define a routine that is expressible by a single statement. Furthermore, the function can be referenced only within the program that defines the function. Note that more than one arithmetic statement function could be used to define a routine that cannot be represented by a single statement; however, such a routine cannot be referenced by other programs. FORTRAN provides two types of subprograms to define a routine that requires more than one statement and can be referenced by many different programs.

The first type of subprogram is the FUNCTION, used for cases in which the routine returns only one result; the second type, the subroutine subprogram, is used where one or more results must be returned by the routine. Unlike arithmetic statement functions, both FUNCTION subprograms and subroutine subprograms are compiled separately from the mainline program and therefore can be referred to by other programs.

14.1 FUNCTION SUBPROGRAMS

The FUNCTION subprogram is a routine that comprises more than one statement but returns only one value. The returned value must be assigned to the name of the FUNCTION subprogram. The END statement must be the last statement of the FUNCTION subprogram, and the subprogram must contain at least one RETURN statement. The general form of the FUNCTION subprogram is:

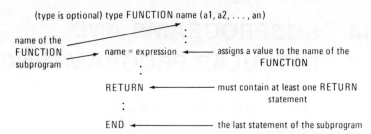

where the type is any FORTRAN variable type such as REAL, INTEGER, or LOGICAL. If the type is omitted, the mode of the FUNCTION's name determines the mode of the returned result. The arguments *a1, a2, . . ., an* are dummy arguments.

Example 14.1

The following FUNCTION subprogram calculates the average of two real numbers:

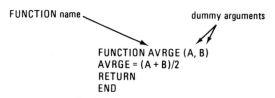

Then, when a statement such as:

in the main program is encountered, control transfers to the first statement of the FUNCTION subprogram. The actual arguments (the arguments within the parentheses following the FUNCTION's name in the main program—in this case, 10.0 and 8.0) must agree in number, mode, and order with the dummy arguments. When control passes to the FUNCTION subprogram, the value of *A* becomes 10.0 and the value of *B* becomes 8.0. Then the computer executes the second statement of the subprogram—namely, AVRGE = (A + B)/2—which makes the value of AVRGE 9.0. The next statement (RETURN) returns control back to the same statement of the main program that relinquished control to the subprogram. Thus, the value of ARM becomes 45.0:

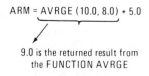

Example 14.2

Write a FORTRAN main program and a FUNCTION subprogram to update a customer's balance and to print out the new balance and interest charge. The main program should read the input record and invoke the FUNCTION subprogram, which calculates the interest charge on the unpaid balance. Also, the main program should compute the new balance and print out both the new balance and the interest charge. The FUNCTION subprogram uses the following table to calculate the interest charge:

UNPAID BALANCE	INTEREST RATE
Less than $500	1.5%
Between $500 and $1,000	1.3%
More than $1,000	1%

The input record is organized in the following manner:

cc	
1–5	Account number
6–11	Old balance
12–17	Payment

The program is shown in Figure 14.1. The pseudo code and the flowchart for the main program are shown in Figure 14.2 and those for the FUNCTION subprogram INTRST in Figure 14.3.

Note that statement 30 of the main program sends control to the FUNCTION subprogram INTRST, and when a RETURN statement is encountered in the FUNCTION subprogram, control returns to this point in the main program.

14.1.1   FUNCTION Subprogram Rules

1. The FUNCTION subprogram is a FORTRAN program; therefore, it can contain any FORTRAN statement except the statements to define a SUBROUTINE, another FUNCTION subprogram, or a BLOCK DATA statement.
2. The FUNCTION subprogram must start with a FUNCTION statement. (See the general form of the FUNCTION subprogram.)
3. The arguments transfer values between the main program and the subprogram. Arguments enclosed in parentheses following the name of the FUNCTION in the subprogram or defined by COMMON statements (explained later) are called *dummy arguments*. The actual arguments are enclosed in parentheses following the name of the function whenever the FUNCTION is referenced in the main program, or are defined by a

```
C THE MAIN PROGRAM
C VARIABLE NAMES USED
C       NUM      ACCOUNT NUMBER
C       BLNS     OLD BALANCE
C       PAYMNT   PAYMENT
C       CHARGE   INTEREST CHARGE
C       NBLNS    NEW BALANCE
        REAL NBLNS
   10   READ (5, 20, END = 70) NUM, BLNS, PAYMNT
   20   FORMAT (I5, 2F6.2)
        UNPAID = BLNS - PAYMNT
        IF (UNPAID .GT. 0.0) GO TO 30
        CHARGE = 0.0
        GO TO 40
C
C THE NEXT STATEMENT TRANSFERS THE CONTROL
C TO THE FUNCTION SUBPROGRAM INTRST.  BOTH
C BLNS AND PAYMNT ARE THE ACTULA ARGUMENT
C
C
   30   CHARGE = INTRST (BLNS, PAYMNT)
C
   40   NBLNS = UNPAID + CHARGE
        WRITE (6, 50) NUM, NBLNS, CHARGE
   50   FORMAT (6X, I5, 6X, F7.2, 6X, F5.2)
        GO TO 10
   70   STOP
        END



C***********************************************************************
C*****        SUBPROGRAM INTRST              ***************************
C***********************************************************************
C
        REAL FUNCTION INTRST (BALANS, PAY)
        UNPAID = BALANS - PAY
        IF (UNPAID .GE. 500) GO TO 10
        INTRST = UNPAID * 0.015
C RETURNS TO THE MAIN PROGRAM
        RETURN
   10   IF (UNPAID .GT. 1000.) GO TO 20
        INTRST = UNPAID * 0.013
        RETURN
   20   INTRST = UNPAID * 0.01
        RETURN
        END
```

FIGURE 14.1   Program for example 14.2

Pseudo Code Form

```
Start
DOWHILE not end of data
     IF Unpaid > 0 Then
            Use function INTRST to find CHARGE
            Compute New balance
       ELSE CHARGE = 0
     Write NUM, NBLNS, CHARGE
End DOWHILE
Stop
```

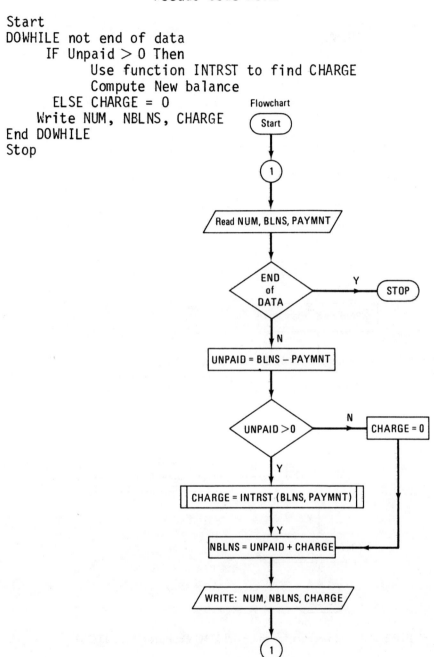

FIGURE 14.2   The pseudo code and the flowchart for the main program of example 14.2

313

Pseudo Code Form

```
Start INTRST
Compute  UNPAID
IF UNPAID < 500 Then
                INTRST = UNPAID * 0.15
                RETURN
   ELSE IF UNPAID ≤ 1000 Then
                INTRST = UNPAID * 0.013
                RETURN
        ELSE  INTRST = UNPAID * 0.01
                RETURN
END IF
```

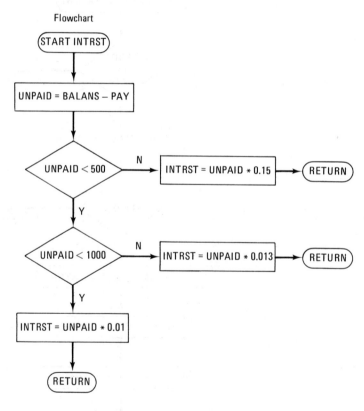

Flowchart

FIGURE 14.3   Flowchart for the FUNCTION subprogram INTRST

COMMON statement within the main program. A dummy argument may be:

a. A nonsubscripted variable

b. An array name

An actual argument may be:

a. A constant

b. A nonsubscripted variable

c. An array element

d. An array name

e. An expression

f. A reference to a FORTRAN subprogram (see the EXTERNAL statement)

Note that if the actual argument is an array, the corresponding dummy argument must be an array as well.

An actual argument and a dummy argument do not have to have the same name; however, corresponding arguments must agree in mode. When the subprogram is referenced, the values of the actual arguments are assigned to the corresponding dummy arguments of the subprograms. It is good practice to assign the same names for both the actual and dummy arguments.

4. The FUNCTION subprogram is referenced by merely using its name within an expression in the main program.

5. The name of the FUNCTION subprogram must appear at least once on the left of an equals sign (=) within the FUNCTION subprogram. In other words, a value must be assigned to the name of the FUNCTION subprogram at least once. In the FUNCTION subprogram INTRST, the name of the FUNCTION appears in three places.

6. After execution of the FUNCTION subprogram, the returned result is stored in the FUNCTION's name.

7. The FUNCTION subprogram must contain at least one RETURN statement. (The FUNCTION subprogram INTRST contains three RETURN statements.) The RETURN statement in the FUNCTION subprogram returns control to the same statement that sent control to the FUNCTION subprogram.

8. The FUNCTION subprogram is compiled and stored separately from the main program. Therefore, it can be used by many different programs.

The following example demonstrates how to use arrays as arguments.

Example 14.3

The main program reads a number of families and their incomes and uses the FUNCTION ARMEAN to find the average incomes of the families. The number of families can be different in each run; however, it cannot be more than 100. The input record is organized as follows:

CC	FIELD
1–2	Number of families
3–9	1st family income
10–16	2nd family income
17–23	3rd family income
•	•
•	•
•	•

The main program and the FUNCTION subprogram are in Figure 14.4, and the flowcharts in Figure 14.5. *Note:* (1) This time, the same names are used for both the actual and dummy arguments; and (2) since INCOM is an array in the main program, then INCOM must be an array in the FUNCTION subprogram as well.

```
C MAIN PROGRAM
C VARIABLE NAMES
C          INCOM(I)          INCOME FOR FAMILY
C          AVARGE            AVERAGE INCOME
C          N                 NUMBER OF FAMILIES IN THE RUN
C
C*********************************************************************
C
          REAL INCOM
          DIMENSION INCOM(100)
          READ (5, 10) N, (INCOM(J) , J = 1, N)
     10   FORMAT (I2, 100F7.2)
C
          AVARGE = ARMEAN (INCOM , N)
          WRITE (6, 20) N, AVARGE
     20   FORMAT (6X, 'THE AVERAGE INCOME FOR', I2, 'FAMALIES IS', F8.2)
          STOP
          END
C
C
C
C*********************************************************************
C*****          SUBPROGRAM ARMEAN                 ***********************
C*********************************************************************
          FUNCTION ARMEAN (INCOM, N)
          REAL      INCOM
          DIMENSION INCOM (100)
C THE FOLLOWING STATEMENT PRINTS THE INCOME
C OF ALL FAMILIES PASSED TO THE FUNCTION SUBPROGRAM
          WRITE (6, 10) N, (INCOM(J) , J = 1, N)
     10   FORMAT (6X, 'THE INCOME FOR', I2, 'FAMILIES ARE:', / 10(6X, F8.2))
C
          SUM = 0.0
          DO 20 I = 1, N
              SUM = SUM + INCOM(I)
     20   CONTINUE
          ARMEAN = SUM/FLOAT(N)
          RETURN
          END
```

FIGURE 14.4   The main program and FUNCTION subprogram to find the income average of a number of families

14.2   SUBROUTINE SUBPROGRAM

As with FUNCTION subprograms, the SUBROUTINE subprogram comprises more than one statement, and it is written by the programmer. The general form of the SUBROUTINE subprogram is:

Flowchart for the Main Program

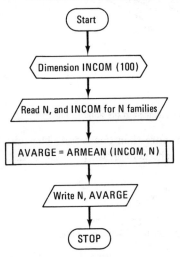

Flowchart for the FUNCTION Subprogram ARMEAN

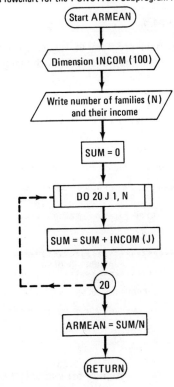

FIGURE 14.5   Flowcharts for the main program and subprogram ARMEAN

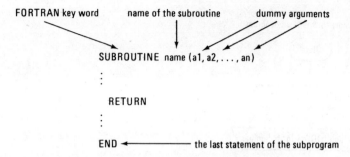

The SUBROUTINE subprogram can return more than one result. The subroutine is referred to by the CALL statement. The general form of the CALL statement is:

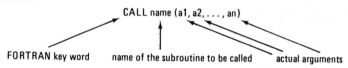

The order, number, and mode of the actual and dummy arguments must be the same.

Example 14.4

The main program in Figure 14.6 reads two numbers and calls subroutine MAVR to find their average and the larger of the two.

```
C                    MAIN PROGRAM
C READ THE VALUES OF A AND B
         READ (5, 10) A, B
    10   FORMAT (2F2.0)
C THE FOLLOWING CALL STATEMENT TRANSFERS CONTROL TO THE
C SUBROUTINE MAVR TO CALCULATE THE VALUE OF ARM
C AND BIG.  AT THIS POINT THE VALUES OF A AND B ARE
C KNOWN, BUT THE VALUE OF ARM AND BIG ARE NOT.
C
         CALL MAVR (A, B, ARM, BIG)
C
C CONTROL IS RETURNED FROM THE SUBROUTINE MAVR.  NOW THE
C VALUES OF ALL ARGUMENTS ARE KNOWN.
         WRITE (6, 10) ARM, BIG
    20   FORMAT (6X, 'MEAN:', F5.2, 'MAXIMUM:', F5.2)
         STOP
         END
C
C***************************************************************
C******          SUBPROGRSM MAVR               *****************
C***************************************************************
C
         SUBROUTINE MAVR (R1, R2, AM, BIG)
         AM = (R1 + R2) / 2.0
         IF (R1 .LT. R2) GO TO 10
         BIG = R1
         GO TO 20
    10   BIG = R2
    20   RETURN
         END
```

FIGURE 14.6 Program for example 14.4

To explain the example, assume that 10 is read as the value of *A* and 20 as the value of *B*. When the CALL statement (the third statement of the main program) is encountered, control transfers to the subroutine MAVR. At this point, the value of *A* is 10, the value of *B* is 20, and the value of both ARM and BIG are unknown. When control enters the subroutine MAVR, the value of the dummy argument *R1* becomes 10, the value of *R2* becomes 20, and the values of AM and BIG are unknown. Next, the computer executes the second statement in the subroutine, AM = (R1 + R2)/2.0. This statement assigns 15.0 as the value of AM. At this point, the value of ARM becomes 15.0 as well; the arguments ARM and AM are different names for the same memory location, which is shared by the subroutine and the main program. For that reason, when one of them changes, the other changes accordingly. Next, because *R1* is less than *R2*, the IF statement sends the control to statement 10, which assigns the value of *R2* (which is 20) to BIG. The RETURN statement returns control to the statement that immediately follows the CALL statement in the main program. In this case, control is returned to the WRITE statement of the main program. Now the WRITE statement prints the value of ARM and BIG.

14.2.1 SUBROUTINE Subprogram Rules

1. The SUBROUTINE subprogram is a FORTRAN program, and it can contain any FORTRAN statement except the statements to define a subroutine and other FUNCTION subprograms, or a BLOCK DATA statement.
2. The SUBROUTINE subprogram must start with a SUBROUTINE statement. (See the general form above.)
3. The actual arguments either are defined by a COMMON statement (explained later) within the main program or appear in the list of the CALL statement. Likewise, the dummy arguments either are defined by a COMMON statement within the SUBROUTINE or appear in the list of the SUBROUTINE statement. The actual and dummy arguments are used to transfer the values between the main program and the subprogram more accurately, to share the values between the subprogram and the main program. A dummy argument may be:
   a. A nonsubscripted variable
   b. An array name
      An actual argument may be:
   a. A constant
   b. A nonsubscripted variable
   c. An array element
   d. An array name
   e. An expression
   f. A reference to a FORTRAN subprogram (see the EXTERNAL statement)

4. A SUBROUTINE subprogram can return more than one result. The results are returned in the dummy arguments. The mode of the arguments determines the mode of the returned results.

5. The SUBROUTINE subprogram must contain at least one RETURN statement. The RETURN statement returns control to the statement that immediately follows the CALL statement that transferred control to the subprogram.

6. The SUBROUTINE subprogram is referenced by means of the CALL statement. In other words, the CALL statement transfers control to the subroutine.

7. The SUBROUTINE subprogram is compiled separately from the main program.

Example 14.5: Using an Array as an Argument

Write a FORTRAN program to read the income of 100 families and to call a subroutine to calculate both the average and standard deviation of these incomes.

```
C VARIABLE NAMES USED
C       INCOM : AN ARRAY TO HOLD FAMILY INCOME
C       AM    : ARITHMETIC MEAN
C       SD    : STANDARD DEVIATION
C
C**********************************************************************
C
        REAL INCOM
        DIMENSION INCOM(100)
        READ (5, 10) INCOM
  10    FORMAT (100F7.2)
C THIS CALL STATEMENT SENDS CONTROL TO THE SUBROUTINE FSDMN
        CALL FSDMN (INCOM, 100, AM, SD)
C NOW BOTH AM AND SD ARE KNOWN
        WRITE (6, 20) AM, SD
  20    FORMAT ('1', 6X, 'THE AVERAGE INCOM'
       +         'FOR 100 FAMILIES IS:',F8.2, 6X, 'THE',
       +         'STANDARD DEVIATION IS:', F8.2)
        STOP
        END
C
C**********************************************************************
C********** SUBROUTINE FSDMN                   **********************
C**********************************************************************
C
        SUBROUTINE FSDMN (INCOM, N, AM, SD)
        REAL INCOM
        DIMENSION INCON(100)
        SUM = 0.0
        SUMSQ = 0.0
        DO 10 J = 1, N
            SUM = SUM + INCOM(J)
            SUMSQ = SUM + INCOM(J) ** 2
  10    CONTINUE
C CALCULATE THE MEAN
        AM = SUM/FLOAT(N)
C CALCULATE THE STANDARD DEVIATION
        SD = (SUMSQ/FLOAT(N) - AM ** 2) ** 0.5
        RETURN
        END
```

FIGURE 14.7   Program for example 14.5

In the program, declare the income of families to be a one-dimensional array. Note that the standard deviation is:

$$SD = \sqrt{\frac{\Sigma(X_i - \overline{x})}{n}} = \sqrt{\frac{\Sigma X_i^2}{n} - (\overline{x})^2}$$

where $\overline{x}$ is the arithmetic mean and X_i is an individual observation.

The program is shown in Figure 14.7 and the flowchart in Figure 14.8.

FIGURE 14.8   Flowchart to find the average and standard deviation of incomes of 100 families

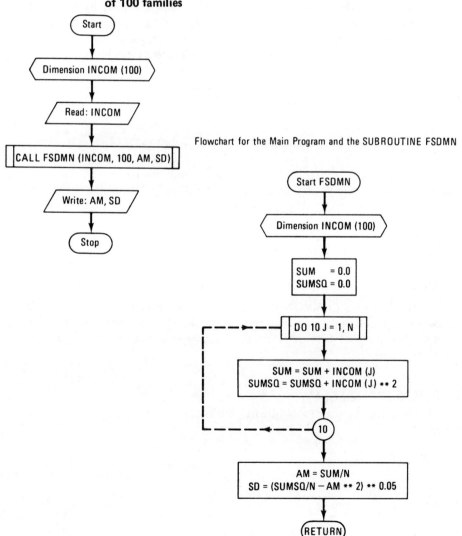

Flowchart for the Main Program and the SUBROUTINE FSDMN

14.3 SOME MORE SPECIFICATION STATEMENTS

In this section, three more specification statements—COMMON, EQUIV-ALENCE, and EXTERNAL—are discussed.

14.3.1 COMMON Statement

The purpose of dummy arguments and actual arguments is to establish communications between a main program and subprograms, or between subprograms themselves. Another way to establish such communication is by use of the COMMON statement. This statement provides the facility to share memory locations between different program units. (A main program or a subprogram is called a program unit.) The general form of the COMMON statement is:

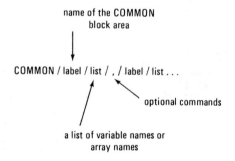

The label (the name) of the COMMON block area is optional.

Example 14.6

The following COMMON statements cause seven memory locations to be shared among the main program, subroutine STLINE, and subroutine SUMYR. Note that the COMMON statement must appear in all program units that share the locations.

```
DIMENSION NAME(4)
COMMON LIFE, SCRAP, COST, NAME
        .
        .
END

SUBROUTINE  STLINE
DIMENSION NAME(4)
```

```
COMMON L, SCR, COST, NAME
      .
      .
END

SUBROUTINE SUMYR
DIMENSION N(4)
COMMON LF, SV, COST, N
      .
      .
      .
END
```

Figure 14.9 demonstrates how the statements above cause the seven locations to be shared.

Main Program	COMMON Storage Location	SUBROUTINE STLINE	SUBROUTINE SUMYR
LIFE		L	LF
SCRAP		SCR	SV
COST		COST	COST
NAME (1)		NAME (1)	N (1)
NAME (2)		NAME (2)	N (2)
NAME (3)		NAME (3)	N (3)
NAME (4)		NAME (4)	N (4)

FIGURE 14.9   Referencing COMMON storage area

While control is in the main program, the name of the first location of the COMMON storage area is LIFE; when control is in the subroutine STLINE, the same location is known by the name L (not LIFE); and when control is in the subroutine SUMYR, the same location is known by the name LF. Note that there is only one location, but it has three different names, depending upon the program unit. Therefore, to avoid confusion, use the same name in all program units for a given location (such as COST, the name of the third location in our example).

When a program interfaces with several subprograms that use variables in the

COMMON storage area, it is not likely that every subprogram will use every variable in the area. One subprogram may reference some COMMON storage locations and others may reference different locations. Therefore, when it is desired to give a subprogram the access to only a part of the COMMON storage area, use the labeled COMMON storage technique.

Example 14.7

In the following example, the COMMON block area BEGIN has 21 locations, and the area LAST has 11 locations:

```
C  MAIN PROGRAM
   COMMON / BEGIN / NUM, RATE(20), / LAST / INCOM(10), B
          .
          .
          .
   END

   SUBROUTINE FACM
   COMMON / BEGIN / NUM, R1, R2, B(18) / LAST /INCOME(10),A
          .
          .
   END

   FUNCTION EDIT(PAY)
   COMMON / BEGIN / N, X(20) /
          .
          .
   END
```

Figure 14.10 illustrates how the COMMON storage memory locations above are referenced.

All 21 locations of the COMMON storage area BEGIN are shared by the main program and both subprograms. The COMMON storage area LAST is shared by the main program and SUBROUTINE FACM. No part of the COMMON storage LAST is available for the FUNCTION EDIT.

COMMON Storage Area	Label of the COMMON Area	Main Program	SUBROUTINE FACM	FUNCTION EDIT
		NUM	NUM	N
		RATE (1)	R 1	X (1)
		RATE (2)	R 2	X (2)
⋮	BEGIN	⋮	B (1) ⋮	⋮
		RATE (20)	B (18)	X (20)
		INCOM (1)	INCOM (1)	
		INCOM (2)	INCOM (2)	
	LAST	⋮	⋮	
		INCOM (10)	INCOM (10)	
		B	A	

FIGURE 14.10

Rules for the use of the COMMON statement:

1. The COMMON statement must precede any executable statement.
2. The order and the mode of the elements in the list (variable and array names) of COMMON statements in the main program and subprograms must match.
3. Any name that appears in the argument list of a subprogram or in the argument list of a CALL statement must not be an element in the list of COMMON statements. For example:

```
C  MAIN PROGRAM        SUBROUTINE CHECK(X,Y)
   COMMON A, B, C      COMMON A, B, C
      .                   .
      .                   .
      .                   .
   CALL CHECK (X, Y)   END
      .
      .
   END
```

The setup above is correct. The arguments X and Y are not permitted to appear in the list of the COMMON statement because they are in the CALL and subprogram lists.

4. The COMMON statement can be used to declare any array. For example:

```
COMMON   B(5),  X(20,5)
```

declares that B is a one-dimensional array of five elements and X is a two-dimensional array with 100 elements, so that there are 105 locations in the COMMON storage area. In the following example, nine locations are shared by the main program and subprogram:

```
C  MAIN PROGRAM
   COMMON J(5), B(4)
       .
       .
   END
   SUBROUTINE CHECK
   COMMON N, I, M(3), R1, R2, B(2)
       .
       .
   END
```

COMMON Storage	Main Program	Subroutine CHECK
	J (1)	N
	J (2)	I
	J (3)	M (1)
	J (4)	M (2)
	J (5)	M (3)
	B (1)	R1
	B (2)	R2
	B (3)	B (1)
	B (4)	B (2)

5. More than one COMMON statement can appear in a program. If several COMMON statements are given (in a program), they are equivalent to one continuous COMMON statement. The following COMMON statements have the same effect:
   a. COMMON A, B, C, PAY(5)
   b. COMMON A, B
      COMMON C, PAY(5)
   c. COMMON A
      COMMON B, C
      COMMON PAY(5)
   d. COMMON A
      COMMON B
      COMMON C
      COMMON PAY(5)

6. The same statement may contain both labeled and unlabeled COMMON storage. For example:

```
COMMON A , B /AREA1/X, J, N/AREA2/D, E//K, R
```

declares two labeled COMMON areas, AREA1 and AREA2, and an unlabeled COMMON area that contains A, B, K, and R. Note that if a block name is omitted but two consecutive slashes are given before the list, then the variables following the two consecutive $//$ are assigned to unlabeled COMMON areas. This explains how K and R are assigned into the unlabeled block area.

7. Unlabeled COMMON areas may be of different sizes in various program units, but labeled COMMON areas must be of the same size in all program units.

8. Entities in unlabeled COMMON areas must be initially defined by a DATA statement; however, the entities of the labeled COMMON can be initialized by the DATA statement.

14.3.2   EQUIVALENCE Statement

The EQUIVALENCE statement is used to assign two or more variable names or array names to the same locations within a given program unit. The programmer can use the storage more efficiently by using the EQUIVALENCE statement. For example, the statement

```
EQUIVALENCE (WAGE, RATE, R) , (PAYMN, PAY) , (ICOUNT, I)
```

reserves three memory locations. The first locations can be referenced by the name WAGE, RATE, or R; the second location by the names PAYMN or PAY; the third location by the names ICOUNT or I. The EQUIVALENCE statement saves computer time, since the locations are allocated during the compilation time rather than the execution time. The EQUIVALENCE statement is useful where a programmer discovers that different spellings for a variable name, such as DISCN and DISCNT, have been used many times in the program. The inclusion of a statement such as:

```
EQUIVALENCE (DISCN, DISCNT)
```

solves the problem. The main drawback of the EQUIVALENCE statement is that it makes the program harder to understand, less readable.

The general form of the EQUIVALENCE statement is:

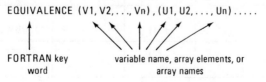

EQUIVALENCE (V1, V2, . . ., Vn) , (U1, U2, . . ., Un) . . . . .

FORTRAN key   variable name, array elements, or
word   array names

The EQUIVALENCE statement specifies that the entities in a list have the same first storage unit. This causes associations for the entities in the list and *may cause associations for other entities as well.*

Example 14.8

```
DIMENSION A(5) , B(8) , C(3)
EQUIVALENCE (A(1) , B(1)) , (B(6) , C(1))
```

This causes A(1) through A(5) to share the same locations as B(1) through B(5), and B(6) through B(8) to share the same locations as C(1) through C(3).

Memory Locations	Names for the Same Locations		
	A (1)	B (1)	
	A (2)	B (2)	
	A (3)	B (3)	
	A (4)	B (4)	
	A (5)	B (5)	
		B (6)	C (1)
		B (7)	C (2)
		B (8)	C (3)

Example 14.9

```
DIMENSION A(5) , J(2) , S(3)
EQUIVALENCE (A(1) , S(1)) , (N, NUM, J(1)) ,
            (M, LAST, J(2)) , (A(4) , R)
```

causes storage to be shared as shown below.

Memory Locations	Names for the Same Locations		
	A (1)	S (1)	
	A (2)	S (2)	
	A (3)	S (3)	
	A (4)	R	
	A (5)		
	J (1)	N	NUM
	J (2)	M	LAST

The rules of the EQUIVALENCE statement are:

1. The EQUIVALENCE statement must appear after DIMENSION and COMMON statement but must precede any executable statement.
2. A unit of storage cannot be specified more than once by an EQUIVA-LENCE statement. For example, the following EQUIVALENCE statement is invalid:

```
DIMENSION B(5)
EQUIVALENCE (B(1) , D) , (B(2) , D)
```

Note that *D* appears twice.

14.3.3   EXTERNAL Statement

The EXTERNAL statement permits the programmer to use the name of a subprogram (excluding the arithmetic statement function) as a dummy or an actual argument. The general form of the EXTERNAL statement is:

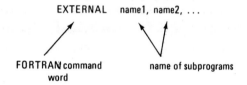

EXTERNAL   name1, name2, ...

FORTRAN command word

name of subprograms

For example:

```
EXTERNAL SQRT
.
.
R = SK(SQRT, Y)
.
.
END
FUNCTION SK(ROOT, Y)
SK = ROOT(Y)
RETURN
END
```

declares that the actual argument SQRT is an external procedure. Therefore, in place of the dummy argument, ROOT, it becomes the built-in function SQRT.

Example 14.10

In Figure 14.11, the FUNCTION name, UNBAL, is used as an actual argument. Therefore, UNBAL must be declared in an EXTERNAL statement.

```
C MAIN PROGRAM
C VARIABLE NAMES
C       OLBLNS          OLD BALANCE
C       PAYMN           PAYMENT
C       CHARG           INTEREST ON BALANCE
C UNBAL, THE NAME OF A FUNCTION SUBPROGRAM, IS USED AS AN
C ARGUMENT.  THEREFORE IT MUST BE DECLARED AS AN EXTERNAL VARIABLE.
C
        EXTERNAL UNBAL
        INPUT = 5
        LINE = 6
C READ BALANCE AND PAYMENT
        READ (INPUT, 10) OLBLNS, PAYMN
    10  FORMAT (2F7.2)
        CALL UPACCN (UNBAL, OLBLNS, PAYMN, CHARG, UPDBL)
        WRITE (LINE, 20) OLBLNS, PAYMN, CHARG, UPDBL
    20  FORMAT (6X, 'OLD BALANCE:' F8.2, 6X, 'NEW BALANCE:', F8.2)
        STOP
        END
C
C*************************************************************************
C
C****    SUBROUTINE   UPACCN          *******************************
C
C*************************************************************************
C
        SUBROUTINE UPACCN (UP, OBL, PAY, CHARG, BAL)
        BAL = 0.0
        CHARG = 0.0
C UP CORRESSPONDS TO THE ACTUAL ARGUMENT UNBAL, NOTE UNBAL IS AN
C EXTERNAL VARIABLE.  THE NEXT STATEMENT TRANSFERS CONTROL TO
C FUNCTION UNBAL.
        DIF = UP (OBL, PAY)
        IF (DIF .GT. 0.0) CHARGE = DIF * 0.015
        BAL = BAL + CHARG
        RETURN
        END
C
C*************************************************************************
C****   FUNCTION UNBAL     ***********************************************
C
C*************************************************************************
C
        FUNCTION UNBAL (OLB,PAY)
        UNBAL = OLB - PAY
        RETURN
        END
```

FIGURE 14.11 Using external statements

14.4 BLOCK DATA SUBPROGRAMS

BLOCK DATA subprograms are used to initialize values of variables and array elements in labeled COMMON blocks. The general form of a BLOCK statement is:

The name is optional. The only other statements that are allowed in a BLOCK DATA subprogram are IMPLICIT, type (such as INTEGER, REAL), DIMENSION, COMMON, EQUIVALENCE, DATA, and END statements. ANSI 77 FORTRAN allows the PARAMETER statement as well.

Example 14.11

```
BLOCK DATA
COMMON /ACNT/ INTRST, PAY, RATE / PERIOD / N, J, K
REAL INTRST
DATA PAY, RATE / 0.0, 0.055 / , N, J / 2*0
END
```

The subprogram above initializes the four variables PAY, RATE, N, and J.

The rules for BLOCK DATA subprograms are:

1. A BLOCK DATA subprogram must not contain any executable statement.
2. It must begin with a BLOCK DATA statement and end with an END statement.
3. A BLOCK DATA subprogram must contain a labeled COMMON statement. The COMMON statement must appear before any DATA statement that initializes entities of the COMMON statement.
4. There must be no more than one unnamed BLOCK DATA subprogram in an executable program.
5. The same name cannot be used for more than one COMMON area in an executable program. In other words, the same named COMMON block cannot be specified in more than one BLOCK DATA subprogram in an executable program.
6. All entities appearing in a DIMENSION, EQUIVALENCE, or type statement must appear in a COMMON block with the DATA BLOCK subprogram.

Note that the BLOCK DATA subprogram is not included in the subset of ANSI 77 FORTRAN.

14.5   MODULAR PROGRAMMING

A program module is a set of instructions written to accomplish a specific task. For example, a SUBROUTINE or a FUNCTION subprogram or a self-contain section within the main program can be considered to be a module. Each program module should (1) be self-contained, (2) have one entry and one exit, and (3) contain no more than 50 lines of coding. The second requirement means that there should be no more than one RETURN statement in a SUB-ROUTINE or a FUNCTION subprogram. The last requirement, no more than 50 lines in a module, is to make the module easy to comprehend and debug.

Modular programming is a very useful technique for designing and programming large systems. The system is divided into smaller, self-contained subsystems (modules), each of which is designed, programmed, and debugged separately. All modules are invoked from the mainline program or from another module. The mainline program often looks like this:

```
C   The MAIN PROGRAM
        CALL MODL1
        CALL MODL2
        CALL MODL3
          .
          .
          .
        CALL MODLn
        STOP
        END
```

where MODL1, MODL2, MODL3, ..., MODLn are module names (subsystems). A modularized program is highly flexible, because a module can be added or deleted from the system without affecting the rest of the modules.

Some languages (such as COBOL or PL/1, and even some FORTRAN compilers) allow statements such as COPY or INCLUDE, which copy previously stored modules into the current program. ANSI FORTRAN and FORTRAN IV provide the programmer with the ability to write modularized programs by means of subprograms.

The advantage of modular designs is that they make the system more flexible, easier to update and to debug, and more manageable.

Example 14.12

Three methods to calculate depreciation for an asset are:

1. Straight-line method
2. Sum-of-years'-digits method
3. Declining-balance method

Write a FORTRAN program to do the following:

1. To read input records. Each record appears as follows:

CC	ITEM DESCRIPTION	TYPE
1–4	Asset number	Integer
5–20	Asset name	Character
21–26	Cost	Real XXXX.XX
27–32	Estimated scrap value	Real XXXX.XX
33–35	Estimated use-life years	Integer
36	Methods	Integer
37–40	I year	Integer

2. To prepare depreciation schedules by any of the methods above. However, the method that should be employed depends on the method indicator: If the method indicator is 1, your main program should call a subroutine that uses the straight-line method; if the method indicator is 2, the main program calls a second subroutine, which uses the sum-of-years'-digits; and if the method indicator is 3, the main program calls a third subroutine, which uses the declining-balance method. If the method indicator is neither 1 nor 2 nor 3, the main program should generate an error message.

3. To print out the depreciation schedule that was prepared in step 2. The output record should contain:

ITEM DESCRIPTION	TYPE
Asset number	Integer
Asset name	Characters
Depreciation method	Integer
Year	Integer
Depreciation for a year	Real
Accumulated depreciation	Real
Undepreciated balance	Real

The year field should begin with IYEAR and increase by one with each line in the schedule. No depreciation should be taken in the first year.

Following are the formulas to find yearly depreciation for the three methods:

1. Straight-line method:

$$\text{Yearly depreciation} = \frac{1}{\text{Use-life}} * (\text{Cost-estimated scrap value})$$

2. Sum-of-years'-digits method:

$$\text{Yearly depreciation} = \frac{P}{q} * (\text{Cost-estimated scrap value})$$

where:

$$q = \frac{(\text{Use-life years} * (\text{Use-life years} + 1))}{2}$$

and P is the year number written in reverse order.

3. Declining-balance method:

$$\text{Yearly depreciation} = \text{Depreciation rate} * \text{Carrying value}$$

where:

$$\text{Depreciation rate} = 1 - \left(\frac{\text{Estimated scrap value}}{\text{Cost}} \right)^{\frac{1}{\text{Use-life years}}}$$

Note: The quantity within the parentheses is raised to the power 1 divided by the number of the estimated use-life of the asset.

Carrying value = Cost − Accumulated depreciation up to the current year

Figures 14.12 through 14.16 show the programs to be used; Figures 14.17 through 14.20 are the flowcharts for these programs.

14.6 SUMMARY

Both FUNCTION and SUBROUTINE subprograms are compiled separately from the main program. A FUNCTION subprogram can return only one result, but SUBROUTINE subprograms can return more than one. Both FUNCTION and SUBROUTINE subprograms must contain at least one RETURN statement, and both should end with the END statement. A FUNCTION subprogram is referenced by its name, but SUBROUTINEs must be referenced by a CALL statement. The COMMON statement is used to share storage locations among the main program and subprograms. Any variable or array name that appears within a COMMON statement cannot appear in the list of actual or dummy arguments.

```
C DEPRECIATION METHODS
C **************************************************************************
C PROGRAM NARRATIVE:
C THE MAIN PROGRAM READS EACH RECORD.  THEN CALLS SUBROUTINE
C GNPRNT TO PRINT GENERAL INFORMATION AND HEADINGS.  BASED ON THE
C VALUE OF THE METHOD INDICATOR A SUBROUTINE IS CALLED TO CALCULATE
C THE DEPRECIATION.  iF THE METHOD INDICATOR IS 1, THE SUBROUTINE
C STLINE WHICH USES STRAIGHT LINE METHOD IS CALLED; IF METHOD INDICATOR
C IS 2 THE SUBROUTINE SUMYRD WHICH USES SUM OF YEARS DIGITS IS
C CALLED AND F THE METHOD INDICATOR IS 3 THE SUBROUTINE DBLMTHIF
C WHICH USES DECLINING BALANCE MEHTOD IS CALLED.
C **************************************************************************
C
C VARIABLE NAMES USED:
C    NUM:          ASSET NUMBER
C    NAME:         ASSET NAME
C    SCRAP*        SCRAP VALUE
C    MIND:         METHOD INDICATOR
C    LIF:          USEFUL LIFE OF THE ASSET
C    IYEAR:        THE CURRENT YEAR
         INTEGER CARD
         COMMON / PRINF / NUM, NAME(4), MIND / DEPR /
      +  COST, SCRAP, LIFE, IYEAR
         CARD = 5
         LINE = 6
C PRINT THE REPORT HEADING
         WRITE (LINE, 10)
   10    FORMAT ('1', 30(/), T50, 'CACULATION OF DEPRECIATION
      +           BY THREE METHODS')
   20    READ (CARD, 30, END=80) NUM, NAME, COST, SCRAP, LIFE, MIND, IYEA
R
   30    FORMAT (I5, 4A4, 2F6.2, I2, I1, I4)
C CALL MODULE GNPRNT
         CALL GNPRNT
C EACH OF THE SUBROUTINES STLINE, SUMYRD, AND DBLMTH IS A
C MODULE TO CALCULATE THE DEPRECIATION BY STRAIGHT LINE METHOD,
C SUM-OF-YEARS DIGITS AND DECLINING BALANCE METHODS, RESPECTIVELY.
C
C THE METHOD INDICATOR DETERMENES THE MODULE WHICH SHOULD BE EXECUTED.
C
         IF (MIND .NE. 1) GO TO 40
C METHOD INDICATOR IS 1 CALL SUBROUTINE STLINE
         CALL STLINE
         GO TO 20
   40    IF (MIND .NE. 2) GO TO 50
C METHOD INDICATOR IS 2
         CALL SUMYRD
         GO TO 20
   50    IF (MIND .NE. 3) GO TO 60
C METHOD INDICATOR IS 3
         CALL DBLMTN
         GO TO 20
C METHOD INDICATOR IS NEITHER 1, 2, OR 3
C THEREFOR GENERATE AN ERROR MESSAGE
   60    WRITE (LINE, 70) MIND
   70    FORMAT (T20, 'INVALID METHOD INDICATOR:', I2)
         GO TO 20
   80    STOP
         END
```

FIGURE 14.12

```
C MODULE TO PRINT HEADING AND GENERAL INFORMATION
      SUBROUTINE GNPRNT
      COMMON/PRINT/NUM,NAME(4),MIND/DEPR/COST,SCRAP,LIFE
      LINE = 6
      GO TO (10, 30, 50) MIND
   10 WRITE (LINE, 20)
   20 FORMAT ('1',5(/),T50,'STRAIGHT LINE METHOD')
   30 WRITE (LINE, 40)
   40 FORMAT ('1',5(/),T50,'SUM OF YEARS DIGIT METHOD')
   50 WRITE(LINE,60)
   60 FORMAT('1',5(/),T50,'DECLINING BALANCE METHOD')
C PRINT INITIAL INFORMATION
   70 WRITE(LINE, 80)NUM,NAME,COST,SCRAP
   80 FORMAT(20X,'ASSET NUMBER:',4X,I5/
     +        20X,'ASSET NAME:',6X,4A4/
     +        20X,'ORIGINAL COST:',2X,F7.2/
     +        20X,'SCRAP VALUE:',6X,F7.2/
     +        20X,'ESTIMATED USEFUL LIFE:',4X,I2)
C PRINT COLUMN HEADINGS
      WRITE(LINE,90)
   90 FORMAT(5(/),T10,'YEAR',T20,'DEPRECIATION
     +   PER YEAR',T50,'ACCUMULATED DEPRECIATION',
     +   T80,'CARRYING VALUE',T10,4('-'),T20,
     +   21('-'),T50,24('-'),T80,14('-'))
      RETURN
      END
```

FIGURE 14.13

```
C THE MODULE TO CALCULATE DEPRECIATION BY THE STRAIGHT LINE METHOD
      SUBROUTINE STLINE
      COMMON/DEPR/COST,SCRAP,LIFE,IYEAR
      LINE = 6
      ACMDPR=0.0
      DEPYR=(1.0/FLOAT(LIFE))*(COST-SCRAP)
      DO 20 J=1,LIFE
         IYEAR=IYEAR+1
         ACMDPR=ACMDPR+DEPYR
         CARVAL=COST-ACMDPR
         IF(CARVAL .LT. SCRAP) GO TO 30
         WRITE(LINE,10)IYEAR,DEPYR,ACMDPR,CARVAL
   10    FORMAT(T10,I4,T25,F7.2,T60,F7.2,T75,F7.2)
   20 CONTINUE
   30 RETURN
      END
```

FIGURE 14.14

```
C
C THE MODULE TO CALCULATE DEPRECIATION BY SUM-OF-YEARS-DIGIT METHOD
      SUBROUTINE SUMYRD
      COMMON/DEPR/COST,SCRAP,LIFE,IYEAR
      Q=(FLOAT(LIFE)+1.0)*FLOAT(LIFE)/2.0
      DIFR=COST-SCRAP
      ACMDPR=0.0
      DO 20 J=1,LIFE
         IP=LIFE-J+1
         IYEAR=IYEAR+1
         DEPYR=Q/FLOAT(IP)*DIFR
         CARVAL=COST-ACMDPR
         IF (CARVAL .LT. SCRAP) GO TO 30
         WRITE(LINE,10)IYEAR,DEPYR,ACMDPR,CARVAL
   10    FORMAT(T10,I4,T25,F7.2,T60,F7.2,T75,F7.2)
   20 CONTINUE
   30 RETURN
      END
```

FIGURE 14.15

```
C THE MODULE TO CALCULATE DEPRECIATION USING THE
C DECLINING BALANCE METHOD
      SUBROUTINE DBLMTH
      COMMON/DEPR/COST,SCRAP,LIFE,IYEAR
      DPRATE=1.0-(SCRAP/COST)**(1.0/FLOAT(LIFE))
      CARVAL=COST
      ACMDPR=0.0
      DO 20 J=1,LIFE
         IYEAR=IYEAR+1
         DEPYR=CARVAL*DPRATE
         ACMDPR=ACMDPR+DEPYR
         CARVAL=COST-ACMDPR
         WRITE(LINE,10)IYEAR,DEPYR,ACMDPR,CARVAL
   10    FORMAT(T10,I4,T25,F7.2,T60,F7.2,T75,F7.2)
   20 CONTINUE
   30 RETURN
      END
```

FIGURE 14.16

Pseudo Code Form

```
DOWHILE not end of data
    Read NUM,NAME, COST, SCRAP, LIFE,MIND, YEAR
    IF MIND = 1 CALL STLINE
     ELSE IF MIND = 2 CALL SUMYRD
         ELSE IF MIND = 3 CALL DBLMTH
             ELSE Write an error
End DOWHILE
Stop
```

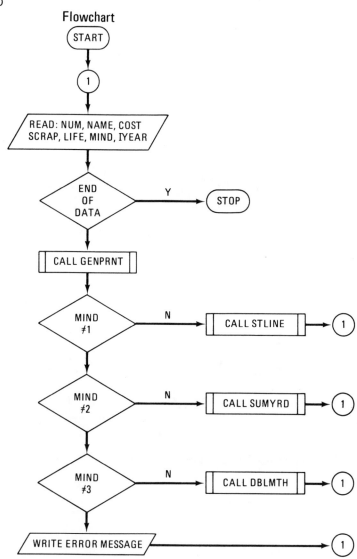

FIGURE 14.17 Flowchart and pseudo code for the main program

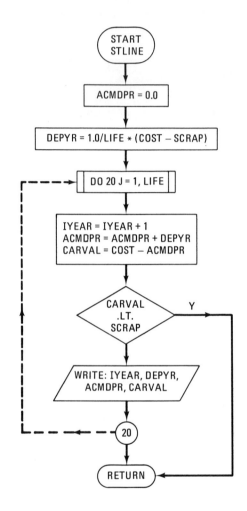

FIGURE 14.18   Flowchart for subroutine STLINE

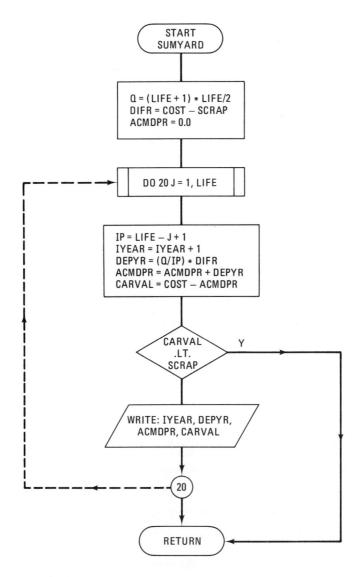

FIGURE 14.19   Flowchart for subroutine sum-of-years'-digits

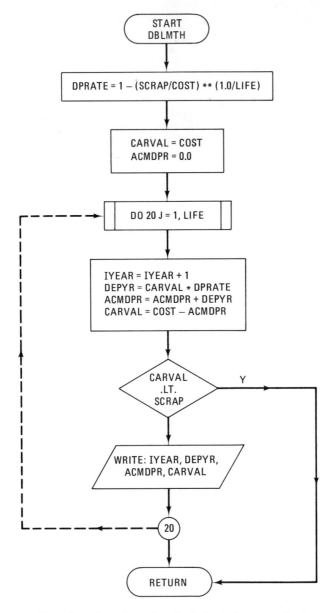

FIGURE 14.20 Flowchart for subroutine declining-balance method

The EQUIVALENCE statement is used to share storage area between variable names or array names within a given program unit. The EXTERNAL statement is used to declare that the name of a procedure is used as an argument in the actual argument list. The BLOCK DATA subprogram is used to initialize the value of variables or array names in the labeled COMMON statements.

**14.7   REVIEW QUESTIONS AND
          SUGGESTED PROBLEMS**

1. *True or False.* FUNCTION AND SUBROUTINE subprograms are compiled within the main program.

2. *True or False.* The mode of a FUNCTION's name determines the mode of the result.

3. *True or False.* The mode of a SUBROUTINE name determines the mode of the result.

4. *True or False.* The FUNCTION subprogram can return more than one result.

5. *True or False.* The SUBROUTINE subprogram can return more than one result.

6. *True or False.* The FUNCTION subprogram must be referenced by a CALL statement.

7. *True or False.* A SUBROUTINE subprogram must be referenced by a CALL statement.

8. *True or False.* A FUNCTION subprogram can be referenced by many programs.

9. *True or False.* SUBROUTINE subprograms can be referenced by many programs or programmers.

10. *True or False.* A BLOCK DATA subprogram may contain an executable statement.

In problems 11 through 15, assume the following statements in the main program:

```
INTEGER COUNT
REAL RATE, COMS
DIMENSION COUNT(20),COMS(5),RATE(5)
```

11. Write the necessary COMMON statements to make the array COUNT available to both SUBROUTIN SUB1 and FUNCTION subprogram FUN1.

12. WRITE the necessary COMMON statement to make the array COUNT available to subroutine SUB1, and the array COMS available to both subroutine SUB2 and FUNCTION subprogram FUN1.

13. Write a BLOCK DATA subprogram to initialize every element in the array COUNT to 20 and COMS to:

$$\begin{pmatrix} 0.05 \\ 0.06 \\ 0.07 \\ 0.08 \\ 0.09 \end{pmatrix}$$

14. Write an EQUIVALENCE statement to make every element of the arrays COMS and RATE equal.

15. Write a COMMON statement so that the first element of RATE is shared with R1, the second element with R2, and the third through the fifth elements share the storage locations of the first through the third elements of COMS.

16. Write a main FORTRAN program and both FUNCTION subprogram FACTOR and SUBROUTINE subprogram PRINT, which are invoked by the main program. The main program reads each number and uses FUNCTION FACTOR to calculate the factorial of the number. After that, the main program calls subroutine PRINT to print out the results. Note that the mathematical notation for factorial is n! and $n! = n(n - 1)(n - 2) \ldots 1$. For example: $4! = 4 * 3 * 2 * 1 = 24$.

17. **The Binomial Probability Distribution.**

$$P(r \mid n, p) = \frac{n!}{r!\,(n - r)!}\, P^r q^{n-r}$$

computes the probability of r successes in n trials, where p is the probability of success and q is the probability of failure for a given trial (note that $q = 1 - p$). Write a FORTRAN program to calculate binomial probability distribution for all r less than or equal to n for each P varying from 0.1 to 1.0 by step 0.1 and for each n that equals 1, 2, 3, or 4. Use the previously defined function FACTOR to find $n!$, $r!$, and $(n - r)!$

18. IPROD is the type of product; COMR is a table containing commission rates.

```
      DIMENSION COMR(5), NAME(4)
      READ(2,10) COMR
 10   FORMAT(5F3.2)
 20   READ(2,30,END=50) NUM, NAME, SALE, IPROD
 30   FORMAT(I5,4A5,F7.2,I1)
      CALL COMSN(SALE,PAY, ..........................)
      WRITE(3,40) NUM, NAME, PAY
 40   FORMAT(6X,I5,6X,4A5,F8.2)
      GO TO 20
 50   STOP
      END
```

The FORTRAN mainline program above reads a table of commission rates, then calls a subroutine COMSN to calculate the commission. The amount of commission paid to a salesman depends on the type of product. COMR(1) is the rate for product 1, COMR(2) is the rate for product 2, and so on.

a. Complete the CALL statement in the mainline program to pass the value of COMR and IPROD in addition to the other arguments in the CALL list to the subroutine COMSN.

b. Write the subroutine COMSN to find the amount of commission for each sale.

19.

```
10 READ(2,20,END=40) X,Y
20 FORMAT(2F2.0)
   CALL PROC1 (X,Y,AVERG,BIG)
   WRITE(3,30) AVERG,BIG
30 FORMAT(6X, 'AVERAGE IS: ',F6.2,'LARGEST NUMBER: ',F6.2)
   GO TO 10
40 STOP
   END
```

The program above calls subroutine PROC1 (below) to find the average of X and Y and their largest value.

```
   SUBROUTINE PROC1(R1,R2,A,B)
   A=(R1+R2)/2.
   IF(R1.LT.R2) GO TO 10
   B=R1
   GO TO 20
10 B=R2
20 RETURN
   END
```

Assume we have only one input data card:

2030

a. When the programs above are executed, then: AVERG = _____ ; BIG = _____ ; R1 = _____ ; R2 = _____ ; A = _____ ; B = _____ .

b. Eliminate the arguments in the list of SUBROUTINE and the list of CALL statements in the mainline program by using the COMMON statement.

20. What is a program module?

21. What are the advantages of modular programming?

15 SORTING, MERGING, STORING, AND SEARCHING TECHNIQUES

Data structures is the portion of computer science concerned with techniques and methods for organizing information within the computer so that it can be stored and retrieved efficiently. In this chapter, we discuss four data-structure techniques: sorting, searching, merging, and storing. In data-structures literature, the terms *list* and *array* are often used interchangeably.

15.1 SORTING

Sorting means organizing data in a certain order (ascending or descending) according to certain fields, called *keys*. For example, the following four employee records are sorted in ascending order on the key "employee last name":

    5555   Linda Brown
    2222   George Ogden
    1111   Wendy Smith
    4444   John Wilson

But when these records are sorted in ascending order on the field (key) "employee number," their order will be:

    1111   Wendy Smith
    2222   George Ogden
    4444   John Wilson
    5555   Linda Brown

Several texts have been written about different sorting algorithms. In general, sorting techniques are classified as external or internal, depending upon whether the data being sorted require secondary storage or fit in main memory. The four most popular external sorting algorithms are balanced, or Von Neumann; cascade; polyphase; and oscillating. Some examples of internal sorts are selection sort, bubble sort, quick sort, tree sort, and merge sort.

Sorting algorithms may also be classified as comparative or distributive sorts. Comparative sorts compare and exchange two keys at a time. Distributive sorts separate keys into subsets so that the items in one subset are greater than all those in the other subset. Popular comparative sorts are selection sort and bubble sort; some popular distributive sorts are quick sort, radix sort, and merge sort.

Storage requirements and average number of comparisons required to sort an unordered array are the two factors used to determine the best sorting algorithm. It has been determined empirically that the quick sort is the fastest sorting technique for many machines.

Many of the aforementioned algorithms are beyond the scope of this text. We will limit ourselves to discussing the selection, bubble, and merge sorts.

15.1.1 Selection Sort

The selection sort is sometimes referred to as linear sort. To sort an array in ascending order by this technique, compare the first element of the array to the second, then to the third, then to the fourth, and so on. If the value of any element is less than the value of the first element, swap its value with that of the first element. After the array is gone through once, the first element will be the smallest value in the array. Repeat the process, this time comparing the second element with the third, fourth, fifth, and so on. Again, if the value of any element (from third on) is less than that of the second element, swap its value with the second element. Now the second element of the array is the second smallest. Repeat the process for the remaining elements. Figure 15.1 is a flow-chart diagram for sorting an array X in ascending order.

Explanation: In the flowchart in Figure 15.1, assume that X is

$$\begin{pmatrix} 10 \\ 6 \\ 20 \\ 15 \\ 4 \end{pmatrix}$$

—a one-dimensional array with five elements. The variable N is the size of the array. In box 2, the variable N becomes 5. Note that the same algorithm can be used for any size array by merely changing box 2. Boxes 3 through 7 contain the selection-sort algorithm. The DO loop in box 3 is the outer DO, and the DO loop

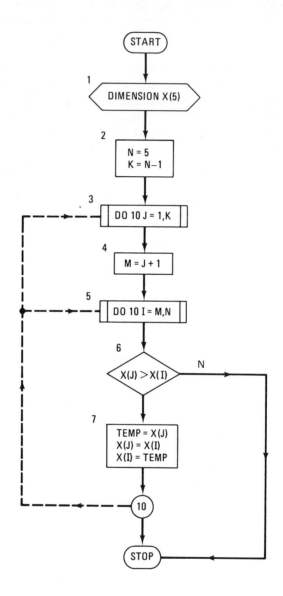

FIGURE 15.1 Sorting an array in ascending order by selection-sort algorithm

in box 5 is the inner one. Both DO loops end in statement 10. In box 3, the value of J is initialized to 1. In box 4, the value of M becomes 2. Let us follow the first iteration of the loop in boxes 5 through 7:

Outer loop

ITERATION	J	X(J)	M
1	1	10	2

Inner loop

ITERATION	I	X(J)	X(I)	X(J) > X(I)?	SWAP
1	2	~~10~~ 6	~~6~~ 10	YES	YES
2	3	6	20	NO	NO
3	4	6	15	NO	NO
4	5	~~6~~ 4	~~4~~ 6	YES	YES

At this point, the inner iteration is exhausted, and the outer DO has made one iteration. The value of the elements of the array X, as indicated above, are compared and changed in the inner loop in the following manner:

FIRST ITERATION	SECOND ITERATION	THIRD ITERATION	FOURTH ITERATION	RESULT
$\begin{pmatrix} 10 \\ 6 \\ 20 \\ 15 \\ 4 \end{pmatrix}$	$\begin{pmatrix} 6 \\ 10 \\ 20 \\ 15 \\ 4 \end{pmatrix}$	$\begin{pmatrix} 6 \\ 10 \\ 20 \\ 15 \\ 4 \end{pmatrix}$	$\begin{pmatrix} 6 \\ 10 \\ 20 \\ 15 \\ 4 \end{pmatrix}$	$\begin{pmatrix} 4 \\ 10 \\ 20 \\ 15 \\ 6 \end{pmatrix}$

After the inner DO loop has completed all its iterations, the index of the outer DO loop (J) is increased by 1. At box 4, the value of M becomes 3. Then the instructions in boxes 5 through 7 compare the second element with third, fourth, and fifth element, and the value of the second element is swapped with the value of these elements if any of them is less than the second element. The process is repeated for the rest of the elements. At the end of the second iteration of the outer DO loop, the value of X is

$$\begin{pmatrix} 4 \\ 6 \\ 20 \\ 15 \\ 10 \end{pmatrix}$$

At the end of the third iteration, X is

$$\begin{pmatrix} 4 \\ 6 \\ 10 \\ 20 \\ 15 \end{pmatrix}$$

And at the end of the fourth iteration, X is

$$\begin{pmatrix} 4 \\ 6 \\ 10 \\ 15 \\ 20 \end{pmatrix}$$

Note that the variable TEMP is needed to keep the value of any element that will be swapped; otherwise, either $X(J)$ or $X(I)$ would be lost. To sort the same array in descending order, change the direction of the inequality in box 6.

Example 15.1: Sorting an Employee File in Ascending Order

Write a FORTRAN program to sort a file of employee records in ascending order on employee number. The file contains 50 records. Each employee record is punched on a card in the following manner:

CC	FIELD	TYPE
1–4	Employee number	Integer
5–16	Employee name	Character

(*Note:* The program above is easier to write in ANSI FORTRAN 77 than in FORTRAN IV, because ANSI FORTRAN 77 has character variables. (See Appendix II.) Because many organizations do not yet have an ANSI FORTRAN 77 compiler, we will write the program in FORTRAN IV.)

The approach is to have four one-dimensional arrays, each with 50 elements. The first array, NUM, contains employee numbers. The second array, NPAR1, contains the first four characters of each name. NPAR2 contains characters 5 through 8 of each name, and NPAR3 contains the last four characters of each name. For example, the representation of the following records:

    5555   Linda Brown
    2222   George Ogden
    1111   Wendy Smith
    4444   John Wilson

in terms of the arrays above, will be:

ELEMENTS	ARRAY NAME NUM	NPAR1	NPAR2	NPAR3
1	5555	LIND	AⱡBR	OWNⱡ
2	2222	GEOR	GEⱡO	GDEN
3	1111	WEND	YⱡSM	ITHⱡ
4	4444	JOHN	SONⱡ	ⱡWIL
·	·	·	·	·
·	·	·	·	·
·	·	·	·	·

Figure 15.2 is the FORTRAN program for this problem.

FIGURE 15.2   FORTRAN program to sort an employee file in ascending order using selection sort

```
C SELECTION SORT
C PROBLEM NARRATIVE: THIS PROGRAM USES SELECTION SORT ALOGORITHM
C                    TO SORT AN EMPLOYEE FILE IN ASCENDING ORDER
C                    ON EMPLOYEE NUMBER.
C
C ARRAY NAMES USED:
C              NUM    EMPLOYEE NUMBER
C              NPAR1 CONTAINS THE FIRST 4 CHARACTTERS OF EACH NAME
C              NPAR2 CONTAINS CHARACTERS 5 THROUGH 8 OF EACH NAME
C              NPAR3 CONTAINS THE LAST 4 CHARACTERS OF EACH NAME
C
        INTEGER CARD
        DIMENSION NUM(50), NPAR1(50), NPAR2(50), NPAR3(50)
        DATA CARD,LINE/5,6/
C
C READ ALL 50 RECORDS
C
        DO 10 J = 1, 50
            READ(CARD, 20) NUM(J),NPAR1(J), NPAR2(J), NPAR3(J)
  20        FORMAT(I4, 3A4)
  10    CONTINUE
C
C START SORTING
C
        DO 30 J = 1, 50
          M = J + 1
          DO 30 I = M, 50
            IF (NUM(J) .LE. NUM(I)) GO TO 30
C           ELSE SWAP NUM(J) AND NUM(I) AND CORRESPONDING ELEMENTS
C           OF ARRAYS NPAR1, NPAR2, AND NPAR3
            TEMP = NUM(J)
            NUM(J) = NUM(I)
            NUM(I) = TEMP
C
C
C SWAP CORRESPONDING ELEMENTS OF NPAR1
            TEMP1 = NPAR1(J)
            NPAR1(J) = NPAR1(I)
            NPAR1(I) = TEMP1
C
C SWAP CORRESPONDING ELEMENTS OF NPAR2
            TEMP2 = NPAR2(J)
            NPAR2(J) = NPAR2(I)
            NPAR2(I) = TEMP2
C
C SWAP CORRESPONDING ELEMENTS OF NPAR3
            TEMP3 = NPAR3(J)
            NPAR3(J) = NPAR3(I)
            NPAR3(I) = TEMP3
  30    CONTINUE
C
C PRINT OUT THE SORTED FILE
        DO 40 N = 1, 50
            WRITE(LINE, 50) NUM(N), NPAR1(N), NPAR2(N), NPAR3(N)
  50        FORMAT(1X,5X,I4,5X,3A4)
  40    CONTINUE
        STOP
        END
```

15.1.2 Bubble Sort

The bubble sort compares successive pairs of elements in the array and swaps two elements if necessary. The scanning of the array is repeated until no further exchanges are required. For example, to sort an array of size n in ascending order using a bubble sort, compare the first element with the second. If the first element is greater than the second, interchange them. Next, compare the second element with the third. If the second element is greater than the third, interchange them. Continue the process of comparison and interchange if necessary of the third and fourth, fourth and fifth, and so on. When the first scan is finished, you know that the nth element is the largest in the array. Now repeat the process from the first element until you reach the last element that was interchanged in the previous scan. Repeat the process until no further exchanges are required. Figure 15.3 is a flowchart diagram for sorting an array X in ascending order using bubble sort.

Explanation: In the flowchart, assume that X is:

$$\begin{pmatrix} 5.0 \\ 2.0 \\ 3.0 \\ 4.0 \\ 6.0 \end{pmatrix}$$

At box 4, M is assigned the value 4 (one less than the size of the array). At box 5, the value of the variable IFLAG becomes 0. IFLAG is used to check on whether any exchange has been performed during one complete scan. If the value of IFLAG remains 0, no exchange has been performed, that is, the sort is completed. However, if the test in box 7 requires an exchange, then control transfers to box 8, where the elements $X(J)$ and $X(J + 1)$ are swapped and the value of IFLAG is changed to 1. Variable K is assigned the current value of J. Thus, K contains the index where the last exchange is performed. At box 9, if IFLAG is still 0, no values have been exchanged during the scan. However, IFLAG $\neq \emptyset$ indicates that some elements have been interchanged, so that control transfers to box 10. At box 10, M is assigned the value K (the index of the last interchange) and the whole process is repeated. The first iteration of the outer loop causes the inner loop to be executed four times:

M	INNER LOOP ITERATION	IFLAG	J	X(J)	X(J + 1)	SWAP	K
4	1	∅	1	5.0	2.0	YES	
		1		2.0	5.0		1
	2	1	2	5.0	3.0	YES	1
				3.0	5.0		2
	3	1	3	5.0	4.0	YES	3
				4.0	5.0		
	4	1	4	5.0	6.0	NO	3

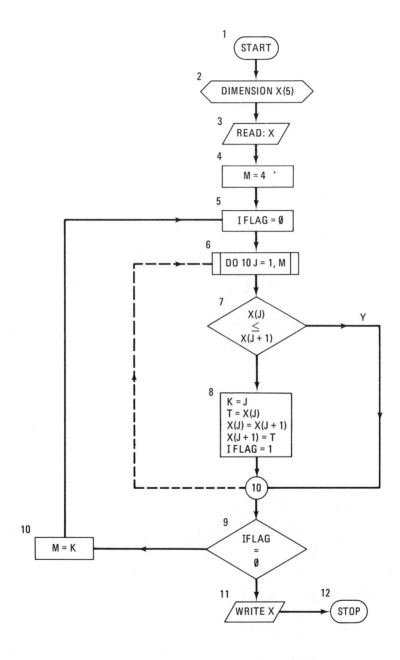

FIGURE 15.3   Sorting array X in ascending order using bubble sort

```
C FORTRAN PROGRAM TO SORT AN EMPLOYEE FILE IN
C ASCENDING ORDER ON EMPLOYEE NUMBER USING BUBBLE SORT
C
C ARRAY NAMES USED
C   NUM CONTAINS EMPLOYEE NUMBER
C   NPAR1 CONTAINS THE FIRST 4 CHARACTERS OF EACH NAME
C   NPAR2 CONTAINS CHARACTERS 5 THROUGH 8 OF EACH NAME
C   NPAR3 CONTAINS THE LAST 4 CHARACTERS OF EACH NAME
C
C
        INTEGER CARD
        DIMENSION NUM(50), NPAR1(50),NPAR2(50),NPAR3(50)
        DATA CARD, LINE/5,6/
C
C READ ALL 50 RECORDS
        DO 20 J = 1,50
            READ(CARD,10)NUM(J),NPAR1(J),NPAR2(J),NPAR3(J)
   10       FORMAT(I4,3A4)
   20   CONTINUE
C
C START SORT
        M = 49
C
C
   30   IFLAG=0
C START INNER LOOP
        DO 40 J = 1,M
            IF(NUM(J) .LE. NUM(J+1)) GO TO 40
C INTERCHANGE NUM(J) AND NUM(J+1)
            T = NUM(J)
            NUM(J)=NUM(J+1)
            NUM(J+1)=T
C
C INTERCHANGE CORRESPONDING ELEMENTS OF NPAR1
            T1 = NPAR1(J)
            NPAR1(J)=NPAR1(J+1)
            NPAR1(J+1)=T1
C
C INTERCHANGE CORRESPONDING ELEMENTS OF NPAR2
            T2 = NPAR2(J)
            NPAR2(J)=NPAR2(J+1)
            NPAR2(J+1)=T2
C
C INTERCHANGE CORRESPONDING ELEMENTS OF NPAR3
            T3 = NPAR3(J)
            NPAR3(J) = NPAR3(J+1)
            NPAR3(J+1) = T3
C
C SET K TO CURRENT INDEX
            K=1
C
C CHANGE IFLAG
            IFLAG=1
   40   CONTINUE
C
C IF IFLAG EQUALS 0 END SORT
        IF(IFLAG .EQ. 0) GO TO 50
C
C ELSE SET M TO K AND REPEAT THE LOOP
            M=K
            GO TO 30
C
C PRINT OUT THE SORTED FILE
   50   DO 70 J = 1,50
            WRITE(LINE,60)NUM(J),NPAR1(J),NPAR2(J),NPAR3(J)
   60   FORMAT(1X,5X,I4,5X,3A4)
   70   CONTINUE
        STOP
        END
```

**FIGURE 15.4   FORTRAN program to sort employee file in
ascending order using BUBBLE sort**

The array X during the iterations is as follows (showing the comparisons and interchanges):

$$\begin{pmatrix} 5.0 \\ 2.0 \\ 3.0 \\ 4.0 \\ 6.0 \end{pmatrix} \quad \begin{pmatrix} 2.0 \\ 5.0 \\ 3.0 \\ 4.0 \\ 6.0 \end{pmatrix} \quad \begin{pmatrix} 2.0 \\ 3.0 \\ 5.0 \\ 4.0 \\ 6.0 \end{pmatrix} \quad \begin{pmatrix} 2.0 \\ 3.0 \\ 4.0 \\ 5.0 \\ 6.0 \end{pmatrix} \quad \begin{pmatrix} 2.0 \\ 3.0 \\ 4.0 \\ 5.0 \\ 6.0 \end{pmatrix}$$

Second iteration of outer loop:

M	INNER LOOP INTERATION	IFLAG	J	X(J)	X(J + 1)	SWAP	K
4	1	0	1	2.0	3.0	NO	3
3	2		2	3.0	4.0	NO	
	3		3	4.0	5.0	NO	

Since IFLAG is 0 at box 9, the loop is terminated, and at box 11 the sorted array is printed.

Example 15.2: **Sorting an Employee File in Ascending Order**

Redo example 15.1, this time using the bubble sort algorithm. Figure 15.4 shows the required FORTRAN program.

15.2   MERGE

Merging means combining two or more sorted files or arrays so that the combined file or array is also sorted. Merging is used very often in the business data-processing environment. Files or arrays that are to be merged must be sorted before the merge routine starts. Figure 15.5 is the flowchart for merging two arrays, *A* and *B*.

Explanation: Assume that array A is

$$\begin{pmatrix} 4 \\ 10 \\ 15 \\ 16 \\ 18 \end{pmatrix}$$

and array B is

$$\begin{pmatrix} 5 \\ 20 \\ 30 \end{pmatrix}$$

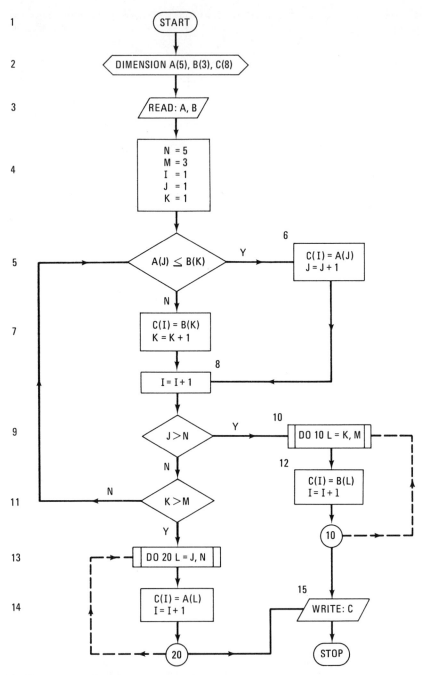

FIGURE 15.5 Flowchart for merging two arrays. Both arrays must be sorted before merge is applied

At box 4, the indices I, J, and K are initialized to 1, and N is set to the size of A and M to the size of B. The instructions in boxes 5 through 8 test whether the current element of A is less than the current element of B. If so, make the current element of C equal to the current element of A; otherwise, box 7 makes the current element of C equal to the current element of B. These instructions are repeated until J is greater than N (that is, all elements of A have been used) or K is greater than M (that is, all elements of B have been used). If all elements of A are used, the instructions in boxes 10 and 12 move the remaining elements of B to C. However, if all elements of B are used before A (in other words, B contains fewer elements than A), then the instructions in boxes 13 and 14 move the remaining elements of A into C. Here is how the values of the indices change and how the elements of C are assigned when the flowcharted algorithm is applied to the arrays A and B:

N	M	I	J	K	
5	3	1	1	1	
		2	2	2	
		3	3		
		4	4		
		5	5		
		6	6	2	← At this point, all elements of A are
		7		3	used.
		8		4	

$$A = \begin{pmatrix} 4 \\ 10 \\ 15 \\ 16 \\ 18 \end{pmatrix} \quad B = \begin{pmatrix} 5 \\ 20 \\ 30 \end{pmatrix} \quad C = \begin{pmatrix} 5 \\ 10 \\ 15 \\ 16 \\ 18 \\ 20 \\ 30 \end{pmatrix}$$

← At this point, copy the remaining elements of B.

15.3   STORING AND SEARCHING

Searching is the process of scanning a data structure (file or array) to find some desired information. For example, to find in the employee file the name and address of an employee whose employee number is 2222, we must perform a search routine to retrieve the information from the file. The nature of such retrieval processes depends on the organization of the data structure—that is, on the manner in which data are stored and organized.

15.3.1   Storage Techniques

In general, data may be stored and organized in the following ways:

1. Sequential
2. Sorted
3. Block structure (indexes)
4. Direct (random)
5. Hashing

The sequential storage technique is the simplest. The first record read is stored in the first position, the second record in the second position, and so on. Assume the following input records:

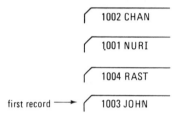

first record ⟶

1002 CHAN

1001 NURI

1004 RAST

1003 JOHN

and assume also that NUM is an array containing employee numbers and NAME an array containing names. When the input cards above are read and stored sequentially in the arrays, then NUM and NAME contain:

ARRAY NAME INDEX	NUM	NAME	
1	1003	JOHN	← Sequential storage
2	1004	RAST	
3	1001	NURI	
4	1002	CHAN	

As explained in the previous section, information can be sorted on certain keys. When the array NAME is sorted in ascending order and the array NUM is changed accordingly, the organization of the data becomes:

ARRAY NAME INDEX	NUM	NAME
1	1002	CHAN
2	1003	JOHN
3	1001	NURI
4	1004	RAST

In direct organization, the position of the record within the file is determined by a key whose value must be numeric. For example, suppose a company must organize a file of 1,000 employees and decides to use employee numbers from 1 to 1,000. The employee number can then be used to create the random file (direct file). The record with employee number 8 will be stored as the eighth record, and the record with employee number 567 as the 567th record. In general, the record with employee number n is stored as the nth record.

Suppose the following input records are read and stored in the random file:

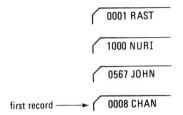

Then the random file becomes:

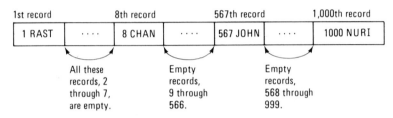

Note that record number 8 was the first record stored in the file, because the first record read had employee number (file key) 8. If the records above were read into a sequential file, then the file would contain:

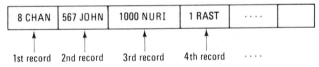

Hashing is a technique in which functions (formulas) are used to derive the file key from information in the record. For example, suppose we wish to create a file for 1,000 employees, using the Social Security number as the file key. Then either we have to have a file that can contain 999,999,999 records (because the Social Security number has nine digits)—which is obviously not desirable, because it would waste a huge amount of storage—or we must use a hash function to convert a Social Security number to a number between 1 and 1,000. One such simple function is:

$$\text{File key} = \text{Remainder of} \left(\frac{\text{Social Security number}}{1,000} \right) + 1$$

Then the file keys for the following Social Security numbers would be:

SOCIAL SECURITY NUMBER	REMAINDER OF S.S. NUMBER DIVIDED BY 1,000	FILE KEY
497 56 2565	565	566
497 56 2500	500	501
497 56 2000	0	1
497 56 2999	999	1,000
497 57 3999	999	1,000

Note that the last two cases have the same key (this is called collision). In such cases, we must design a routine (which is beyond the scope of this text) to handle collisions.

The last storing technique, block structure, is a combination of direct and sequential techniques. This is usually called indexed sequential. Blocks are stored and retrieved directly; information within a block is stored and retrieved sequentially.

15.3.2 Searching

Information can be retrieved either sequentially or directly, or by some combination of both (such as index sequential search). In the remainder of this chapter, the sequential search and binary search are explained.

15.3.2.1 SEQUENTIAL SEARCH

To search an array or file sequentially, start with the first element (record). If this is the desired element, stop the search; otherwise, search the next element. Continue the search until the element is found or all elements of the array or records of the file have been examined.

Example 15.3

Suppose we have three arrays. The first contains account numbers; the second contains the type of account–C for checking and S for saving; and the third array contains balances. Typical data would be:

ACCOUNT NUMBER	TYPE OF ACCOUNT	BALANCE
1112	C	500.25
1543	S	9750.45
1678	C	2600.18
2945	S	5000.20

Thus, the customer with customer number 1112 has a checking account and his balance is $500.25.

Write a FORTRAN program to print the account numbers and balances of all customers who have savings accounts, and also the total savings and numbers of customers who have savings accounts. Figure 15.6 is the flowchart diagram to search an array sequentially, and Figure 15.7 is the FORTRAN program for the problem.

15.3.2.2 BINARY SEARCH

Binary search is faster (on the average) than sequential search for retrieving a specific element of an array or a record of a random (direct) file (discussed in Chapter 16). Binary search can be applied to sorted arrays or to files or arrays that are ordered lexicographically (either alphabetically or numerically).

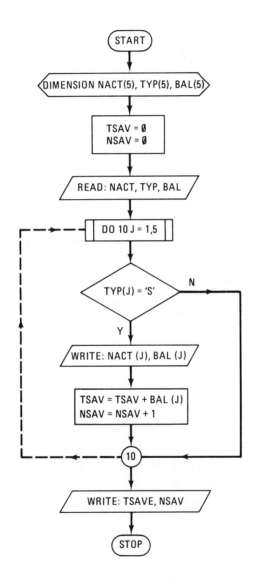

FIGURE 15.6 Sequential search of an array

```
C SEQUENTIAL SEARCH
C VARIABLE NAMES USED
C    ARRAY NACT CONTAINS ACCOUNT NUMBER
C    ARRAY TYP CONTAINS TYPE OF ACCOUNT
C    ARRAY BAL CONTAINS BALANCES
C    TSAV TOTAL SAVES
C    NSAVE NUMBER OF SAVING ACCOUNTS
C
         INTEGER CARDS
         DIMENSION NACT(5),TYP(5),BAL(5)
         CARDS=5
         LINE=6
         TSAVE=0.0
         NSAVE=0.0
C
C PRINT HEADINGS
         WRITE(LINE,10)
   10    FORMAT('1',T20,'ACCOUNT NUMBER',T50,'BALANCE')
C READ INFORMATION FROM CARDS
         DO 15 I=1,5
             READ(CARDS,20)NACT(I),TYP(I),BAL(I)
   20        FORMAT(I5,A1,F9.2)
   15    CONTINUE
C
C LOOP TO SEARCH
C
         DO 40 J=1,5
             IF(TYP(J) .NE. 'S')GO TO 40
C            ELSE
                 WRITE(LINE,30)NACT(J),BAL(J)
   30            FORMAT(T25,I5,T50,F10.2)
                 TSAV=TSAV+BAL(J)
                 NSAV=NSAV+1
   40    CONTINUE
         WRITE(LINE,50)NSAV,TSAV
   50    FORMAT('1',T10,'NUMBER OF SAVING ACCOUNTS:',I3,T50,
     +   'TOTAL SAVING AMOUNT:',F10.2)
         STOP
         END
```

FIGURE 15.7   FORTRAN program for example 15.3 using sequential search

To understand binary search, assume the following two arrays:

NACT	BALANS
1112	1567.28
1543	2450.20
1678	670.90
2945	218.67
5672	5450.25
8345	8618.30
9728	592.12

The first array contains account numbers that are sorted in ascending order, and the second array contains their balances. Suppose we have both these arrays stored and we want to retrieve the balance of the customer whose account number is 5672. If we used sequential search, we would need to retrieve and examine five elements of the array NACT before the account number (the target key) is found in the array. Since 5672 is the fifth element in the array, BALANS (5), which is $5,450.25, is the balance corresponding to account number 5672. When binary search is used, first we retrieve the middle element of the array and compare it with the target key (5672). The middle element of NACT is NACT(4), which is 2945. Since 5672 is bigger than 2945 and because array NACT is sorted in ascending order, we know that 5672 will lie in the second half of the array; therefore, we disregard the first half. Next, we compare 5672 with the element in the middle of the second half of the array. If they are equal, stop the search; if the target is less than the middle element, disregard the higher half; and if the target is greater than the middle element, disregard the lower half. By successively halving the remainder of the array, we can close in on the desired item.

Example 15.4

Write a FORTRAN program to read account numbers and balances and store them in two arrays. The program then reads an individual account number and calls a subroutine that uses a binary search to retrieve the balance for the specific account number. First type data are punched in the following manner:

CC	FIELD	TYPE
1–5	Account number	Integer
6–13	Balance	Real

The second type data are punched on the card as follows:

CC	FIELD	TYPE
1–5	Account number	

Figure 15.8 is the flowchart for the subroutine of the binary search. Figure 15.9 shows the main program and Figure 15.10 the subroutine for the binary search.

15.4   SUMMARY

Sorting means storing and organizing data in a certain order. Two comparative sorting techniques, bubble and selection sort, were explained. Searching is the process of scanning a data structure to find and retrieve the desired information. The retrieval process is dependent on the specific storage technique used. Sequential, sorted, block structure, direct, and hashing are the different types of storage technique. Accessing (retrieval) can be either sequential, direct, or some combination of both.

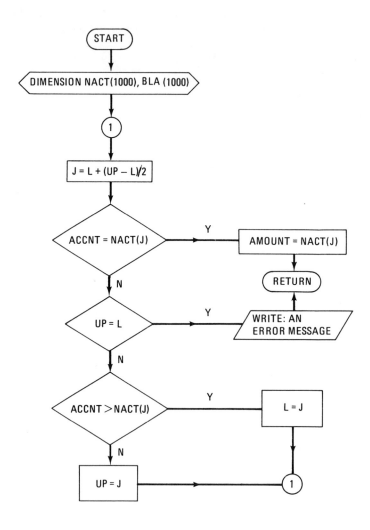

FIGURE 15.8 Binary search

```
C MAIN PROGRAM CALLS SUBROUTINE BISRCH FOR BINARY SEARCH
C PROBLEM NARRATIVE: THE MAIN PRGRAM READS ACCOUNT NUMBERS,  BALANCES,
C                    AND STORES THEM IN TWO SEPARATE ARRAYS. THEN THE
C                    MAIN PROGRAM READS AN INDIVIDUAL ACCOUNT NUMBER AND
C                    CALLS SUBROUTINE BISCH TO RETRIEVE THE BALANCE.
C
C VARIABLE NAMES USED
C    ARRAY NACT CONTAINS ACCOUNT NUMBERS
C    ARRAY BAL CONTAINS BALANCES
C    ACCNT ACCOUNT NUMBER FOR THE SECOND TYPE CARD.
C
        INTEGER ACCNT,CARDS
        DIMENSION NACT(1000),BAL(1000)
        CARDS=5
        LINE=6
C READ IN DATA. THE DATA IS SORTED IN ASCENDING ORDER ON ACCOUNT NUMBERS
C
        DO 10 I=1,1000
   10       READ(CARDS,20,END=40)NACT(I),BAL(I)
        CONTINUE
   20       FORMAT(I5,F8.2)
C NOW ALL DATA ARE STORED
C READ AN ACCOUNT NUMBER FROM SECOND TYPE OF INPUT CARDS
C
   40   READ(CARDS,50,END=70)ACCNT
   50   FORMAT(I5)
        CALL BISRCH(ACCNT,AMOUNT,NACT,BAL)
        WRITE(LINE,60)ACCNT,AMOUNT
   60   FORMAT(6X,'THE BALANCE FOR ACCOUNT:',I5,5X,'IS:'F9.2)
        GO TO 40
   70   STOP
        END
```

FIGURE 15.9 Main FORTRAN program

```
                       SUBROUTINE BISRCH(ACCNT,AMOUNT,NACT,BAL)
                       INTEGER ACCNT,UP
                       DIMENSION NACT(1000),BAL(1000)
C VARIABLE NAMES USED
C    UP CONTAINS UPPER INDEX
C    L  CONTAINS LOWER INDEX
C    J  CONTAINS THE INDEX OF MIDDLE ELEMENT
C
C INITIALIZE UPPER AND LOWER INDICES
C
                       UP=1000
                       L =1
C
C START BINARY SEARCH
C
   10       J=L+(UP-L)/2
C
C IF TARGET EQUAL MIDDLE ELEMENT END SEARCH
C
            IF(ACNT .EQ. NACT(J)) GO TO 30
C
C                ELSE IF UPPER AND LOWER INDEXES ARE
C                     EQUAL, IT MEANS ELEMENT IS NOT IN
C                     THE ARRAY SO WRITE ERROR MESSAGE
C
            IF(UP .EQ. L) GO TO 35
C
C                ELSE, IF TARGET .GT. MIDDLE ELEMENT
C
            IF(ACCNT .GT. NACT(J)) GO TO 20
C
C                   ELSE THE TARGET .LT. MIDDLE ELEMENT
C                        DISREGARD THE UPPER HALF
C
            UP=J
            GO TO 10
C
C DISREGARD THE LOWER HALF OF THE ARRAY
C
   20       L=J
            GO TO 10
   30       AMOUNT=BAL(J)
            GO TO 60
   35       WRITE(LINE,40) ACCNT
   40       FORMAT(6X,'SEARCH FAILED FOR:',I5)
   60       RETURN
            END
```

FIGURE 15.10 Binary search subroutine

15.5 REVIEW QUESTIONS AND SUGGESTED PROBLEMS

1. How many comparisons are required to sort a one-dimensional array of size 10 by using (a) selection sort? (b) bubble sort?

2. What is the average number of searches required to locate an element in a one-dimensional array of size 10 using (a) sequential search? (b) binary search?

3. Can a record be accessed directly from a sequentially organized data structure?

4. What are the five techniques for storing information?

5. Describe sequential search.

6. Describe direct search.

7. Which requires more storage, sequential or direct storage?

8. Assume that GRADE is a one-dimensional, 31-element array, which contains the grades of students in an Introduction to Computer Science class. Write a FORTRAN program to read the array GRADE, and a SUBROUTINE subprogram to find the average and median of the grades. *Note:* To find the median, sort the array GRADE in ascending order and pick the middle element. Your subroutine should use the selection sort algorithm.

9. Repeat problem 8, this time using bubble sort algorithm.

10. Write a FORTRAN program to read an employee file and store the records as elements of arrays of your choice. The input records are punched on cards in the following manner:

CC	FIELD	TYPE	VALUE
1–5	Employee number	Integer	XXXX.XX
6–12	Salary	Real	M Married
13	Employee marital status	Character	S Single
			D Divorce
14	Employee sex	Character	M Male
			F Female
15	Employee status	Character	F Full-time
			P Part-time
16–35	Employee name	Character	

Your FORTRAN program should call a subroutine to sort the file in ascending order on employee number using the bubble sort algorithm. The main program should also call a second subroutine to print the sorted file along with appropriate headings.

11. Redo problem 10, this time sorting the file on marital status; the subroutine should use the selection sort algorithm. The print subroutine should print the data on married, single, and divorced employees in three separate groups, along with appropriate headings.

12. Redo problem 10, this time sorting the file in ascending order on employee sex. The sort subroutine should use the bubble sort, and the print subroutine

should print all males and females in separate groups along with appropriate headings.

13. Redo problem 10, this time sorting in ascending order on salary. Make your choice of sort subroutine. The print subroutine should find the range of salaries and print the list of employee names (starting with smallest salary first) along with their salaries under appropriate headings. *Note:* The range is the difference between the largest and the smallest salaries.

14. Redo problem 10, this time assuming that the input data cards of problem 10 will be followed by a second type of input card, punched in the following manner:

CC	FIELD	TYPE
1-5	Employee ID	Integer

After the main program reads the employee records, the first type of input card, it should read the second type and call a search subroutine to retrieve the employee record. The search subroutine should use sequential search. There should then be another call to a print subroutine to display the retrieved record.

15. Redo problem 14; this time the search subroutine should use binary search.

16. Redo problem 14, this time assuming that the second type of input card contains employee name instead of employee number—that is, the second type of card is punched in the following manner:

CC	FIELD	TYPE
1-20	Employee name	Characters

The main program should be organized as follows:

```
      CALL INTIAL
      CALL SORT
   10 READ(5,20,END=30) NAME
      CALL SEARCH
      CALL PRINT
      GO TO 10
   30 STOP
      END
```

The INTIAL subroutine reads the input records and stores them in the appropriate arrays. The SORT subroutine sorts the file in ascending order on the employee name, using bubble sort. The SEARCH subroutine uses binary search to retrieve an employee record, and the PRINT subroutine prints the retrieved record. Complete and run the main program and subprograms.

17. Write a FORTRAN program to merge two files. The records of both files are punched on cards in the following manner:

CC	FIELD	TYPE
1–5	Student number	Integer
6–9	Grade point average	X.XX
10–29	Name	Character

Call the first file the master file, and the second the transaction file. The records of the master file should be read first. A student record with zero student number should be used as a signal (flag) to indicate that all records of the master file have been read. The main program should read both files and store them in the appropriate arrays. The subroutine SORT should be called to sort both files in ascending order on student grade point average. Next, the subroutine MERG should be called to merge these two files into a third file. The program should print the merged file under appropriate headings.

18. Redo problem 17, this time merging both files on student number.

19. Redo problem 18, merging them on student name.

16 FILE ORGANIZATION

In the preceding chapter, we discussed different storage and accessing techniques. In this chapter, we will concentrate on two types of file organization—namely, sequential and random (direct).

Files are classified according to their organization—that is, their construction techniques. In general, files can be organized as (1) sequential, (2) random (direct), (3) indexed sequential, and (4) relative indexed sequential.

FORTRAN provides the facilities to organize sequential and random files directly. No facilities are provided to create indexed sequential or relative indexed sequential directly (as in the COBOL language). However, programmers can create indexed sequential files indirectly by means of sequential and random files. ANSI FORTRAN 77 provides support for sequential, random, and stream files.

Different computers and compilers have slightly different techniques to create and manipulate disk and tape files. Because disk and tape file manipulation on the DECSystem 10 differ only slightly under ANSI FORTRAN 77, the creation and manipulation of sequential and random files will be first discussed on the DECSystem 10. Later, we will point out the difference between DEC-System 10, ANSI FORTRAN 77, and IBM FORTRAN IV.

16.1 SEQUENTIAL FILES

Sequential storage techniques are used to create a sequential file. Creation of a sequential file is quite simple. Records are written to the file one after another without any gaps (empty records) between them. The order of the records of a sequential file is the order in which they were written.

Sequential files can be created on disk, tape, or even punched cards. They can be accessed only sequentially; that is, to read the twentieth record of a sequential file, one has to read (or to forward) the first nineteen records to reach it.

16.1.1   Required Commands to Create Disk or Tape Files

An OPEN statement is required to create a new disk or tape file or to open an already existing disk or tape file to make it available for processing and manipulation. One simple form of an OPEN statement on the DECSystem 10 is:

```
OPEN(UNIT=n,DEVICE='DSK',FILE=filename,
ACCESS=access method)
```

where OPEN is a FORTRAN keyword to open a file, UNIT$=n$ assigns a logical unit number to the file, DEVICE='DSK' tells the system that this file is on the disk, FILE$=$filename assigns a name to the file, and ACCESS$=$access method identifies the access method.

Example 16.1

The following OPEN statement creates an output sequential file on the disk named EMPL.DAT, and 10 is assigned as its logical unit number.

```
OPEN(UNIT=10,DEVICE='DSK',FILE='EMPL.DAT',
ACCESS='SEQOUT')
```

Note that even though the file is still empty, it has been created. Pictorially, the file is:

EMPL.DAT   ☐

the filename.

Note that this logical unit number 10 must be used in the WRITE statement to write a record to the file above.

The OPEN statement above does not tell the system how large each record of the file is or how many records can be held in such a file. To give such information, you must add two more arguments to the list of the OPEN statement. These are FILE SIZE$=n$ and RECORD SIZE$=n$, where n is an integer constant.

To create this file on magnetic tape, change the argument DEVICE='DSK' to DEVICE='MTA'; and to create a file on dectape, DECSYSTEM 10's special version of magnetic tape, change it to DEVICE='DTA'. The access method can be one of the following:

ACCESS = SEQIN   The file is to be read in sequential mode.
ACCESS = SEQOUT   The file is to be written in sequential access mode.
ACCESS = 'SEQINOUT'   The file may be first read, then written to.
ACCESS = 'RANDOM'   The file is to be read or written directly (randomly).

One other argument that specifies the action to be taken regarding a file at close time is DISPOSE. These actions are:

DISPOSE = 'SAVE'   Save the file on the device.
DISPOSE = 'DELETE'   Delete the file.

Note that a sequential file cannot be accessed randomly.

The file name on the DECSystem 10 is constructed from two parts: Part 1. ext. The first part can be from one to six characters long and the second part (the extension) from one to three characters long. The first part and the extension part are separated by a period. The following are valid file names on the DECSystem 10: EMPLOY.DAT, INVTRY.INF. SAMPLE.F4, PROF.CBL.

Before the program is stopped, a CLOSE statement should be issued. The general format for the CLOSE statement is:

```
CLOSE(arg1,arg2, . . ., argn)
```

where the arguments are the same as those used in the OPEN statement. Generally, the arguments such as DISPOSE should be written within the CLOSE statement rather than within the OPEN statement.

Example 16.2

The following CLOSE statements are valid on the DECSystem 10. The statement

```
CLOSE(UNIT=10,DEVICE='DSK',FILE='EMPL.DAT',DISPOSE
='SAVE')
```

closes the file EMPL.DAT, which is on the disk, and saves it. The statement

```
CLOSE(FILE='EMPL.DAT',DISPOSE='DELETE')
```

closes the file EMPL.DAT and deletes it from the disk storage area. See FORTRAN-10, DECSystem 10 Manual, Sixth Edition, for other options of the OPEN and CLOSE statements.

Some other instructions required to manipulate disk or tape sequential files are these:

1. READ statement. The READ statement that reads the records of a sequential file is the usual READ, whose general format is READ ($n1$, $n2$,END=$n3$,ERR=$n4$) *list*, where $n1$ is the logical unit number, $n2$, $n3$, and $n4$ are statement numbers, and END=$n2$ and ERR=$n4$ are optional. *List* is the list of variables. Note that after the OPEN statement is executed, the first execution of the READ statement of the sequential file reads the first record of the file, the second execution of the READ causes the second record of the sequential file to be read, and so on. For reading of the file from the beginning again, the file must first be closed,

then reopened. In other words, a CLOSE statement must be executed, then an OPEN statement.

2. WRITE statement. To write a record to a sequential file, the usual WRITE statement is used. Recall that the general format of the WRITE statement is:

WRITE(n1,n2)list

where *n1* is the logical unit number, *n2* is the format statement number, and *list* is the list of variables. After writing the last record in the file, the computer writes the end-of-file record automatically. Therefore, caution must be taken when adding or changing records of a sequential file. This will be clarified later in this chapter.

3. REWIND statement. The general format of the REWIND statement is REWIND *n*, where *n* is the logical unit number of the sequential file. The REWIND statement rewinds the tape on the designated unit. On some systems, such as the DECSystem 10, REWIND can be issued for sequential files on the disk as well. After the REWIND statement is executed, the first record of the sequential file becomes accessible.

4. SKIP RECORD *n* or SKIP *n* causes one record of the file whose logical unit number is *n* to be skipped.

5. BACKSPACE *n*. This statement backspaces the designated tape file one record.

Example 16.3

Write a FORTRAN program to read the records of an employee file that are punched on cards and to store the information in a disk sequential file, EMPLOY.DAT. After all the records have been processed, CLOSE the disk file EMPLOY.DAT and reopen it as an input file. Now read the EMPLOY.DAT file and create from it a sequential file EMTAPE.DAT on magnetic tape and a second file on the line printer to print the records of the file EMPLOY.DAT.

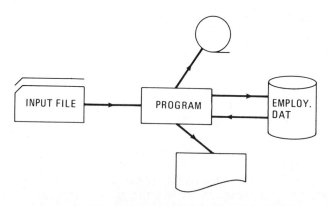

FIGURE 16.1 System flowchart to create disk and tape files

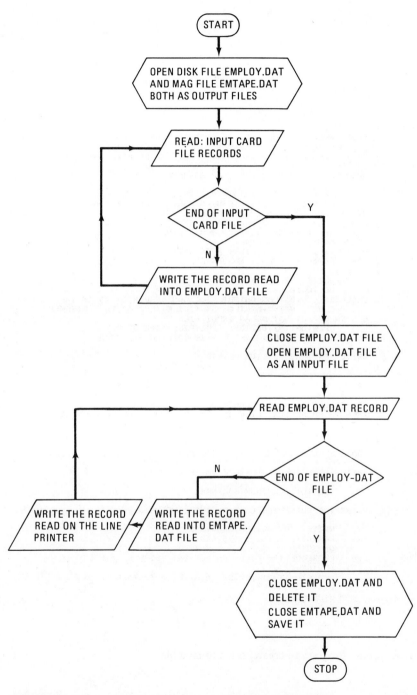

FIGURE 16.2 Program flowchart to create disk and tape file

371

```
C FORTRAN PROGRAM TO CREATE DISK AND TAPE FILES
        DIMENSION NAME(4)
        INTEGER CARDS
        DATA CARDS, LINE/2,3/
C
C OPEN EMPLOY.DAT ON DISK AS AN OUTPUT FILE
        OPEN(UNIT = 7,DEVICE='DSK',FILE='EMPLOY.DAT',
     +  RECORD SIZE=27,ACCESS='SEQOUT',FILE SIZE=1000)
C
C OPEN EMTAPE ON MAGNETIC TAPE AS AN OUTPUT FILE
C
        OPEN(UNIT=21,DEVICE='MTA',FILE='EMTAPE.DAT',
     +  RECORD SIZE=27,ACCESS='SEQOUT',FILE SIZE=1000)
C START LOOP TO READ INPUT  RECORDS AND
C STORE THEM IN THE SEQUENTIAL DISK FILE EMPLOY.DAT
   10   READ(CARDS,20,END=30)NUM,SAL,NAME
   20   FORMAT(I4,F7.2,4A4)
C WRITE IN EMPLOY.DAT FILE. NOTE UNIT=7
C MAKE THE LOGICAL UNIT NUMBER FOR EMPLOY.DAT
C FILE TO BE 7
        WRITE(7,20)NUM,SAL,NAME
        GO TO 10
C CLOSE EMPLOY.DAT AS OUTPUT FILE AND REOPEN IT AS AN INPUT FILE
   30   CLOSE(UNIT=7,DEVICE='DSK',FILE='EMPLOY.DAT',DISPOSE='SAVE')
C REOPEN EMPLOY.DAT AS AN INPUT FILE
        OPEN(UNIT=7,DEVICE='DSK',FILE='EMPLOY.DAT',
     +  RECORD SIZE =27,FILE SIZE=1000,ACCESS='SEQIN')
C
C WRITE HEADINGS ON LINE PRINTER
C
        WRITE(LINE,40)
   40   FORMAT(1X,T10,'ID',T30,'NAME',T60,'SALARY')
C
C START LOOP TO READ RECORDS OF EMPLOY.DAT AND WRITE
C THEM IN EMTAPE.DAT FILE AND ON THE LINE PRINTER AS WELL.
C
C READ EMPLOY.DAT RECORDS
C
   50   READ(7,20,END=70)NUM,SAL,NAME
C
C WRITE THE RECORD IN EMTAPE.DAT FILE
C
        WRITE(21,20)NUM,SAL,NAME
C
C PRINT THE CURRENT RECORD ON THE LINE PRINTER
C
        WRITE(LINE,60)NUM,NAME,SAL
   60   FORMAT(1X,T10,I4,T30,4A4,T60,F8.2)
        GO TO 50
   70   CLOSE(UNIT=7,FILE='EMPLOY.DAT',DISPOSE='DELETE',
     +  DEVICE='DSK')
        CLOSE(UNIT=21,DEVICE='MTA',FILE='EMTAPE.DAT',
     +  DISPOSE='SAVE')
        STOP
        END
```

FIGURE 16.3   Program to create disk and tape file

The input file is punched on the card in the following manner:

CC	FIELD	TYPE
1–4	Employee number	Integer
5–11	Salary	Real XXXX.XX
12–27	Employee name	Character

Assume that we want the file to have the capacity of 1,000 records. Note that the record size is 27 characters. Figure 16.1 is the system flowchart and Figure 16.2 is the program flowchart for the program in Figure 16.3, which solves the problem.

The pseudo code form for the program in Figure 16.3 is:

```
Start
Open Output disk file EMPLOY.DAT, Tape file EMTAPE.DAT
DOWHILE Not End of Input card file
        Read Number, Salary, Name From Card file
        Write Number, Salary, Name Into EMPLOY.DAT
END DOWHILE
Close EMPLOY.DAT
Open Input disk file EMPLOY.DAT
DOWHILE Not End of EMPLOY.DAT file
        Read Number, Salary, Name From EMPLOY.DAT
        Write Number, Salary, Name Into EMTAPE.DAT
        Write Number, Salary, Name On the Line Printer
END DOWHILE
Close all files
Stop
```

16.2   RANDOM FILES

Random files are constructed differently from sequential files. Random files can be easily organized on direct-access storage devices such as disk. Usually, strictly sequential storage devices, such as magnetic tapes, are not used for random files.

A random file always has a key, called the *file key*. The numerical value of the file key represents the location of the record in the file. Because of the file key, random files can be accessed randomly (directly). To gain access to a particular record in a random file—say, the fifth record—you must set the file key to 5 and request an input or output operation. The computer will then read or write the record specified by the key—in this case, record number 5. In addition to direct access, random files can be accessed sequentially.

16.2.1   Command to Create and Manipulate Random Files

The OPEN statement of a random file should contain the clause ACCESS= 'RANDOM'. The remaining parts of the OPEN and CLOSE statements are the same as those for sequential files.

The READ and WRITE statements used in conjunction with random files are different from READ and WRITE statements of sequential files. The general format for READ and WRITE statements of random files is:

```
READ(n1#i,n2)list        WRITE(n1#i,n2)list
READ(n1'i,n2)list        WRITE(n1'i,n2)list
```

where $n1$ is the logical unit number, $n2$ is the format statement number, *list* is list of variables, and i is the record key, which must be an integer constant or an integer variable. The following examples clarify the creation and manipulation of random files.

```
C PROGRAM TO CREATE A RANDOM FILE
C
C    VARIABLE NAMES USED
C       ID    EMPLOYEE NUMBER
C       SAL   SALARY
C       NAME  EMPLOYEE NAME
C
C VARIABLE ID USED AS THE RECORD KEY
        DIMENSION NAME(3)
        INTEGER CARDS
        CARDS=2
C OPEN RANDOM FILE
        OPEN(UNIT=8,DEVICE='DSK',FILE='RANEM.DAT',RECORD SIZE=20,
     +  FILE SIZE=10,ACCESS='RANDOM')
C LOOP TO READ  RECORDS AND WRITE THEM IN THE RANDOM FILE
C
   10   READ(CARDS,20,END=30)ID,SAL,NAME
   20   FORMAT(I2,F6.2,3A4)
        WRITE(8#ID,20)ID,SAL,NAME
        GO TO 10
   30   STOP
        END
```

Example 16.4

Suppose that employee data are punched on cards in the following manner:

CC	FIELD	TYPE
1–2	Employee number	Integer
3–8	Salary	Real XXX.XX
9–20	Name	Character

Below is the FORTRAN program from which to read the input employee card file above and to create disk random file RANEM.DAT.

Let us assume the following input data:

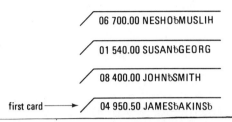

first card ⟶   04 950.50 JAMESbAKINSb

To create a random file, we must identify the record key. The key is one of the fields (available), which determines the position of the record within the file. In this case, we will choose "employee number" as the record key. The following program created a random file, with a capacity of ten records, each 20 characters long.

After execution of the program, the contents of the random file are:

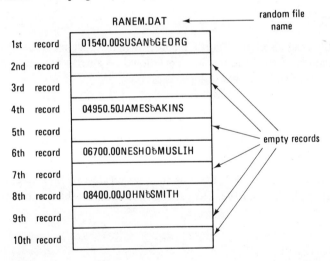

Note the following:

1. ID is the file key, because ID follows the # in the WRITE statement. When the first card is read, the value of ID becomes 04; then the statement WRITE(8#ID,20)ID,SAL,NAME commands the system to write the values of the variables ID, SAL, and NAME in the fourth record in the file. Note that the first, the second, and the third record are bypassed and are still empty.

2. When the second card is read, the value of ID becomes 8; hence, the WRITE(8#ID,20)ID,SAL,NAME writes the values of the variables ID, SAL, and NAME in record number 8 in the file.

Now it should be clear why such a file organization is called direct or random file; it is because a record can be directly read or written.

In sequential files, the access of the next record is dependent on the position of the current record. For example, if you just read record number 5 of a sequential file, the next record available to be read can be only record number 6. In contrast, access to the next record in random files is independent of the position of the current record in the file. The execution of the following statements:

```
    ID=4
10  READ(8#ID,20)ID,SAL,NAME
    IF(ID .GE. 8)STOP
    IF(ID .EQ. 4) GO TO 20
    IF(ID .LE. 1)ID = 8
    GO TO 10
20  ID=ID-3
    GO TO 10
```

causes the reading of the fourth record, then the first record, and finally the eighth record of the random file. You should be able to note that ID assumes the values 4, 1, and 8 in that order.

Example 16.5

We redo example 16.4, but this time we create two files, one random and the other sequential disk file. The pseudo code form for the program is:

```
Start
Open random file RANEM.DAT,Output sequential
     file SEQEM.DAT
DOWHILE Not End of Input Employee card file
     Read ID,Salary,Name From Employee file
     Write ID,Salary,Name In RANEM.DAT
        based on the file key ID
     Write ID,Salary,Name Im SEQEM.DAT
END DOWHILE
Close all files
Stop
```

The program is:

```
C THIS PROGRAM CREATES BOTH SEQUENTIAL AND RANDOM DISK FILES
C
C VARIABLE NAMES USED:
C       ID         EMPLOYEE NUMBER. USED AS THE FILE KEY FOR THE RANDOM FILE
C       SAL        SALARY
C       NAME       EMPLOYEE NAME
C
C
        DIMENSION NAME(3)
        INTEGER    CARDS
        CARDS = 2
C
C OPEN RANDOM FILE RANEM.DAT
        OPEN (UNIT=8, DEVICE='DSK', FILE='RANEM.DAT', RECORD SIZE=20,
     +  FILE SIZE=10, ACCESS='SEQOUT')
C
C OPEN SEQUENTIAL FILE
C
        OPEN (UNIT=17, DEVICE='DSK', FILE='SEQEM.DAT', RECORD SIZE=20,
     +  FILE SIZE=10, ACCESS='SEQOUT')
C
C START THE LOOP TO READ INPUT RECORDS AND WRITE THEM IN BOTH RANDOM AND
C SEQUENTIAL OUTPUT FILES
C
  10    READ (CARDS, 20, END=30) ID, SAL, NAME
  20    FORMAT (I2,F6.2,3A4)
C
C WRITE THE RECORD IN THE RANDOM FILE
C
        WRITE (8#ID, 20) ID, SAL, NAME
C
C WRITE THE RECORD IN THE SEQUENTIAL FILE
C
        WRITE (17, 20) ID, SAL, NAME
        GO TO 10
  30    CLOSE (UNIT=8, DISPOSE='SAVE')
        CLOSE (UNIT=17, FILE='SEQEM.DAT', DISPOSE='SAVE')
        STOP
        END
```

After execution of this program, the contents of the random and sequential files are:

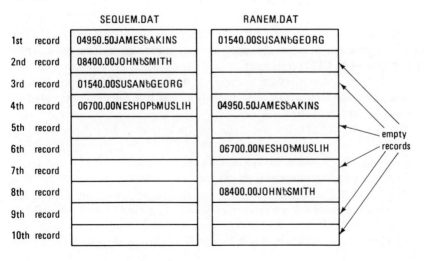

	SEQUEM.DAT	RANEM.DAT
1st record	04950.50JAMESჼAKINS	01540.00SUSANჼGEORG
2nd record	08400.00JOHNჼSMITH	
3rd record	01540.00SUSANჼGEORG	
4th record	06700.00NESHOPჼMUSLIH	04950.50JAMESჼAKINS
5th record		
6th record		06700.00NESHOჼMUSLIH
7th record		
8th record		08400.00JOHNჼSMITH
9th record		
10th record		

empty records

Note the following:

1. When the first card is read, the value of ID becomes 4; then the statement WRITE(8#ID,20)ID,SAL,NAME causes the values of the variables ID, SAL, and NAME to be written in record number 4 of the random file. However, the statement WRITE(17,20)ID,SAL,NAME causes the value of these variables to be written as record number 1 in the sequential file.
2. The second execution of the loop in the program reads the second card, and writes the second record of the sequential file and the eighth record of the random file. You should be able to understand how the remaining records of the random and sequential files are written.

16.3   ANSI FORTRAN 77 COMMANDS

The general format for the OPEN statement in ANSI FORTRAN 77 is:

OPEN(*argument-list*)

where *argument-list* is a list of specifiers:

UNIT = $n1$ ($n1$ becomes the logical unit number)
ERR = $n2$ ($n2$ is a statement number)
FILE = file name
STATUS = file status
ACCESS = access method
FORM = formatted or unformatted
RECL = record length
MAXREC = maximum number of records in the file
BLANK = NULL or ZERO

The argument list of the OPEN statement must contain UNIT = $n1$. The other specifiers are optional. No specifier can appear more than once in the argument list of an OPEN statement.

The first three specifiers are the same as those on the DECSystem 10. Note that the file name depends on the installation, but it is usually constructed of from one to eight characters.

The specifier STATUS = file status can be in one of the following forms:

STATUS = NEW means this is a new file.

STATUS = OLD means this is an old file.

STATUS = SCRATCH indicates that this file is used as a scratch file. No file name is needed for a scratch file. Scratch files are automatically deleted when a CLOSE statement is executed.

STATUS = UNKNOWN means the status is processing-dependent.

The option UNKNOWN is assumed if the STATUS specifier is omitted.

The ACCESS specifier can be in one of the following forms: ACCESS = DIRECT, or ACCESS = SEQUENTIAL, or ACCESS = STREAM. The SEQUENTIAL access is assumed if this specifier is omitted. See Appendix II for STREAM file.

The forms of the specifier FORM are FORM = FORMATTED, or FORM = UNFORMATTED. The specifier FORM may be specified only for direct-access files. If this specifier is omitted for the file being created, the UNFORMATTED form is assumed.

The specifier RECL = record length is mandatory for direct-access files. It specifies the length of each record. If the records are formatted, record length is the number of characters; if the records are unformatted, the length is the number of noncharacter storage units.

The specifier MAXREC specifies the maximum number of records in the file. The specifier BLANK has two forms: BLANK = ZERO and BLANK = NULL. The first option treats all blanks (spaces) except leading blanks as zeros. The second option causes all blank characters in a numeric formatted input field to be ignored, except that a field of all blanks is treated as zero.

The general form of the CLOSE statement is:

CLOSE(UNIT=*n1*, ERR=*n2*, STATUS= *file status*)

The specifier UNIT = $n1$ must be specified. The STATUS specifier has the forms STATUS = KEEP or STATUS = DELETE. The first option keeps the file permanently and the second deletes the file. If the status specifier is omitted, then STATUS = KEEP is assumed.

In addition to CLOSE and OPEN statements, ANSI FORTRAN 77 permits the INQUIRE statement, which may be used to inquire about the properties of a particular named file. For different forms of the INQUIRE statement, see section 12.1.3.3 of *SIGPLAN NOTICES*, Vol. 11, No. 3 (March 1976).

The following file position statements are permitted: BACKSPACE n, END-FILE n, and REWIND n, where n is the logical unit number of the files. The same actions are performed as those on the DECSystem 10.

The input/output statements are very similar to those on the DECSystem 10. The general form of the READ statement to read a sequential file is:

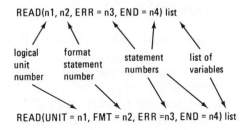

Incidentally, the first form is the same as the one on DECSystem 10.

The READ for direct (random) access must contain an additional specifier, REC = n, where n is the record number—that is, the record key. In other words, the general format for a READ of a direct file is:

READ(n1, n2, REC = n3, ERR = n4, END = n5) list

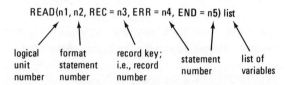

| logical
unit
number | format
statement
number | record key;
i.e., record
number | statement
number | list of
variables |

The general format of the WRITE statement for a sequential file is the same as the one on the DECSystem 10:

WRITE($\underline{n1},\underline{n2}$)list

where $n1$ is the logical unit number, $n2$ is the format statement number, and *list* is the list of variables. The general form of the WRITE statement for a direct (random) file is:

WRITE($\underline{n1},\underline{n2}$,REC=$\underline{n3}$)list

where $n1$ is the logical unit number, $n2$ the format statement number, $n3$ the number of the record to be written (the record key) and *list* the list of variables.

Another output statement that is permitted is the PRINT statement. The general form of the PRINT statement is:

PRINT $\underline{n1}$, list

where $n1$ is the format statement number and *list* is the list of variables. Note that PRINT writes the output on the line printer.

Example 16.6

Convert the program in example 16.5 (p. 376) to ANSI FORTRAN 77.

16.4　IBM FORTRAN IV COMMANDS

16.4.1　Sequential Files on Tape

The familiar commands READ, WRITE, END FILE, REWIND, and SKIP RECORD are used to create and manipulate sequential files on tape. Unlike FORTRAN IV on the DECSystem 10 and ANSI Fortran 77, the logical unit number of the file, the file name, and record size, along with other information regarding the tape file, are not assigned within the FORTRAN program but by means of job control statements. The following examples show how to create and manipulate tape files. Note that job control commands are part of the operating system's commands. All job control commands start with // in the first and second columns of each card. In our example, we separated the job control commands from the FORTRAN program by solid lines.

```
C THIS PROGRAM CREATES BOTH SEQUENTIAL AND RANDOM FILES
C THE PROGRAM IS WRITTEN IN ANSI FORTRAN 77
C
C VARIABLE NAMES USED:
C
C       ID    EMPLOYEE NUMBER. USED AS THE FILE KEY FOR THE RANDOM FILE
C       SAL   SALARY
C       NAME  EMPLOYEE NAME
C
        DIMENSION NAME(3)
        INTEGER CARDS
        CARDS=5
C
C OPEN RANDOM FILE
        OPEN (UNIT=8, FILE=EMPLOYDAT, STATUS=NEW, ACCESS=DIRECT,
     +  FORM=FORMATTED, RECL=20, MAXREC=10, BLANK=ZERO)
C
C OPEN SEQUENTIAL FILE
        OPEN (UNIT=17, FILE=SEQEMDAT, STATUS=NEW, ACCES=SEQUENTIAL,
     +  RECL=20, MAXREC=10, BLANK=ZERO)
C
C START LOOP TO READ INPUT RECORDS AND WRITE THEM IN BOTH SEQUENTIAL
C AND RANDOM OUTPUT FILES
    10      READ(CARDS,20,END=30)ID,SAL,NAME
    20      FORMAT(I2,F6.2,3A4)
C WRITE IT IN THE RANDOM FILE
            WRITE(8,20,REC=ID)ID,SAL,NAME
C WRITE IT IN THE SEQUENTIAL FILE
            WRITE(17,20)ID,SAL,NAME
            GO TO 10
    30      STOP
            END
```

Example 16.7

Write a program to read an employee payroll list from cards and store it in a file on tape. Then read each record of the tape file and print it on the line printer. Each employee record is punched on a card in the following manner:

CC	FIELD	TYPE
1–2	Employee number	Integer
3–8	Salary	Real
9–20	Name	Character

Figure 16.4 is the program to accomplish these requirements. Following is a brief discussion of the job control statements in the program. The job card is:

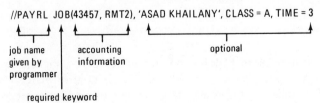

//PAYRL JOB(43457, RMT2), 'ASAD KHAILANY', CLASS = A, TIME = 3

job name given by programmer   required keyword   accounting information   optional

381

```
//PAYRL JOB (43457,RMT1),'ASAD KHAILANY',CLASS=A,TIME=3
//        EXEC FORTGGO
//FORT.SYSIN DD*
C
C SYSTEM :PAYROLL
C PROGRAM NARRATIVE: THIS PROGRAM READS THE LIST OF EMPLOYEES FROM
C                    CARDS AND STORES THEM ON A MAGNETIC TAPE FILE.
C                    AFTER PROCESSING ALL THE RECORDS, THE TAPE FILE
C                    IS REWOUND, AND THE RECORDS OF THE TAPE FILE
C                    ARE READ AND PRINTED ON THE LINE PRINTER.
C
C
C
C VARIABLE NAMES USED
C    ID      EMPLOYEE NUMBER
C    SAL     SALARY
C    NAME    EMPLOYEE NAME
C
         DIMESION NAME(3)
         INTEGER CARDS
         DATA CARDS, LINE/5,6/
C
C LOOP TO READ INPUT RECORDS AND STORES THEM IN MAGNETIC TAPE FILE
C
    10   READ(CARDS,20,END=30)ID,SAL,NAME
    20   FORMAT(I2,F6.2,3A4)
C NOTE THE JOB CONTROL CARD //GO.FT08001 AT THE
C END OF THE FORTRAN PROGRAM WHICH ASSIGNS
C 8 AS THE LOGICAL UNIT NUMBER FOR THE TAPE FILE
C WRITE THE RECORD IN THE TAPE FILE
         WRITE(8,20)ID,SAL,NAME
         GO TO 10
C WRITE THE END OF TAPE FILE
    30   END FILE 8
C REWIND THE TAPE FILE
         REWIND 8
C LOOP TO READ RECORDS OF THE TAPE FILE AND PRINT THEM ON THE LINE PRINT
ER
C
    40   READ(8,20,END=60)ID,SAL,NAME
         WRITE(LINE,50)ID,SAL,NAME
    50   FORMAT(1X,T10,I2,T30,F7.2,T50,3A4)
         GO TO 40
    60   STOP
         END
/*
//GO.FT08001  DD   DSN = PRYLFILE,
//               UNIT=TAPE9,VOL=SER=011111,
//               LABEL=(,SL),
//               DCB=(RECFM=FB,LRECL=20,BLKSIZE=200),
//               DISP=(NEW,CATLG,DELETE)
//GO.DATA DD*
/*
//
```

FIGURE 16.4   Program for example 16.7

The clause CLASS=A identifies the memory size that is required by this program, and TIME=3 limits the CPU time of the program by three minutes. In the card:

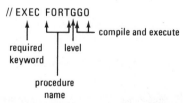

The procedure name FORT stands for FORTRAN compiler. Several levels of FORTRAN compilers are available. The letter *G* after FORT identifies FORTRAN compiler level G as the one to be used to compile the program. The word

382

GO refers to compile-link-and-go; that is, after compilation, start executing the program.

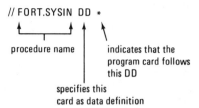

```
// FORT.SYSIN DD *
```

procedure name | indicates that the program card follows this DD

specifies this card as data definition

The card /* is the delimiter card.

The tape file is defined by the following control statement:

```
//GO.FT08F001   DD   DSN=PRYLFILE,
//                   UNIT=TAPE9,VOL=SER=011111,
//                   LABEL=(,SL),
//                   DCB=(RECFM=F,LRECL=20,BLKSIZE=200)
```

Let us discuss different parts of this statement.

GO.FT08F001

GO. is a required keyword, FT is a required keyword, and 08 is the logical unit number (data-set reference) that the programmer has assigned to the file. Thus, FT08 assigns 8 as the logical unit number for the file. This number is used in the READ or WRITE statement with respect to this file. See the statement WRITE(8,20)ID,SAL,NAME of our example. F001 is a data-sequence set number that indicates that this is the first reel in the tape.

DD   DSN=PRYLFILE

DSN means data-set name (the name of the file). PRYLFILE is the name of the file chosen by the programmer. The file name can be from one to eight characters long and must start with a letter.

UNIT=TAPE9,VOL=SER=01111

UNIT=TAPE9 indicates that the file will be on nine-track tape. VOL=SER= 01111 indicates that the tape file is on one tape (VOL), and its serial number (the number to identify the tape) is 011111.

LABEL=(,SL),

This asks the system to write the standard label. The comma indicates that the tape contains one file.

DCB=(RECFM=F,LRECL=20,BLKSIZE=200)

DCB stands for data control block. RECFM=F indicates that the size of each record is fixed; LRECL=20 that the record size is 20 bytes; and BLKSIZE=200 that each block contains ten records. Therefore, there are ten records per block.

DISP=(NEW,DELETE)

DISP stands for disposition—status of the file. The first parameter, NEW, indicates that this is a new file, and the second, DELETE, that after the execution of the program is completed, the tape will be rewound for dismounting from the tape drives.

The card

//GO.DATA   DD *

indicates that the data cards following this card are the program's data cards. Finally, the card

//

indicates end of job.

16.4.2   Creating Files on Direct-Access Devices

There are four statements to create and manipulate files on direct-access devices. These are DEFINE FILE, READ, WRITE, and FIND statements.

The general form for the DEFINE FILE statement is:

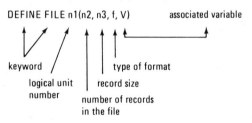

where:

- *n1* is an integer constant that represents the logical unit number of the file (data reference).
- *n2* is an integer constant that represents the size of the file.
- *n3* is an integer constant that represents the size of the record.
- *f*   specifies whether the file is to be read or written, either with or without a FORMAT statement. One of the following is permissible for *f*:
    - *L* indicates that the file is to be read or written either with or without a FORMAT statement. In such a case, the maximum record size is measured in number of bytes (characters).
    - *E* indicates that the file is to be read or written with a FORMAT state-

ment. The maximum record size is measured in number of bytes (characters).

U indicates that the file is to be read or written without a FORMAT statement. The maximum record size is measured in number of computer words. Four bytes make one computer word.

v is a nonsubscripted integer variable known as an associated variable. After each read or write statement, the value of the associated variable is set to the number of the record that immediately follows the one being processed. In other words, at the conclusion of each READ or WRITE operation, a value 1 more than the number of the record being processed is automatically assigned to the associated variable.

The DEFINE FILE statement of a file must appear prior to any READ or WRITE statement referencing the file.

Example 16.8

Write a DEFINE FILE statement to create a file on disk. Each record of the file is organized in the following manner:

CC	FIELD	TYPE
1–2	Employee number	Integer
3–8	Salary	Real
9–20	Name	Character

The file is to be read or written under format control, and the file size should be 1,000 records:

```
DEFINE FILE 9(1000,20,E,J)
```

Note that 1,000 is the size of the file, and 20 (number of characters) bytes is the record size. *E* indicates that the file is to be read or written under format control, *J* is the associated variable, and 9 is the logical unit number. This logical unit number, along with the file name and other information, must be supplied to the system by means of the job control statement

```
//GO.FTnnFnnn   DD
```

An appropriate job control statement for our example is:

```
//GO.FT09FT001 DD   DSN=DS43457.PAYRL,
//               UNIT=3300,VOL=SER=DSKA1,
//               LABEL=(,SL),SPACE=(20,(1000,50)),
//               DCB=(RECFM=F,LRECL=20,BLKSIZE=200),
//               DISP=(NEW,DELETE)
```

As you can see, the job control statements above are almost the same as the ones used for a tape file, except for UNIT=3300, which indicates the type of disk pack, and SPACE=(20,(1000,50)), which indicates the space to be reserved for the disk file. 20 represents the record size; 1000 represents the primary disk space to be allocated to hold 1,000 records (that is 1,000 units of 20 bytes each); 50 represents the secondary amount of storage allocated to hold up to 50 extra records if the primary area is exhausted.

Example 16.9

The following DEFINE FILE statement defines a file with logical unit number 22. The file size is 500 records, and the size of each record is 61 bytes. The file can be processed formatted or unformatted.

```
DEFINE FINE 22(500,61,L,I)
```

Change the DEFINE FILE statement above so that the file can be processed only in an unformatted manner.

```
DEFINE FILE 22(500,16,U,I)
```

Note that the record size is 61 bytes, which is equivalent to 15.25 words (61/4 = 15.25), but this number must be rounded up to the nearest integer greater than the number. Thus, the record size is 16.

The other statements for manipulating files on direct-access devices are READ, WRITE, and FIND. The general form of READ is:

```
READ(n1'i,n2,ERR=n3)list
```

where $n1$ is the logical unit number, i is an integer constant or an integer variable that is the file key (the number of the record to be read), and $n2$ is the format statement number. If the file is unformatted, $n2$ is omitted. The ERR part is optional; $n3$ is a statement number; and *list* is the list of variables.

Note that this is the second form of the READ statement given in section 16.2.1 to read direct file on DECSystem 10 and ANSI FORTRAN 77.

The general form for the WRITE statement is:

```
WRITE(n1'i,n2)list
```

where $n1$, i, and $n2$ are the same as those with the READ statement.

Finally, the general form of the FIND statement is:

```
FIND(n1'i)
```

where $n1$ is the logical unit number and i is the number of the record (file key) that should be retrieved. The FIND statement causes the next input record to be found while the present record is processed. This speeds up the processing. The FIND statement does not read the record but makes it available for the next read. There is no advantage to using FIND with the WRITE statement.

Example 16.10

Write a FORTRAN program to read employee records from cards and create from them two files on disk. The first file should be a random file and the second should be a sequential file. Use "employee number" as the file key for the random file. The input records are punched on cards in the following manner:

CC	FIELD	TYPE
1–2	Employee number	Integer
3–8	Salary	Real
9–28	Employee name	Character

The file size should be 1,000 records. Figure 16.5 is the complete FORTRAN program, along with required job control cards.

Note that the first time the value of ISEQ is set to 1 and whenever there was a WRITE statement, ISEQ (the associated variable) was automatically increased by 1. As you can see, the same DEFINE FILE, READ, and WRITE statements are used for both sequential and random files on IBM equipment. However, as is the case with DECSystem 10 and ANSI FORTRAN 77, the organization and access mechanism of random and sequential files are quite different, as discussed at the beginning of this chapter.

16.5   GENERAL MANIPULATION OF FILES

16.5.1   Creating a Sequential File

1. Open both input and output files.
2. Repeat steps 3 through 5 until the end of input file is encountered.
3. Read a record of the input file. If end of file is encountered, close all the files and stop run.
4. Move the record of the input file to the record of the output file.
5. Write the record to the output file.

16.5.2   Adding New Records to the End of a Sequential File

1. Open input file and open as input–output the old sequential file.
2. Repeat step 3 until the end of old sequential file is found.

```
//EMPSAM  JOB(43457,RMT2),'ASAD KHAILANY'CLASS=A,TIME=10
//    EXEC FORTGGO
//FORT.SYSIN  DD*
C
C FORTRAN PROGRAM
C SYSTEM:  EMPLOYEE LIST
C PROBLEM NARRATIVE: THIS PROGRAM READS EMPLOYEE NPUT RECORDS
C                    AND STORES THEM IN TWO FILES; ONE OF THESE
C                    TWO FILES IS RANDOM AND THE OTHER IS SEQUENTIAL.
C
C INPUT FILES: CARD FILE
C OUTPUT FILES:
C    1.  RANDOM FILE RANEMP. 20 IS ASSIGNED AS ITS LOGICAL UNIT NUMBER
C
C    2.  SEQUENTIAL FILE  SEQEMP. 22 IS ASSIGNED AS ITS LOGICAL
C        UNIT NUMBER
C
C VARIABLE NAMES USED:
C   ID  EMPLOYEE NUMBER USED AS FILE KEY
C   SAL SALARY
C   NAME EMPLOYEE NAME
C   IRAN ASSOCIATED VARIABLE FOR RANDOM FILE
C   ISEQ ASSOCIATED VARIABLE FOR SEQUENTIAL FILE
C
        DIMENSION NAME(5)
        INTEGER CARDS
        DATA CARDS/5/
C DEFINE RANDOM FILE
        DEFINE FILE 20 (1000,28,E,IRAN)
C DEFINE SEQUENTIAL FILE
        DEFINE FILE 22(1000,28,E,ISEQ)
C INITIALIZE THE ASSOCIATED VARIABLE OF
C SEQUENTIAL FILE TO 1
        ISEQ=1
C  LOOP TO  READ CARDS AND WRITE RECORDS IN BOTH FILES
    10  READ(CARDS,20,END=30)ID,SAL,NAME
    20  FORMAT(I2,F6.2,5A4)
C WRITE IT IN THE RANDOM FILE
        WRITE(20'ID)'SAL'NAME
C WRITE IT IN THE SEQUENTIAL FILE, NOTE THAT
C ISEQ IS USED  AS THE RECORD KEY WHICH
C WAS INITIALIZED TO 1
        WRITE(22,ISEQ)ID,SAL,NAME
        GO TO 10
    30  STOP
        END
/*
//GO.FT20F002  DD DSN=DS43457.RANEMP9,
//             UNIT=3300,VOL=SER=DSKA1,
//             LABEL=(,SL),SPACE=(28,(1000,50)),
//             DCB=(RECFM=FB,LRECL=28,BLKSIZE=280),
//             DISP=(NEW,KEEP)
//GO.FT22F002  DD  DSN=DS43457.SEQEMP9,
//             UNIT=3300,VOL=SER=DSKA2,
//             LABEL=(,SL),SPACE=(28,(1000,50)),
//             DCB=(RECFM=FB,LRECL=28,BLKSIZE=280),
//             DISP=(NEW,KEEP)
//GO.DATA DD*
/*
//
```

FIGURE 16.5   Program for example 16.10

3. Read a record of old sequential file. If end of old sequential file is encountered, perform step 4.

4. Repeat steps 5 through 7 until end of input file is encountered. If end of file, close all files, stop run.

5. Read a record of the input file. If end of the input file is found, close all files and stop run.

6. Move the input record to the record of old sequential file.

7. Write the record of sequential file.

16.5.3   Merging Files

A better way to add a record to an already existing sequential file is to merge the existing file with a transaction file (a file of new records to be added to the existing sequential file) and create from them a new file, which is sorted on the same sort key and in the same order as the old sequential file.

Note that all merging files must be sorted before the merging process starts. The new file resulting from merging becomes sorted on the same sort key in the same order as the merging files without a separate sorting routine.

The following steps describe how to merge file 1 and file 2 into file 3. Before the merge process is started, both file 1 and file 2 must be sorted on the same sort key (such as employee number) and in the same order (such as ascending order). We assume that both are sorted in ascending order.

1. Open both file 1 and file 2 as input files, and file 3 as an output file.
2. Read a record of file 1. If end of file 1 is encountered, perform steps 5 through 7 until end of file 2 is found.
3. Read a record of file 2. If end of file 2 is encountered, perform steps 8 through 10 until end of file 1 is encountered.
4. If the sort key of the record of file 1 is less than the sort key of file 2:
   Move the record of file 1 to the record of file 3.
   Write the record of file 3, perform step 2.
   Repeat step 4.
   Otherwise:
   Move the record of file 2 to the record of file 3.
   Write the record of file 3, perform step 3.
   Repeat step 4.
5. Read a record of file 2. If end of file 2 is encountered, close all files, stop run.
6. Move the record of file 2 to the record of file 3.
7. Write the record of file 3.
8. Read a record of file 1. If end of file 1, close all files, stop run.
9. Move the record of file 1 to the record of file 3.
10. Write the record of file 3.

16.5.4   Changing a Record of a Sequential File

Do not write on the file whose records need to be changed. Instead, make a new file so that an audit trail can be preserved. Suppose that file 1 is the old file, some of whose records need updating, that file 2 contains keys of the records along with new updated information, and that file 3 is the new file.

1. Sort both file 1 and file 2 on the same sort key and in the same order.
2. Open both file 1 and file 2 as input files, and file 3 as an output file.
3. Repeat steps 4 through 6.

4. Read a record of file 2. If end of file 2, perform steps 7 through 10.
5. Read a record of file 1. If end of file 1, write an error message indicating that file 1 does not contain the record that requires updating, close all files, stop run.
6. If sort key of file 1 is equal to the sort key of file 2:
   Update the record of file 1.
   Move the updated record to record of file 3.
   Write the record of file 3, repeat steps 4 through 5.
   Otherwise:
   Move the record of file 1 to the record of file 3.
   Write the record of file 3.
   Repeat steps 5 through 6.
7. Read a record of file 1; if end of file 1, close all files, stop run.
8. Move the record of file 1 to the record of file 3.
9. Write the record of file 3.
10. Repeat steps 7 through 10.

16.6   COMPARISON BETWEEN SEQUENTIAL AND RANDOM FILES

1. Sequential files are easier to create than random files.
2. Sequential files can be accessed sequentially only. Random files can be accessed both sequentially and directly.
3. Sequential files require less storage than random files, because random files must reserve space for unfilled records in addition to other records.
4. Updating a sequential file is harder than updating a random file.
5. It is better to have a direct file organization when the file is not very active, in the sense that most work with the file requires a small percentage of the records of the file. If the file is very active—i.e., 15% or more records of the file need to be accessed—then the sequential file is more efficient.
6. Direct files are also preferable when records have to be located quickly, such as for an airline reservation system or a bank customer-account system. Sequential files are best for files such as payroll, where most of the records of the file must be processed at the end of each payroll period.

16.7   SUMMARY

Sequential files can be created on both sequential-access devices such as magnetic tape and direct-access devices such as disk. Random (direct) files are easily created on direct-access devices. Sequential files can be accessed sequentially only; random files can be accessed both sequentially and directly.

A random file always has a file key. The numerical value of the file key represents the location of the record in the file. Sequential files are generally more compact than random files in terms of storage usage, and random files are more efficient for retrieving a few records at once, or where records need to be retrieved quickly.

16.8   REVIEW QUESTIONS AND SUGGESTED PROBLEMS

1. *True or False*. Random files can be created on a direct-access device.

2. *True or False*. Sequential files can be created on both sequential- and direct-access devices.

3. *True or False*. Random files can be accessed sequentially or randomly.

4. *True or False*. Sequential files can be accessed sequentially only.

5. *True or False*. The records of a sequential file always occupy the physical front of the file.

6. *True or False*. Random files may contain empty records.

7. *True or False*. Sequential file organization is more compact than direct organization in terms of storage.

8. *True or False*. The record key must be known in order for a specific record of a random file to be read or written.

9. *True or False*. If a good percentage of the records of the file must be accessed, then a sequential file, not a direct-access file, should be used.

10. *True or False*. Before a merging procedure is started, all merging files should be sorted on the same sort key and in the same order.

11. **Creating an Inventory Sequential File on Magnetic Tape.** Write a FORTRAN program to read inventory records from cards and create a permanent inventory tape file. Each inventory record is punched on two cards in the following manner:

CC	FIELD	TYPE
1–3	Item number	Integer
6–26	Item name	Character
27–29	Unit price	Real
30–34	Number of units on hand	Integer
35–39	Number of units requested	Integer
40–44	Number of units on order	Integer
45–74	Name of manufacturer	Character
1–50	Description (2nd card)	Character

After all records have been written to the tape file, read the tape file and write all the records on the line printer.

12. Redo problem 11, this time creating a disk file instead of a tape file.

13. **Random Inventory File Using the Item Number as the File Key.** Redo problem 11, this time creating a random file, not a sequential file. Use the item number as the file key.

14. **Updating Inventory Random File.** Suppose that the inventory file that was created in problem 13 is for XYZ Retail Store. From past data, the XYZ Retail Store has established two levels for each inventory item: upper and lower critical numbers. At the end of each week, the inventory level of each item is reviewed to see if it is below its critical number. If it is, an order is placed for the following amount: Upper critical number − Current critical number.

Write a FORTRAN program to read a card file in which each record is punched in the following manner:

CC	FIELD	TYPE
1–3	Item number	Integer
4–8	Current inventory level	Integer
9–13	Lower critical number	Integer
14–18	Upper critical number	Integer

Update the random disk file above and print any orders that need to be placed and the dollar cost of each order. Do not forget to print pertinent information such as name of item, name and address of manufacturer, etc., for the item that should be ordered.

15. Write a FORTRAN program to sort the file of problem 12 in ascending order using "item number" as the sort key.

16. Redo problem 15 using "item name" as the sort key.

17. Write a FORTRAN program to merge the sorted file of problem 15 with a transaction inventory file that is sorted in ascending order on item number. The layout of the transaction inventory file is the same as the sorted file described in problem 11.

18. You were asked to create a random file for Informatic Associate Corporation's employees. The employee records are punched on the cards in the following manner:

CC	FIELD
1–4	Employee number
5–21	Employee name
22–52	Employee address
53–59	Salary, with rightmost two digits being decimals
60–61	Number of exemptions

You decided to use the employee number as the file key and the following layout of the record of the random file:

RC	(RECORD CHARACTER)
1–4	Employee number
5–21	Employee name
22–52	Employee address
53–59	Salary XXXXX.XX
60–66	Federal withholding taxes XXXXX.XX
67–73	State withholding taxes XXXXX.XX
74–81	Year-today pay XXXXXX.XX
81–82	Number of exemptions

a. First, write a FORTRAN program to read the specified input cards and create a random file by the name INASCR.RAN. Note that initially, each of the federal and state withholding taxes and the year-today pay are zero.

b. Second, write a second FORTRAN program to read cards from the card reader. Each punched card has at least the first punched field, and it may have six fields. These fields are punched in the following manner:

CC	FIELD
1	Type
2–5	Employee number
6–12	Salary XXXXX.XX
13–29	Employee name
30–60	Employee address
61–62	Number of exemptions

Your program should test the first field, Type.

a. If the Type field contains U, then the punched record contains only the first three fields; hence, your program should add the salary to the year-today pay and calculate federal and state taxes, and then add to their corresponding fields within the random record of that employee. Use the following formula to calculate the federal and state taxes:

$$\text{Federal taxes} = 0.20 \, (\text{Salary} - 750/12 * \text{Number of exemptions})$$
$$\text{State taxes} = \text{Federal taxes} * 0.15$$

b. If the field contains N, then the punched record contains all the fields. This indicates that this is a new employee record, and it should be added to the file.

c. If the Type field contains D, then the punched card has only two fields— namely, the type and employee number; hence, your program should retrieve the random record for this employee and display it on the line printer.

d. If the Type field contains A, then the punched card has only the Type field; therefore, your program should print out all the records of the random file.

e. If the Type field contains S, the punched card has only one field, and your program should STOP the execution.

19. Redo problem 18, this time making the file sequential and naming it INASCR.SEQ.

APPENDIXES

I NUMBER SYSTEMS

Any number system depends on its base. Once the base is decided on, the digits of the system will be identified. The largest digit of any number system is equal to its base minus 1, and the digits of the system will be from 0 to the largest digit. Ancient Babylon used a number system with a base 60. A very familiar number system to us is the decimal system, which uses 10 as its base. In this appendix, decimal, binary, octal, and hexadecimal number systems are discussed briefly.

DECIMAL NUMBER SYSTEM

The base of the decimal number system is 10. Its largest digit is Base − 1 = 10 − 1 = 9. The digits of the decimal number system are 0, 1, 2, 3, 4, 5, 6, 7, 8, and 9.

Examples of decimal numbers:

567 is an integer number (no fraction).

65.78 is a mixed decimal number. The number to the left of the radix (decimal point) is the integer part, and the number to the right of the radix is the fraction part.

0.67 is a decimal number with an integer part of 0.

The number 234.25 is actually equal to:

$$234.25 =$$

$$5 \times 10^{-2} = 5 \times \frac{1}{100} = 0.05$$
$$2 \times 10^{-1} = 2 \times \frac{1}{10} = 0.2$$
$$4 \times 10^{0} = 4 \times 1 = 4$$
$$3 \times 10^{1} = 3 \times 10 = 30$$
$$2 \times 10^{2} = 2 \times 100 = 200$$

$$\overline{234.25}$$

BINARY NUMBER SYSTEM

The binary system's base is 2. The largest digit in this number system is Base $- 1 = 2 - 1 = 1$. The digits of the binary system are 0 and 1. Examples of binary numbers:

BINARY INTEGERS	BINARY MIXED NUMBER	BINARY FRACTIONS
11001011	1001.1011	0.00111
11111000	111.01001	0.11011
11111111	111.11111	0.11111
10101100	10010.111	0.10010

OCTAL NUMBER SYSTEM

In the octal number system, the base is 8. The largest digit is 7, because Base $- 1 = 8 - 1 = 7$. The digits of the octal number system are 0, 1, 2, 3, 4, 5, 6, and 7.
Examples of octal numbers:

INTEGERS	MIXED NUMBERS	FRACTIONS
56723	56.723	0.672
123450	1.34567	0.03456
10076	12345.654	0.345601
−32	−11.34536	−0.002345

HEXADECIMAL NUMBER SYSTEM

The hexadecimal base is 16; the digits are those from 0 to 15 (Base $- 1 = 16 - 1 = 15$). To avoid confusion, the digits after 9 are represented by letters. The hexadecimal digits A, B, C, D, E, and F are equivalent to the decimal integers 10, 11, 12, 13, 14, and 15 respectively. In other words, the hexadecimal digits are 1, 2, 3, 4, 5, 6, 7, 8, 9, A, B, C, D, E, and F.
Examples of hexadecimal numbers:

INTEGERS	MIXED NUMBERS	FRACTIONS
AB5DE	10.FDE2	0.0013
71456789	AD4.987	0.ABC
D45AC	EF5.BACD	0.123ADB
FFFFF	F00.372D	0.67EF

CONVERTING BINARY NUMBERS TO DECIMAL NUMBERS

To convert a binary number to a decimal number, the integer and the fraction parts must both be calculated. The fraction part is found by multiplying the first binary digit to the right of the radix by 2^{-1}, the next digit by 2^{-2}, and so on. Then add up the sum of these multiplications. The integer part is calculated by multiplying the first digit to the left of the radix point by 2^0, the next digit to the left of this by 2^1, the next digit to the left by 2^2, and so on. Finally, add the results of all these multiplications. The following example demonstrates how to convert a binary number to a decimal number.

Example: Convert the binary number 1011011.01 to a decimal number. In other words, $(1011011.01)_2 = (?)_{10}$.

CONVERTING DECIMAL NUMBERS TO BINARY NUMBERS

The conversion of a decimal number to a binary number is performed in two steps: converting the integer part and converting the fraction part. The following example shows how such a conversion is performed.

Example: Convert the decimal number 91.25 to a binary number.

$$(91.15)_{10} = (?)_2$$

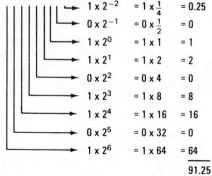

Step 1: Converting the integer part

NUMBER	INTEGER PART RESULTING FROM DIVIDING THE NUMBER BY 2	REMAINDER OF THE DIVISION	
91	45	1	rightmost
45	22	1	
22	11	0	
11	5	1	
5	2	1	
2	1	0	
1	0	1	

Thus, $(91)_{10} = (1011011)_2$.

Step 2: Converting the fraction part

FRACTION PART	RESULT OF MULTIPLYING THE FRACTION BY 2	INTEGER PART OF THE RESULT	
0.25	0.50	0	
0.50	1.0	1	rightmost

Therefore, $(0.25)_{10} = (0.01)_2$. And the whole number $(91.25)_{10} = (1011011.01)_2$.

The same procedure is used to convert an octal or hexadecimal number to a decimal number, or vice versa. The only difference is that in the case of the octal number, the base is 8, and the hexadecimal base is 16. In other words, to convert an octal number to a decimal number or vice versa, replace 2 in the procedure above by 8, and replace it by 16 when the conversion is between hexadecimal and decimal numbers.

Example: Convert the octal number 173.54 to a decimal number.

$$173.54 =$$

$$4 \times 8^{-2} = 4 \times \frac{1}{64} = 0.0625$$
$$5 \times 8^{-1} = 5 \times \frac{1}{8} = 0.625$$
$$3 \times 8^{0} = 3 \times 1 = 3$$
$$7 \times 8^{1} = 7 \times 8 = 56$$
$$1 \times 8^{2} = 1 \times 64 = 64$$
$$123.6875$$

Thus, $(173.54)_8 = (123.6875)_{10}$.

Example: Convert 123.6875 to an octal number.

Step 1: Converting the integer part (123)

NUMBER	INTEGER PART RESULTING FROM DIVIDING THE NUMBER BY 8	REMAINDER OF THE DIVISION	
123	15	3	rightmost
15	1	7	
1	0	1	

Thus, $(123)_{10} = (173)_8$.

Step 2: Converting the fraction part

FRACTION PART	RESULT OF MULTIPLYING THE FRACTION BY 8	INTEGER PART OF THE RESULT	
0.6875	5.5	5	
0.5	4.0	4	rightmost

Hence, the fraction $(0.6875)_{10} = (0.54)_8$; therefore, the whole number $(123.6875)_{10} = (173.54)_8$.

Example: Convert the hexadecimal number 52DC.1B to a decimal number.

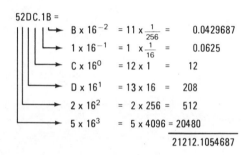

$$52DC.1B =$$

B x 16^{-2}	= 11 x $\frac{1}{256}$ =	0.0429687
1 x 16^{-1}	= 1 x $\frac{1}{16}$ =	0.0625
C x 16^0	= 12 x 1 =	12
D x 16^1	= 13 x 16 =	208
2 x 16^2	= 2 x 256 =	512
5 x 16^3	= 5 x 4096 =	20480
		21212.1054687

Thus, $(21212.1054687)_{10} = (52DC.1B)_{16}$.

Example: Convert the decimal number (21212.1054687) to a hexadecimal number.

Step 1: Convert the integer part $(21212)_{10}$ to a hexadecimal number.

NUMBER	INTEGER PART RESULTING FROM DIVIDING THE NUMBER BY 16	REMAINDER OF THE DIVISION	
21212	1325	12 = C	rightmost
1325	82	13 = D	
82	5	2	
5	0	5	

Step 2: Convert the fraction part (0.1054687) to a hexadecimal number.

FRACTION PART	RESULT OF MULTIPLYING THE FRACTION BY 16	INTEGER PART OF THE RESULT	
0.1054687	1.6874992	1	
0.6874992	11	B	rightmost

Thus, the decimal fraction $(0.1054687)_{10} = (0.1B)_{16}$, and the whole number $(21212.1054687)_{10} = (52DC.1B)_{16}$.

It should be mentioned that three binary digits make one octal digit, and four binary digits make one hexadecimal digit.

Example:

$$(1101011111011)_2 = (6573)_8$$
$$(110000111011) = (C3B)_{16}$$
$$(567.5)_8 = (101110111.101)_2$$
$$(567.B)_{16} = (010101100111.1101)$$

II ANSI FORTRAN 77

Character set:

Digits: 0, 1, 2, 3, 4, 5, 6, 7, 8, 9

Letters: A, B, C, D, E, F, G, H, I, J, K, L, M, N, O, P, Q, R, S, T, U, V, W, X, Y, Z

Special characters: +, −, *, /, (,), . , :, =, $, apostrophe ('), comma, and space (blank) character

Variable names: Any variable name must be composed of six or fewer non-special characters, and the first character must be a letter.

Constants: Six different constants are permitted: integer, real, double-precision, complex, logical, and character.

Integer constant: An integer constant is a number that contains no decimal point or letter E or letter D, and has an optional sign. 25, −23, 30, and 0 are valid integer constants.

Real constant: A real constant is a number with a decimal point and/or the letter E and has an optional sign. Each of the following numbers is a valid real constant: −25.36, 0.367, 9.0, 9., −0., .125E+03, 125.E+03, 125E−03, and 125.E03. Note that 125.E + 03 = 125×10^3 = 125000. E + 03 is the scientific notation for 10^3. This type of real constant is a single-precision (in most computers, a single-precision has seven significant digits), because only one computer word is used to store it.

Double-precision constants: Like a real constant in E form, a double-precision constant is composed of three portions. The first is the precision portion, which may contain a decimal point and may be preceded by an optional sign. The precision portion is followed by the letter D, called an exponential indicator, and the letter D is followed by two digits preceded by an optional sign. This portion is called the exponent portion. Examples of double-precision constants are 25.56D + 04, 14.D + 03, 0.567D + 04, 125.D − 03, 125D − 03, and −256.9D + 01.

Two computer words are used to store a double-precision constant or a double-precision variable. In most processors, a double-precision constant has 16 significant digits. As in the E form, the D in the D form means 10 raised to a power equal to the number following the D. Thus, 456.78D + 03 = 456.78 × 10^3 = 456780.

Complex constants: Each complex number is composed of two parts, real and imaginary. In ANSI FORTRAN 77, the format of complex constants is (real,real). Examples of complex constants are (2.5, 30.8), (−2.5, 3.0), (−0.7 9.2), and (−4.5, −7.3). Note that (2.5, 30.8) is equal to 2.5 + 30.8i.

Logical constants: .TRUE. and .FALSE.

Character constants: The character constants in ANSI FORTRAN 77 have the form 'string', where the string is any FORTRAN character string. An apostrophe within the string must be represented by two consecutive apostrophes. Examples: 'PRODUCT', '$*123', 'DON''T', and 'STUDENT''S NAME'.

Variables: The six types of variables permitted are integer, real, double-precision, complex, logical, and character.

The type of an integer or a real variable is determined either by the pre-defined rule (integer variables start with either I, J, K, L, M, or N, and real variables start with a letter other than these) or by the type, or by implicit statements. See the format of type and implicit statements in the table at the end of this appendix. The type of the double-precision, complex, logical, and character variables must be declared by either a type or an implicit statement.

Examples:

```
DOUBLE PRECISION J,A
LOGICAL TEST, CHECK
REAL INTRST, JOB(5,10)
INTEGER COUNT(100) ,NUMBER (50,500)
COMPLEX X,Y Z(100,80)
CARACTER I, 80*CARD, LINE*120,6*X(4,2)
IMPLICIT CHARACTER *6(O–P)
IMPLICT DOUBLE PRECISION (A–D)
IMPLICIT LOGICAL (G–H)
IMPLICIT INTEGER (R–V)
```

Executable statements: The following are executable statements in ANSI FORTRAN 77: Assignment, GO TO, IF, DO, CONTINUE, STOP, PAUSE,

READ, WRITE, PRINT, REWIND, BACKSPACE, END FILE, OPEN, CLOSE, INQUIRE, CALL, RETURN, and END. Note that the END statement must be the last statement in the program.

Specification statements: DIMENSION, EQUIVALENCE, COMMON, DATA, INTEGER, CHARACTER, COMPLEX, LOGICAL, IMPLICIT, PARA-METER, PROGRAM, EXTERNAL, FORMAT, INTRINSIC, SAVE, and ENTRY.

The integer, real, complex, logical, and double-precision variables in ANSI FORTRAN 77 and FORTRAN IV are the same.

Character variables: A variable, an array, or a function name can be declared to have a type of character by either the type statement CHARACTER or an implicit specification statement. The following statements specify that CARD is a one-dimensional array of elements of default length one character, INPUT is a character variable of length 80, LINE is a character variable of length 120, and A is a 3 × 4 array whose elements are six characters long:

```
CHARACTER CARD(80)
CHARACTER 80*INPUT,LINE*120
CHARACTER 6*A(3,4)
```

The value of subscript or nonsubscript variables may be assigned by an assignment statement such as:

```
SIGNAL = 'END'
CHECK  = 'DATA'
```

The concatenation operator is used to combine two substrings. Two consecutive slashes are used for the concatenation operator. The value of the character variable MESSAG after the execution of the following statement is END OF DATA.

```
MESSAG = SIGNAL//' OF '//CHECK
```

Substring: A substring of string V is V(L1:L2), where L1 is the beginning and L2 is the ending character position of the string V. After the execution of the following two statements, the value of SCODE becomes CDEF.

```
CODE = 'ABCDEFG'
SCODE = CODE(3:6)
```

A substring may appear on either side of the equals sign. The statement

```
CODE(2:2) = '$'
```

causes the second character of CODE to be $, and the statement

```
A(1,3) (2:5) = '***'
```

makes the second through the fifth character of the array element A(1, 3) an asterisk. Character strings may be compared using relational operators, may be passed as arguments to functions and subroutines, and may be returned as the value of a function. The intrinsic function LEN has as its value the length of the character string.

Some other intrinsic functions for manipulating character data type are ICAR, CHAR, and INDEX. The function ICAR converts a single character to an integer, CHAR converts a single digit to a character, and INDEX determines whether a string contains a specific substring. The INDEX function returns either zero or a value indicating the starting position of the substring. After execution of the following statements, the value of J will be 7, I will be 4, N will be 0, and M will be 1.

```
J = LEN(CODE)
I = INDEX (CODE,'DEF')
N = INDEX ('ROOT', 'BET')
M = INDEX ('ROOT', 'ROO')
```

Arrays: An array may have up to seven dimensions. The format for a dimension declarator is $d1: d2$, where $d1$ is the lower dimension bound and $d2$ is the upper dimension bound. If $d1$ is omitted, then the lower dimension bound is assumed to be 1. A constant array declarator is an array with each of its dimension bounds being an integer constant. An adjustable array declarator is an array in which one or more of the dimension bounds contains a variable. Further, when the name of the array is a dummy argument, then the array is a dummy array; otherwise, the array is an actual array. A dummy array declarator is permitted only in subprograms and can appear in a DIMENSION or a type statement, but not in a COMMON statement. An actual array declarator may appear in a DIMENSION, type, or COMMON statement. In a dummy array declarator, the last upper bound of the last subscript may be replaced by an asterisk.

Examples:

```
DIMENSION X(-3:7,0:10,20),Y(7,8:60,9,7)
REAL INTRST(5,6,3,4,3:9)
CHARACTER B(-5:10,8,0:20)*20

SUBROUTINE T(N,B)
COMMON N
DIMENSION B(-3:N,3*N+1,-N:0), A(M:N,-3:*)
```

Expression: Mixed-mode arithmetic is permitted. Further expressions may appear as dimension bounds, as subscripts, as parameters in a DO statement, and in many places in input/output statements where previously ANSI FORTRAN did not permit it.

Control statements: Two significant changes in the control statements are the inclusion of IF-THEN-ELSE and the extension of the DO statement. IF-THEN-ELSE construct is discussed in detail in sections 8.4 and 12.1.1.1, and the DO statement is discussed in section 11.1.

Input/output statements: Three different access methods—sequential, random (direct), and stream—are permitted. The new standard allows the programmer to specify a default unit, a default FORMAT, and statements to open files, to close files, to inquire about the status of a file, and to treat a character string as a file. See section 16.3 and the table at the end of this appendix for the details of the input and output statements.

Stream (list-directed) input and output: List-directed input/output is accomplished by using an asterisk in place of the format identifier within the input or output statement. The input data must be separated by blanks, commas, or slashes. This will eliminate the requirement for placing data in certain columns. When the list-directed output is used, the programmer does not have to specify the exact form of the output.

Example:

```
READ(FMT=*,UNIT=5) X,Y,Z
READ(5,*) X,Y,Z
READ * X,Y,Z
WRITE(6,*) X,Y,Z
WRITE *, X,Y,Z
WRITE(UNIT=6,FMT=*) X,Y,Z
```

Format identifier: The format identifier used by a READ, WRITE, or PRINT statement may be a FORMAT statement number, an integer variable, a character constant, a character expression, or an asterisk.

Example:

```
        READ(UNIT=7, FMT=10) J,X,Z
(a)  10  FORMAT(I2,F3.2,F4.2)


        I = 10
        READ(7,I)J,X,Z
(b)  10  FORMAT(I2,F3.2,F4.2)
```

(c)   CHARACTER FRM*12
            FRM = 'I2,F3.2,F4.2'
            READ(7,FRM) J,X,Z

(d)   READ(7, 'I2,F3.2,F4.2') J,X,Z

(e)   READ(7,*) J,X,Z

Internal files: This option is similar to CODE and DECODE facility on some systems; however, the READ and the WRITE statements are used instead of CODE and DECODE. This releases the programmer from remembering which of these two (CODE or DECODE) reads and which writes. This feature is implemented by using a character string or an array in place of a unit identifier.

PARAMETER statement: The PARAMETER statement assigns a name to a constant. Such a name, called a constant name, can be used anywhere a variable may be used. A constant name may also be used in a specification statement, such as a DIMENSION statement.

Example:

PARAMETER (I=0,SPACE ='b')
PARAMETER (J=25, R= 25.2)

Subprograms:

ENTRY statement: The ENTRY statement allows any executable statement of a subprogram to be the first executable statement. The format of ENTRY statement is:

ENTRY subprogram⅜ ENTRY subprogram-name (arg1, arg2, .
. ., argn)

> *SAVE statement:* The specification statement SAVE saves the values of local variables, local arrays, and named COMMON blocks between calls of subprograms. See the table at the end of this appendix.
> *INTRINSIC functions:* The following intrinsic functions are supported by ANSI FORTRAN 77: INT, IFIX, IDINT, FLOAT, SNGL, REAL, DE-FOAT, DBLE, CMPLX, AINT, DINT, ANINT, NINT, IDNINT, DNINT, IABS, ABS, DABS, CABS, MOD, AMOD, DMOD, ISIGN, SIGN, DSIGN, IDIM, DIM, DDIM, MAX0, AMAX1, DMAX1, AMAX0, MAX1, MIN0, AMIN1, DMIN1, AMIN0, MIN1, LEN, AIMAG, CONJG, SQRT, DSQRT, CSQRT, EXP, DEXP, CEXP, LOG, ALOG, CLOG, ALOG10, DLOG10, and all trigonometric functions.

Alternate RETURN statement: The alternate RETURN statement may return control to a statement in the calling program other than the one following the CALL statement itself that sent control to the subprogram.

Example:

```
      CALL B(I,K,*10,C,*20)
100   CONTINUE
         .
10       .
         .
20       .
         .
      END
      SUBROUTINE B(I,K,*,R,*)
      N = (I + R)/K
      RETURN N
      END
```

If the value of N is 1, then control returns to the statement with statement number 10 in the main program, and to the statement with statement number 20 if $N = 2$; otherwise control returns to statement 100.

Following on pp. 410–18 is a table that summarizes the main features of ANSI FORTRAN 77. The words written in capital letters in the table are FORTRAN keywords.

STATEMENTS/FORMATS	MEANING OF SYMBOLS AND REMARKS	EXAMPLES
Specification statements: DIMENSION v(s1:s2)	s1 is the lower and s2 is the upper bound of the subscripts. s1 and s2 must be integer constants or integer variables. Up to 7 subscripts are permitted. 1 is assumed if s1 is omitted.	DIMENSION X(5),Y(1:10),R(5,15) DIMENSION Z(5:15),D(3,2:10,9:20) DIMENSION G(5:100,2:30,1:10) DIMENSION B(1:N),A(K),F(10)
EQUIVALENCE (v1, v2)	v1 and v2 are variable names, array-element names, array names, or substring names.	EQUIVALENCE (A,B), (GREAT,G)
COMMON/name/v1, v2, . . .	v, v2, . . . are variable names, array-element names, array names, or array declarators. The name of the COMMON block area is optional.	DIMENSION Y(5),J(3) COMMON X,J(2),Y,Z(20)
Type Statements: INTEGER v1, v2, . . .	v1, v2, . . . are variable names, array-element names, array names, function names, or array declarators. Type statements are specification statements.	INTEGER FACTS,Y(2,10),X
REAL v1, v2, . . .	v1, v2, . . . are variable names, array-element names, array names, or array declarators.	REAL INTRST,PAY(5),J(20,8)
COMPLEX v1, v2, . . .	v1, v2, . . . are variable names, array-element names, array names, or array declarators.	DOUBLE PRECISION R(20),J,AMOUNT
	In the example, the first part (2.5) is the real part, and the second (9.3) is the imaginary part of the complex number (Y).	COMPLEX Y Y = (2.5,9.3)
LOGICAL v1, v2, . . .	v, v2, . . . have the same meaning as above.	LOGICAL DUE, TEST
CHARACTER n* v1, v2, . . . CHARACTER v1, v2, . . ., vm *n	v1, v2, . . . are variable names, array-element names, function names, or array declarators. n is an unsigned integer constant that specifies the length of the character variable.	CHARACTER 80*CARD CHARACTER R,A(3,5),LINE *120 CHARACTER PAGE*50,6*X(4,5)

Implicit statements: IMPLICIT type (letter-letter) IMPLICIT CHARACTER * n (letter-letter) EXTERNAL v1, v2,...	Type is either INTEGER, REAL, COMPLEX, LOGICAL, or CHARACTER. n is a nonzero integer constant that specifies the length of the character variables. v1, v2,... are subprogram names.	IMPLICIT REAL (A–J) CHARACTER (O–R),COMPLEX (Y–Z) IMPLICIT CHARACTER * 6(O–R) EXTERNAL SQRT,EXP
INTRINSIC v1, v2,...	v1, v2,... are names of intrinsic functions. The intrinsic functions are built-in and other functions that are supplied by the processor.	INTRINSIC SQRT,IABS
SAVE v1, v2,...	v1, v2,... are variable names, array names, or common-block names. SAVE statement is used within subprograms. v1, v2,... do not become undefined as a result of the execution of a RETURN or END statement in subprograms.	SAVE A,B
DATA v1, v2,..., vn/c1, c2,...,cn/ DATA v1, v2,..., vn/n*c/	v1, v2,..., vn are variable names, array-element names, substring names, or implied DO-list. c1, c2,...cn are constant or constant names. n is a nonzero unsigned integer constant or a constant name and * is the repetition factor.	DATA I,J,N,R1,R2/3*0,5.2, '$b'/ DATA (X(J),J=1,5)/5* 20/
Assignment statement: v = expression	v is a variable or an array-element name.	X = Y + 5 * B
ASSIGN n TO v	n is a statement number, and v is a variable name or an array-element name. ASSIGN is used in conjunction with assign GO TO statement.	ASSIGN 50 TO J

STATEMENT/FORMAT	MEANING OF SYMBOLS AND REMARKS	EXAMPLE
Expressions:		
Arithmetic expression:		
Unsigned-arithmetic constant	The type of constant name, variable name, array-element name, and function reference name must be either integer, real, double-precision, or complex. A constant name is defined by a PARAMETER statement.	5 , 9.3
Constant-name		THREE, J
Variable name		I,PAY, J
Array-element name		X(J),N(4)
Function-reference name		PAY(A,B)
(Arithmetic expression)		(5), (R), (ROOTS)
+ Arithmetic expression		+5, +J
− Arithmetic expression		−X, −2.5, −J
Arithmetic expression + Arithmetic expression		x+6.7, B+2.3, I+J
Arithmetic expression * Arithmetic expression		6*J, (A+B)*(K+2)
Arithmetic expression − Arithmetic expression		8−K, R−2.5
Arithmetic expression / Arithmetic expression		k/2, (7.3+B)/6.5
Arithmetic expression ** Arithmetic expression		(X+4.5)**2
Character expression:		
Character constant	The type of constant name, variable name, array-element name, and function reference name must be character. Note that an expression within parentheses is still an expression. // is a concatenation symbol, used to join two character expressions.	'ABCD'
Constant name		I,J,R
Variable name		I, B, PAY, TEST

Array-element name	TEST(5),R(N)
(Character expression)	(J)
Function-reference name	TEST(A,B)
Character expression // Character expression	'ABD'//I
Substring name: v(L1:L2)	A(2:7)

v is either a variable or an array-element name. The type of v must be character. L1 specifies the leftmost character position, and L2 specifies the rightmost character position of the substring.

Relational operators:

.LT.	Less than
.LE.	Less than or equal to
.GT.	Greater than
.GE.	Greater than or equal to
.NE.	Not equal to
.EQ.	Equal to

Relational expression:
a1 .relational operator. a2
b1 .relational operator. b2

a1 and a2 are arithmetic expressions. b1 and b2 are character expressions. In the example, J is a character variable.

I.LT.100
'BAC' .LT. J

Logical Operator:
.NOT., .AND., and .OR.

Logical expression:
Logical constant
Constant name
Variable name
Array-element name
Function-reference name
Relational expression
(Logical expression)

The type of constant name, variable name, array-element name, and function-reference name must be logical.

.TRUE. , .FALSE.
I, TEST
k,RESULT
EXAM(N), N(6,5)
PAID(I,J)
I .LE.10
(I .LT.10)

STATEMENTS/FORMATS	MEANING OF SYMBOLS AND REMARKS	EXAMPLES
.NOT. logical expression Logical expression .AND. logical expression Logical expression .OR. logical expression	A and B are logical variables.	.NOT. B A .AND. B A .OR. B
GO TO statements: Unconditional GO TO: GO TO n	n is a statement number.	GO TO 50
Computed GO TO: GO TO (n1, n2, . . ., nm), v	n1, n2, . . ., nm are statement numbers, and v is a variable name or an arithmetic expression. The comma before v is optional. The integer value of v determines the next executable statement.	GO TO(20,70,50,20),J
Assigned GO TO: GO TO v, (n1, n2, . . ., nm)	v is a variable name. The comma after v is optional. The value of v must be assigned by an ASSIGN statement.	GO TO J,(20,30,70,40)
IF statements: Arithmetic IF: IF (a) n1, n2, n3	a is an arithmetic expression; n1, n2, and n3 are statement numbers.	IF(J − 2*K)50,30,20
Logical IF: IF (a) statement	a is a logical expression.	IF (J .GE.10) STOP

IF-THEN-ELSE statement:
```
IF c1 THEN e
  ELSE d
END IF
```
c1 is a condition, and e and d are blocks of statements. A block may contain only one statement.

```
IF (J.LE.10) THEN
          X=X * 5.0
          I=I + 1
  ELSE X=X +1
          I=I+2
END IF
```

Nested IF-THEN-ELSE:
```
IF c1 THEN e1
  ELSE IF c2 then e2
  ELSE d1
  END IF
END IF
```
c1 and c2 are conditions, d1 and d2 are blocks statements. Nested IF can be repeated to any desired level.

```
IF(J.LT.10) THEN
          X=X+5.0
          I=I+1
  ELSE IF(J .EQ. 20) THEN
                    STOP
          ELSE X=X−1
                    J=J+2
          END IF
END IF
```

Do statement:
```
DO n i = m1, m2, m3
```
m1, m2 and m3 are either integer, real, or double-precision variables or expressions. 1 is assumed if m3 is omitted.

```
DO 50 I=1,100
DO 50 I=100,1,−1
```

Continue statement:
```
CONTINUE
```

```
CONTINUE
```

STATEMENTS/FORMATS	MEANING OF SYMBOLS AND REMARKS	EXAMPLES
Stop statement: STOP		STOP
Pause statement: PAUSE n	n is either a digit or a character constant.	PAUSE 5 PAUSE '$$'
Input-output statements: READ sequential files: Read (u, f) list READ (u, f, END = n1, ERR = n2) list READ (UNIT = u, FMT = f, END = n1, ERR = n2) list	u is the unit identifier which must be an integer constant, a variable name, an array-element name, or a substring name. The format identifier f can be a statement number, a variable name, an array-element name, or a character expression. n1 and n2 are statement numbers, and list is a list of variable names, array-element names, array-block items, and/or an implied DO-list. The keywords UNIT, FMT, END, and ERR are optional. If they are omitted, then the order of u, f, n1, and n2 is significant. The i in the READ of direct files is the record key.	READ(5,10)X,Y,Z READ(5,10,END=70,ERR=90)X,Y READ(UNIT=5,FMT=2,END=7,ERR=9)X,Y,Z READ(UNIT=I,FMT=2,END=50)X,Y,Z READ(UNIT=I,FMT=J,END=40)XX,X,Y,Z
READ direct (random) files: READ (u, f, REC = i) list READ (u, f, REC = i, END = n1) list READ (u, f, REC = i, END = n1, ERR = n2) list READ (UNIT = u, FMT = f, REC = i, END = n1, ERR = n2) list		READ(5,2,REC=20)X,Y,Z READ(5,2,REC=J,NED=10,ERR=6)XX,Y,Z READ(UNIT=1,FMT=7,REC=I,END=6)X,Y,Z
WRITE statement: WRITE for sequential files: WRITE (u, f) WRITE (u, f) list WRITE (u, f, ERR = n2) list WRITE (UNIT = u, FMT = f, ERR = n3) list	The symbols have the same meaning as in READ statement. List is optional. END = option cannot be used with WRITE statement.	WRITE(6,10) WRITE(6,10)X,Y,Z WRITE(6,10,ERR=20)X,Y,Z WRITE(UNIT=6,FMT=3,ERR=4)X,Y,Z

WRITE for direct file:

WRITE (u, f, REC = i)
WRITE (u, f, REC = i) list
WRITE (u, f, REC = i, ERR = n1) list
WRITE (UNIT = u, FMT = f, REC = i, ERR = n1) list

WRITE(10,20,REC=7)
WRITE(10,20,REC=7)Z,X,Y
WRITE(10,20,REC=6,ERR=70)X,Y,Z
WRITE(UNIT=10,FMT=20,REC=9,ERR=2) X,Y,Z

PRINT statement:

PRINT f, list

f and list have the same meaning as in READ statement. The PRINT statement prints a line on the line printer.

PRINT 100,XX,Y,Z

OPEN statement:

OPEN (UNIT = u, ERR = n2,
FILE = filename,
STATUS = OLD or NEW or SCRATCH or UNKNOWN,
ACCESS = DIRECT or SEQUENTIAL or STREAM,
FORM = FORMATTED or UNFORMATTED,
RECL = record length,
MAXREC = maximum number of records in the file,
BLANK = NULL or ZERO)

u and n2 have the same meanings as in the READ statement.

OPEN(UNIT=7,ERR=20,FILE='INVEN-TORY',STATUS=NEW,
ACCESS=DIRECT,FORM=UNFORMATTED,
RECL=90,MAXREC=10000,BLANK=NULL)

OPEN(UNIT=10,STATUS=OLD,FORM= FORMATTED,
ACCESS=SEQUENTIAL,RECL=120,
MAXREC=500)

CLOSE statement:

CLOSE (UNIT = u, ERR = n2,
STATUS = KEEP or DELETE

u and n2 have the same meanings as in the READ statement.

CLOSE(UNIT=10,ERR=40,STATUS=KEEP)
CLOSE(UNIT=20,STATUS=DELETE)

STATEMENTS/FORMATS

INQUIRE statement:
INQUIRE(UNIT = u, ERR = n2,
FILE = filename,
EXIT = ex, OPENED = od,
NUMBER = n, NAMED = nd,
NAME = fn, ACCESS = ac,
FORM = fm, RECL = lr,
MAXREC = mr, NEXTREC = nr)

u and n2 have the same meanings as in the READ statement, and ex, od, n, nd, fn, ac, fm, lr, mr, and nr are either variable names or array-element names. ex, od, and nd must be logical; n, mr, nr, and lr must be integers; and ac, fn, and fm must be character. The value of ex, od, and nd becomes .TRUE. if the file exists, is opened and named respectively. The value of ac becomes one of the access methods, fn the file name, and fm either FORMATTED or UNFORMATTED. The value of n will be the unit identifier, mr the maximum number of records in the file, and nr the key of the next record.

EXAMPLES

INQUIRE(UNIT=10,ERR=20,
EXIT=EXL,OPENED=CHECK,
NUMBER=NU,NAMED=CHNAME,
NAME=FNAME,ACCESS=ACCMTH,
FORM=FORTFM,RECL=LREC
MAXREC=MRECR, NEXTREC=NXTR)
INQUIRE(FILE='INVENT',EXIT=CHEXT,
OPENED=CHOPEN,NAMED=CHNAME,
NAME=NAMFL, ACCESS=MTHACC,
FORM=TYPFRM, RECL=LTHREC,
MAXREC=NREC, NEXTREC=NXTRC)

BACKSPACE u
or
BACKSPACE (UNIT = u, ERR = n)

u is the unit identifier, and n is a label. The unit identifier must be present.

BACKSPACE 10

BACKSPACE(UNIT=10,ERR=20)

ENDFILE u
or
ENDFILE (UNIT = u, ERR = n)

u is the unit identifier, and n is a label. The unit identifier must be present.

ENDFILE 10

ENDFILE(UNIT=10,ERR=20)

REWIND u
or
REWIND (UNIT = u, ERR = n)

u is the unit identifier, and n is a label. The unit identifier must be present.

REWIND 10

REWIND(UNIT=10,ERR=20)

FORMAT statement:
FORMAT (e1, e2, . . . , en)
Format codes:

In
An
Fw.d
Ew.d
Dw.d
Gw.d
kP
'h....h'
nHh1,...hn
Tn
bX
S
SS
SP
Ln
BN
BZ
/
:

419

e1, e2, . . . , en are format codes.

n is a nonzero unsigned integer constant.
I format is used for integer fields. w is a non-zero unsigned integer constant. A format is used for character fields. d is an unsigned integer constant. F format, E format, and D format are used for real, real in exponent form, and double-precision respectively. G format is a general format. k is an optionally signed integer constant. K format is used for scale factor. h1, h2, . . . , hn are FORTRAN characters. Both H format and quotation format are used for character constants. b is a nonzero, optionally signed integer constant. T format to edit starting at nth position. X format to edit forward or backward b positions. S format restores the optional + to the processor. SS to edit to suppress the optional + sign. SP to edit to produce the optional + for any position that contains an optional + sign. L format used for logical fields. BN format used for editing input only to ignore blanks. BZ format used for input editing only to treat blanks as zeros.
The / format is used to skip a record.
And : format is used to edit to terminate the format control, if there are no more items in the input/output list. Otherwise has no effect. Each of the format codes above can be preceded by a repetition factor.

FORMAT(I5,A4,E.4,D10.4)
FORMAT(T5,SP,I6,7x,F7.2)
FORMAT(T50,I6,−20X,F4.2)

FORMAT(6P,I5,−3P,D12.4)
FORMAT('1',5X,'EXAMPLE')
FORMAT(5I4,3L5,:,7A4)

STATEMENT/FORMAT	MEANING OF SYMBOLS AND REMARKS	EXAMPLE
Statement function: function-name (v1, v2, . . ., vn) = expression	v1, v2, . . ., vn are variable names.	ROOT(A,B)=(−B+(B**2−4*A*C)**0.5)/2
CALL statement: CALL subroutine-name (arg1, arg2, . . ., arg3)	arg1, arg2, . . ., arg3 are variable names, array-element names, constants, substrings, array names, subprogram names, or labels.	CALL CHECK (PAY,HRS,RATES)
RETURN statement: RETURN	e is an integer, real, or double-precision variable or expression. Alternate	RETURN
or RETURN e	RETURN is not permitted.	RETURN I

III SUMMARY OF FORTRAN IV

INPUT/OUTPUT STATEMENTS WITH NAMELIST

The NAMELIST statement is used to eliminate the usage of FORMAT statements in conjunction with input/output statements. When NAMELIST is used, the FORMAT statement is not required; input/output statements reference the group name of the NAMELIST instead of the FORMAT statement. The general form of the NAMELIST statement is:

```
NAMELIST /n1/v1, v2, v3, . . ., vn/n2/u1, u2, . . ., un
```

where *n1* and *n2* are variable names, array-element names, or array names. The following simple program demonstrates the use of NAMELIST with input and output statements that reference the group name of the NAMELIST instead of FORMAT statements:

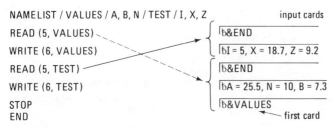

The output printed by the program above is:

```
ƀ&VALUES
ƀA=25.5,B=7.3,N=10
ƀ&END
ƀTEST
ƀI—5,X=18.7,Z=9.2
ƀ&END
```

421

As shown in the example, when NAMELIST is used, no FORMAT statements are required.

The following rules apply to the NAMELIST statement, the input, and the output when NAMELIST is used.

NAMELIST STATEMENT

1. The NAMELIST statement must appear before any READ or WRITE statement that references the group name of the NAMELIST.
2. Any array name appearing in the NAMELIST must have been dimensioned in a prior statement.
3. The same variable name may appear in several lists of the NAMELIST. For example, the following statement is valid:

```
NAMELIST /ONE/A,B,C,N/TWO/A,B,E,M/THREE/A,B,N,M
```

NAMELIST-INPUT RULES

1. The first character of every input card (record) must be a blank character.
2. The first card (record) must contain an ampersand (&) followed by the special group name, such as &TEST or &VALUE.
3. Each variable and its value must be punched in the following manner:

$$variable = value$$

Each variable with its value is separated from the following one by a comma. Blanks are optional.
4. The order of the variables in the input list is significant.
5. Both subscripted and nonsubscripted variables must appear in the form:

$$variable\text{-}name = value$$

An example of an input card is:

```
ƀX=5.3,Y(1)=8.9,N(2)=8
```

If an array name appears without subscripts, then the values of all elements of the array must be presented. When an array has more than one dimension, the values are transmitted in column order. For example, assume that

$$N = \begin{pmatrix} 5 \\ 7 \\ 8 \\ 2 \end{pmatrix} \quad \text{and} \quad X = \begin{pmatrix} 4.2 & 3.1 & 0.0 \\ 5.2 & 6.2 & 0.0 \end{pmatrix}$$

```
DIMENSION NDAT(4), X(2,3)
NAMELIST /ONE/NDAT,X
```

then the input cards would be:

```
b&END
bNDAT=5,7,8,2,X=4.2,5.2,3.1,6.2,2*0
b&ONE
```

The asterisk in the input data is the repetition factor (2*0. is equivalent to 0., 0.).

6. Trailing blanks are considered zeros. For example:

```
bA=25b,C=0.25E2b,B=0.25D3b
```

is read as:

```
bA=250,C=0.25E20,B=0.25D30
```

7. The last input card (record) of each group name of NAMELIST must be b&END card.

NAMELIST-OUTPUT RULES

The output associated with NAMELIST has a fixed format. Each line of the output starts with a blank character. The first line of the output contains the ampersand, followed by the group name of the NAMELIST. The last line of the output is bEND. The variables and their values are printed between these two lines. The programmer has no control of the specific form in which the values will be displayed.

NAMELIST is relatively new, and some FORTRAN compilers do not support NAMELIST option.

Following on pp. 424–31 is a brief review of FORTRAN IV in table form.

STATEMENTS/FORMATS	MEANING OF SYMBOLS AND REMARKS	EXAMPLES
Specification statements: DIMENSION (n1, n2, n3, n4, n5, n6, n7)	n1, n2, n3, n4, n5, n6, and n7 are integer constants. Up to 7 dimensions are allowed. All subscripts must be nonzero, non-negative integer constants. n2 through n7 are optional.	DIMENSION X(5),J(5,6),Y(5,8,9)
EQUIVALENCE (a1, a2, . . .), (b1, b2, . . .)	a1, a2, . . ., b1, b2, . . . are variable names or array-element names.	EQUIVALENCE (A,B,C),(X,Y(2)) EQUIVALENCE (N,J(1),IC),(X,Y,Z)
COMMON statement: COMMON /name/v1, v2, v3, . . .	v1, v2, v3, . . . are variable names, array-element names, or array names. *Name* is the name of the COMMON block area, which is optional.	COMMON A1, XX, Y, H(1) COMMON /B/X,Y,N,J,Z
Type statements: INTGER v1, v2, . . .	v1, v2, . . . are variable names, array-element names, array names, or array declarators.	INTEGER XX,B,Y(3,4),RES(5,6,7)
REAL v1, v2, v3, . . .	v1, v2, . . . are variable names, array-element names, array names, or array declarators.	REAL INTRST,PAY(12,500),J(70)
DOUBLE PRECISION v1, v2, v3, . . .	v1, v2, . . . are variable names, array-element names, array names, or array declarators.	DOUBLE PRECISION X(80),K,J,N
COMPLEX v1, v2, v3, . . .	v1, v2, . . . are variable names, array-element names, array names, or array declarators.	COMPLEX X,N,Z
LOGICAL v1, v2, v3, . . .	v1, v2, . . . are variable names, array-element names, array names, or array declarators.	LOGICAL TEST,RESULT(60),CHECK

Implicit statement: IMPLICIT type (a1, a2, . . .) or IMPLICIT type (a1−a2)	a1, a2, . . . is each a single letter. *Type* is either INTEGER, REAL, COMPLEX, or LOGICAL.	IMPLICIT INTEGER(A,B,N,F) IMPLICIT REAL (M−P),LOGICAL(A−D)
EXTERNAL v1, v2,. . .	v1, v2, . . . are subprogram names.	EXTERNAL SQRT,EXP
DATA v1, v2, . . ., vn/c1, c2, . . ., cn/ or DATA v1, v2, v3, . . ., vn/n*c1/	v1, v2, . . ., vn are variable names, array-element names, array names, or DO-list. c1, c2, . . ., cn are constants, n is a non-zero, unsigned integer constant, and * is a repetition factor.	DATA I,J,B(2),R,Y/2*0,5.2,2*3.5/
Assignment statement: v = expression	v is a variable or an array-element name.	I = I+1 B(2)= X(J)*4 + T
or ASSIGN n TO v	ASSIGN is used in conjunction with assigned GO TO statement.	ASSIGN 10 TO J
Expressions: Arithmetic expression: An arithmetic constant A variable name An array-element name Function reference name (a1) +a1 − a1 a1+a2 a1 − a2	The type of the variable, array-element name, or function name must be either INTEGER, REAL, DOUBLE PRECISION, or COMPLEX. a1 and a2 are arithmetic expressions.	5, −3,0,0.7.89,0.4E02,2.4D01 I, RI,J,JI,XX,BX X(J),Y(5,4)N(3),K(I,L,M) SQRT(Y),EXP(3.),NP(A,N,B) (X),(2.5),(Y(I,J)) +X,+(Y(I,J),+2.7 −2.7,−(X(I,J)),−0.9, BB X+2.5,X+Y(I,J)+N,I+1 X−Y,9.5−X,J(3,4)− I

STATEMENTS/FORMATS	MEANING OF SYMBOLS AND REMARKS	EXAMPLES
a1 * a2 a1/a2 a1**a2		8*N(I,J),B*X*XG(6),R1*9*A I/2,R1/7,B/K,C1/C2,90/J X**0.2,I**2,N**I**2
Relational operators: .LT. .GT. .LE. .GE. .EQ. .NE.	Less than Greater than Less than or equal to Greater than or equal to Equal to Not equal to	
Relational expression: a1 .relational operator. a2	a1 and a2 are arithmetic expressions.	I .LT.100 J .NE. K+1
Logical operators: .NOT. .AND. .OR. Logical expressions:		
A logical constant		.TRUE. , .FALSE.
A logical variable	J, TEST, and R must be declared as logical variables.	J, TEST , R
An array-element name		TEST(I), J(2)
A function reference name	Function name must be logical.	NP(A,B),TYPE(K,N)
Relational expression		I.LE.110

	Example	Description
(Logical expression)	(I.LE.100)	
.NOT. logical expression	.NOT. TEST	
logical expression .AND. logical expression	(I.LT.100) .AND. (I.NE.K)	
logical expression .OR. logical expression	(I.LT.100) .OR. (I.NE.K)	
GO TO statement:		
Unconditional GO TO: GO TO n	GO TO 50	n is a statement number.
Computed GO TO: GO TO (n1, n2, n3, . . . , nm), v	GO TO (20,30,20,50,100),J	each n1, n2, . . ., nm is a statement number, and v is an integer variable.
Assigned GO TO: GO TO v, (n1, n2, . . ., nm)	GO TO J,(20,50,30,100)	each n1, n2, . . ., nm is a statement number, and v is an integer variable. The value of v must be assigned by an ASSIGN statement.
IF statements:		
Arithmetic IF: IF (a) n1, n2, n3	IF (I*2−K)60,50,20	a is an arithmetic expression. Each n1, n2, and n3 is a statement number.
Logical IF: IF (a) statement	IF (I,LE.100)STOP	a is a logical expression.
DO statement: DO n i = m1, m2, m3	DO 50 J=1,100 DO 20 N=100,1,−1 DO 70 K=40,500,10	i (an index of DO) is an integer variable; n is the statement number of the last statement in the range of DO. m1, m2, and m3 are nonsubscripted integer variables or integer constants. The parameter m3 is optional. If it is omitted, its value is assumed to be 1.

STATEMENTS/FORMATS	MEANING OF SYMBOLS AND REMARKS	EXAMPLES
CONTINUE statement: CONTINUE		CONTINUE
STOP statement: STOP or STOP n	n is a string of 1 through 5 decimal digits.	STOP STOP 5
PAUSE statement: PAUSE or PAUSE n or PAUSE 'characters'	n is a string of 1 through 5 decimal digits. n is a string of 1 through 5 decimal digits. None of them can be greater than 7.	PAUSE PAUSE 12 PAUSE 'DATA'
Input/output statements: input/output for sequential files: READ(n1, n2, END = n3, ERR = n4) list	n1 is the logical unit number, n2 is the FORMAT statement number, n3 and n4 are statement numbers. *List* is a list of variables. Both END = n3 and ERR = n4 are optional. The list may contain subscripted variables, array names, or implied DO-list.	READ(10,20,END=60)X,Y,Z READ(2,6,ERR=5,END=7)X,Y,Z READ(5,90)I,X,Z,N(L)
WRITE (n1, n2) list	n1, n2, and *list* have the same meanings as in the READ statement. The list may contain no variables.	WRITE(6,10)X,Y,Z,I,N WRITE(3,40)
Input/output for direct (random) files: READ (n1'i, n2, ERR = n3) list	n1, n2, n3, and *list* have the same meanings as in the READ statement. The parameter i is the record key.	READ(10'I,30,ERR=50)X,Y,N READ(20'7,40,ERR=50)X,N,K READ(10'JK,30)X,,Y,Z

PRINT statement:
PRINT n, list

Some FORTRAN IV compilers accept **PRINT** statement. List is the same as in the READ statement, and n is the FORMAT statement number. **PRINT** statement prints on the line printer.

PRINT 40,XX,Y,N

OPEN, CLOSE, and DEFINE files:

See Chapter 16.

BACKSPACE n

n is the logical unit number of the file (unit identifier). BACKSPACE returns the file backward by 1 record.

BACKSPACE 10

END FILE n

n is the logical unit number of the file.

END FILE 10

REWIND n

n is the logical unit number of the file.

REWIND 10

RETURN
or
RETURN i

i is an integer constant or an integer variable whose value is the nth statement number in the list of SUBROUTINE statements.

RETURN

RETURN I

ENTRY name (a1, a2, . . ., an)

Name is the name of the entry point in the SUBROUTINE. a1, a2, . . ., an are arguments.

ENTRY BEG(J,X,Z,N(5))

CALL name (a1, a2, . . ., an)

Name is the name of a subroutine. a1, a2, . . ., an are arguments. Any variable that appears in the CALL list cannot appear in a COMMON list.

CALL STDM(A,B,N,X)

Subprograms:
Statement functions:
Name (a1, a2, . . ., an) = expression

Name is the name of the function: a1, a2, . . ., an are arguments.

$RT(R,N)=(1+R)**N$

STATEMENTS/FORMATS	MEANING OF SYMBOLS AND REMARKS	EXAMPLES
FUNCTION subprogram: Type FUNCTION name (a1, a2, . . ., an)	*Type* is either INTEGER, REAL, LOGICAL, or COMPLEX. *Name* is the name of the function. *Type* is optional. If it is omitted, the mode of the name of the function determines the mode of the result. One result is returned, and that is placed in the name of the function. Each a1, a2, . . ., an is an argument. Any variable in the function list cannot appear in the COMMON list.	REAL FUNCTION AV(N1,N2) AV=(N1+n2)/2 RETURN END
Subroutine subprogram: SUBROUTINE name (a1, a2, . . ., an)	*Name* is the name of the subroutine; a1, a2, . . ., an are arguments. Any argument that appears in a COMMON area cannot appear in the list of the subroutine.	SUBROUTINE SUMM(A,B,N,J) A=(N+J)/2 B=N+J RETURN END
	If *N* is greater than *J*, then RETURN I returns control to the statement whose label is 10 in the main program. Otherwise, control is returned to the statement whose statement number is 100 in the main program.	SUBROUTINE SUMM(A,*10,B,*100,N,J) B=(N+J)/2 A=N+J I=4 IF(N.GT.J)I=I−2 RETURN I END
FORMAT statement: n FORMAT (e1, e2, . . ., en)	n is the statement number; e1, e2, . . ., en are format codes.	50 FORMAT('1',5(5X,I6,4X,F7.2)/)
Format codes: rIn rAn prFn.d	For integer fields For character fields For real fields	I1,5I4,I6 A1,6A3,A6 F5.2,F1.3,5F7.3

prEn.d	Real field, scientific notation (exponent) single precision	E7.4,3E10.2
prDn.d	Real field double precision	D10.2,D16.4
rGn.d	Integer, real, logical, or complex fields	G7.2,5G6.3
rLn	Logical fields	L1,5L4
rZn	Hexadecimal fields	Z4,6Z3
'character'	Literal constant	'1', 'STUDENT'S NAME', 'DATA'
nHstring	String is a string of characters	1H1,14HSTUDENT'S NAME,4HDATA
nX	Skip n positions	5X,1X,10X
Tn	Starts the transmission in nth position	T10,T120,T50
/	Skips a record	/, ///, /////
r(.,.,.)	Group format	(I2,F6.2,E10.3), 5(T6,I2,3X)

The parameter n is an integer constant, r is an optional integer constant that is a repetition factor, and p is the scale factor, which must be in the form nP.

NAMELIST statement:
NAMELIST /V/v1, v2, v3, . . . , /U/
u1, u2, . . . , un

V and U are NAMELIST names; v1, v2, . . . , u1, u2, . . . are variable or array names.

NAMELIST/INPUT/X,Y,I,N
NAMELIST /OUT/ I,J,X,Z

Carriage controls:

'b' or 1Hb	Next line (b stands for a blank.)
'1' or 1H1	Top of a new page
'0' or 1H0	A blank line
'+' or 1H+	Suppress spacing

INDEX

A

Absolute address, 73
Access clause, 368, 378
Access time, 2
Actual arguments, 303–4, 311, 319
A-format code, 8, 113–15
Algorithms, 44–45
Arithmetic assignment statements,
    150–52
Arithmetic expressions, 149–50
Arithmetic IF, 196–98
Arithmetic/logical section, 28
Arrays, 211–25
Arithmetic statement function,
    303–6
ASCII codes, 4
Assigned Go To, 194–96

B

Batch processing systems, 31
BCD codes, 4
Binary language, 3

Binary search, 358, 360–1
Block DATA subprogram, 330–32
Blocked Records, 17
Bubble memory, 25–27
Bubble sort, 350–53

C

CALL statement, 318
Career in computer field, 318
Card reader, 9
Card punch format, 6
Carriage control, 109–10
Cathode Ray Tube (CRT) terminal,
    11
Central processing unit (CPU):
    arithmetic/logical section, 28
    control section, 1, 27–29
    registers, 28–29
Coding FORTRAN statements, 76
Channels, 29–30
Character set, 70–71
CLOSE statement, 369, 379
Comment statement, 68
COMMON statement, 322–27